HOLMAN
Old Testament Commentary

Isaiah

GENERAL EDITOR
Max Anders

AUTHOR
Trent C. Butler

**HOLMAN
REFERENCE**

NASHVILLE, TENNESSEE

Holman Old Testament Commentary
© 2002 B&H Publishing Group
Nashville, Tennessee
All rights reserved

ISBN: 978–0–8054–9473–0
Subject Heading: BIBLE.OT. ISAIAH

Library of Congress Cataloging-in-Publication Data
Butler, Trent C.
    The book of Isaiah
        p. cm. — (Holman Old Testament commentary)
    Includes bibliographical references.
    ISBN 0–8054–9473–1
    1. Bible. O.T. Isaiah—Commentaries. I. Title. II. Title: II. Series

BS1515.3.B877 2002
224'.107—dc21   2002071201
                                                                        CIP

5 6 7 8 9 10 11 12   13 12 11 10 09
R

To

Roanna Brynn Butler the

granddaughter who brings new

joy each day and lets me see

pure love and joy of living.

Acknowledgments

John R. Sampey, Old Testament scholar and former president of The Southern Baptist Theological Seminary, called a portion of Isaiah the heart of the Old Testament. Students who studied under Sampey said that he could not teach Isaiah 52:13–53:12 without weeping. Here in these verses is revealed in vivid detail the Suffering Servant.

We come to know this Suffering Servant through Scripture and those who have been our teachers. My life has been touched and shaped by many suffering servants. I would like to acknowledge and thank a few of them. Martin Luther saved the church from itself and willingly gave his life to reform the church. Martin Luther King marched through America preaching that we will overcome, unknowingly making an indelible impression on a young Texas preacher-boy named Trent Butler. In the civil rights movement, I learned what it meant to give oneself totally and sacrificially for Jesus Christ and the good of his people.

LeRay Fowler and George R. Wilson pastored my home church in days when our church seemed more willing to sacrifice the pastor for human desires rather than to sacrifice themselves as cross-carrying suffering servants. In the midst of church struggle and chaos, two pastors taught me the meaning of loving Jesus and led me to salvation and to dedication to the Christian ministry.

Ben Brock was as handsome a person as I ever met and probably the most talented and dedicated high school journalism teacher in the land. But he spent much of his time teaching youngsters at church the love of Christ and setting a model for his journalism students of what it meant to be a self-giving Christian striving for perfection in a most imperfect world.

Paul Redditt, a seminary roommate from Arkansas, restored self-respect and self-esteem to a discouraged Texas preacher-boy and has remained a confidante, friend, colleague, fellow scholar, and pilgrim on the way through all sorts of trials and tribulations of life.

Lee Keck gave an Old Testament graduate student a dose of excitement in studying the New Testament and then led me to the realization that I had the ability to interpret the text for myself.

Penrose St. Amant and his beloved Jesse took a young professor onto a prestigious European faculty and opened doors of opportunity for me to develop the teaching, writing, and research skills that God had given me. With sufficient material resources to retire and enjoy life, Penrose and Jesse moved to Europe to labor tirelessly for an institution in whose mission they believed. They showed the spirit of the Suffering Servant and encouraged each of us on the faculty to do the same for our students.

Sibley Burnett accepted me as his son-in-law with the reminder that parenthood is permanent. Then he continued his Suffering Servant ministry, traveling the United States at great personal sacrifice to teach people how to conduct Vacation Bible Schools in a way that God could use to lead children to know Jesus as Savior. Then he and his beloved Anita retired to serve as missionary pastor and wife among young military people in Germany.

Finally, dare I include the most current example of the Suffering Servant in my life? Some would say this inclusion is self-serving on my part, but I would be totally remiss not to recognize the meaning Dr. James Draper has given to my life. He has shown time after time a servant's heart in ministering to people far removed from his current responsibilities and seen by many an outsider as far removed from his theological home base. I will never forget standing in the church doorway before the funeral of my beloved wife Mary and seeing Dr. Draper with his dear Carol Ann come in, give me a strong hug and word of encouragement, and then sit quietly in the pew for the hour-long service. That typifies so many ways in which Jimmy Draper has been a friend, encourager, and Suffering Servant model for my family.

I regret having to leave so many people off this list, but hopefully you see the direction this heads. Each of us stands where we do in Christian commitment because special people put aside the world's call to fame to assume the Master's call to the cross and to the role of Suffering Servant for him. We take time to thank these people who have molded our lives and to commit ourselves anew to follow the paths they showed us. Then we can join the crowd that testifies to the greatness of God's unique Suffering Servant and walk the servant's path ourselves.

Editorial Preface

Today's church hungers for Bible teaching, and Bible teachers hunger for resources to guide them in teaching God's Word. The Holman Old Testament Commentary provides the church with the food to feed the spiritually hungry in an easily digestible format. The result: new spiritual vitality that the church can readily use.

Bible teaching should result in new interest in the Scriptures, expanded Bible knowledge, discovery of specific scriptural principles, relevant applications, and exciting living. The unique format of the Holman Old Testament Commentary includes sections to achieve these results for every Old Testament book.

Opening quotations stimulate thinking and lead to an introductory illustration and discussion that draw individuals and study groups into the Word of God. "In a Nutshell" summarizes the content and teaching of the chapter. Verse-by-verse commentary answers the church's questions rather than raising issues scholars usually admit they cannot adequately solve. Bible principles and specific contemporary applications encourage students to move from Bible to contemporary times. A specific modern illustration then ties application vividly to present life. A brief prayer aids the student to commit his or her daily life to the principles and applications found in the Bible chapter being studied. For those still hungry for more, "Deeper Discoveries" takes the student into a more personal, deeper study of the words, phrases, and themes of God's Word. Finally, a teaching outline provides transitional statements and conclusions along with an outline to assist the teacher in group Bible studies.

It is the editors' prayer that this new resource for local church Bible teaching will enrich the ministry of group, as well as individual, Bible study, and that it will lead God's people truly to be people of the Book, living out what God calls us to be.

Contents

Contents

Holman Old Testament
Commentary Contributors

Vol. 1 Genesis
ISBN 978-0-8054-9461-7
Kenneth O. Gangel and Stephen Bramer

Vol. 2 Exodus, Leviticus, Numbers
ISBN 978-0-8054-9462-4
Glen Martin

Vol. 3 Deuteronomy
ISBN 978-0-8054-9463-1
Paul Douglas McIntosh

Vol. 4 Joshua
ISBN 978-0-8054-9464-8
Kenneth O. Gangel

Vol. 5 Judges, Ruth
ISBN 978-0-8054-9465-5
Gary W. Phillips

Vol. 6 1 & 2 Samuel
ISBN 978-0-8054-9466-2
Stephen Andrews

Vol. 7 1 & 2 Kings
ISBN 978-0-8054-9467-9
Gary Inrig

Vol. 8 1 & 2 Chronicles
ISBN 978-0-8054-9468-6
Winfried Corduan

Vol. 9 Ezra, Nehemiah, Esther
ISBN 978-0-8054-9469-3
Knute Larson and Kathy Dahlen

Vol. 10 Job
ISBN 978-0-8054-9470-9
Stephen J. Lawson

Vol. 11 Psalms 1-72
ISBN 978-0-8054-9471-6
Steve J. Lawson

Vol. 12 Psalms 73-150
ISBN 978-0-8054-9481-5
Steve J. Lawson

Vol. 13 Proverbs
ISBN 978-0-8054-9472-3
Max Anders

Vol. 14 Ecclesiastes, Song of Songs
ISBN 978-0-8054-9482-2
David George Moore and Daniel L. Akin

Vol. 15 Isaiah
ISBN 978-0-8054-9473-0
Trent C. Butler

Vol. 16 Jeremiah, Lamentations
ISBN 978-0-8054-9474-7
Fred C. Wood and Ross McLaren

Vol. 17 Ezekiel
ISBN 978-0-8054-9475-4
Mark F. Rooker

Vol. 18 Daniel
ISBN 978-0-8054-9476-1
Kenneth O. Gangel

Vol. 19 Hosea, Joel, Amos, Obadiah, Jonah, Micah
ISBN 978-0-8054-9477-8
Trent C. Butler

Vol. 20 Nahum, Habakkuk, Zephaniah, Haggai, Zechariah, Malachi
ISBN 978-0-8054-9478-5
Stephen R. Miller

Holman New Testament
Commentary Contributors

Vol. 1 Matthew
ISBN 978-0-8054-0201-8
Stuart Weber

Vol. 2 Mark
ISBN 978-0-8054-0202-5
Rod Cooper

Vol. 3 Luke
ISBN 978-0-8054-0203-2
Trent C. Butler

Vol. 4 John
ISBN 978-0-8054-0204-9
Kenneth Gangel

Vol. 5 Acts
ISBN 978-0-8054-0205-6
Kenneth Gangel

Vol. 6 Romans
ISBN 978-0-8054-0206-3
Kenneth Boa

Vol. 7 1 & 2 Corinthians
ISBN 978-0-8054-0207-0
Richard Pratt

Vol. 8 Galatians, Ephesians, Philippians, Colossians
ISBN 978-0-8054-0208-7
Max Anders

Vol. 9 1 & 2 Thessalonians, 1 & 2 Timothy, Titus, Philemon
ISBN 978-0-8054-0209-4
Knute Larson

Vol. 10 Hebrews, James
ISBN 978-0-8054-0211-7
Thomas Lea

Vol. 11 1 & 2 Peter, 1, 2, 3 John, Jude
ISBN 978-0-8054-0210-0
David Walls & Max Anders

Vol. 12 Revelation
ISBN 978-0-8054-0212-4
Kendell Easley

Holman Old Testament Commentary

Twenty volumes designed for Bible study and teaching to enrich the local church and God's people.

Series Editor	Max Anders
Managing Editor	Steve Bond
Project Editor	Dean Richardson
Product Development Manager	Ricky D. King
Marketing Manager	Stephanie Huffman
Executive Editor	David Shepherd
Page Composition	TF Designs, Mt. Juliet, TN

Bible versions used in this book:

ASV	American Standard Version
GW	God's Word
JPS	Jewish Publication Society
KJV	King James Version
NAB	New American Bible
NASB	New American Standard Bible, 1995 Update
NEB	New English Bible
NIV	New International Version
NJB	New Jerusalem Bible
NKJV	New King James Version
NLT	New Living Translation
NRSV	New Revised Standard Version
REB	Revised English Bible
TEV	Today's English Bible (Good News Bible)

Abbreviations for Reference Books Cited

AB	Anchor Bible
ABD	Anchor Bible Dictionary
BK	Biblischer Kommentar
EBC	Expositor's Bible Commentary
FOTL	Forms of the Old Testament Literature
HALOT	Hebrew and Aramaic Lexicon of the Old Testament
ICC	International Critical Commentary
IDB	Interpreter's Dictionary of the Bible
ITC	International Theological Commentary
JSOTS	Journal for the Study of the Old Testament Supplements
NCB	New Century Bible
NICOT	New International Commentary on the Old Testament
NIDOTTE	New International Dictionary of Old Testament Theology and Exegesis
OTL	Old Testament Library
TLOT	Theological Lexicon of the Old Testament
WBC	Word Biblical Commentary

Introduction to

Isaiah

Isaiah was a prophet in Judah over a period of forty years (about 740–700 B.C.). His ministry paralleled the rule of four kings: Uzziah, Jotham, Ahaz, and Hezekiah. The name Isaiah means "the Lord saves," which is a concise summary of his prophecy.

Isaiah 6:1 tells us Isaiah received his call in the year that King Uzziah died, which can be dated at approximately 740 B.C. Yet Isaiah 44:28 and 45:1 name the Persian king Cyrus as the agent God would use to deliver Judah from exile. Cyrus became king of Persia in 559, almost 200 years after Isaiah began his ministry. The deliverance referred to in Isaiah did not begin until 538 B.C. (see Ezra 1:1). This has led many scholars to doubt that Isaiah could have written all of the book that bears his name.

The first we hear of doubts about the likelihood of such a predictive prophecy, however, is from the Jewish rabbi Ibn Ezra, about A.D. 1167. At that time and later, in the eighteenth century, the argument was made that the author of Isaiah 40–66, who eventually came to be known as "Deutero-" or "Second-Isaiah," likely lived among the Jewish exiles in Babylon. By the end of the nineteenth century the multiple authorship of Isaiah was widely held by critical scholars, who also began to identify another author of Isaiah 56–66 as "Trito-" or "Third-Isaiah."

Some sort of multiple authorship view for Isaiah is often treated as an assumption. Two types of evidence support this view. One is that the style, themes, and historical settings—at least of chapters 1–39 and 40–66—reflect some differences. The first section presupposes a world in which Assyria was the dominant foreign power, whereas the latter section presupposes that Babylonia had taken Assyria's place. Assyria began to have serious trouble with rebellious Babylonia during the reign of Ashurbanipal (668–627 B.C.) and finally fell to the Medes, Babylonians, and Scythians in 614–612 B.C. Thus, Isaiah's prophecy of a Babylonian exile of the Jews (Isa. 39:6–7), and then even further of the Persian king who would conquer Babylonia, strains the credibility of many.

Furthermore, the first section of Isaiah emphasizes God's anger and the coming judgment, while chapter 40 introduces a section dominated by "comfort ye my people" (KJV). The second type of evidence centers on the theological themes in the two parts of the book. The first section is dominated by themes of God's election of Jerusalem, the temple, and the king, while the themes of exodus, creation, wilderness, and conquest are the important elements in chapters 40–66.

Nevertheless, few critical scholars today maintain a simple division of the book into three separate sections from three different authors. Most would allow an original prophet Isaiah, whose disciples continued to supplement and interpret Isaiah's words for the following centuries, updating his message for their day. This perspective, however, is far from that of the biblical text, which presents its contents as a revelation received from God by the eighth-century prophet Isaiah. The view of multiple authorship, in fact, is fraught with difficulties.

One is that the testimony of early Judaism is uniform that the Book of Isaiah as a whole came from the prophet whose name it bears. This includes the book of Ecclesiasticus from the second century B.C., Josephus in the late first century A.D., and the earliest manuscript of the book from the Dead Sea Scrolls. As Alec Motyer explains, "In the oldest manuscripts available, dating back to 100 B.C., the first two lines of chapter 40 (which is where many scholars say the book should be divided) come without any break in the text at the bottom of the column on which chapter 39 ends" (Motyer, IVP, p. 27). There is, in fact, no manuscript evidence that the book was ever circulated in parts.

Furthermore, Isaiah is mentioned in the New Testament twenty-two times, and quotations of many parts of both sections of the book are found there ascribed to the prophet Isaiah. Jesus, for example, cited Isaiah 40:3 as "spoken of through the prophet Isaiah" (Matt. 3:3), and the apostle Paul quoted Isaiah 65:1–2 as what Isaiah "boldly says" (Rom. 10:20–21).

In spite of the obvious difference in tone between chapters 1–39 and chapters 40–66, judgment and comfort appear in both. The term "the Holy One of Israel" is found twelve times in chapters 1–39 and thirteen times in chapters 40–66 (and only seven times in the rest of the Bible). Both parts of Isaiah reflect the same sins and evils: falsehood (10:1; 59:4–9), bloodshed and violence (1:15; 59:3,7), hypocrisy (29:13; 58:2,4), and idolatry (1:29; 57:5).

If Isaiah 40–66 had been written in the community of the exiles in Babylon, we should expect evidence of that physical environment. The author of chapters 40–66 demonstrates a knowledge of Palestine, mentioning trees found in Palestine (41:19). Judean cities are still in existence (43:6), supporting the view that this portion of Isaiah was written prior to Nebuchadnezzar's invasions, which began in 605 B.C.

How could Isaiah have named Cyrus as God's servant in restoring his people to Jerusalem? Isaiah's naming Cyrus and foretelling something of his role in restoring Israel to Jerusalem is strongly consonant with the view of God presented in Isaiah 40–55. God is contrasted with the idols of the nations. Idols cannot tell what is going to happen. Their prophets describe what happened after the fact. By contrast, God tells the things that are to come. If Cyrus were written into Isaiah's prophecy after the fact, this contrast between God and the gods is negated. God's prophets are no better than prophets of idolatry.

The view taken in this commentary is that there was only one author of the Book of Isaiah—the man Isaiah who prophesied "during the reigns of Uzziah, Jotham, Ahaz and Hezekiah, kings of Judah" (1:1). The book presents this one prophet as having a message featuring events of his own day (chs. 1–39; about 740 to 690 B.C.), events in the days of Cyrus of Persia (chs. 40–55; 559–530 B.C.), and events in the days after the temple had been rebuilt (chs. 56–66; 515–480 B.C. or so). The people in Isaiah's lifetime needed not only a look at the dangerous situations they faced as they came under attack from Assyria, but they also needed to see the times of hope God had planned for later generations. As they lost power in their day, they needed assurance that God was still in command of history in the long run.

Thus, as we study each segment of the book, we will try to place as close a date as possible on the passage and show the type of language being used. For chapters 40–66, we cannot easily determine either when the passages were first preached or the precise date in the period of Cyrus or the new temple that was addressed. We will try to describe some parts of the religious situation of the people that the prophetic message spoke to.

Our dating and historical description are based on the following outline of the history of Israel, bearing in mind that different scholars will assign different dates for various kings and events due to the fact that many kings first reigned with their fathers as co-rulers before taking full control after the father's death.

OUTLINE OF HISTORY

I. The Assyrian Period
- A. Tiglath-Pileser III (745–727)
  1. Collects tribute from Menahem (742) of Israel and Rezin of Damascus (738)
  2. Israel and Damascus join in revolt and try to force Judah to participate by besieging Jerusalem in Syro-Ephraimitic War (734)
  3. Ahaz (735–715) of Judah summons Tiglath-Pileser to help, bringing destruction of Damascus and reduction of Israel to a small city-state around Samaria (732) with a new king, Hoshea (731–723) (2 Kgs. 16:5–17:1)
- B. Shalmaneser V (727–722) besieges Samaria (724–722), which was then captured either by him or by Sargon II
- C. Sargon II (722–705)

1. Subdues rebellions in Babylonia, Hamath, Gaza, and Samaria, while collecting tribute from Judah (720). Egypt defeated for first time
2. Hezekiah (715–687) becomes king of Judah, bringing religious and political reforms (2 Kgs. 18)
3. Ashdod revolt is put down (712)
4. Babylonian revolt fails (710)

D. Sennacherib (705–681)
1. Subdues rebels in Assyria and Babylonia
2. Defeats Phoenicians, Philistines, Egyptians (701)
3. Destroys most Judean cities and besieges Jerusalem (701), but has to retreat to Nineveh (2 Kgs. 18:13–19:37; Isa. 36–37)
4. Manasseh begins reign as Judean king (687–642)

E. Esarhaddon (680–669)

F. Ashurbanipal (668–631) marks beginning of end of Assyrian power with major revolts in 642—a contributing factor to assassination of Ammon of Judah (642–640) and rise of independent Josiah (640–609) (2 Kgs. 22–23)

II. The Babylonian Period

A. Nabopolassar (626–605)
1. Fall of Asshur and fall of Nineveh (614–12) mark end of Assyrian empire
2. Josiah killed at Megiddo (609) by Egyptians (2 Kgs. 23:29–30), succeeded by Jehoahaz, then Jehoiachim (609–598)

B. Nebuchadnezzar II (605–562)
1. Defeats Pharaoh Necho of Egypt at Carchemish to gain control over Syria-Palestine (605)
2. Invasion of Egypt fails (601), encouraging Judah's revolt
3. Defeats Jerusalem (597), sends large numbers including Ezekiel and new king Jehoiachin into exile, and names Zedekiah (597–587) king (2 Kgs. 24:1–17)
4. Judean rebellions in 594, then 589, with Egyptian encouragement, lead to final destruction of Jerusalem (587/586) (2 Kgs. 24)
5. Further exile of Jewish citizens in 582 (Jer. 52:30)

C. Amel-Marduk (562–560; Evil-Merodach in NIV, KJV, NRSV) releases Jehoiachin from prison (2 Kgs. 25:27; Jer. 52:31)

D. Nabonidus (555–539) busies himself with travels and archaeology projects, so that much responsibility falls on his son and co-regent Belshazzar; allows Babylonia to be conquered by Persians without resistance

III. The Persian Period

A. Cyrus the Great (559–530)

      1. Founds Persian Empire (559)

      2. Captures Babylonia without resistance (539)

      3. Issues edict (538) allowing Jews to return home (Ezra 1:1)

      4. Work begins on Jerusalem temple (538–537) (Ezra 3:6–8)

   B. Cambyses (530–522) conquers Egypt (525)

   C. Darius (522–486) leads revolution

      1. Work on temple begins anew under Zerubbabel, Joshua, Haggai, and Zechariah (520–518).

      2. New temple dedicated (515) (Ezra 6:15–18)

      3. Darius loses battle of Marathon to Greeks (490)

Within this historical framework, we can understand each of the short sermons preserved in the Book of Isaiah. We will refer to this chart and to the information on prophetic language below to place each of the sermons in context.

THE PROPHETS AND PROPHETIC LANGUAGE

Isaiah ushers us into the wonder-filled world of the prophets. Heroic visions race through our minds at the mention of the word *prophets*. But what is the job description of a prophet? What common factors bind Samuel and Malachi, Elisha and Amos, Isaiah and Obadiah? Why does the ministry of an Elijah produce stories in Kings, while Amos's ministry results in a collection of his sermons? A student of the Bible must face such questions before he can hope to understand biblical prophecy. We can give only brief hints for reflection here by discussing prophetic culture, community, calling, context, content, collection, and canonization.

THE PROPHETIC CULTURE

The culture in which prophecy was at home extended far beyond Israel, appearing in various forms in Egypt, Babylonia, Syria, and Phoenicia. Prophets bringing words to kings appeared in Mari, a Syrian town on the Euphrates River, seven hundred years before Saul or David. The Bible records that other gods had their prophets (1 Kgs. 18:19–20; 2 Kgs. 10:19; Jer. 29:9). Prophecy was something Israel monopolized. It was also not something that stayed static. Prophecy changed as the culture changed and as the individuals whom God called to prophesy were different from their predecessors. A look at the prophetic school surrounding Samuel and Saul with ecstatic utterances and a glance at Jonah first preaching to Jeroboam and then fleeing to Tarshish so he would not have to preach shows the great differences in the phenomenon called prophecy. A further look at Isaiah confronting King Ahaz and Jeremiah being taken out of the well that served as his prison again highlight the wide variety of people and events that create and compose the prophetic culture.

THE PROPHETIC COMMUNITY

Such change is seen in the prophetic community. For Samuel the prophetic community included a group of prophets living together at the place of worship (1 Sam. 10:5). At other times, prophets lived at the king's court (1 Kgs. 1; 18; 22). Some simply followed prophetic leaders (2 Kgs. 4:1; 9:1; cp. Isa. 8:16). Prophetic groups could be large (1 Kgs. 18:4; 22:6), but prophets could feel lonely and isolated (1 Kgs. 19:10; Jer. 15:17). They even faced prophetic competition (1 Kgs. 22:24; Jer. 27–28). At times they faced public contempt for their unusual conduct (1 Sam. 10:6; 19:24; 2 Kgs. 2:23–25; Isa. 20:1–5; Hos. 1; Ezek. 4). These changing prophetic communities performed an important task for God's people. They preserved the accounts and sermons of the prophets.

THE PROPHETIC CALLING

At the center of these communities stood the prophetic calling. This was a very personal experience. Each was different, coming in visions (Isa. 6), dreams (1 Sam. 2), or in a sense of destination from birth (Jer. 1). Each brought a sense of inadequacy. Each brought a compulsion to preach. Each resulted in continuing experiences with God that brought new messages for new historical situations.

THE PROPHETIC CONTEXT

The prophet can be understood only within the context of history. Prophets preached to Israel for at least seven hundred years, from the time of Deborah the prophetess (Judg. 4:4) to the time of Malachi or even later. Each faced different problems, temptations, and needs. The same prophet saw drastic changes in his context, as we will see with Isaiah. Only new experiences with God could provide the needed word for the moment. Not only the historical context but the social context changed as well. Samuel and Isaiah were closely related to the temple (1 Sam. 2; Isa. 6). Amos and Jeremiah were forbidden to enter the temple (Amos 7; Jer. 36:5). Ezekiel lived in exile, far removed from the temple. Haggai and Zechariah sought to rebuild a destroyed temple.

Amos came from the south to preach to the north, while Hosea was a northerner preaching to his own people. The other prophets apparently preached in the Southern Kingdom. Many spoke directly to the king in private conversation (Isa. 7; 38; Jer. 22). We understand the preacher and his message better when we know when, where, and to whom he preached. Most prophetic words do not directly state where and when they were preached. It is the work of the commentator to help us find this information.

THE PROPHETIC CONTENT

Most importantly, we search for the content of prophetic preaching. Theologically, we claim that the words of the prophet are words of God. This is the starting point for any statement about prophetic preaching. Yet each prophet had his own vocabulary, his own themes, his own way of speaking. How do we interpret this? At least three types of evidence crack the door just a bit for us to understand this awesome mystery and power of inspiration.

First, the prophet could speak and identify with his audience because of his own deeply personal experiences. The word of God was based on the agonizing marriage experience of Hosea, the life-changing encounter with the holy God by Isaiah, the fantastic visions of Ezekiel, the impatient waiting on the watchman's stand by Habakkuk, and the painful personal struggle with God by Jeremiah. God showed his spokesmen how to formulate into language their deeply personal experiences.

God gave his prophets yet another tool—the basic language formulas which alerted the audience to the moods and scenes the prophet was setting. An understanding of such language formulas helps us understand the prophetic books. We will look briefly at the most obvious ones.

The *prophecy of disaster* begins with a call to listen as in Isaiah 1:10 or 7:13. It is followed by an accusation listing the sins of the audience as in Isaiah 1:11–12; 7:13b. The conclusion is the prediction of disaster beginning "Therefore saith the Lord" (see 1:24–25, KJV). When the audience heard this "therefore," they knew bad news was coming.

The *prophetic woe oracle* was borrowed from Israel's funeral ceremonies. First, the prophet cried out "Woe," the word of sorrow and grief. This showed the emotional empathy of the prophet for his people. Then the prophet listed the sins of the people, followed by the announcement of judgment. Isaiah 5:8–10 is a good example.

The prophet often imitated a *courtroom trial.* He summoned witnesses to court (1:2; 5:3), reported the lawyer's questioning of defendant and witnesses (5:4), and announced the verdict and sentence (5:5–6).

The prophet borrowed language for his *oracle of salvation* from the temple priests, whose job it was to assure the worshiper who came to the temple in time of trouble. The oracle of salvation begins, "Do not fear." It promised God's help and described the result of such help (Isa. 7:4-7).

These were the major linguistic tools of the prophetic trade—tools which the prophets borrowed from the courtroom, the funeral parlor, and the temple, among other places. Such tools help us today as we try to separate individual prophetic sermons from one another. They help us in our search for the social context of the prophet and in our attempts to recreate the mood of the congregation as the prophet preached. They alert us to the fact that the prophets borrowed their language from all areas of daily life. We must be alert to discover new forms of speech which the prophets transformed for their own purposes. The commentary in this book begins each major section by showing the type of language the prophet used. You may want to find the various parts of each language type as you study a section of prophecy.

The prophets had still another tool as they preached God's word to his people. This was the religious *tradition of Israel*. The prophets did not speak in a vacuum. They spoke to people who worshiped the creator God who had led Israel's fathers from Mesopotamia into the land of Canaan then into Egypt and back out again in the exodus. Their God had directed a murmuring people through the wilderness to Sinai, given them the law, and led them on through the wilderness to the promised land.

God's history did not end there. Kingship was requested and accepted, a temple was built, and temple worship practices developed. All of these gave new language that the prophets used to explain God's new purposes to the audiences. We can learn much if we observe which traditions the particular prophet used and how he used old language to proclaim the new word of God in the new historical context.

Isaiah was particularly adept at transforming the traditions of creation, exodus, wilderness wandering, gift of the land, and kingship from their ancient, original meanings to apply to a new action of God in a new moment of history. Thus he pointed to a new creation, a new exodus from Babylon, a new highway in the wilderness from Babylon to Israel, a renewed possession of the land, a new king from the stump of Jesse.

With these linguistic and historical tools, the prophet followed God's inspiration in shaping the divine word into an emotion-filled call to God's people to listen, learn, and let God lead. In so doing they taught great theological truths about the nature of the God/man relationship. For Isaiah, many of those truths are captured in powerful Hebrew words. These are studied in some depth in the various "Deeper Discoveries" sections throughout the commentary. Throughout the sixty-six chapters of his book, Isaiah sought to lead a people to repent of their false religion and their unjust, oppressive treatment of the financially and socially disadvantaged; to tell the truth; to trust God instead of themselves, other gods, or foreign rulers; and to recognize ultimately that only one God exists—the Creator God who had chosen Israel to be his people.

Isaiah used every method possible to help Israel see that the present circumstances were God's way of calling them back to him. He wanted them to see the new actions God had planned to save his people on this earth and in a new heaven and a new earth.

SUMMARY OF ISAIAH

The Book of Isaiah speaks to us through its great themes: trust, holiness, political and religious allegiance, justice and righteousness, and hope. But we must realize that the structure of the book provided a message in itself to those who had experienced all the long history through which the book sought to lead Israel. Having seen the fall and rebirth of a people, what was the nation of Israel centered in the rebuilt Jerusalem to expect in her relationship with God? What did God expect from her?

The remarkable summary in chapter 1 shows us that the basic message of the book was a call to accept the judgment of God on the fallen city as justified, to repent from the sins which had caused that fall, and to look forward to God's new day of salvation in their city. Chapters 1–12 spell out this theme of restoration through repentance and provide a song for the people to sing as they celebrate God's new day of salvation for them.

Chapters 13–23 list the nations God would punish as he worked to bring salvation to his people. The list shocked God's people because they found themselves on the list. Still, looking back, they could rest assured that just as God had brought judgment upon many of these nations, so he would complete his word of promise and bring judgment on the others. Could the community which had joined the nations in suffering God's judgment wait in expectant trust as God completed his task?

Chapters 24–27 take up the language of apocalyptic to announce that God's new work in the history of his people would cover the entire universe. No class of people, no geographical location, no political power could escape. Everyone would be included. While the people of God waited for the great event, they should occupy themselves with two responses. They should prepare the great hymn of thanksgiving that God had provided for them to sing at the appropriate moment, and they should rid themselves of evil practices which had brought God's judgment and which could not be tolerated in the day of salvation.

Chapters 28–39 show Israel that her own military might and that of her allies did not supply the final answer. God could bring victory in the midst of great chaos and overwhelming odds. However, God demanded absolute trust in the prophetic word, not in that of foreign ambassadors. God's people must not seek security for the moment but permanent security in the Word of God for his people forever.

Chapters 40–55 bring a call of comfort to those who had suffered, but the call is also to trust in the comfort. Israel must forget past complaints and must forsake present complacency to join in God's day of salvation—a day led by the divine servant, who suffers for his people. Israel must identify herself and her history with that of the servant and become an instrument of God's salvation for the world. Only then would they be part of God's covenant people.

Chapters 56–66 bring the book to a close with a renewed definition of God's salvation. Divine salvation could not be limited to one people or one place. It was for all who would help the needy, providing justice for society, and would worship God properly in his temple. People from all nations could be involved. They all could also be involved in God's judgment upon the people who refused to meet God's call for trust. The matter came down to a call to confession of sin and to thanksgiving for what God had done and was doing for his people.

God had committed himself to do his part. Would his people respond faithfully and do their part, or would they choose to hide behind the protective walls of the temple, avoid contact with all other peoples, and complain that God had not fulfilled his promises?

The people of Israel had a long history of prophetic proclamation. This history stretched even further back to the moment of God's great redemption in the wilderness when he had proved his power to save his people from foreign exile. They had the witness of history that stretched even further back to the creation when God proved that all earth had its hope in him. Still Israel hesitated to heed God's word, to believe God's hope, to trust God's promise.

We have seen God's history with his people stretch even further through the history of the Christian church. We have seen the promised Messiah come and fulfill the divine promises to his people. We have seen that divine word reach out to encompass the nations of the world. Yet, we still wait in our churches, much like Israel behind the walls of the second temple. We know the Messiah who took the role of the Suffering Servant, accepted the commission of the prophet (see ch. 61), and sent his followers into the world with an even more challenging and comprehensive commission (Matt. 28:19–20).

How do we react to this call to service? Is our reaction any different from that of Isaiah's reluctant readers?

Isaiah 1

Restoration Through Repentance

I. INTRODUCTION
Country Club Conversion

II. COMMENTARY
A verse-by-verse explanation of the chapter.

III. CONCLUSION
A Trip to Court

An overview of the principles and applications from the chapter.

IV. LIFE APPLICATION
The Realistic Road to Repentance

Melding the chapter to life.

V. PRAYER
Tying the chapter to life with God.

VI. DEEPER DISCOVERIES
Historical, geographical, and grammatical enrichment of the commentary.

VII. TEACHING OUTLINE
Suggested step-by-step group study of the chapter.

VIII. ISSUES FOR DISCUSSION
Zeroing the chapter in on daily life.

"*The keenest sorrow is to recognize ourselves as the sole cause of all our adversities.*"

S o p h o c l e s

Isaiah 1

IN A NUTSHELL

The Heavenly Father asks a rebellious people why they do not turn to him even after experiencing his discipline for their sin. He wants justice, not mere religious behavior.

Restoration Through Repentance

I. INTRODUCTION

Country Club Conversion

*E*velyn Christenson tells of the woman she took to lunch at the country club. Since the woman's husband owned most of the club's stock, she got her choice of tables and the best of service at the club. So they chose a secluded corner table where they could talk. What did two women talk about in a secluded corner of the town's fanciest restaurant? Evelyn told the woman how she was a sinner and needed to repent. After much discussion, they left the restaurant and went to the woman's Cadillac. There the woman confessed her sins, asked Jesus to forgive her sins, and gave her heart to Christ.

How, you may ask, could you possibly lead a leading socialite to Christ in a country club? Evelyn thought she knew the answer. She had eight prayer warriors chosen to pray for her as she witnessed. She found the rest of the story on Thursday morning when the woman who helped clean her house appeared for work. Mary had one question for Evelyn: "What happened on Tuesday afternoon?"

"Why do you ask?" Evelyn inquired.

"Because on Sunday the Lord told me to quit eating and drinking and start praying. He did not let me eat again until Tuesday afternoon. Then he said, 'It's okay now. You may eat.' I prayed for you Sunday through Tuesday. What happened Tuesday?"

Evelyn hugged the woman as she shared the conversion story. People could repent and find God's salvation because God's people were praying (Christenson, pp. 16–17).

Isaiah knew this was God's way. He went to Israel's social headquarters and called the entire nation to repentance and obedience. He showed them exactly what kind of life they would live after they repented.

Doom dominates the content of Isaiah 1–12. This we expected from the prophet's commission to harden the hearts and blind the eyes of his people (ch. 6). The order and structure of the twelve chapters, however, show that disaster was not the last word. Light shone through the darkness. Rays of hope brightened the stage at the climax of the section (Isa. 9:2–7; 10:1–11:16), bringing forth the great hymn of thanksgiving in chapter 12. In spite of all the dark moments, the theme of the opening section of Isaiah is restoration for a repentant remnant.

II. COMMENTARY

Restoration Through Repentance

> **MAIN IDEA:** *A sinful people who have rebelled against God and suffered his punishment for their sins must demonstrate repentance in moral actions, not in religious rituals.*

A Calling the Confused to Court (1:1–3)

Summons to witness (about 740 B.C.)[1]

> **SUPPORTING IDEA:** *Sinners who continue in their rebellion eventually get to the point where they do not recognize their Heavenly Father when he speaks to them.*

1:1. A preface (v. 1) describes Isaiah's words as based on visions. This preface shows the dating for the prophet's ministry from about 740 B.C. to 690 B.C. The time of Isaiah's ministry can be dated by reference to the four kings of Judah mentioned in verse 1. A vision (Hb. *chazon*) represented an experience in which God revealed his will and his future plans (Hos. 12:10). Such an experience could occur while awake (Ezek. 12:27) or during sleep (Mic. 3:6). A vision was not the same as a dream.

God's judgment brought a period of time without visions (1 Sam. 3:1; Lam. 2:9; Mic. 3:6). Both true and false prophets (Jer. 14:14; Ezek. 13:16) claimed to have such visions, but historical fulfillment was the final test showing which prophet was authentic (Deut. 18:22; Jer. 28:9). The true prophets often had disciples like Isaiah's who collected their prophecies and placed them in a book (Hab. 2:2). Even the record of a king could be included in a prophet's vision (2 Chr. 32:32). The entire book was then labeled a vision or revelation of God through the prophet's entire ministry (Nah. 1).

1:2–3. The message of Isaiah begins by calling the universe to the jury box to hear God's accusation. The charge is blunt: God's people are dumber than beasts of burden, who at least know the hand that feeds them. God's people don't even know their Heavenly Father. Israel shared this concept of God as Father with her neighbors, who used it literally in fertility worship (Jer. 2:27). So Israel used the concept cautiously. Isaiah described God as a

---

1. The notations introducing each section give the date of the situation the prophet addressed and the type of speech he gave. See the "Introduction to Acts" to understand the context of each of these notations throughout this volume.

Father who was concerned for his children (Deut. 1:31; Hos. 11:1), whom he educates in vain (Prov. 3:12). Deuteronomy 32 says God is Father because he is Creator (vv. 5–6) and uses "Father" in the context of the birth of the nation (Deut. 32:18; cp. Exod. 4:22–24). In Deuteronomy as in Isaiah the emphasis lies on unfaithful, rebellious children (Deut. 32:5,19–21; cp. Jer. 3:4,19; Mal. 1:6).

B Lamenting the Lost (1:4–9)

Woe oracle (701 B.C.)

> **SUPPORTING IDEA:** *God punishes his disobedient people not as an independent judge but as a caring Father seeking to bring them back to him.*

1:4. Not a stern, impassive judge, but a mourning father brought the accusation against the defendant Israel. The accusation is loaded with theological words. **Sinful** (Hb. *chote'*) refers to breaking a personal relationship, not just a single law (Gen. 50:17). **Guilt** (Hb. *'won*) is a lifestyle bent out of shape, crooked (Isa. 30:13). **Evildoers** are wicked in the most general and encompassing sense. **Corruption** (Hb. *mere'im*) is a military term referring to destruction which eliminates the possibility for human well-being. Such action showed that the people had **forsaken** and **spurned** God.

The sad truth was that the people were unaware of the consequences of their actions and attitudes. They thought they continued to be the people of God. The prophet had to reveal the reality to them. The personal relationship of mutual love and trust similar to that between parent and child had disappeared.

God is here called the **Holy One of Israel**, a favorite expression of Isaiah (otherwise the phrase appears only in 2 Kgs. 19:22; Pss. 71:22; 78:41; 89:19; Jer. 50:29; 51:5). Isaiah's call (ch. 6) gave a new intensity of meaning to this descriptive title of God, who is totally pure. Mankind's sinfulness stood in stark contrast to the purity of God.

1:5–9. God used rhetorical questions as he tried to argue sense into Israel's head, describing the nation's desperate condition after the invasion of Sennacherib of Assyria. The nation was almost destroyed. But they would not let someone bandage their wounds and apply soothing oil. In more literal terms, the country had become a stretch of uninhabited desolation, the cities burned with fire. Foreign soldiers had reaped and burned the fields, stripping away the nation's food supply. The people—now described as the Father's **Daughter**—no longer had housing. It was as if God's people had to spend their entire life in the watchman's tower overlooking the devastated vineyards. Only God's grace in leaving a few **survivors** as a remnant had allowed them to escape the fate of **Sodom** and **Gomorrah**, the two immoral cities that God had destroyed in Abraham's time when he could not find ten righteous people (Gen. 18–19). God had diagnosed Israel's pains, but Israel would not return to him for healing. (For daughter of Zion, see "Deeper Discoveries," chs. 9–11; for survivors/remnant, see "Deeper Discoveries," chs. 2–4.)

Ⓒ Reviving the Religious (1:10–17)

Courtroom accusation, based on prophetic instruction (about 740 or 715 B.C.)

SUPPORTING IDEA: *God calls his people to show repentance through acts of justice and morality, not through acts of religious ritual.*

1:10. On a national holiday the prophet saw the herds of animals being brought for sacrifice. He then stood up in his role as teacher. He identified the congregation with the ancient people from Sodom and Gomorrah. His listeners stood in stunned silence. Were they really Sodomites?

1:11. The prophet followed with a question that seemed to be out of place in the setting of a religious festival: "Why are you sacrificing?" They responded: "Moses told us to; we've always done so!" The prophet shocked them further: God says, in effect, "I'm full up to here; I'm sick of all this!" (For sacrifices and burnt offerings, see "Deeper Discoveries.")

1:12–15. The prophet had a new teaching, a new law: no more offerings, no more festivals, no more prayers. Did Isaiah want to close the doors of the temple? No! He wanted to set priorities straight. Worship must not shield people from God's claim upon their lives. Gifts cannot replace personal action. Ritual does not make people right. Sacrifice does not substitute for service. Justice must be provided for all people before the jury allows the temple doors to open. Then ritual can be in response to the riches of God, our redeemer.

New Moons represented the first day of each month when Israel brought burnt offerings to God (Num. 28:11; cp. Num. 10:10; Ps. 81:3). Saul and his family routinely celebrated these festivals (1 Sam. 20:5,18,24; cp. 2 Chr. 8:13; Neh. 10:34). In Amos's day people did not open their shops for commerce on the new moon. Ezekiel expected new moon worship in his new temple (Ezek. 45:17). But Isaiah saw the new moon festivals as ritual for ritual's sake without any commitment to God or to his way of life (Isa. 47:13; Hos. 2:11).

The observance of **Sabbaths** rested in the teaching of the creation (Gen. 2:2–3) and in the experience of the exodus (Exod. 16). It was a humanitarian day of rest and a religious memorial of God's acts. Israel often saw worship occasions only as traditional teaching they had to obey (Exod. 31:12–17). Too often they regarded it as unnecessary restriction of economic opportunities.

Convocations were officially called meetings of the community for worship, especially in connection with annual festivals such as the Feast of Unleavened Bread and the Feast of Weeks (Num. 28:18,25–26; cp. Lev. 23:2,37).

Isaiah condemned the central acts of Israel's worship. They should stop worshiping until they could begin working God's works of justice. Even prayer made God's "I Hate It" list. Prayer accompanied by heinous sin did not provide entrance to God's holy throne.

1:16–17. Isaiah's teaching began to sound much like the priests'. Washing was a regular part of worship. These ritual washings were meant to cleanse a person of ritual impurity so he could be admitted to worship (2 Sam. 12:20; cp. Exod. 29:4; 40:12; Lev. 17:15).

Isaiah had another type of washing in mind—a washing that did not require water. It required a cleansing of the heart, a change of attitude and practice. Worship and prayer could be practiced only when other practices ceased. There was no half-way compromise in Isaiah's charge. Stop evil. Stop wrong. Do right. Seek justice. Aid the oppressed. Go to court for the fatherless child and widow. God's priority is how you live normal days of life, not how you perform on special days set aside for ritual. (For justice, see "Deeper Discoveries.")

Ⅾ Reasoning for Repentance (1:18–20)

Prophetic call to repent (705 B.C.)

SUPPORTING IDEA: *God is reasonable and offers his people a choice: obey and find cleansing for your sins, or rebel and be destroyed.*

1:18–20. The judge did not pronounce the sentence. He laid a choice before the accused. The evidence was clear. The verdict: guilty. But the divine judge offered one more chance for a new start. Would Israel obey and prosper or remain rebellious and die? The reasonable course of action was clear. They were sinners. They needed cleansing. God offered to cleanse them from their sin. First, they must be willing to obey. Then God would restore the desolate land so that abundant crops would cover the hillsides. Resist and rebel, however, and cleansing would be impossible. They would not **eat the best from the land**. Instead, the enemy's army would consume them. Give reasonable repentance and obvious obedience, or receive the rebel's reward. God had spoken the final word.

Ⅲ Recycling the Righteous (1:21–26)

Funeral lamentation and woe oracle (740 B.C.)

SUPPORTING IDEA: *A faithful people who rebel against God find God purging them of sin to bring them back to himself as a pure, righteous, faithful people.*

1:21. While the city was enjoying the height of prosperity, the prophet described Jerusalem's funerals. He pictured the city as a bride who had forsaken her husband for the world's oldest profession. The bride had had three essential qualities.

The first quality was to be **faithful** (Hb. *'munah*), meaning "strong and enduring," as well as "loyal and believing." Faithfulness is the basic demand of Isaiah (see Isa. 7:9; 8:2; 28:16).

Justice (Hb. *mishpat*) is a quality that creates and encourages equal rights and peace among people and nations. It has particular reference to situations of judgment where innocence and guilt are established. Every personal decision, every court case, every verdict, every sentence, every law, every act that assists someone in need can be described as *mishpat*. Individuals may claim it is the government's or the temple's responsibility to create the atmosphere of justice, but God places responsibility for justice on each person. Every decision a person makes should lead to justice and wholeness in some part of society.

Righteousness (Hb. *tsedeq*) is a relationship term. It refers to the condition where all is right in the world. It is the world order that stands true to all of God's expectations. It includes a commitment of loyalty among all members of society that results in all actions being beneficial to all society's members, rich and poor.

God condemned Jerusalem because she was no longer qualified to be his bride. She was totally transformed—for the worse. Murder reigned.

1:22–23. Nothing in the city was pure, not even its money or its drink. Stealing and self-interest dominated the rulers. Bribes became more important than belief. God's people ignored the needs of the land's neediest—the **fatherless** and the **widow**—for whom God's law gave the highest protection (Deut. 16:11,14; 26:12–13; Job 24:9; Ps. 94:6; Jer. 5:28; Ezek. 22:7; Zech. 7:10).

1:24–25. The Lord of Hosts (NIV, LORD **Almighty**) could not ignore this. In sorrowful anger the **Mighty One of Israel** moved. Here are two ancient titles for Israel's God. The military designation "Lord of Hosts" was connected to the ark of the covenant, which had led Israel's armies to victory (1 Sam. 6:2). It referred to all forces at God's command, heavenly and earthly. (For Lord Almighty/Lord of Hosts, see "Deeper Discoveries.") "Mighty One of

Israel" occurs only in this passage in the Old Testament, but the related term "Mighty One of Jacob" rings forth in Genesis 49:24 and Psalm 132:2,5. God was the might and power behind all that his people Israel or Jacob did.

Isaiah's announcement sounded like good news for Israel. God's armies were finally going to march. Isaiah, as usual, had a surprise in his language. Israel was God's enemy. The divine armies would march *against* Jerusalem, not out *from* Jerusalem. Yes, God would attack his own people. The mighty, divine General must put his hand to the smelter to recycle his rebellious people. Isaiah had hope for the nation, but only after it had been punished and humiliated by the Lord.

1:26. Judges (*shophet*) exercised military, political, judicial, and, supposedly, moral leadership. But the Book of Judges showed that from the beginning such leaders often followed rather than led. David and Solomon depended on the advice of wise **counselors** as they organized and initiated Israel's monarchy (2 Sam. 16). God decided to go back to the way government was run in Israel's beginning days when God was recognized as king of Israel. Then Jerusalem would be just what God wanted: **the City of Righteousness, the Faithful City.**

F Burning the Baal-Lovers (1:27–31)

Announcement of Zion's redemption (715 B.C.)

SUPPORTING IDEA: *God's beloved city will be redeemed but only after God has caused the rebellious people to perish.*

1:27. The combination of hope and threat that repeats itself in this chapter finds explicit interpretation. Apparently life was going well as demonstrated in Israel's worship (Isa. 1:29–31). The Assyrian threat was not yet serious. The question at issue was **Zion**, a word filled with theological importance. Zion was the southeastern hill of the city of Jerusalem (2 Sam. 5:7), the site where Solomon built the temple. The term was then extended to designate all of Jerusalem as the Holy City. Temple worshipers raised hymns of praise to the city (Pss. 46; 84; 132). It was God's "resting place for ever," which he had chosen (Ps. 132:14).

But Isaiah disagreed with this view. He modified popular opinion. Zion had to be **redeemed** by God because she was sinful. Such redemption would bring human **justice**. To be redeemed is to be set free, liberated. Redemption is needed when a person has lost personal freedom. Someone must pay the price to restore one's freedom from slavery (Exod. 21:8,30; Lev. 19:20–22; Job 6:23). Redemption is needed by firstborn sons and animals who belong to God and must be redeemed (Num. 18:16; 1 Sam. 14:45). God paid the price for the redemption of persons, resulting in human justice on earth. Sinners take the first step toward justice when they repent and become agents of God's **righteousness**.

1:28–29. Isaiah gave justice an unusual interpretation. It begins with destruction, pronouncing the sentence of death on **sinners** because they rebelled and forsook God rather than obeying and creating justice. Justice also produced embarrassment at improper religion. Israel's sin was their worship of the pagan Canaanite god Baal in **sacred oaks** and **gardens**.

1:30–31. The Divine Judge would ultimately pronounce his sentence—death by burning. Like drooping, withering plants without water, the people would be easily set ablaze by a spark. Yet the conflagration would blaze out of control, and no one would be able to put it out. No hope remained for those who thought they were so mighty because they were so religious. Still, with the judgment, hope remained for those who repented.

> **MAIN IDEA REVIEW:** *A sinful people who have rebelled against God and suffered his punishment for their sins must demonstrate repentance in moral actions, not in religious rituals.*

III. CONCLUSION

A Trip to Court

God's people need a trip to court where they find themselves on trial. The court wants more than ritual worship. The court demands evidence of a changed life. Are you liberated and redeemed from the world's values? The court demands that religious people show concrete evidence that they are working for justice by helping others.

Isaiah issued God's decree of "guilty" against a very religious people. They were so religious they could sacrifice to God in the temple and to Baal on the hillsides and in the fertility cult gardens. People who thought they were lily white found they were blood red. People secure in their religion found a death sentence hanging over their heads. God's people must measure the sincerity of their religion by the way they treat those in need. God wants agents of justice, not observers of rote ritual.

PRINCIPLES

- Religious people may be deceived, thinking they know God when they do not.
- Sin is turning against God and not obeying him.
- God's discipline should lead a person to repent and obey him.
- Religious ritual without righteous living does not gain God's favor.

- God does not listen to the prayers of people who constantly do wrong.
- God's way of life leads believers to help those who cannot help themselves.
- Religious tradition does not win a person favor with God in the present.
- God has a plan to restore and save a remnant of his people.

APPLICATIONS

- List your own personal sins and confess them to God.
- Repent of your sins now.
- Ask God to forgive your sins and make you clean.
- Quit depending on participation in religious services and rituals to win favor with God.
- Find a ministry to help someone in need.
- Admit to God that he has been right in disciplining you.
- Ask God to teach you his way of doing right.
- Thank God for his plan of salvation.

IV. LIFE APPLICATION

The Realistic Road to Repentance

What story do you expect to hear to illustrate God's call to repentance and confession of sin? The town drunk? A woman-chaser turned preacher? A famous conversion like Charles Colson's? Probably these are too extreme for you to identify with. You cannot repent of sins in the way these people did. You may be more like me. As a youngster in elementary school, I went to church every Sunday and many other days. I was a quiet kid, stayed by myself reading much of the time, so that I seldom got into trouble. People would tell my parents what a good child I was and how proud they should be.

Then one day, the pastor stopped to talk with me. He asked me if I knew Jesus Christ as my Savior. Suddenly, I realized I had committed the worst sin of all. I had not believed God. I had not trusted his way of salvation. I had not accepted his invitation to eternal life. I prayed with the pastor. I told God I was sorry for my sins, and I listed the little lies I had told, the times I had disobeyed my parents, the things I had done in anger. Most of all I told God I had not believed in Jesus, and I wanted to believe in him. God forgave my sins that day.

From that day forward, I have never gotten into what we call the "big sins" of life. But each day I have to ask God to forgive sins that the world would never see or suspect. I know that my faithful record at church does not impress God. He continues to look at my heart and to see my attitudes, my anger, my selfishness, my devotion to self rather than to him and others.

You may be more like me than the town drunk. Sin saturates your life, like alcohol does his. Yours may be a more subtle kind of sin that you hide from others, try to hide from yourself, and may even think you can hide from God. God is waiting to bring great things to your life and to your church. He waits for you to ask forgiveness of your sin and to dedicate yourself to his service.

V. PRAYER

God Almighty, you know my religious acts and are quite unimpressed. Forgive me for depending on acts of worship that make me feel good, and for ignoring the acts of justice that you expect. Cleanse me. Take away my sin, for I repent of it. Show me where you are working to bring justice and righteousness. Show me how to join you in your work. Amen.

VI. DEEPER DISCOVERIES

A. Kings of Judah (1:1)

Isaiah 1:1 places the ministry of the prophet Isaiah during the lifetime of four kings of Judah. Dating their reigns is a perennial problem for biblical students. Uzziah (also known as Azariah) ruled for fifty-two years (2 Kgs. 15:2) as one of Judah's strongest kings. Most scholars set his dates as 792–740 B.C., most of it as coruler with his father Amaziah (796–767) or his son Jotham (750–731). The people assassinated Uzziah's father and installed the sixteen-year-old Uzziah as king (2 Kgs. 14:19–21). Uzziah firmly established his rule, gaining power over southern sea routes and over the highways along the Philistine coast (2 Chr. 26:2–6). He apparently strengthened the defenses in Jerusalem and Judea and reorganized the army (2 Chr. 26:6–10). In his last years a horrible skin disease forced Uzziah to let his son have most of the power (2 Kgs. 15:5).

Jotham continued Judah's prosperity (2 Kgs. 15:33–38), although he faced opposition from the strong Northern Kingdom allied with Syria (2 Kgs. 15:37). He rebuilt many of the nation's defenses (2 Chr. 27:3–4).

Ahaz ruled Judah from about 735 until about 713 (2 Kgs. 16:2). The kings of Syria and Israel tried to force Ahaz to join them in fighting the king of Assyria, but Isaiah warned Ahaz to trust God and not listen to the kings (Isa. 7). Syria took away Judah's control of Edom and the southern sea routes (2 Kgs. 16:6) and had to fight Edom (2 Chr. 28:17–18) and the Philistines. Ahaz paid some type of homage to Tiglath-Pileser of Assyria and adopted religious practices of Syria (2 Chr. 28:23).

King Hezekiah (729–686 B.C.) brought spiritual renewal to Judah (2 Chr. 29:1–31:21) by destroying Canaanite worship, refurbishing the temple in Jerusalem, and restoring traditional worship practices. He instituted religious reform with political wisdom, so that he avoided confrontation with Assyria when the Philistines revolted in 712. Then he prepared his country militarily for Sennacherib's invasion in 701 (Isa. 22:8–11), insuring sufficient water for the city (2 Kgs. 20:20).

Hezekiah showed his religious faith by following Isaiah's advice rather than giving in to Assyrian threats. Thus, he avoided capture of Jerusalem and experienced God's miraculous deliverance. But Hezekiah still lost many cities, including Lachish, and had to pay tribute to Assyria (2 Kgs. 18:13–19:37; Isa. 36–39). Many of Isaiah's sermons came from the period of Hezekiah's confrontation with Assyria.

B. Holy One of Israel (1:4)

Isaiah's encounter with God in the temple (ch. 6) shaped his understanding of God as the Holy One of Israel, the God who was pure beyond all human understanding and who could not endure the presence of sin (1 Sam. 6:20). Israel was not the first people to view a god as holy. The Canaanites also described their gods as holy. But Israel was apparently the first to use "holy" as a moral term that separated God and man (Isa. 17:7). Holiness thus became a reason for God to bring judgment on human sin and to discipline his own people. Isaiah uses "Holy One of Israel" over thirty times to describe the God who warns his sinful people and woos them to repentance (30:12). This title for God also appears in Psalms 71:22; 78:41; Jeremiah 50:29; and Ezekiel 39:7.

Israel rejected the Holy One of Israel (Isa. 1:4), depended on Egypt instead of him (30:15; 31:1), mocked his warnings (30:11), and responded in anger to his call to trust him (30:11). They despised and rejected their Holy One (30:12) and so deserved his judgment. By enforcing righteousness and justice among his people, God showed himself to be holy (5:16). He sought to make his people trust him and have confidence in him (17:7; 29:23). After all, he is their Creator (43:15) and Redeemer (43:3,14; 48:17). He will glorify Israel and bring the nations to himself (55:5). His people will praise their Holy One (17:7; 29:19)

C. Sacrifices and Burnt Offerings (1:11)

Old Testament worship featured a sacrificial system with specific offerings set out for specific life situations and occasions of worship as prescribed in the opening chapters of Leviticus. Such worship was not the creation of human minds. God had given the entire system to Moses for the people to follow. During the monarchy the system became a problem in several ways.

First, where did one sacrifice: at Jerusalem only or at Bethel and Dan if you lived in the Northern Kingdom? Second, could you also follow the sacrifice rituals of other nations and other gods if you faithfully sacrificed to the God of Israel? Third, what was the difference between Israel's sacrificial system and Canaan's? Fourth, did God expect anything else from you if you faithfully carried out the system of annual festivals and ongoing daily and weekly sacrifices? Finally, what did God get out of Israel's sacrifices; that is, in what way did he need them?

Isaiah burst on the scene with a different emphasis: first things first. Follow God's covenant expectations of justice and righteousness before you even think of worship ritual and sacrifice. Until you get daily living correct, such rituals as daily sacrifice, weekly Sabbath worship, monthly new moon observances, and annual festivals and assemblies are meaningless. God can live without them. They do nothing to enhance his being or ensure his existence.

Sacrifices and worship services were intended to show people the proper ways to approach God, show their gratitude to and dependence on God, and show them the way God offered atonement and forgiveness of sin. Atonement and forgiveness were not available for a people who were devoted to sin rather than righteousness. Worship was unacceptable from a person whose lifestyle was not accepted by the Lord. Isaiah's message is clear: live right; then you can worship right.

D. Justice (1:17)

The Hebrew term *mishpat* ("justice") occurs about 425 times in the Old Testament, forty-two of those in Isaiah. The term ranges over a wide spectrum of Israel's legal system. In different contexts, the word is translated as "God's instructions," "God's laws," "the court," "the case before the court," "the judgment of the court," "the verdict rendered by the court," and "the sentence imposed by the court." It may also refer to the entire system of justice the court on earth or in heaven attempts to establish. The NIV uses more than eighty different words to translate this one Hebrew word.

According to Isaiah, God is a God of justice (30:18), and he expects his leaders, especially his king, to establish justice (5:7; 32:1). The basic measurement of justice is how one treats the poor, the fatherless, the orphan (3:14; 10:2). Human legal judgment oppresses the Suffering Servant (53:8) and is part of the sin of God's people (58:2). Thus God's goal for his future kingdom is that justice is established (9:7; 32:16; 34:5; 61:8). God's people thus must learn to seek and carry out justice (1:17; 56:1). They must rely on God to hear and defend their case (41:1; 54:17).

E. Lord Almighty/Lord of Hosts (1:9,24)

The term "LORD Almighty" or "Lord of Hosts" is used 285 times in the Old Testament and sixty-two times in Isaiah to refer to God as the all-powerful commander of the heavenly and earthly armies (1 Sam. 17:45; Isa. 13:4). Most of the occurrences of this divine title are in the prophetic books with none in Genesis-Judges. Such armies may even be used against his own people (Isa. 1:24–25) but are usually aimed at other nations (13:4–6). The armies are led by the Divine King who is enthroned on the cherubim of the ark of the covenant (2 Sam. 6:2; 2 Kgs. 19:15).

For Isaiah, "Lord of Hosts" or "Lord Almighty" is one of the most significant titles for the God of Israel (Isa. 5:16,24; 21:10; 44:6), the Holy One (8:13; 47:4). The Lord Almighty summoned and commanded the heavenly armies to accomplish his will (13:4; 45:12). One way of doing this is to establish justice through a messianic king (24:23). Another is to bring judgment on a sinful people (28:22). Another is to bring a punished people back to himself (9:13; 19:20) and punish their enemies (10:16–26; 17:3; 29:6). This will lift up the Lord of Hosts or Lord Almighty by displaying and proving his justice (5:16).

The will of the Lord Almighty is to punish the proud (2:12; 10:33; 23:9), which can mean his people in his city (5:24; 39:5), and to protect the helpless (3:15). He provided a remnant for Israel after its punishment (1:9; 37:32). And he planned salvation for all nations (25:6)

VII. TEACHING OUTLINE

A. INTRODUCTION

1. Lead Story: Country Club Conversion
2. Context: Isaiah spoke God's word boldly to Israel and Judah for half a century. He saw four kings come and go on the throne of Judah. He outlined God's ways with his people not only for his generation but for two centuries beyond his lifetime. Thus he pointed Israel to God's destruction of the Northern Kingdom, his deliverance of Hezekiah from Sennacherib of Assyria, the eventual fall of the Southern Kingdom, the exile in Babylon, the return from exile, and the new start with the new temple. Those who collected his preaching and formed it into a book carefully placed the sermons of chapter 1 together as an introduction of Isaiah's preaching.
3. Transition: In chapter 1 we hear Isaiah's call to repent and his warning for those who refuse to repent. Here the prophet painted a picture for religious people, people who thought they were right with God. He showed them the futility of religious ritual without correct conduct. He pleaded with his people to let God wash away their guilt by

repenting of their sin and turning to justice and righteousness as the marks of daily life.

B. COMMENTARY

1. Calling the Confused to Court (1:1–3)
2. Lamenting the Lost (1:4–9)
3. Reviving the Religious (1:10–17)
4. Reasoning for Repentance (1:18–20)
5. Recycling the Righteous (1:21–26)
6. Burning the Baal-Lovers (1:27–31)

C. CONCLUSION: THE REALISTIC ROAD TO REPENTANCE

1. Wrap-up: God called his people to court. They expected to be on the witness stand testifying to their faith in God and what he had done for them. Instead, they found they were the defendants, accused of rebelling against God, pretending to be religious and faithful when they had missed the whole point of a relationship with God. These "oh-so-religious" people were declared lost. They needed to be revived, to be turned back to God and his priority. Here came the surprise: God's priority had nothing to do with temple worship and religious ritual, even though Scripture taught these. God's priority centered on daily life, dealing with the less fortunate of the world and fighting for justice and righteousness for them. If "God's people" would not repent of unrighteous living and let God wash them clean, they would face a new round of judgment and discipline. Only a remnant had hope.
2. Personal Challenge: Take yourself to court. Face Isaiah's penetrating examination of your life. Has religion replaced right living? Has a "just get by" attitude replaced justice as your life's goal? Do you need to plead guilty before God and ask him to forgive your sin and wash you clean? Or do you want to face another round of his judgment and discipline as he tries to woo you back to himself?

VIII. ISSUES FOR DISCUSSION

1. Why is religious living not good enough to meet God's requirements?
2. What sins do people in the church most frequently commit today?
3. Is it possible to be guilty before God while thinking you are in good standing with him? How?
4. In what ways does God bring discipline and judgment on his people today?
5. What causes God to hide his eyes from our prayers?

Isaiah 2–4

Payday on the Way

I. **INTRODUCTION**
Fear—the Fatal Flaw

II. **COMMENTARY**
A verse-by-verse explanation of these chapters.

III. **CONCLUSION**
Disaster and Hope

An overview of the principles and applications from these chapters.

IV. **LIFE APPLICATION**
Achieving the Unachievable

Melding these chapters to life.

V. **PRAYER**
Tying these chapters to life with God.

VI. **DEEPER DISCOVERIES**
Historical, geographical, and grammatical enrichment of the commentary.

VII. **TEACHING OUTLINE**
Suggested step-by-step group study of these chapters.

VIII. **ISSUES FOR DISCUSSION**
Zeroing these chapters in on daily life.

"*G*od does not pay weekly,

but he pays at the end."

Dutch proverb

Isaiah 2–4

IN A NUTSHELL

*I*n these chapters Isaiah wraps descriptions of God's glorious future for his righteous remnant around a series of sermons condemning Israel's lax leadership and luxury-loving ladies. The final day of the Lord will bring peace and protection for the pious remnant but judgment and destruction for the sinful majority.

Payday on the Way

I. INTRODUCTION

Fear—the Fatal Flaw

*M*aggie represents so many of us. A casual observer thinks Maggie has everything a person could want. She is president of the neighborhood homeowners' association, coach of the soccer team, and social hostess with a humorous story and good word for everyone she meets. And she never meets a stranger. She ran her own business before she married, is a gourmet cook, and loves to garden. Her devoted husband and children are so proud of Maggie, but Maggie is not proud of herself. She still looks for that one great achievement to show she really amounts to something. The problem is that this one great achievement changes every couple of weeks. She's going to open the town's biggest interior decoration shop, start a gourmet coffee bar, remodel a country home into a quaint bed and breakfast stop. One thing apparently squashes each of Maggie's plans—fear of failure.

The women of Israel had everything going for them, too. Parties, clothes, status, family, religious involvement—they were on top of the world doing everything right. Deep down inside lurked the fear that something was going to ruin their party and destroy their dream life. Along came Isaiah to confirm their fears and then point the way to hope. Perhaps life is too good to be true for you, too. Does some indefinable fear keep raising its quiet voice in the depth of your heart? Could it be that you are in the same situation as the lovely ladies of Israel? (This is adapted from Breathnach, pp. 159–160.)

II. COMMENTARY

Payday on the Way

> **MAIN IDEA:** *God's ultimate plan is for all people to live in peace, worship him, and enjoy his holy presence among them. But God's judgment will humble and purify the sinful people—male and female, leader and common citizen.*

A The Way to Warless Worship for the World (2:1–5)

Prophetic announcement of salvation in Zion (701 B.C.)

> **SUPPORTING IDEA:** *God's ultimate plan is to bring all nations to worship him at his temple, to learn to obey his ways, and to declare universal peace.*

2:1. This section begins with another introduction much like Isaiah 1:1, but this one only introduces the following sermons, not the entire book. What follows is a vision, **what Isaiah . . . saw**. Interestingly, the first part of this vision also appears in Micah 4:1–5. The form of this sermon sounds like a call to worship introduced by a prophetic announcement of salvation. Apparently Isaiah and his younger contemporary Micah both used the same call to worship from the Jerusalem temple to speak to God's people. This would mean that God used the temple hymnody as a source for his inspired word.

2:2. While the destruction of Jerusalem dominated chapter 1, the city's function as the center of salvation for all nations introduces this section. The **last days** are still within world history with separate nations acting. Israel used the same language as her Near Eastern neighbors in talking about the national temple as the highest mountain on earth where the deity fights battles for his people (cp. Pss. 46; 48). The prophet Isaiah applied this language to the temple in Jerusalem even though Jerusalem was obviously not the highest of the mountains Israel could see. Jerusalem would be high and lifted up because God was at work there, causing his purpose for the world to be realized in historical events. The emphasis is not on the height of Jerusalem. The emphasis is on the unheard-of foreign nations coming to Jerusalem to worship. God's hope always encompasses the world, not just one small nation (see Gen. 12:1–4).

2:3–4. The prophet, as he often did, took up the popular theology of the people's hymnody and subtly shifted it from present to future tense. Only in the last days would Zion occupy such an exalted position. God would no longer battle the nations. Jerusalem could no longer glory in the hope that nations would march to her with large gifts and tribute for her victorious king. The prophetic hope is that God's word will become the world's weapon. Military academies and weapons will vanish. People will learn to live according to God's ways. They will obey his teachings. Nations will come to Jerusalem, not because a victorious king forces them to, but because they are attracted to Jerusalem by the God who lives there and the wisdom he gives there. No longer will they have to fight to settle their differences. In Jerusalem God will be the great Mediator who settles all human disputes without battle. Military weapons will become obsolete. The world's only war will be on poverty and hunger. (For law, see "Deeper Discoveries"; for word of the Lord, see "Deeper Discoveries," chs. 28–33.)

2:5. The prophet knew only one way for this to happen. Thus he issued his own call to worship. This worship is not limited to the temple but shines forth in everyday life as people walk in the light of God's word. Israel could not hope for world domination through military superiority. They could become the hope for the world if they obeyed God's teaching, walked where he led them, and showed the world the superiority of God's way of life.

B Reasons for Rejection (2:6–9)

Announcement of judgment in that day (about 740 B.C.)

SUPPORTING IDEA: *Rich, successful people who ignore God for this world's gods face humiliation on the day of God's exaltation.*

2:6. The prophet sets out a dialog between the people and God. They accuse God of being unfaithful, abandoning his people in their time of greatest need. His reply shows why he abandoned them: they have imported every kind of superstitious religion they can find from east and west. In a day of peace and prosperity, Israel profited from international trade. But her imports stretched too far, because they imported religion along with consumer goods. Israel had a covenant with God, not a partnership with pagan practices. Israel's original enemy—the Philistines (Judg. 3:31; 1 Sam. 4:1–2 Sam. 8:12)—was a major trading partner and source of temptation.

We must be very careful in studying this section of God's Word. Several parts of the Hebrew text are difficult to read. Verse 6b reads literally: "They are full from the east and diviners as the Philistines." Translators usually add a word very similar to "from the east" meaning "diviners." The word translated **clasp hands with** occurs only here, so its meaning is not really known. The Dead Sea Scrolls do not contain verses 9b–10.

2:7–9. Isaiah spoke to a people who were rich and told them why they were headed for ruin. They listened to magicians rather than prophets, practiced foreign rites, worshiped foreign gods, then strutted proudly around and wondered why God was displeased. Traditionally, the prophet's task had been to plead to God on behalf of the people. The situation had become so desperate that Isaiah could only raise the terrifying curse: **do not forgive them**.

C Preaching Against Pride (2:10–22)

Prophecy of disaster (about 740 B.C.)

SUPPORTING IDEA: *Pride, self-reliance, and false gods face a day of terror when God reveals his majesty and splendor.*

2:10. Isaiah caught the people's attention quickly as he exhorted the people to hide from God's terror. The irony is that they might try to hide but there is no escape from God. Israel had gloried in God's majesty, the beauty and splendor that revealed him to be greater than anything in nature and superior to any of the gods so gloriously decorated by human hands. But sinful Israel could not enjoy that splendor. It blinded them and destroyed them.

They had to run for the rocks to hide from their own God. Only a redeemed Israel could look on God's majesty (Isa. 35:2).

2:11. The oracle points back (**in that day**) to the opening of chapter 2 to remind the readers that no one is guaranteed a part in the "last days" (v. 2). God is the only one sure to be exalted then. A disobedient people may exalt themselves in pride now, but they will finally be **brought low**.

2:12. Isaiah joined the prophet Amos in transforming a favorite expression of the popular piety. Everyone believed the day of Yahweh, Israel's God, would be a day of victory in battle against her enemies. The prophets said it would be a day of victory for Yahweh against his enemies, who were his own people (Amos 5:18–22)! Isaiah underlined his previous condemnation of the people of God. God's day is victory only for those who are truly God's people, not for the proud. (For day of the Lord, see "Deeper Discoveries," chs. 13–14.)

2:13–16. The marvels of creation and of human handiwork represent the most magnificent realities the human eye can see. Yet each of these splendid objects will vanish from sight on God's day of judgment.

2:17–19. The good days of prosperity will soon give way to economic disaster. Human pride and achievement will vanish. Only God will remain high and lifted up, exalted above his world. The idols so valued (Isa. 2:6) will **disappear**. The arrogant and proud will have to follow the prophet's advice (v. 10) and **flee to caves in the rocks**. Why? Because as men are **brought low**, God **rises to shake the earth**.

2:20–21. As God shakes the earth in judgment, the idols people fashioned for the purpose of worship will be fit only for the animals who inhabited the darkest places of the earth and who could not appreciate their beauty. So again the refrain: **flee to caverns in the rocks**. Those who did not fear the Lord will now stand in dread of him. Those who did not praise his majesty will shrink away from it in horror.

2:22. The prophet concluded with another curse, calling upon his faithful followers not to put their confidence in human beings. Humans are only dust, given the breath of life by God (see the same expression in Gen. 2:7). A sarcastic rhetorical question is a fitting conclusion. People have no basis for pride. In the end they will crawl trembling into the cave to finish their days. The arrogant will have to admit they are worth no more than the dust of the ground.

D A Lack of Leadership (3:1–12)

Prophecy of disaster climaxing in woe oracle (740 B.C.)

SUPPORTING IDEA: *A lack of loyal leadership mixed with public sin causes God to bring judgment on his people while bringing
assurance to the righteous.*

3:1–12. Again the Hebrew text calls us to be cautious. **Skilled craftsman**
(v. 3) is usually translated "magician" (see TEV, NLT, NRSV), in light of Aramaic and Syrian words meaning "magician." **Mere children** (v. 4) means "ill-
treatment, affliction, capricious use of power." **Remedy** (v. 7) represents a
play on a word that means "to tie up" and can be used both to tie up a wound
and to saddle (be in the saddle), thus to rule.

Look (v. 9) occurs only here in the Bible, so its meaning is uncertain. It
may mean "partiality" as a related term does in Deuteronomy 1:17. A quick
glance at several translations reveals the difficulty of translating verse 12. The
first half may mean "taskmasters oppress them" or "a child oppresses them"
(author's translation). There follows either "money-lenders rule over them"
or "women rule over them" (author's translation).

The central message of the text is clear. One of the consequences of failure to worship God wholeheartedly will be a leadership vacuum. For leaders
who simply seduced and swallowed God's people (v. 12), God had a remedy:
Assyrian exile. Isaiah described this exile in some detail. The leaders of every
area of the country's life—religious, political, legal, military—would be
snatched from their homeland and sprinkled over the far reaches of the
Assyrian Empire. This would leave the land at the mercy of foreign governors. Experienced local leadership would not exist.

3:1–3. Amid Judah's pride in her prosperity, the prophet described her
imminent fate. Siege warfare would remove all their food supplies. Then exile
would remove the leadership.

3:4–7. Inexperienced leadership would lead to anarchy. Society would be
turned upside down. The only qualification for the highest position in the
land would be possession of life's necessities. But the nominee would lie and
connive to avoid election.

3:8–9. All this would happen because God's people had acted like little
children, defiantly disobeying God even when his glory was clear. So brazen
and proud were they that they flaunted their sin openly. Sodom offered the
only possible comparison (Gen. 13–14; 18). In face of such pride and flagrant
rebellion, the divine response is especially noteworthy. God entered into
mourning for his people, taking up the **woe** of the funeral lamentation for
them.

3:10–12. Still, God offered assurances of hope for the righteous remnant. They had no reason to worry. Then God resumed his mourning tones to announce the judgment of the wicked. Payback time was approaching. Lack of leadership was both the cause and result of their situation. This brought divine judgment and a real sense of loss in the heart of God. He could cry mournfully, **O my people**, as he described their hopeless situation.

E Princes Prey on the Paupers (3:13–15)

Courtroom trial (740 B.C.)

SUPPORTING IDEA: *The divine judge states his case against leaders who gain power and wealth at the expense of the poor and helpless.*

3:13. Isaiah moved from the language of the funeral home to that of the courtroom as he condemned the leaders of the people. Cleverly, the prophet pictured the divine judge standing in the courtroom ready to judge "peoples" (author's translation). His audience stood immediately to attention, eager to hear the prophet proclaim the expected word of judgment on their enemies.

3:14. Only with verse 14 would the audience suddenly awake to what was happening. The prophet placed his audience under arrest and dragged them into God's courtroom for judgment and sentencing. Primary focus is on the leadership. The **elders** originally formed the governing body of the nomadic tribe. Once settled in the land, they functioned in the same way as did the elders in the Canaanite cities (Josh. 9:11), making political decisions for their tribe. In national affairs they became advisors to the king. In Ruth 4, elders functioned as the local court of justice at the city gate. Laws for this function appear in Deuteronomy 19:11–12; 21:1–9,18–21; 22:13–21; 25:5–10. But in Isaiah's day the elders used their legal and political powers to feather their own nests. This, among other things, brought God's judgment on Israel.

These **leaders** were royal officials who traced their positions of power back to Moses (Exod. 18:25). As such they had rigid qualifications (Exod. 18:21). They were military officials. They had power to imprison people (1 Kgs. 22:26). Gradually the term came to be generalized to include all royal officials (1 Kgs. 4:2). At times they represented a threat to the king (Jer. 38:24–27). They also represented a threat to the poor country farmers, using their political power to demand payments and gifts. Farmers who did not pay found their vineyards burned. Isaiah bluntly called this stealing.

3:15. The elders and princes saw no significance in such oppressive acts. But God took notice. These acts formed the basis for his condemnation of the nation to destruction. **Declares the Lord** represents a technical expression for "oracle of Yahweh," which occurs 365 times in the Bible. It appears most often in the prophetic literature to lend authority to the prophetic word, since that word was not usually believed by the audience.

F Too Late for the Ladies (3:16–4:1)

Prophecy of disaster (740 B.C.)

SUPPORTING IDEA: *Party-loving women must share the blame with their V.I.P. husbands and face God's judgment on their pride.*

3:16. The courage of the prophet knew no limits. He even attacked the Jerusalem women's circle. Again, the punishment pronounced on the flirts of Zion matched the crime.

3:17. Lovely hairdos would fall down as scratching fingers struck at dandruff or a more serious scalp disorder. God would finish the process and make them bald.

3:18–23. Then God would remove all their feminine finery, not because it was evil in itself but because it was contributing to their false pride. Here Isaiah used a vocabulary that is not seen in other biblical books, so the translation remains uncertain at many points. The student of the Bible should compare several translations.

3:24–26. New clothing would be laid out. These clothes should be suitable for a pilgrimage into exile rather than a pilgrimage to the temple. Such a pilgrimage would be lonely, because the men would die in battle. Funeral rites would be the only social activity.

4:1. The women would lose all their pride as they fought over whatever sort of man happened to remain alive. The women would want no material goods from the man, only a married name and children to remove the disgrace of being unmarried and barren. What a contrast to the proud prancers whose greed and arrogance brought such judgment on themselves.

G Protection for the Pious (4:2–6)

Prediction of hope (701 B.C.)

SUPPORTING IDEA: *After judgment God will cause his people to branch out in glory and safety as he redeems and cleanses them so he can live among them in holiness.*

4:2. That day cannot be totally dark. This section of the book thus ends, as it began, with a note of hope (see 2:1–5). The date of "that day" remains vague and undefined. The point is not to circle a day on a calendar but to affirm the saving purpose of God for his people. The only chronological note is that such salvation comes after judgment. A bouquet of images describes the day of hope.

First, agricultural language describes the blossoming and fertility of the trees for the remnant left in the land. Such language had wider overtones. The **Branch** or "sprout" is related to the verb "sprout" connected with kingship hopes in 2 Samuel 23:5 (NIV, "bring to fruition") and Psalm 132:17 (NIV, "grow"). The noun designated the hoped-for king who would bring salvation (Jer. 23:5; 33:15; Zech. 3:8; 6:12). Early in its history, Judaism used this passage as a basis of future hopes for a king. **Survivors** form the root of salvation hope in Isaiah 10:20 and 37:31–32.

4:3. He who is left (NIV, **those who are left**) appears twenty-seven times in Isaiah with the double meaning of disaster and hope. Here it points to the hope that a chance for survival and new life remained. (For survivors/remnant, see "Deeper Discoveries.")

This remnant hope ranges through much of the Old Testament literature (see Gen. 7:23; 1 Kgs. 19:9–18; Amos 5:15). Those chosen for inclusion among the remnant are **recorded among the living in Jerusalem**. This is a figure of speech taken from the political practice of taking a census and recording genealogies (see Neh. 7:64). Here such a remnant will be declared **holy**. This reflects cultic practice by which the priest declared a worshiper fit to enter the temple and worship (Exod. 22:31; Lev. 17–26, particularly ch. 19).

4:4. Isaiah said no priest would proclaim man holy. Nor could ethical actions provide such holiness. God himself must perform the cleansing. This can be done only through acts of judgment and destruction.

4:5–6. The prophet turned to creation language. Hope for the remnant lay only in the power of God to start all over again and give his preserved people a new place to live. The glory of the place is the protective presence of God as symbolized in the exodus event (Exod. 14:20–24). Not just the holy of holies in the temple (1 Kgs. 8:10–11), but the entire site of Mount Zion would become God's dwelling place on earth.

The concluding statements (5b–6) represent a very difficult text, reading literally, "for upon all glory a shelter, a booth will be for a shade daily from devastating heat and for a refuge from cloudburst and from rain" (author's translation). The glory of the divine presence is thus roofed in so that it remains with Jerusalem and cannot depart (cp. Ezek. 10:18–19.). Israel would find protection from all life's threats. Such protection is not dependent upon human leaders or pride. Divine presence guarantees it, removing all reason for human pride.

> **MAIN IDEA REVIEW:** *God's ultimate plan is for all people to live in peace, worship him, and enjoy his holy presence among them. But God's judgment will humble and purify the sinful people— male and female, leader and common citizen.*

III. CONCLUSION

Disaster and Hope

God has a marvelous future planned for his people. He can use various kinds of language to describe that future. It is a time without war when the nations of the world stream to God's chosen place to learn his teaching. It is a time of fertility and beauty when God lives with the remnant of his people, having cleansed them with judgment. It is a new exodus when God fulfills his purposes that the original exodus generation rebelled against.

No matter how the day of hope is described, it comes only after disaster. God must bring the arrogance and pride of his people low before he can give them his promised day of hope. Leaders must be forced to realize they have responsibility to help the needy, not show off their ill-gained wealth and finely-clad beauty. God must bring mourning before he can bring the new morning of hope.

Pride pokes its ugly face into each of our lives. Where are you most susceptible to pride's temptation? Where have you fallen victim to pride? List before God the ways pride is present in your life and ask him to forgive you. Commit yourself to using the resources and talents he has given you to help those whom society ignores and abuses. Pray that you will be able to enjoy the fruit of righteous deeds, enjoying God's deliverance rather than facing his doom.

PRINCIPLES

- World peace depends on God's actions and on our obedience to his law.
- War is not God's plan for his people.
- Superstitions, divinations, and astrology do not reveal God's will or help us face the future.
- Riches do not bring happiness or eternal success.
- Products of human hands are not worthy of worship.
- People have no reason for pride.
- Only God is worthy of our trust and worship.
- God has a day of final judgment in store for the world.

- God protects the righteous from his terrible judgment.
- Women as well as men will be judged for their sins of materialism and pride.
- God will save a remnant of his people and make them holy so he can live among them.

APPLICATIONS

- Invite people of all classes, races, and nations to join you in worshiping God.
- Join a Bible study class where you can learn God's ways and word.
- Work in God's ways for peace in the world.
- Dedicate your material possessions to God, and do not depend on them to protect you in times of trouble.
- Confess your pride to God, and ask him to forgive you and take it away.
- Are you trusting in human ability and human resources rather than in God?
- Confess any sins you may have against the poor and needy.

IV. LIFE APPLICATION

Achieving the Unachievable

One bookshelf in my office is filled with books I have written, edited, or contributed to. It is easy to look up from my computer and see the *Holman Christian Standard New Testament,* the *Holman Bible Dictionary,* or the *Holman New Testament Commentary* on Luke, or any of the other works and begin to think: "Hey, look what I have accomplished. I am quite a guy, am I not?"

It is easy to go to church and join a self-congratulatory society where we tell one another how good we are, how wonderful it is to have so many good people in our church, and how glad we are that we are not like such-and-such, a feuding and fussing bunch. Yes, everywhere I go temptation reaches out to tell me what a good boy I am. Then I turn to Scripture and hear Isaiah reminding us that our only hope rests in God and what he does, not in me and what I do. I realize that all the work I do to produce new books and new products often brings only fret, worry, and long hours of work. Is that what I want out of life? Is there something more, something better?

Isaiah uses one word to describe what I want—*shalom*—peace, wholeness, fulfillment. I want that, but I cannot achieve it. I must accept it as God's gift to me and praise him for such a marvelous gift. Devotion to and worship of God bring what I want and need, not devotion to work and achievement.

How about you? Can you list impressive achievements in your life? Do you find yourself resting on your laurels from such achievements rather than resting in God's peace? Join me now in asking God to deliver you from a religion and life of self-achievement and to introduce you to the life of worship and peace that only he can give.

V. PRAYER

Thank you, O God, that you are a God of hope. Thank you that you have a plan to bring peace and protection to your people. Forgive my arrogance and pride. Take away the temptation to concentrate on what I have accomplished and what I own. Teach me your ways and your law. Give me the heart to follow where you lead so I may truly participate in your day of deliverance. Amen.

VI. DEEPER DISCOVERIES

A. Law (2:3)

God is a teacher who wants his people to be good learners. The subject God teaches is *torah,* his instruction or law. The word occurs 220 times in the Old Testament, twelve of these in Isaiah. On the daily human plane, *torah* is the oral teaching of the wise men that created Proverbs (Prov. 5:13; 7:2; 13:14) as well as parental instruction for children (Prov. 4:1,4,11; 31:26).

Priests also had important teaching responsibilities (see Lev. 10:11; Deut. 17:11; 2 Kgs. 17:27–28; Jer. 18:18; Mic. 3:11), which they often failed to carry out properly (Ezek. 22:26; Zeph. 3:4). The priest must let people know what is clean and unclean, what is acceptable before God and what is not (Lev. 11:46; Ezek. 44:23; Hag. 2:11–13). He must show how worship ritual is to be carried out properly.

When the priests took bribes and did not teach God's true law and the people refused to follow God's true law (Isa. 24:5; 42:24), then the prophets claimed to have God's true teaching (Amos 2:4). Isaiah called Israel to hear God's law (Isa. 1:10), which they had rejected (5:24). Their rejection provided God the opportunity to "make his law great" (42:21). They knew God's law, having memorized it and hidden it in their hearts (51:7). Isaiah pointed to God's day when the nations would come to Jerusalem to hear God's word (2:3). When the people refused to listen to Isaiah's words, he could seal them up in written form with his disciples and call them God's law (8:16) to which future generations would refer for God's authoritative word (8:20).

God's servant will bring his law as a source of hope for the scattered peoples of earth (42:4). God will send out his law to establish justice as a light for the nations (51:4). Israel thus should listen to their Teacher (30:20) as he gives torah in the form of wisdom teaching, priestly instruction, and prophetic warning. Eventually, all such instruction is bound up into a written collection (see Deut. 4:8; 28:61; 31:26; 32:46). This written torah serves as God's final authoritative teaching which judges all human conduct and serves as the revelation of God himself (Josh. 1:7–8; 22:5; 2 Kgs. 21:8; 1 Chr. 22:12; 2 Chr. 15:3; 35:26).

Torah is not something forced on people against their will. Torah is God's way of life that should bring joy and delight to the person who learns it and obeys it (Ps. 19:7).

B. Survivors/Remnant (4:2)

A survivor is one who escapes the death sword in war (Jer. 44:28; Amos 9:1) or the messenger who escapes battle with the message of horrendous defeat (Gen. 14:13; Ezek. 24:26–27).

God is the one who enables people to escape (2 Chr. 12:7; Isa. 31:5). The psalms often use the term in laments (Pss. 17:13; 89:48) and thanksgivings (107:20; 116:4). In times of trouble God's people listen for his word of hope and deliverance. They have endured his judgment and discipline. Their only hope lies in his providing a way for them to escape or survive (Isa. 49:24–25). In the day of the Lord he will bring salvation to those whom he allows to escape his final judgment (Isa. 4:2; 37:30–32; cp. Dan. 12:1). God's survivors have a mission to the nations (Isa. 66:19).

Those who are left in Zion (4:3) represent God's remnant. Isaiah used forms of this Hebrew term twenty-seven times. The basic meaning is "to remain." Food (1 Sam. 9:24), grain and oil (Deut. 28:51), parts of the harvest (Jer. 49:9), money (Gen. 47:18) can all remain. It can be used in a military context to say no one remained (Josh. 8:17; 2 Kgs. 10:21). A family that is eradicated is said to have its name and remnant destroyed (Isa. 14:22).

God threatens to destroy a people's remnant (Jer. 47:4–5; Amos 1:8). Even Israel's remnant after judgment could be threatened (Deut. 7:20). God's anger at a disobedient people causes him to come in judgment. That judgment may leave a small helpless remnant (Isa. 6:13; Amos 5:3), no remnant, or a remnant with which God plans to complete the work of his plan of salvation for the world. The first remnant came with Noah (Gen. 7:23) who found grace in God's eyes (Gen. 6:8). Here God promised never to destroy the entire remnant of mankind (Gen. 8:21–22). Thus God sent Joseph to preserve a remnant (Gen. 45:7). God seeks not just a remnant but a faithful remnant true to him (1 Kgs. 19:10–18). Leaving a remnant is God's decision and may not happen (Amos 5:15).

The center of Isaiah's remnant thinking is reflected in his son Shear-Jashub, whose name means "a remnant will return" (see Isa. 7:3). This child stood as a warning to King Ahaz. The king must faithfully follow Isaiah's instructions or his nation would see only a small remnant return from war. That remnant, however, has a strong hope (Isa. 10:20–23). Such a remnant must rely totally on God (10:20). It must be a holy seed, bringing the justice and righteousness God expected (6:13; cp. 28:5–6).

For the generation who suffered exile in Babylon, Isaiah provided hope. God will surprise his people with the blessings of fertility (49:21–23).

VII. TEACHING OUTLINE

A. INTRODUCTION

1. Lead Story: Fear—the Fatal Flaw
2. Context: The summary of Isaiah's preaching in chapter 1 leads to a new introduction in 2:1. Hope (4:2–6) encases the announcement of judgment on the day of the Lord. God will create a people who know his law and obey it, and he will give them life without military threats or danger. The present situation, however, is far different and so demands God's judgment.
3. Transition: The call to repentance in chapter 1 leads to promises of peace in chapter 2. This glorious hope is tempered by a look at the present reality. God's salvation fades into the future in light of present disobedience and false worship. The day of the Lord may sound like a glorious moment in eternal history, but in current history it will bring only judgment and discipline. A people who parade their sin, bow to the products of their own hands, and lift their faces in arrogant pride will soon march away to a foreign land.

B. COMMENTARY

1. The Way to Warless Worship for the World (2:1–5)
2. Reasons for Rejection (2:6–9)
3. Preaching Against Pride (2:10–22)
4. A Lack of Leadership (3:1–12)
5. Princes Prey on the Paupers (3:13–15)
6. Too Late for the Ladies (3:16–4:1)
7. Protection for the Pious (4:2–6)

C. CONCLUSION: ACHIEVING THE UNACHIEVABLE

1. Wrap-up: God promised his people a wonderful day of victory. Military power would vanish. The glories of family farm life would prevail. God's holy people would again inhabit Jerusalem, led by God's selected Branch as their leader. Discipline and cleansing would be

past history. People would live under God's glory. But first things first. Present prosperity would soon disappear, because it was based on a lifestyle of pride and idolatry. God would remove all Jerusalem's resources. He would appear to Israel in all his glory decked out in battle array against his people. Trust in humans would cease. Caves would be the refuge as people attempted to hide from God. God would remove all Jerusalem's resources. People would search in vain for competent leaders and then for anyone at all who would lead. Pompous women would be reduced to begging old men to be their husbands and protectors. Amid the misery of divine judgment, God would preserve the righteous.

2. Personal Challenge: Take a personal spiritual inventory. Find the sins Israel had to pay for. How many of these inhabit our life? What are you doing to gain forgiveness and renewal in your spiritual life? Do you see yourself as being among the righteous whom God will preserve or among the proud idolaters whom he will punish?

VIII. ISSUES FOR DISCUSSION

1. What do you look for when God brings his final day of victory to the earth?
2. What kinds of idolatry do church members practice today?
3. In what ways are women today similar to those Isaiah described?
4. How do church members express and show unhealthy pride today? What can the church do for such people?
5. In what ways does God express his judgment on his people in today's world?

Isaiah 5

Vindication Against the Vineyard

I. **INTRODUCTION**
You Are What Your Heart Is

II. **COMMENTARY**
A verse-by-verse explanation of the chapter.

III. **CONCLUSION**
A Blind, Undiscerning People
An overview of the principles and applications from the chapter.

IV. **LIFE APPLICATION**
Dealing with Disappointment
Melding the chapter to life.

V. **PRAYER**
Tying the chapter to life with God.

VI. **DEEPER DISCOVERIES**
Historical, geographical, and grammatical enrichment of the commentary.

VII. **TEACHING OUTLINE**
Suggested step-by-step group study of the chapter.

VIII. **ISSUES FOR DISCUSSION**
Zeroing the chapter in on daily life.

"*T*hough the mills of God grind slowly;

yet, they grind exceedingly small."

Friedrich von Logau

Isaiah 5

IN A NUTSHELL

*G*od sang the song of the vineyard to his people, warning them of disaster because they did not meet his expectations. Then he pronounced woes on them for their materialistic, self-righteous, unjust way of life. Foreign armies would be his agents of judgment.

Vindication Against the Vineyard

I. INTRODUCTION

You Are What Your Heart Is

*M*ax Lucado relates a legend from India. A mouse lived his poor life terrified of cats. One day he persuaded a magician to help him, so the magician turned the mouse into a cat. But the mouse-become-cat then met a ferocious dog and insisted he could not live as a cat, since his every moment was consumed with fear of the dog. Again the magician accommodated him, turning him into a dog. Things went all right until the mouse-turned-cat-become-dog chanced upon a tiger. One more time the magician did his stuff, resulting in a new member of the tiger family. But the tiger inevitably met a hunter. Again he came running to the magician. He was still haunted by fear. The magician stood adamant: "I will make you into a mouse again, for though you have the body of a tiger, you still have the heart of a mouse" (Lucado, *The Applause of Heaven*, p. 77).

Isaiah described Israel in similar terms. God had done everything he knew for the people he loved. He had given them the most productive environment possible for them to become precisely what he wanted them to be. But Israel did not produce. Israel remained a sinful, rebellious nation. God had to act.

Two major types of prophetic literature appear in the next section of the Book of Isaiah. Poetic oracles (5:1–30) surround prose stories about the prophet (6:1–8:22). These have been artistically joined together. The woe statements of 5:8–23 are resumed in 10:1–4, and the chorus of 5:25 reappears in 9:12,17,21; 10:4. Prophetic condemnation and judgment again provide the bulk of the material, but the climax shows that hope and salvation for a remnant is the controlling theme (10:5–11:16).

II. COMMENTARY

Vindication Against the Vineyard

MAIN IDEA: *Having done everything possible for his people, the Lord announced woes upon them for rejecting his ways and becoming champions of immorality.*

A An Unproductive Vineyard (5:1–7)

Harvest love song changed ironically into a courtroom trial (740 B.C.)

SUPPORTING IDEA: *When God provides everything his people needs and they still produce rotten fruit, they will lose all he has supplied.*

5:1. We stand before one of the great pieces of prophetic literature; indeed, one of the greatest pieces of literature ever written. The prophet donned the actor's grease paint to perform for his audience. He sang a love song, fitting into the frivolous mood of gaiety permeating the harvest holidays. In so doing, he assumed the role of the friend of the bridegroom. This was like today's best man. He represented the groom before the bride, since the bride and groom were not allowed to see each other before the wedding. He used the language of agriculture, a common custom in Israelite love poetry (see Song of Songs).

5:2. He showed the faithfulness of the bridegroom in preparing every detail. He prepared the land in the best way he knew so grapevines would grow. Thus the bridegroom had great expectations. This should be among the nation's best vineyards.

5:3–4. Suddenly the prophet changed his mood and image. He called the court into session with the citizens of his country as the jury. First, he put the bridegroom in the defendant's chair and asked how he could have done more than he did to produce an outstanding crop of **grapes**.

5:5–6. Then he quickly pronounced the verdict. The bride was guilty! The sentence: death! The unproductive **vineyard** had no more life, no more chances.

5:7. Abruptly, the prophet changed his speech form once more. He interpreted the entire love song/court trial as a parable, indeed an allegory. Yahweh, the God of Israel, was the bridegroom; **Judah**, the bride. God's expectation is described in beautiful alliteration, which might be rendered: "He hoped for righteousness, but here are riots; for legality, but here is lamentation" (author's translation). The divine lover had suffered ultimate disappointment and rejection. He must discipline his beloved (cp. Hos. 1–3). But he again made his basic expectations known—righteousness and legality or justice. (For justice and Lord Almighty/Lord of Hosts, see "Deeper Discoveries," ch. 1.)

Ⓑ Woes on the Worldly (5:8–30)

Woe oracles (740 B.C.)

SUPPORTING IDEA: *Champions of economic oppression, social misbehavior, deceit, wickedness, mistrust, moral blindness, conceit, injustice, and oppression face God's judgment from unexpected sources because they have rejected God.*

5:8–30. The note of condemnation and death does not come easily to the prophet nor to God. As so often, the funeral mourning cry of "**Woe, alas, how horrible!**" follows. We have here a series of such woe oracles just as in Isaiah 28–31, Habakkuk 2, and Amos 5–6. A few points in the text provide difficulties. Verse 9 reads literally, "By (or in) my ears, Yahweh of Hosts" (author's translation), which must be an abbreviated oath formula. Translators must supply some verb of swearing. "Dying of hunger" (v. 13) is the reading of the earliest translations; the Hebrew text reading is "its honored ones are men of hunger" (author's translation). The Hebrew probably seeks to make a word-play between two words, "men" and "dying," which share similar appearance and sound.

Verse 17 is filled with rare words and forms, giving rise to many possible translations. The proper translation is, "The lambs will graze as if it were their pasture, while strangers eat the ruins of the fatlings" (author's translation), but note the variety among modern translations and commentaries.

The grammar and syntax of verses 25–30 present great uncertainty. Some translations place the events in the future tense, others in the present, and still others in the past. The Hebrew word at the end of verse 30 occurs only here in the Bible and is of uncertain meaning: suggestions include "clouds," "hilltops," and "shadows."

5:8. Uncertainties aside, the passage pours judgment upon a prosperous people so intent on gaining wealth and enjoying themselves that they ignore the real world. They have robbed the poor farmers through unjust economic practices and have taken farms until they have only a lovely country mansion with no neighbors.

5:9–14. The people have eaten and drunk so much at the temple parties that they do not miss the guest of honor, when God departs to bring judgment upon them (v. 12). God's judgment is appropriate to the crime. Mansions become lonely haunted houses. The work of the farmer produces only one-tenth of the expected crop. Landed nobility marched into **exile**, their feasting turned to enforced fasting. Only the **grave** (Hb. *Sheol*, "the home of the dead") finds its appetite satisfied. (For grave or Sheol, see "Deeper Discoveries.") Apparently biblical measures changed through Israel's history (see Deut. 25:13–16; Ezek. 45:11). The **bath** was about twenty-two liters. A **homer** equaled one hundred liters, and an **ephah** was ten liters.

5:15–17. The contrast is complete. The mighty of Judah have been **humbled**, while the very action of God in judgment has proved the pure holiness and **righteousness** of God. (For the Holy One of Israel, see "Deeper Discoveries," ch. 1.) God stands **exalted**. Men have been humbled. God has retained his position as the High and Mighty One. The promised land and Holy City are reduced to occupation by flocks and foreigners. Lambs will graze among the ruins of the rich.

5:18–19. The situation became even worse. Rather than carry the produce of the land to market, Israel has tied up its sin and carried it to market in an ox-drawn cart. Its sin is so fruitful that only such a cart can hold it. But the cart itself comes into question, for its lines tying it to the ox are **cords of deceit**, a picture of bad ropes and bad people. The people were so occupied in their evil that they taunted the prophet and his God, daring God to act and to do so in a **hurry**.

5:20–23. The prophet claimed that the people had their priorities upside down. In Genesis Adam and Eve sought the power to decide **good** and **evil** for themselves (Gen. 3:5–6). Isaiah said his generation had confused the two things. They had lost the moral capacity to distinguish between right and wrong. Living in **darkness**, they could not see the light of God's goodness and his good plan for them. Having caused bitterness for the people who looked to them for leadership, they no longer knew how **sweet** life could taste. So long had they depended on their own wisdom and **clever** plans that they were blind to what God was doing. This could be seen in their uncontrolled use of liquor and their mockery of the system of social justice.

5:24–25. The ominous, prophetic **therefore** sounds forth twice to predict punishment on God's worldly wise but wicked people. They took pride in possessing God's law, his instruction for living. (For law, see "Deeper Discoveries," chs. 2–4.) Knowledge was not enough. They refused to live by it. By refusing to obey God's teachings, they **spurned the word of the Holy One of Israel**. This could be a parallel way of talking about the law, or it may introduce the prophetic word into the picture. If that is so, then the people had a double sin: refusing to live by God's teachings and ignoring the warnings of God's prophets. The divine wrath would become insatiable. The result: Jerusalem's streets lined with unburied corpses, the price of war and of rejecting God.

5:26–30. Exactly how would judgment come? God would whistle for Assyria and other **distant nations**. Nations that normally ignored Israel's God as insignificant would respond **swiftly**. They would resemble hungry **lions** on the prowl for whatever **prey** they could find. The sounds and fury of warfare would thunder over the land. Hope had vanished for that generation. The generation that could not distinguish between light and darkness would now experience only **darkness**. Storm clouds hung over all of life.

> **MAIN IDEA REVIEW:** *Having done everything possible for his people, the Lord announces woes upon them for rejecting his ways and becoming champions of immorality.*

III. CONCLUSION

A Blind, Undiscerning People

In spite of God's blessing on his people, they ignored and rejected him. The result: a people blind to reality, unable to judge between good and evil, light and darkness, sweet and bitter. The people of the Book ridiculed God, his plans, and his demands. They made their own laws to fit their own desires. God said, Enough! Time for judgment. Darkness is all you will see. King of Assyria: About face! Forward march! My people are yours for the taking.

PRINCIPLES

- God has done everything possible to make you a part of his people.
- God disciplines his people who do not produce the fruit he expects.
- God expects justice and righteousness from his people.
- Riches may lead only to isolation, not to contentment.
- Ignoring God and giving him no respect lead to disaster.
- Sin leads to spiritual blindness that cannot distinguish between good and evil.
- God punishes pride and conceit.
- God rules over all political and military powers.

APPLICATIONS

- Describe ways God has shown his love for you.
- Describe the fruit that your life is producing for God.
- Describe how you expect God to react to the fruit of your life.
- Describe ways you promote justice and injustice in the world.

- Make a written plan to follow in using your material resources for God's purposes.
- Confess to God any sins you commit—drinking, eating, and partying. Ask him to forgive and change you.
- Repent of pride and conceit in your life.
- Tell God you are content to let him rule the world in the way he chooses and that you will no longer complain about how he is doing it.

IV. LIFE APPLICATION

Dealing with Disappointment

Blake was almost born in the church. He got a rose bud his first Sunday in the cradle roll. He had perfect attendance records, won Scripture memory contests, attended Vacation Bible School and church summer camps, sang in the youth choir, and was always chosen for a leadership role when the youth organized themselves for some mission event or youth Sunday at church. Then Blake went off to college. There he learned many things his parents had warned him about—drinking, doing drugs, cheating on tests, stealing. Blake ended up spending some time in jail.

Everything Blake's parents had expected, they didn't get from him. Their "reward" was heartache, disappointment, worry, guilt, and self-recrimination in spite of the fact that those who knew the situation said they had done everything possible for Blake. Still Blake rebelled.

God knows that experience. He chose Israel to be his people. He provided everything they needed to live on. He showed them exactly what he expected of them and promised that they would have the best possible life if they met his expectations. But God was disappointed. Israel turned every way but the right way. Israel seemed to do everything possible not to meet God's expectations. Finally, Israel had to face judgment just as Blake did in jail.

V. PRAYER

Holy God, you have done everything for me that I could possibly ask and even more. You have created your plan of salvation from before the creation of the world and have carried it out to the very letter through your Son Jesus, my Savior. Forgive me when I decide to go my own way and not yours, decide to listen to my desires and not your teachings, decide to treat others for my advantage rather than with your love. Change my heart, and turn your anger away. Amen.

VI. DEEPER DISCOVERIES

The Grave or Sheol (5:14)

The Hebrew word *Sheol* occurs over sixty times in the Old Testament to refer to the residence of those who have lived and died. Sheol is the underworld to which people go down (Num. 16:30; Ps. 88:3–4; Isa. 7:11; Amos 9:2). Sheol is pictured as a geographical location with city gates protecting it (Job 38:17; Isa. 38:10; cp. Jer. 15:7; Rev. 1:18). Apparently, all people go there at death (Ps. 89:48; cp. Gen. 37:35). One can even enter Sheol alive (Ps. 55:15). Ultimately, God sends people to Sheol (Gen. 42:38; 1 Sam. 2:6; Ezek. 31:16). No light penetrates this place of the dead (Job 17:13; cp. Job 18:18). Neither does sound (Pss. 31:17–18; 94:17; Isa. 47:5).

Sheol was a place a person could never leave (Job 7:9). In Sheol one felt tied in ropes or chains like a criminal (2 Sam. 22:6). To lie in Sheol was to lie in the dust from which one was made and to which one returned (Job 17:16; Ps. 7:5). Whatever type of existence one had in Sheol was weak and shadowy (Isa. 14:9–10).

The Old Testament has described Sheol in very personal terms: an insatiable appetite (Prov. 27:20; 30:15b–16; Isa. 5:14; cp. Ps. 141:7); ability to arouse its sleeping inhabitants (Isa. 14:9).

Still, God retains power over Sheol and its inhabitants (Hos. 13:14). He can redeem his servant from Sheol (Ps. 49:15), deliver one's soul from Sheol (Ps. 86:13), and guide people in the upwards path away from it (Prov. 15:24), because Sheol lies open before God (Prov. 15:11). The New Testament gives a much clearer picture of the separation of the wicked and the righteous in the afterlife and of God's victory over death and the grave (see 1 Cor. 15).

VII. TEACHING OUTLINE

A. INTRODUCTION

1. Lead Story: You Are What Your Heart Is
2. Context: Having wrapped the horrible picture of the judgment day of the Lord in two snapshots of God's ultimate promise of hope for his people in chapters 2–4, the prophet Isaiah turns to show why that judgment is necessary.
3. Transition: God is not to blame. He planned and executed everything to perfection. He loved his people and gave them everything they needed to grow up just as he planned. God's people did not cooperate. They embraced materialism, greed, injustice, and debauchery rather than God, who had delivered them from captivity and given

them a bountiful land. As a result, God's sorrowful woes poured forth on his beloved.

B. COMMENTARY
1. An Unproductive Vineyard (5:1–7)
2. Woes on the Worldly (5:8–30)

C. CONCLUSION: DEALING WITH DISAPPOINTMENT
1. Wrap-up: God did everything he could do. He provided the best possible environment for you to grow in his love and grace. You joined the rest of the human race in choosing sin over obedience. You rejected God and decided you knew more about good and evil than he did. The result is that he declared the coming of the day of the Lord as a day of judgment and discipline. He has already signaled for the enemy forces to come destroy. How do you respond?
2. Personal Challenge: Take time to list everything God has done for you to make your life as good as it can be. Thank him for every item on the list. Now list things you have done to load yourself up with the burden of sin. How have you rejected the law of the Lord of Hosts? How have you spurned the word of the Holy One of Israel? What is your next step now?

VIII. ISSUES FOR DISCUSSION

1. What does it mean for God to sing a love song for his people?
2. What charges do people today make against God? How would you answer those charges?
3. Do the people of God today handle financial success any better than the people of Isaiah's day?
4. What does the Bible teach about using alcoholic beverages?
5. Give examples from our culture of people confusing what is good and what is evil.

Isaiah 6–8

Called, Cleansed, and Commissioned

Quote

"*H*oliness on the one hand creates distance between him and mankind, on the other hand his holiness creates a renewing fellowship between God and mankind."

S . H . W i d y a p r a n a w a

Isaiah 6–8

I N   A   N U T S H E L L

*C*hapter 6 serves as a foundation stone to prove the authority of the prophetic preaching. Isaiah did not preach destruction from his own desires but from the call of God. The prophet shrank from the task and pleaded for his people, but God sent him out to accomplish divine, not human, purposes.

Called, Cleansed, and Commissioned

I. INTRODUCTION

One Day You Can Be . . .

*L*arry Crabb recalls an eventful moment that transformed the direction of his life. He entered fifth grade and met Mr. Erb, freshly graduated from the university and determined to be the best fifth grade teacher ever. He looked for the potential in each child he taught. He made kids work extra hard, probably harder than they had ever worked in their lives. They worked because they knew he liked them and believed in them. A month into the school year Mr. Erb dismissed the class for afternoon recess, but motioned to Larry. "Larry, I want to see you for a moment."

What now? Larry wondered. The young teacher stared through Larry for a moment, then pronounced the life-changing words: "I've noticed you like words. I've been thinking about that. Larry, one day you could be a writer." To encourage Larry, the educator challenged him with a special daily assignment. Larry was to find a new word in the dictionary and write a sentence showing he knew what it meant. He would then discuss the sentence with the teacher.

Those were the first sentences of Larry Crabb's distinguished writing career. He sees them as confirmation of the Holy Spirit's work in his life leading him to write. In a true sense, God used a youngster just out of college to call a talented kid to his vocation (Crabb, pp. 157–158).

God used a worship service to call Isaiah to his prophetic vocation. He overwhelmed the prophet with a sense of awe and reverence, leading to a deep conviction of sin and a strong willingness to answer God's call to a mission.

II. COMMENTARY

Called, Cleansed, and Commissoned

MAIN IDEA: *God called his prophet to confront a faithless king and declare judgment for the present but hope for the future.*

A Called to Condemn (6:1–13)

Prophetic call narrative (740 B.C.)

SUPPORTING IDEA: *The holy God called a sinful man as his prophet to announce his judgment to his sinful people.*

6:1. A brief moment of biography provides a glimpse of how such dire predictions as we have seen in the preceding chapters came to be uttered. The basic explanation comes from God's commission to his prophetic messenger. The disease-ridden but successful and powerful **King Uzziah died** in 640 B.C. In those difficult circumstances a young man went to worship and had his life changed forever. Isaiah **saw the Lord**. This occurred within the Jerusalem **temple**, perhaps indicating that the prophet had been a professional minister on the temple staff. The earthly temple was suddenly transformed, allowing the prophet to enter the heavenly court, where God was enthroned, **high and exalted** over all creation in heaven and in earth. His greatness is indicated by the size of the train of his robe which occupied all the available room in the magnificent earthly temple.

6:2. God's ministers were serving him. **Seraphs** (the traditional seraphim is a letter-for-letter transliteration of the Hebrew word *seraph*, including the plural ending *-im*) are literally the "searing or burning ones" and appear only here in the Old Testament as members of God's court. They covered their faces so they would not see the holiness of God. Covering their feet is probably a euphemism for covering one's private parts so that one could not be thought to be unclean in the holy presence. They were flying so they could maintain their position over the holy throne. (For seraphs and divine messengers, see "Deeper Discoveries.")

The heavenly council is one of many ideas Israel had in common with its Near Eastern neighbors. Other religions saw a king of the gods ruling over a council of lesser gods. Israel claimed that her God, Yahweh, the only real God, ruled over a group of beings who served him, particularly in the role of messengers (see 1 Kgs. 22:19). Israel also made the radical assertion that God was the king of the nation rather than simply king of the gods.

6:3–4. The setting of Isaiah's call was the doxology sung responsively by two members of the heavenly court (cp. Rev. 4:8). They looked down upon the earth and saw that it reflected the divine glory—that is, the prestige, wealth, and honor of God, literally, his weightiness. Yes, looking at earth gave heavenly messengers another view of God's greatness. (For glory of God, see "Deeper Discoveries"; for divine holiness, see the commentary on 1:4.) Burnt offerings and incense often filled the temple with a special aura and aroma. Heavenly voices filled it with something more tantalizing and awe-inspiring. The framework of the building shook at such an awesome experience. As God first led Israel through the wilderness in a cloud, so now his cloud of smoke infiltrated the temple, the building whose worship the previous chapters condemned.

6:5. Isaiah realized that he had no business in such a holy setting. He was able to see what was forbidden even to Moses (Exod. 33:20). Isaiah was not, however, the first to see God (Gen. 16:13; Judg. 6:22; Pss. 11:7; 27:4; 63:2). (For seeing God, see "Deeper Discoveries.") *Pg 69*

The vision turned Isaiah's eyes inward to realize his own sinfulness. The **woe** language Isaiah used to express sorrow at the nation's fate now pointed to the prophet's problem. He had to endure what he proclaimed to others. Language predicting the death of a nation now confessed that his own death appeared to be certain. **I am ruined** may mean "I am silenced, still, cannot reply" (author's translation) since this is most often the meaning of the Hebrew word.

The prophet stood in the divine council but identified himself with his people on earth. He and his people were **unclean,** a term used in the temple worship to designate a person who had not followed the laws properly or who had come into contact with a substance that rendered him unclean (see "Deeper Discoveries").

6:6–7. God's heavenly ministers performed the proper rituals for Isaiah. Here the dynamic character of Old Testament worship dramatizes both the odious nature of sin before God and the power of God to forgive and forget. The **coal** was so closely connected to the holy **altar** that it shared the altar's holy character. The heat and holiness joined to singe the sin from the prophet's lips and prepared him to use those lips as God's messenger. God accepted the prophet's confession. He was a person of "unclean lips" (v. 5). He was a sinner. He did not have to stay that way. God took away his **guilt and atoned** for his sin. (For atoning for sin and guilt, see "Deeper Discoveries.")

6:8–10. Isaiah was fully accepted into the heavenly council to stand in God's presence. He heard the question God posed to the holy council, **Who will go for us?** Rather than let one of the seraphs answer (1 Kgs. 22:21), Isaiah himself boldly volunteered, **Here am I. Send me!** He received an impossible assignment—the hardening of Israel. Here is the Old Testament's bluntest statement of God's total freedom over his world. As God once hardened

Pharaoh (Exod. 7–14), so he hardened his enemy Israel. Here human understanding must bow before the sovereignty of God and his purposes with people. Jesus took up the same words and applied them to his generation (Matt. 13:10–15; Luke 8:10; John 12:37–43).

At times God must destroy a generation before he can work out his purpose of salvation. The people have walked so far along the road of sin and rejection that divine intervention would send the wrong message about divine holiness and divine justice. In such times, God gives his messenger a hard word of judgment that leads neither to a great following among the people nor personal happiness. As Walter Brueggemann phrases it: "The purposes of God are at work in the midst of severe human obduracy. There are no easy healings. There are no ready turnings. The healings are not readily available, and the turnings are too demanding. There is no easy gospel. There is no cheap grace, no good word that gives assurances to those who drop by hoping for a quick and comfortable deal. And that leaves in these cases only obtuseness and its terrible consequences" (Brueggemann, p. 63).

6:11–13. The prophet backed away from the task, asking **How long**? The divine answer painted an ugly picture: total destruction (vv. 11–12). Verse 13 apparently gives a glimmer of hope in the darkness, but the text is almost impossible to read (cp. the translations of NRSV, NEB, KJV, JPS). A very literal reading says, "And still in its tenth, then it will return to (or again) be for burning as an oak tree (possibly a cultic marker of pagan worship) and as a terebinth (probably a cultic marker of pagan worship) that when it is felled a stem (or memorial stone) in them. A holy seed its stem (or memorial stone)" (author's translation).

Most of the language belongs to the high places of worship with holy trees and stones, for which it appropriately appears to picture repeated destruction. But the conclusion surprises us totally, for the result is a **holy seed**. The darkest moment in Israel's history—that when its hardening and destruction are announced without relief—still finds the light of God's forgiveness. Hope is always his last word. A remnant is his way of bringing salvation even in the face of judgment.

🅑 Faith or Failure (7:1–9)

Prophetic report (733 B.C.)

> **SUPPORTING IDEA:** *God is sovereign over world history, and his people can trust him and not their enemies.*

7:1–2. The biographical report continues, turning to experiences of the prophet amid royalty and nobility. These show that the prophet faithfully carried out his commission. His message achieved exactly what God said (ch. 6), hardening the heart of the people and their king. **Rezin** (2 Kgs. 16:5,9) apparently usurped the throne of Syria. In 738 he paid tribute to Tiglath-Pileser III of Assyria. Against further Assyrian threats Rezin gained support from the usurper **Pekah** of Israel, from the Philistines, and other neighboring kingdoms. About this time **Jotham**, king of Judah, died. Rezin then beckoned to Judah to join. **Ahaz**, the young king, refused. (For kings of Judah, see "Deeper Discoveries," ch. 1.) Rezin and Pekah besieged Jerusalem to force Ahaz to join forces against Assyria (2 Kgs. 15:37). They succeeded in taking some Judean territory (2 Kgs. 16:5–9).

7:3–4. In the midst of decision, a fearful Ahaz met the prophet **Isaiah**, who came at God's command (v. 3). Isaiah took with him his son **Shear-Jashub**, who bore the ominous, symbolic name "a remnant shall return." This is a play on words. "Remnant" may mean a hopeless handful or the basis for a new society. "Return" may point to literal returning from war or to spiritual return, being the normal Hebrew word for "repent." In the military setting, the name suggested defeat in battle. The child's presence was a warning to the king not to enter battle, as well as a challenge to God's people to be part of the repentant remnant.

The geographical setting of the confrontation (v. 3) was apparently outside the city at a good place to examine the military situation. God's word for the situation was clear—an oracle of salvation (v. 4) calling on the king to do nothing. His enemies had burned themselves out and were simply dying embers.

7:5–6. Verse 5 has an opening formula "Because" (not reflected in NIV translation) which introduces a new oracle. It describes the situation for the following sermon. The situation was desperate for Ahaz. The enemies sought to take control of Judah and replace Ahaz with a **son of Tabeel**, that is, a man with an Aramaic name and, thus, Syrian connections (since Syria spoke the Aramaic language and was called Aram in the Bible). He would be more open to the plans of his Syrian countrymen and apparently had no connections with the God of Israel or the family of David. This certainly went against God's plan, because he had promised to keep a son of David on the throne of Judah (2 Sam. 7).

7:7–9. The prophetic messenger formula, "Thus says the Lord" (NIV, **this is what the Sovereign LORD says**), introduced the divine decision. This formula indicated that the prophet was God's messenger delivering God's authorized word to his people. God simply stated that the weak opposition kings would not succeed, since they depended on their political position and not on God. Syria, its capital Damascus, and its king Rezin were too weak to succeed against God. So were Ephraim—the Northern Kingdom, Israel—its capital in Samaria, and its king Pekah.

Ahaz had no reason to fear Ephraim. In a generation or so the country would be so shattered that it would lose its identity. Israel had lost all political power by 722 B.C., but the prophet pointed ahead to an even greater loss of identity. This came to pass about 670 B.C. when Esarhaddon and Ashurbanipal of Assyria deported the majority of Ephraim's population and brought foreigners in to occupy the country (cp. Ezra 4:2,10).

The prophet turned to Ahaz and his advisers with God's plan, expressed in a wordplay. The Hebrew word means both "to believe" and also "to be established, made stable, stand firm." We can translate: "If you all do not confirm (this), you will not be confirmed" (author's translation). Ahaz's reaction is not reported. A principle God uses in working with his people stands firm: he expects our actions to come from faith in him, not from faith in political or military powers.

C Confounding Conception (7:10–17)

Prophetic report (733 B.C.)

SUPPORTING IDEA: *Failure to trust and obey God brings certain judgment even though there is final hope.*

The interpretation of this passage has stirred some of the greatest controversy in the Christian church and has led many people to words and actions that displayed anything but the spirit of Christ. The passage is presented in dialogue between Isaiah and Ahaz and must be interpreted along with the rest of the Book of Isaiah and of the Old Testament in the historical context of the people originally involved. The meaning there and the use of the passage in later texts, particularly New Testament texts, may indicate that the passage has a still fuller meaning and fulfillment at a different time in history. We must seek to understand that meaning also, but not to the neglect of the original meaning.

7:10–11. The king had not obeyed God's final word. Isaiah confronted Ahaz again. The king could display his faith by asking God for a sign that would confirm the divine help. Here is a unique example of a prophet given opportunity to prove his word true immediately. The Hebrew text of verse 11b is not clear, reading, "Go deep, ask, or go high to the heights" (author's translation). Most translators slightly change the vowels of the Hebrew word for *ask*, creating a text close to the NASB reading: "make it deep as Sheol or high as heaven" (cp. REB, NIV, NRSV). God set no limits. The king could ask any kind of sign anywhere he wanted it. (For grave or Sheol, see "Deeper Discoveries," ch. 5.)

7:12–13. The king refused the offer, but with the most pious language: "Who am I to test God?" (author's translation). God did not want pious language. He sought faith. Ahaz was too busy working his poor people until they were dead tired, or according to the NIV interpretation until their patience with him wore thin. The prophet charged that Ahaz's pious language made God just as tired or impatient. God would act on his own and give the king a sign.

7:14. The sign is given in the traditional manner of announcing the birth of a child (Gen. 16:11; Judg. 13:3,5). The birth would be a sign for the king in the immediate circumstances. The Hebrew text reads, "The young woman has conceived and is giving birth to a son" (v. 14, author's translation). (See REB, TEV, NRSV, NJB, JPS; for interpreting Isa. 7:14, see "Deeper Discoveries.")

Ahaz probably knew the woman of whom the prophet spoke. Some have suggested it was Isaiah's wife and son. Others believe it was some other woman in Israel. The most likely candidate may have been a wife of Ahaz, since this would have been the surprise fulfillment of the oracle, a royal prince becoming a sign to the king, his name—Immanuel—constantly reminding the king that "God is with us." Such a sign would give hope to a king who trusted God, but would be a constant threat to one who followed his own strategy. As Childs phrases it: "The sign of Immanuel . . . now has a double edge. For those of unbelief—Ahaz and his people—the sign is one of destruction (v. 17), but for those of belief, the sign of Immanuel is a pledge of God's continuing presence in salvation (v. 16)" (Childs, pp. 67–68).

The Septuagint interpreted this, "The virgin will conceive," a translation taken up in Matthew 1:23 and the continuing Christian tradition. The church has seen and continues to see that God often gives fuller and deeper meaning to his word at a stage after its original fulfillment. This is definitely the case here, for the New Testament shows us that Jesus Christ was virgin-born and is Immanuel, God with us. He still represents God's double-edge sign to us. Those who believe in him find salvation, but those who do not see God with us in Jesus find God with them in judgment.

7:15–16. The ambiguous wordplay continues. Curds and honey represent extreme blessing and paradise for people who live outside the settled land and look for a land that provides food "automatically" (Josh. 5:6). For people in a land devastated by enemy armies, curds and honey represent the only food available, a diet much more sparse than has been previously enjoyed. In the present context, it would appear to be a promise of blessing for the child in the near future, a matter of a few years before he could made his own moral choices.

Promise for the child would mean judgment on the enemy kings of Syria and Israel. With these words of hope, Ahaz prepared to bid the prophet farewell, but Isaiah had one last word.

7:17. The prophet knew the obstinate mind-set of the king. The result was obvious. Judgment would come to Judah, too. The prophet used shocking words to announce it. Isaiah compared this judgment to the rebellion of the Northern Kingdom separating from Judah in 928 B.C. (1 Kgs. 12). The instrument of judgment was also clear—the king of Assyria. He threatened not only Syria and Israel but Judah as well.

Poor Ahaz would not listen. The cringing king was afraid to trust his fathers' faithful God and ran rebelliously to the king of Assyria for help (2 Kgs. 16:7–9). But the prophet did not simply bury his word along with his hopes for Ahaz. Rather, he preserved it among his followers (Isa. 8:16), waiting for a new royal child, who would come from a family of faith and show that God's intention was to bestow his gracious blessing on humanity. The people of God waited seven hundred years before such a child was born. Even then, the paradise remained a promise. The church continues waiting for that day.

D Day of Destruction (7:18–25)

Prophetic report announcing disaster (733 B.C.)

SUPPORTING IDEA: *Lack of faith leads to God's day of destruction from God's surprise visitor.*

7:18–19. To make sure the meaning of the previous section is totally clear, a series of oracles follows. These define the expected day of disaster. Traditional enemies would come from north and south (Hos. 9:3; Jer. 2:36) and settle into all the places Judah thought would provide safety. These enemies would control the country's water supply.

7:20. God had a surprise visitor for Judah—the king on whom Ahaz called for help (2 Kgs. 16:7–9). **Assyria** would give Judah a **shave** too close for comfort. Such a shave would be a mark of shame for a people who expected its men to wear **beards** and have a full **head** of hair.

7:21–22. Judgment would be almost total, leaving the smallest of remnants. A herdsman would have only three animals left after the devastation, but God would be with the poor. Using these animals and wild honey, he would supply food in abundance for the remnant in the land.

7:23–25. The rich farmer, however, would see his vineyards become weed patches, even though their price made them the most valuable in the land. The only people using the land would be hunters seeking wild game. Otherwise, the land would be left to pastureless animals searching desperately for a morsel to eat among the thorns and briers. What a day God has for a king and his people who will not believe!

Ⓔ Child of Condemnation (8:1–4)

Prophetic report of symbolic act (713 B.C.)

SUPPORTING IDEA: *God used the prophet's family as a sign of the speed and certainty of coming destruction.*

8:1. Childbirth became a sign for the king and his people in a different way. The prophet interpreted the birth of his own son as a sign from God. Before the birth God called upon the prophet to prepare a public billboard, "Belonging to Speedy is the spoil, quick the plunder" (author's translation). But who is speeding, and who forms the "spoil"? The sign is ambivalent. Will Judah plunder her enemies, or will the enemies plunder Judah? Certainly, the prophet hoped the sign would mean salvation for Judah, but he knew the demand placed on the king for faith. We can be sure the king also knew!

8:2. The prophet worked his way through all the legal red tape, getting **two witnesses** (Deut. 17:6; 19:15). And what witnesses they were—the leading **priest** of the temple (2 Kgs. 16:10–11) and **Zechariah**, who may have been a relative of the king (2 Kgs. 18:2). Isaiah had access to people in high places, another sign that he may have been employed in the temple (see ch. 6 notes).

8:3–4. Isaiah was also married to a woman who may have worked on the temple staff as a **prophetess**. The birth event gave clearer indication of the meaning of the sign. Before the child began to say his first "Mommy, Daddy," the king of Assyria would do away with all claims to power made by Judah's two enemies.

Ⓕ River of Rage (8:5–8)

Prediction of disaster (733 B.C.)

SUPPORTING IDEA: *Judgment shows one side of God's presence with his people.*

8:5–6. That the sign was not totally good for Judah becomes clear in the next word from the prophet, given only a little while later. The Hebrew of verse 6b uses a word that normally means "joy, rejoicing" (see Isa. 24:8,11; 60:15; Jer. 49:25). The word may be related to one which sounds much the same and means "to lose courage" (cp. NRSV, TEV).

The **waters of Shiloah** is a water system about four hundred meters long that brought a trickle of water from the Gihon spring to the pool of Siloam in Jerusalem. God promised to use this system, which did not look promising from a human standpoint, to provide all the resources the city needed to withstand any siege by Syria and Israel.

8:7-8. The people refused to trust God's protection, preferring to call on Assyria for help. So the prophet described Assyria—pictured as its most notable geographical feature, the Euphrates River. Yes, Assyria was a mighty flood, branching out until it covered not only Damascus and Samaria but also all of Judah. Judah would be up to its **neck** in floodwaters, with no one to help.

Then the image changed. Assyria is pictured as a **bird** soaring above its prey on **outspread wings**, a terrifying image of an enemy army dispatching its units throughout the country. This bird is so big it covers the entire land of Judah. The only reaction is the cry, **O, Immanuel**, referring to the sign of Isaiah 7:14. God is with us in destructive rage. Yet at the same time the cry remained a prayer, hoping for divine intervention. Again we see the ability of the prophet to use language with double meanings.

Ⓖ Present to Protect (8:9-10)

Sarcastic use of a military call to battle (733 B.C.)

SUPPORTING IDEA: *Proud nations must hear God's call to battle in which he reveals his presence by defeating the nations.*

8:9-10. Using military language, the prophet summoned the nations to fight and lose. Again, this gave hope to his own people. The basis of such hope is Immanuel, **God is with us**. But it is a hope after defeat and destruction. God would be present to judge his people, then to judge the nations.

Ⓗ Falling Before Our Fear (8:11-15)

Prophetic teaching (733 B.C.)

SUPPORTING IDEA: *A time of crisis reveals whom one fears and worships, and calls for unity in the face of terror.*

8:11-12. The prophet imitated the priest, whose duty was to teach the people how to behave before the holy God. He subtly turned the teaching into a word of judgment. Isaiah set himself apart from his people. God had given him a new lifestyle. This was the basis for his new teaching. The new lifestyle centered in a new politics, since crisis had produced panic. Everyone was on the outlook for traitors. The least word or action beyond the normal aroused the cry, **Conspiracy . . . conspiracy.** Within Judah an Assyrian party faced a Syrian party, which in turn faced a Yahweh party. The level of trust was low. Everyone feared everyone else.

8:13. The voice of Yahweh called for calm and trust, not panic and **fear**. No enemy king is worth the time spent worrying, plotting, or trembling in fear. In fact, only the **holy** God deserves our fear. Here is the most obvious of the many wordplays in this section. Fear of God is, of course, a central concept in the divine-human relationship, but the particular Hebrew term used here appears elsewhere only in Malachi 1:6 and 2:5 to designate this relationship. Elsewhere this word expresses the horrible terrors of war. Isaiah deliberately used this war terminology to make a wordplay within the military context. The same type of wordplay occurs in Psalm 71:11. Judah must not fear the terrors of war, but her "Holy Terror." The military context also determines the use of the Lord of Hosts title with its reference to God as the commander of the armies. (For Lord Almighty/Lord of Hosts, see "Deeper Discoveries," ch. 1.)

8:14–15. A similar wordplay occurs here in the use of **sanctuary**. This is literally a holy place where the holy God is worshiped. It can also mean the place where a person fleeing from his enemies seeks sanctuary or protection from his pursuer. God is often called Israel's rock, an image of protection and strength. Now, however, Israel and Judah would **stumble** on the rock. Without faith, Israel would **fall**. Hunters often placed a **trap** or **snare** in the rocks to catch animals or even to trap enemy soldiers. Now God had become a trap into which faithless Jerusalem would fall.

⬛ Tie Up the Teaching (8:16–22)

Prophetic instruction (733 B.C.)

> **SUPPORTING IDEA:** *A time of crisis calls for people to trust God, ignore solutions rising from panic, and study the teachings of God's word.*

8:16. Knowing he would win the war, Isaiah realized when he had lost a battle. He retreated from confrontation with the king and people into the sanctuary of his faithful followers. He devoted his time to teaching his students. He had faith in the words he had uttered and wanted them preserved for a day when they would be heeded. God provided faithful **disciples** who took the first step in canonizing Isaiah's prophecy.

8:17. Ahaz refused to listen and trust God. So did the people of Israel and Judah. The faithful remnant seemed to be reduced to the prophet himself, his family, and his disciples. In such dire circumstances, Isaiah continued to confess his **trust** in God alone. For the moment God was in hiding, refusing to reveal his face or his word to his people. Isaiah knew God would come out of hiding one day and complete the plan of salvation and the prophetic promises. For the moment the prophet would **wait**.

8:18. Even when he did not preach, Isaiah remained faithful to his prophetic commission. His silence spoke louder than words. His presence with his sons, who bore symbolic names (7:3; 8:3), recalled every word of his message to the king and his aides. In silence Isaiah exercised his prophetic office. God, though silent, still claimed his house on **Mount Zion**.

8:19. People should have sought the will of God from Isaiah, but Judah ran to **mediums**, believing these people could **consult** the dead and find the fate of the **living** (cp. 1 Sam. 28; see also Lev. 19:31; Isa. 19:3). Isaiah said the chirps of birds were all they found. Yet, such mediums reigned supreme in the crisis situation. (For mediums and spiritists, see "Deeper Discoveries.") They put the true prophet out of work. But not for long! Isaiah knew that God would act to bring fulfillment to the prophetic word and that people would come running to him again.

8:20. The prophet remained confident of the superiority of his preaching over the words of the wizards. He called people to return to his preaching preserved by his disciples. Without light from the prophetic words, they would live in darkness with no hope of dawn.

8:21–22. In such a situation, the prophet could only draw a picture of the famine and hunger sure to follow the inevitable defeat—a defeat ensured for a people who sought hope for the living by consulting the dead. Here the Hebrew text is difficult. We do not know who the subject is or where the action takes place. Gloom, darkness, and anger dominate. The prohibition of cursing in Exodus 22:28 is broken. Despair has brought the subject to doubt both the king and God as leaders of the people. As a result, all will live in darkness.

MAIN IDEA REVIEW: *God called his prophet to confront a faithless king and declare judgment for the present but hope for the future.*

III. CONCLUSION

God Is in Control

God called his prophet to a dark task. Isaiah would be used to harden the hearts of a people who refused to trust him. King Ahaz exhibited that unbelief in a dramatic way. He would not accept a sign God offered him. Still God provided him with several signs: three babies. Two belonged to the prophet Isaiah. Their names pointed to destruction so that the nation's identity would rest with a small repentant remnant. The third baby apparently belonged to the king himself. This baby represented Immanuel, God with us.

But how is God present with us—in promise or in punishment? The prophet said it all depends. Do you trust God or not? He saves the trusting but devastates the doubting. A king who called on Assyria for help rather than trusting God would get his punishment from Assyria. A rejected God had become a stumbling stone, a snare for his own people. So the prophet waited faithfully for God to carry out the judgment. Then the prophet would see his hope in God justified as God saved his remnant who remained faithful to the prophet's preaching. Until then, darkness would prevail.

PRINCIPLES

- God rules over all the world's political powers.
- God is holy so that nothing sinful can enter his presence.
- Humans stand as sinners before the holy God, and they need to be cleansed.
- God calls people to be a part of his mission.
- God wants people to volunteer to go where he wants to send them.
- Most people will not listen and cannot understand what God is saying.
- God's people have no reason to fear worldly political powers but should fear God alone.
- Faith in God is the only basis on which to make life's decisions.
- God uses pagan peoples to discipline his people.
- God gives his people signs of his presence with them.
- God preserves his word for the time when people will listen and learn from it.

APPLICATIONS

- Listen for God's call and volunteer to go on mission for him.
- Confess your sins to God and ask him to blot them from his record.
- Thank God that he used the virgin Mary to bring Jesus to die for our sins.
- Pray to God, confessing how great, holy, and majestic he is.
- Ask God to forgive you for the times you have refused to listen to him and obey his word.
- Dedicate yourself to studying God's Word and learning about him.
- Ask God to remove all fear from your life.
- Ask God to help you make all of life's decisions in a spirit of obedience to him.

IV. LIFE APPLICATION

A Consecrated Commoner

D. L. Moody was an ordinary shoe salesman. God began working in his life, calling him to preach the gospel. But how could such an uneducated, unsuccessful person preach the gospel with any success? One day he joined Henry Varley and other friends in a hayfield where they gathered to confess their sins, consecrate themselves to God's service, and pray. Varley reminded the group, "The world has yet to see what God can do with and for and through and in a man who is fully and wholly consecrated to Him."

Later Moody listened to Charles Haddon Spurgeon preach. Suddenly he realized this was not Spurgeon's doing; this was God at work. If God could work through Spurgeon as he was doing, why could he not also work through Moody? He determined then and there to be the man God could fully use. The results are written all over the pages of the history of world evangelism. Thousands of people came to know Jesus Christ as Savior because an uneducated shoe salesman heard the call of God on his life and determined to be wholly dedicated to him.

Moody and Spurgeon followed the footsteps of Isaiah as they listened to God's call and went where God led. Isaiah is gone. Spurgeon is gone. Moody is gone. A new generation of lost people wait to hear God's word. God continues to call people to see what he can do through a fully dedicated person. Are you listening for God's call? Are you encouraging your children and family members to listen? Imagine what God could do through a fully and wholly dedicated you!

V. PRAYER

God, we do not like hard times. We want prosperity and joy. But our sins and faithlessness bring your judgment. Give us faith to believe when everyone else doubts. Give us protection when judgment comes. Create us as your faithful remnant to carry on your kingdom work here on earth. Amen.

VI. DEEPER DISCOVERIES

A. Seraphs and Divine Messengers (6:2)

Seraphs (Hb. plural is *seraphim*) are citizens of God's heaven related to heavenly messengers or angels. The word appears only in this one passage in Scripture. It basically means "the fiery ones." A similar Hebrew word means "fiery serpents," so that some interpreters think the seraphim were snakelike in appearance. But the description in Isaiah seems to make them appear more like humans with wings. Literature written between the time of the Old Testament and the New Testament lists classes or categories of angels, including a category of seraphim. Isaiah seems to indicate that seraphs were present at meetings of God's council, they prevented unwanted beings from attending, and they sang praise to God.

B. Glory of God (6:3)

The Hebrew word for "glory" (*kabod*) means "weight" or "heavy." It refers to the reputation, importance, or weight a person carries in a society. People can give glory to God, that is, acknowledge his importance and reputation, by honoring him (Isa. 24:15; see 1 Chr. 16:29; Ps. 96:8; cp. Mal. 2:2). Foreigners are invited to glorify God (Isa. 25:3). In God's day of salvation even the animals will glorify him (Isa. 43:20). One honors God from wealth (Prov. 3:9), by helping the poor (Prov. 14:31), and by keeping the Sabbath (Isa. 58:13).

God's glory is seen in his high position over the universe and his dignity (Pss. 57:5; 113:4). The heavens reveal God's glory (Ps. 19:2; cp. Num. 14:22; Isa. 60:22). So do his saving acts (Isa. 40:5). God created his people so they would bring glory to him by their actions and honorable characteristics (Isa. 43:7). God is Israel's glory, but Israel refused to accept this and went after other gods, other glories (Jer. 2:11). In prayer the psalmist asks God to help so as to bring glory to God (Ps.79:9).

The Old Testament uses the term *glory of Yahweh* about thirty times, ten of these in the Book of Ezekiel. Here glory takes on a tangible form. It is the experienced presence of God as it fills God's dwelling place to consecrate it (Exod. 29:43; 1 Kgs. 8:11; Ps. 26:8; Ezek. 9:3). It can also fill the whole earth (Num. 14:21; Hab. 2:14). But he can remove his glory from Israel's temple (Ezek. 10:18–19). Isaiah sees God's glory returning to the temple after judgment (Isa. 24:23; 40:5; 60:1–2,13; 66:18–19).

Such glory can be seen (Exod. 16:7,10). It is "like a consuming fire on top of the mountain" (Exod. 24:17). God is thus the "King of glory" (Ps. 24:7–10). His glorious appearance and presence bring fear (Isa. 59:19).

But Moses was not permitted to see God's glory (Exod. 33:18,22). On the last day when the Root of Jesse appears, glory will be God's resting place (Isa. 11:10).

C. Seeing God (6:5)

God is invisible because he is spirit and not flesh; yet many people claim to see God. Having spoken with a messenger of God, Hagar exclaimed in surprise, "Have I even remained alive here after seeing him?" (that is, "the God who sees," Gen. 16:13). Jacob wrestled all night and then claimed that he had seen God face to face. The marvel was that "my life was spared" (Gen. 32:30).

In the Book of Judges Gideon saw the "angel of the LORD" (Judg. 6:22), while Manoah feared death because he and his wife had "seen God" (Judg. 13:22).

Thus many exceptions occur to the theological rule that you will die if you see God's face (Exod. 33:20). Behind this stood opposition to pagan theology in which people could easily see the face of the idol. Thus Moses was allowed to see the glory pass by and witness only the back of God (Exod. 33:18–23). God expected his people to appear before him—that is, be seen by him—three times a year at the annual festivals (Exod. 23:15,17). In worship a person often claimed to see God (Pss. 27:4; 63:2; Hos. 5:15). Seeing God, then, is an experience of worship in which a person recognizes the presence of God in a very personal way. As entry to the presence of the holy God, seeing God is an awesome and fearful experience made possible only by the grace of God himself.

D. Unclean (6:5)

The expression "to be unclean" or "to be defiled" occurs 160 times in the Old Testament: 85 of them in Leviticus, 30 in Ezekiel, 23 in Numbers, and in Isaiah 30:22. The adjective occurs 89 times, including: 47 in Leviticus and 5 in Isaiah. To be unclean is to be disqualified from participating in the worship of Israel's God. Much impurity is related to practices of pagan religion. Others come from hygienic and health concerns. Others simply echo long-held beliefs based on generations of experience.

Leviticus 12–21 shows many ways in which people become unclean. Such uncleanness, even through unconscious or unintentional means, still involves an element of guilt before God that must be purified by atoning rituals (cp. Num. 6:9–11). Even the place and furniture of worship can become unclean (Lev. 16:18–20). Cleansing or purifying comes through rituals involving washing, sacrificing, application of blood, oil, and/or salt, cutting the hair, etc. (Lev. 14:8–9; 17:15; Num. 19:19; Ezek. 36:25). In specific instances sacrifices are required (Lev. 14:4–7,10–20). Ultimately Israel knows no one can be pure (Prov. 20:9) and that atonement depends on God's mercy (Ps. 51:3–4; cp. Ezek. 36:25,33; Mal. 3:3).

Isaiah had the ultimate experience of impurity. He was in God's holy presence in the temple when he realized he had seen God. Being unholy and seeing the holy revealed his unclean state and demanded purification, but the unclean state forbade him to stand in the sanctuary. Thus Isaiah, like Hagar and Jacob and Manoah, expected to die because he had seen God. No normal temple ceremony was sufficient to bring cleansing. Indeed, God in his grace initiated a unique ritual, one with burning coals from the holy altar, scorching the prophet's lips and making them clean.

Isaiah promised the community returning from exile that the Holy City would no longer see unclean people (Isa. 52:1). Indeed, those returning would walk the highway of holiness where no unclean person could walk (35:8). Those who joined the return had to purify themselves and be sure they were not unclean (52:11).

E. Atoning for Sin and Guilt (6:7)

Israel knew the meaning and experience of sin. The people of his nation knew they had rebelled against God and done that which was unjust, not maintaining equality in the social order that God demanded for the weak and helpless. This meant they had to have a means to be reconciled to God, to cut down the barrier that sin created between them and God. The process of removing the guilt and barrier created by sin is called atonement (*kippurim*). The priest made atonement for the guilty parties (Lev. 4:26,31,35; 14:18,20; 19:22). This was done through specific sacrifices, depending on who sinned and what their sin was (see Lev. 4:1–5:13; cp. Ezek. 45:15,17). The Day of Atonement is described in Leviticus 16. Central to the atonement ritual are the blood rites (Lev. 17:11).

Such atonement not only reestablished a relationship with God; it also involved dedicating and sanctifying the person forgiven to the service of God. The result was forgiveness for the guilty party. Such forgiveness came from God, not from the mechanical observance of a ritual. The individual had to recognize the need for atonement and initiate the proper activities to bring atonement.

Atonement reaches its ultimate explanation in texts that have nothing to do with sacrifice and ritual. Here God alone brings atonement (Pss. 65:3; 79:9, all involving the Hebrew word for "atone"). God remains free to refuse atonement (1 Sam. 3:14; Isa. 22:14). Isaiah belongs here, for God chooses to bring atonement for Isaiah through the acts of his seraphs at the altar (Isa. 6:7). This takes away his sin, qualifies him to see God, and prepares him for involvement in the divine council and for volunteering for assignment in God's mission.

F. Interpreting Isaiah 7:14

This passage requires careful study. It stems from King Ahaz's adamant refusal to respond to God's invitation and ask for a sign that would lead him to believe the prophet's words. God countered by announcing he was bringing Ahaz (literally, "you" plural, referring to the Davidic dynasty) a sign anyway. Three verbs carry the message. *Be with child* or *conceive* is a verb form normally used for past tense, but often found in prophetic contexts with a future sense. This results in the verb being rendered differently in different translations. *Give birth* is a participle which can indicate continuous or imminent action. *Will call* is a verb form usually indicating the future tense.

The most natural way to translate this string of verbs is past tense, imminent future, and future tense. This also represents the normal chain of events in a birth situation: become pregnant, giving birth, will name. This certainly makes sense in the context of Isaiah and Ahaz. God did not plan to wait nine months to give the sign. The girl was pregnant, on the point of labor, and would soon name the child. (It is possible, however, to understand the verbs as timeless—the girl conceives, gives birth, and names the child.)

Who is the woman? The text only says she is an 'almah. This Hebrew word occurs seven times in the Hebrew Bible (Gen. 24:43; Exod. 2:8; Ps. 68:25; Prov. 30:19; Song 1:3; 6:8; Isa. 7:14—apparently a woman who has conceived and is ready to deliver).

A masculine equivalent 'elem appears in 1 Samuel 17:56 (young David fighting Goliath) and in 1 Samuel 20:22 (lad assisting Jonathan).

Apparently the 'almah is female, young, and able to bear children. Hebrew's explicit word for "virgin"—bethulah—is not used here. (Some, however, understand bethulah as referring to a woman of marriageable age and 'almah as an unmarried girl.) Nor do we expect a virgin birth in the time of Isaiah. John Walton concludes that the important component of meaning here is childbearing: "a woman ceases to be an 'almah when she becomes a mother—not when she becomes a wife or a sexual partner" (Walton, NIDOTTE, 3, p. 417). Its counterpart applies to youthful virility for a man.

Thus for Isaiah, the 'almah was a young woman about to bear a child, a woman known to the king, and probably one who had been "known" by the king. Matthew used a Greek word parthenos with practically identical meaning to 'almah and emphasized one element that belonged to its meaning in many cases, that of not only not having borne a child but also not having had sexual experience. He saw greater meaning in Isaiah's vocabulary item and in Isaiah's prophecy as a whole than was seen in the original setting.

As Oswalt phrases it, "it is the dual focus of the oracle that explains the use of 'almah here. In the short term, the conception does not seem to have had primary importance. Rather, the significance is that a child conceived at that moment would still be immature when the two threatening nations would have been destroyed (vv. 16,25). Had Isaiah used bethulah here, Ahaz would probably have been so caught up with that thought that he would have missed the specific linkage to his own time. On the other hand, the very two-sidedness of the sign in Ahaz's time demanded something more. . . . No child born to a young woman in Ahaz's day is proof of God's presence in all times. But if a virgin overshadowed by God's Spirit should conceive and give birth, it would not only be a sign of God's presence with us. Better than that, it would be the reality of that experience. . . . For such a twofold task 'almah is admirably suited" (Oswalt, p. 211).

The child of Ahaz's day, born by normal means, represented only a sign of God's presence with the people. Jesus, born in a miraculous, virginal way, was literally Immanuel, God with us in the flesh, God incarnate.

G. Mediums and Spiritists (8:19)

Isaiah used two terms for pagan religious personnel who claim spiritual powers—*mediums* (Hb. *'oboth*) and *spiritists* (Hb. *yidde'onim*). The meanings are closely related, the two terms appearing in parallel with each other in eleven of the sixteen appearances of mediums in the Hebrew Bible. Moses' law forbade Israel to have anything to do with such people (Lev. 19:31; cp. Deut. 18:10–11). The penalty for such practice was death (Lev. 20:27). Kings are judged for their consultation of mediums (2 Kgs. 21:6) and are praised for ridding the country of mediums (2 Kgs. 23:24). First Samuel 28 shows how such people work, establishing communication with the dead. The medium contacted the dead, and then the spirit of the dead spoke through the body of the medium.

Deuteronomy 18:10–11 shows us activities associated with such people— sacrificing children; practicing divination, sorcery, and witchcraft; interpreting omens, casting spells, and consulting the dead (cp. 2 Kgs. 21:6). Despondent people often resorted to these practices in desperate crises, seeing no other way out. Of these activities the medium concentrated on consulting the dead (Isa. 29:4). First Samuel 28 seems to indicate that some had the real ability on occasion to make such contacts. Isaiah 29:4 may be imitating those who used tricks and mimicry to imitate ghostly sounds and fool their "customers." Thus the Septuagint translates *'ob* as *engastrimythos* or "ventriloquist."

Isaiah charged Israel with making horrible choices. Needing to know the divine will and the opportunities in the future, they should naturally turn to God and his prophets. Instead they turned to forbidden servants of pagan practices who could not give a clear word but only a mutter or whisper, ghostlike sounds. Isaiah was infuriated at such nonsense. The dead have nothing to offer the living. Only the living God has a word for the living. So Isaiah stored up his prophecies with his disciples until the people were ready to listen to him and not to the dead.

VII. TEACHING OUTLINE

A. INTRODUCTION

1. Lead Story: One Day You Can Be . . .
2. Context: Isaiah 6–8 forms the central core of the first section (chs. 1–12) of his prophecy. Here biographical stories show how God confronted Isaiah in his call and kings in their stubborn unbelief. Here we see how Isaiah preserves prophecies that only harden stubborn hearts to prepare for a future generation who will listen and respond to God's word.
3. Transition: The prophet was more than just an inspired writer who left a book of sixty-six chapters behind for us. The prophet got down

in the trenches to do God's work with people of importance. Isaiah sought to bring God's word to bear on current political policy. He was so dedicated to the word of God that he let his own children become walking symbols of what God would do for the nation. The greatest symbol was yet another child. This section shows us the immediate importance of that child and the long-range importance for us.

B. COMMENTARY

1. Called to Condemn (6:1–13)
2. Faith or Failure (7:1–9)
3. Confounding Conception (7:10–17)
4. Day of Destruction (7:18–25)
5. Child of Condemnation (8:1–4)
6. River of Rage (8:5–8)
7. Present to Protect (8:9–10)
8. Falling Before Our Fear (8:11–15)
9. Tie Up the Teaching (8:16–22)

C. CONCLUSION: A CONSECRATED COMMONER

1. Wrap-up: Personal call and personal confrontation pointed to a people hardened to God's word, destined to destruction. Still there was a strong hope for the remnant.
2. Personal Challenge: Look back to the day God called you to a special task in his kingdom. How did you respond? How are you still responding? Have you faithfully carried out God's commission to you? Do you need to recommit yourself to the mission he gave you? How is your family involved in carrying out God's mission?

VIII. ISSUES FOR DISCUSSION

1. Is God still in the business of calling people and commissioning them to a specific task in his mission? What evidence do you have to support your answer?
2. What does it say about God when he calls people to a task but acknowledges they will have few positive results?
3. What is a sign from God? Does he still give signs to his people?
4. Explain your understanding of the virgin birth prophecy in Isaiah and Matthew's use of it. In what way is belief in the virgin birth important for Christian faith?
5. God with us can represent both a threat and a promise. Explain the meaning of this statement and tell how God is with you today.

Isaiah 9–11

Punishment by Proxy

I. INTRODUCTION
No Hugs, No Home, No Hope

II. COMMENTARY
A verse-by-verse explanation of these chapters.

III. CONCLUSION
Preparing the Way for a Savior

An overview of the principles and applications from these chapters.

IV. LIFE APPLICATION
God of the New Beginning

Melding these chapters to life.

V. PRAYER
Tying these chapters to life with God.

VI. DEEPER DISCOVERIES
Historical, geographical, and grammatical enrichment of the commentary.

VII. TEACHING OUTLINE
Suggested step-by-step group study of these chapters.

VIII. ISSUES FOR DISCUSSION
Zeroing these chapters in on daily life.

"*N*early all men can stand adversity,

but if you want to test a man's character,

give him power."

A b r a h a m   L i n c o l n

Isaiah 9–11

IN A NUTSHELL

*G*od promised a newborn child to bring hope and leadership for his people, but his anger remained against a people who proudly practiced injustice and led his people astray. He was also angry at Assyria, that overstepped its bounds as God's agent for punishment of Israel and Judah. After judgment, God's remnant would trust him, and his anger would cease. He would send his Messiah from the roots of Jesse with his Spirit to deliver his people and to bring the exiles home.

Punishment by Proxy

I. INTRODUCTION

No Hugs, No Home, No Hope

*G*ary Smalley tells of his daughter's first experience teaching school. She taught in the low-rent district which had a low love quotient for its kids. She determined to give each child a hug before they left the classroom. Each day little Juan found a way to escape her good-bye hugs. Kari determined to find out why. She discovered that Juan lived with his grandmother along with a house full of other grandchildren. Occasionally Juan's mother would leave one of her lovers to come and visit. Even then the mother ignored Juan, the product of a marriage she wanted to forget. To her other children she showed affection and took them on outings, but she ignored Juan.

Kari went to work. She raised money and moved this grandmother's house to a safer neighborhood near the school and then helped furnish the home. Gradually, Juan shifted directions. His schoolwork improved. Fighting and fear faded from his life. He waited eagerly for hug times. Finally, Juan's life had hope, love, and meaning. Why? He found someone who had faith and love for him. This gave him faith and love for himself (Smalley and Trent, pp. 13–14).

Isaiah used his own family to symbolize what God would do with an Israel that had no faith in God and none in itself. He pointed the way through suffering and deprivation to a time of hope. He promised a people walking in darkness that a great light would shine for them. This light would come from a messianic king who would bring justice and righteousness.

II. COMMENTARY

Punishment by Proxy

MAIN IDEA: *God will destroy a proud, sinful people who oppress the poor, but he will also judge the nation he used to punish his people. He will also send a gifted child as the promised Messiah to take up again his promises to David.*

Sons of Salvation (9:1–7)

Thanksgiving (732 B.C.)

> **SUPPORTING IDEA:** *God has a word of hope for a people who have suffered punishment. Hope is coming in the form of a newborn child. This child will bear royal titles and rule David's kingdom in justice and righteousness.*

9:1. This verse is in prose and concludes chapter 8 in the Hebrew text, while verses 2–7 are poetry and begin a new section with hope as the theme. The first verse joins the previous picture of darkness with the light that follows. To do so, it contrasts the former situation with the new hope. The Assyrians had annexed both the northeastern (**Naphtali**—Josh. 19:32–39) and the northwestern (**Zebulun**—Josh. 19:10–16) portions of the Northern Kingdom in 732 B.C. The prophet, stepping out of his Jerusalem context for a moment, spoke a word of hope to the North. A new day was coming. Isaiah used Assyrian geographical divisions—**way of the sea**, land beyond/**along the Jordan**, **Galilee of the Gentiles** (nations)—to depict a new glory. The basis of this glory is explained in verses 2–7. Geoffrey W. Grogan notes: "These lands, the first to feel the ominous tread of the warrior's boot (v. 5), would be the first to see the new and great light God would focus on Israel (cp. 60:1–3). Matthew rightly saw the fulfillment of this in the ministry of Jesus in Galilee (Matt. 4:15–16; cp. Luke 1:79; John 8:12; cp. John 7:52 with its reference to Galilee)" (Grogan, EBC, commentary on Isaiah 9:1).

9:2–5. A song of thanksgiving joins harvest and military language to praise a new act of God. The reason for rejoicing is not just military victory, but eternal peace, because uniforms become fuel for the fire. This future act is guaranteed by the event that has actually happened—the birth of a son.

9:6–7. These verses contain a royal birth announcement. For once the prophet and king stood together, rejoicing over the happy event. A touch of irony appeared in the prophet's voice as he looked at the baby and described Israel's hope for peace. Such hope lay not in the baby's royal father. Nor did the hope of the nation lie in the baby as the father hoped. Even in joining the royal family's thanksgiving, the prophet succeeded in condemning Ahaz.

The psalms show us that the names used for the new baby belong to the Judean understanding of kingship. The king devised plans and counsel which were too wonderful for men, almost like God (cp. 2 Sam. 16:23), because ultimately God is the **Wonderful** in counsel. **Mighty God** or "heroic God" (author's translation) reflects the thinking behind Psalm 45:6, where the Hebrew text addresses the king as "god." This reflects the respect and authority due the king as distinguished from other men and his closeness to Yahweh, the only God. Psalm 2:7 shows that the king was adopted as son of God when he ascended the throne (see Ps. 89:26–27). Thus Mighty God, which belongs only to God in its real meaning, can be transferred to the obedient king. **Everlasting Father** is yet another divine attribute used among the traditional royal titles. **Prince of Peace** reflects the role of the king in all areas of the nation's life. Peace is more than the opposite of war. It is a sense of personal well-being. It is also material prosperity. It is the complete life of fulfillment and hope. Would this baby, the new king, truly be the Father of his country rather than the servant of Assyria? The king and people certainly hoped so, and they heard the prophet saying so.

But the prophet had a longer view. This baby might improve greatly on the work his father was doing, but he would not live up to God's expectations of his king. "The description of his reign makes it absolutely clear that his role is messianic. There is no end to his rule upon the throne of David, and he will reign with justice and righteousness forever. . . . The language is not just of a wishful thinking for a better time, but the confession of Israel's belief in a divine rule who will replace once and for all the unfaithful kings like Ahaz" (Childs, p. 81).

9:7. Such lasting peace was dependent upon a king whose chief goals are **justice and righteousness**. Justice is the center of the prophetic demand on the people of God. But the same Hebrew word also means the law which establishes justice (Isa. 26:9), the correct teaching (28:26), and the judgment which enforces the law (4:4). Justice ultimately does not rest on human law or judgment, but upon the nature of God (5:16). The prophetic hope rests not on the power of the new king, but upon the **zeal of the LORD Almighty** (see "Deeper Discoveries").

Ahaz's new baby did not fill the prophetic demands. Nor did any other occupant of David's throne. The people of God had to wait over seven hundred years for Jesus of Nazareth, who did fulfill and even surpass such expectations. He did not bring all to immediate fulfillment, but he set his followers on a course of expectation, looking to the final coming of the Prince of Peace. These events were backed by the zeal of a jealous God who would defeat all his end-time enemies and establish justice and righteousness forever.

B The Abiding Anger of the Almighty (9:8–10:4)

A prophecy of disaster against the Northern Kingdom (734 B.C.)

> **SUPPORTING IDEA:** *A punished people who do not return to God find further judgment forecast as God displays his anger against his people because of their injustice and oppression.*

This passage is distinctive in Isaiah because its subject is the Northern Kingdom rather than the Southern Kingdom. Isaiah was a minister to the South. Isaiah 9:8–10:4 is really an oracle against a foreign nation, similar to those found in chapters 13–23. Such sermons were addressed rhetorically to the enemy. Yet the enemy never heard them. The audience that listened was the prophet's own people. When he pronounced judgment on the enemy, he was normally proclaiming salvation for his people.

We have seen in 7:4–9,16 and 8:4 that Isaiah promised salvation to Judah in the midst of the war with Syria and Ephraim. Such salvation, however, was connected with the demand for faith and ultimately accompanied by judgment upon Judah because she would not believe, relying instead upon Assyria. The chorus (9:12,17,21; 10:4) joins the section to 5:24–25, while the woe oracle in 10:1–4 connects back to the series in 5:8–23. This ties the present section back to chapter 5. Why? The writer wanted to show that the judgments applied also to the Southern Kingdom. By itself 9:8–10:4 could be read as hope for the South and judgment only for the North. Pointing it back to chapter 5 shows that judgment was pronounced on the South also, because Judah imitated the action of the North and had to repeat its history.

9:8–10. God had spoken, but the judgment had not yet fallen. The word of God was sent as a messenger that brought to pass that which it proclaimed. **Jacob**, **Israel**, **Ephraim**, and **Samaria** are distinctive ways of referring to the Northern Kingdom by reference to its patriarch (Gen. 35:10), its official national name, its major tribe, and its capital city. The prophet left no doubt about his attitude toward the North: they were proud and arrogant. Only God has a right to such majesty and pride. The pride was evident in their contempt for God's discipline. He had defeated and destroyed. They thought they could build everything back with better materials.

9:11–12. Syria and Israel ignored the Assyrian threat even when some of their land was occupied. Isaiah assured them that God was on their enemies' side. He let Syria and Philistia attack and defeat Israel. Now Syria would experience God's judgment. God's **anger** had **not turned away.**

9:13–17. God's punishment of his people had a definite purpose. He sought repentance, which would turn his people away from other gods and back to him. To repent is literally "to turn or return." Repentance has a still greater effect, because it restores relationship with God. In this section the refrain echoes the sad complaint that God had not returned, because the people had not. Instead, God extended his judgment, eliminating the people's leaders. He had turned from his normal course of action. God no longer took **pleasure** in the strong young warriors, nor did he express compassion or **pity** for the **widows** and **fatherless,** who could normally depend upon his special protection. Instead, in **a single day** God would swoop down unexpectedly and take away all their worthless leaders. Still the anger remained.

9:18–21. Israel did not turn to God; so God would not turn to them. His judgment burned the land. Still, Israel paid no attention. They fought among themselves for political leadership or turned against their brothers in the kingdom of Judah. The only image that could describe the magnitude of their sin was cannibalism. God disciplined them, but to no avail.

10:1–4. All that remained for the prophet was to whine out his funeral song in mourning over his dying people. **Unjust, oppressive** people who fed on the poor and helpless deserved the death sentence. Their evil conduct left no doubt about their future—exile! The enemy was coming! Where could they **run**? Who could help? Even then, God's anger **is not turned away**. The implication is that the remainder of God's people, Judah, are next in line!

◖C◗ Rattling the Rod (10:5–19)

Ironical woe oracle (705 B.C.)

> **SUPPORTING IDEA:** *The sovereign God can use godless people for his purposes, but he will punish them when they refuse to realize they are not in command.*

10:5–6. The woe continues. Unexpectedly, the subject is Assyria, not Judah. Verse 5b reads literally: "A staff! It is in their hand my fury" (author's translation). This explains the role of Assyria in punishing God's people. Assyria was God's secret agent. She did not know that Yahweh was using her to punish Israel.

10:7–10. Assyria proudly attributed their success to their own power and purpose. Assyria captured the Syrian cities of **Calno** (738 B.C.), **Carchemish** (717 B.C.), **Hamath** (738 B.C. and again 720 B.C.), and **Arpad** (740 B.C. and 720 B.C.). **Damascus** was the capital city of Rezin in Syria, while **Samaria** was the capital of Israel. All were alike to Assyria. Some had gods even better than Israel and Judah, so the Assyrians thought. Isaiah knew better. Yahweh alone gave Assyria permission to attack Samaria.

10:11. Suddenly the prophet stunned his Judean audience. The great Syrian cities with their famous gods fell. Samaria was no different. And, the prophet shouted, Jerusalem is also no different! She, too, will fall! Only then would God punish Assyria. The prophetic irony is complete. The mourning cry over the enemy, raising hopes in the hearts of his Judean listeners, turned into a blazing threat against Judah because of its idolatry.

10:12–19. The climax turned to a threat against proud Assyria, that claimed credit for all the accomplishments rather than serving as a rod of anger in God's hand. Assyria was compared to a forest burned so completely that a child could scribble the number of trees left. God would be the spark that set the forest ablaze.

Rewarding the Remnant (10:20–27)

Promise of salvation (711 B.C.)

> **SUPPORTING IDEA:** *God's punishment leaves a faithful remnant who return to him and rely on him for protection.*

10:20–23. Remnant theology is interpreted precisely in these verses. Remnant theology has two sides. God disciplined the nation that leaned on Assyria for help until that nation turned back to God. This return had to be in truth, in loyal faithfulness. Such a remnant fulfilled the name of the prophet's son (7:3) but reflected only a shadow of former glory (v. 22), since God's righteous judgment had to be completed (v. 23).

10:24–27. Once such judgment was finished, an oracle of salvation could be sounded. This would show that the God of the exodus from Egypt and of the judges could repeat his former victories for Israel. Then Assyria would no longer be a burden of oppression against Israel. Remnant theology thus presupposes almost total destruction before God acts to create a new community out of the faithful few. Remnant theology calls on God's people to trust his plan of salvation—not enemy armies—even in the most difficult times.

Marching to Murder (10:28–32)

Battle report with prophetic warning (712 B.C.)

> **SUPPORTING IDEA:** *God uses his prophetic spokesman to warn his people of imminent danger.*

10:28–32. The Assyrian army of King Sargon repelled rebellions in Philistia, centering in Ashdod from 713–711 B.C. (cp. ch. 20). Apparently Sargon sent troops from the north to make sure Jerusalem did not become involved. The prophet imitated a military scout's report as he warned Jerusalem of the enemy's approach on an unexpected path through the toughest terrain north of Jerusalem. The enemy might surprise Jerusalem. It could not surprise God.

Pruning the Powerful (10:33–34)

Image-filled oracle against a foreign nation (712 B.C.)

> **SUPPORTING IDEA:** *The Lord can bring down the most powerful human rulers as he judges the world in his sovereignty.*

10:33–34. Isaiah issued a warning, intentionally left open to interpretation. He pictured God as a lumberjack chopping down the tall trees. The tall trees could refer to Jerusalem's leaders as they contemplated joining the rebellion. They could refer to the approaching Assyrian army. The prophet said in effect, "If the shoe fits, wear it and suffer the consequences."

Ⓖ The Spirit's Stump of Salvation (11:1–9)

Ironical use of prophetic coronation oracle (700 B.C. [?])

SUPPORTING IDEA: *God's Spirit will start over with Israel, going back to the root of David's family tree to provide a righteous, just ruler to bring peace and knowledge of God to the world.*

11:1–2. At some time within his ministry, Isaiah lost all hope for the present kingship. This could have been during the crisis with Ahaz in 733 B.C. or again with Hezekiah in 713 B.C. or 701 B.C. Perhaps during an actual coronation ceremony or at a festival celebrating the role of the king, Isaiah stepped up to perform the traditional prophetic role of announcing God's blessing of the king (cp. Ps. 2). Isaiah's first words shocked the audience. He did not speak of a Davidic king. He did not refer to the present king. Instead, he pointed to a coming king from the **stump of Jesse**, a **Branch** growing out of roots. He presupposed that the present line of Davidic kings was dead. Similarly Isaiah's contemporary Micah sent Judah back to Bethlehem for a new king (Mic. 5:2). Samuel's search in 1 Samuel 16 would have to be repeated. Israel needed a new kind of king, one filled with the Spirit like David was (1 Sam. 16:13; cp. 1 Sam. 10:6,10; 11:6; 18:10).

The prophet no longer used military imagery to describe the king (as in ch. 9). He turned, instead, to the language of the wise men, the court counselors. The divine **Spirit** would reveal itself in the king's **Spirit of wisdom**, so that he could make proper plans and give proper advice and teaching. The center of such thought is **fear of the LORD**. This is an awesome respect and reverence for God that directs every area of a person's life.

11:3–5. The wise king would enter the royal courtroom to judge his nation correctly. As judge, the king would be empowered with **the breath of his lips**, the same word translated "Spirit" in verse 2. By this he would protect the poor from the wicked, establishing the economic **justice** so central to prophetic preaching. The new age established by the new king would bring **righteousness**, a dominant theme for Isaiah. Coupled with **faithfulness**, this clothed the king for his royal reign.

11:6–9. Such a king would not bring just a transformation of the social order. Nature, too, would be restored to paradise. Natural enemies would feed together. A lad would surpass even the wildest childhood dreams, becoming king of the jungle. Human power, alone, could not accomplish this. The **holy mountain**, where God resided, provided the center. From there, personal acquaintance with Yahweh, the God of Israel, would flood out over the entire world. No Israelite king took Isaiah's role description for a proper king seriously. This was not just Isaiah's view. God himself was the source of this description. Centuries later, when the Jews least expected it, the stump of Jesse blossomed into life once more. Jesus Christ, filled with the divine Spirit, came to minister to the poor and outcast of society, and to give his wise teachings to the world. Since that moment, the **knowledge** of God has gradually flowed through the world. The bold goal of letting the world know of Jesus of Nazareth has not yet been reached, yet his church continues the mission of proclamation on which he sent them. One day he will return to realize fully the vision of Isaiah.

⊞ The Day of Decision (11:10–16)

Prophecy of salvation (700 B.C.)

SUPPORTING IDEA: *God will work a new exodus to unite a remnant of his people, overcoming their jealousy to create a new rule that makes the nations come running.*

11:10–11. This prose description of the coming "day of Yahweh" interprets and connects the two poetic oracles in 11:1–9 and 12–16 (cp. 7:18–25). It takes up language from both oracles. The messianic king would function specifically for the nations, an idea only hinted at in verse 9. The holy mountain where God dwelt would entice the nations with its splendor and glory. Such an action of God can only be described as a **second** exodus (vv. 11,15), a purchase or ransom of Israel's **remnant** from slavery among the nations of the world (see Ps. 74:2). Elam was the land east of Babylonia and the lower Tigris River on the Persian Gulf. Its capital was at Susa. The coastlands of the sea probably refer to the Phoenician coast.

11:12–16. The salvation hope in these verses includes both the Northern and Southern Kingdoms. The Northern Kingdom went into exile first in 732 B.C. and finally in 722 B.C. (2 Kgs. 17). The invasion of Sennacherib and Hezekiah's dependence upon Egyptian help in 701 B.C. (2 Kgs. 19) may have driven some Jews into exile in Egypt, but the major flight to Egypt came only in the Babylonian crisis of 609–587 B.C. (2 Kgs. 23:29–25:30).

This oracle apparently looked to the time when both kingdoms would have lost their independence and would rely on Yahweh for a new miracle to recreate his people. Then God would raise his signal flag to the nations, who would allow God's people to return home. God would reunite the two parts of his people, with the result that jealousy and hostility would disappear. Israel would then conquer anew their neighbors to the east and west, restoring the Davidic kingdom (cp. 2 Sam. 8). God's new exodus (vv. 15–16; cp. Exod. 14) would lead across a special **highway** laid **from Assyria**, where the Northern Kingdom was captive (2 Kgs. 18:9–12). Similar language appears in the second half of Isaiah to describe the return of Judah from Babylon (Isa. 40:3; 62:10).

> **MAIN IDEA REVIEW:** *God will destroy a proud, sinful people who oppress the poor, but he will also judge the nation he used to punish his people. He will also send a gifted child as the promised Messiah to take up again his promises to David.*

III. CONCLUSION

Preparing the Way for a Savior

God's punishment may appear unjust and extreme. That is the short-sighted view. The long-term perspective shows that God knows what he is up to. He is disciplining his people, preparing a faithful remnant who will rely on him and no one else. He is showing his sovereign control of all world history, preparing the way for a Savior to come who will offer salvation to everyone who will rely on him.

PRINCIPLES

- God has a plan to establish his kingdom with peace and justice.
- God expresses his anger against pride and arrogance.
- God disciplines his people so they will seek him and turn to him.
- God can use people for his purposes even when they are unaware that he is using them.
- God will fulfill his promises to David and his descendants and establish his kingdom of righteousness and fairness.
- God brings salvation through a holy remnant.

APPLICATIONS

- When life reaches its darkest moment, look to God for help.
- Express your joy for what God is doing in your life today.
- Worship the child whom God sent to give you salvation.
- Determine where pride and arrogance are in control of your life. Ask God to take them out of your life and forgive you.
- Turn away from your sin and seek God.
- Create ways you can help care for the people in your community who are in great need.
- List your fears; then ask God to take charge of them.

IV. LIFE APPLICATION

God of the New Beginning

What an experience I have had in the last couple of years! As I write this commentary, I have a new wife, a new eleven-year-old daughter, a new daughter-in-law, and a new granddaughter. Having emptied my nest of children and then lost my wife to cancer, I am in a real sense learning what it is to be a remnant and begin anew with God. I have learned what it means to lose much of what I held dear and what gave a sense of hope, security, and continuity to life. I have seen God work to weed out the sins and bad habits of my life to prepare me for a new beginning. I have seen God bring new people, new territory for ministry, new responsibilities, new love, and new challenges into my life. He is a God of new beginnings.

Through Isaiah, God promised Israel a new beginning. Suffering and loss came first. But a remnant would come back to the land and return to their God. God would send his promised Messiah to start over again with his work of salvation among his people. God is still in the business of starting over again. Perhaps your life needs a new start. Significant losses and disappointments may have you joining Israel in wondering where God is and why he is not doing what you expect. Renew your faith and trust in him. Ask him to show you where he is at work right now. Ask him to give you the patience to wait for his timing to begin anew his work of grace in your life. Be ready to change your lifestyle as God starts over again in your life.

V. PRAYER

Disciplining God, we accept your discipline for our sins. We confess that we have relied on so many resources rather than depending totally on you. Forgive us our sins. Lead us into your paths of righteousness and justice. Accept our thanks for the Branch from the root of Jesse, even Jesus Christ, who has become our counselor, our wisdom, our mighty God. Amen.

VI. DEEPER DISCOVERIES

A. Zeal of the Lord (9:7)

God's zeal is at the same time jealousy. It is a term which in the Ancient Near East referred to the relationship between the gods, one god being jealous of another. Israel used it to describe God's attitude toward his own worshipers, a usage not known elsewhere in Israel's environment. This attitude is the foundation of the Ten Commandments that prohibit worship of any other gods (Exod. 20:5). Such jealousy brings judgment upon a disobedient people. But suffering under judgment, Israel could pray in hope on the basis of divine jealousy (Isa. 63:15) and find God acting in zeal and jealousy to restore his people (Isa. 37:32). In our passage the jealousy and zealousness of God are the hope for Israel's kingship. Only when God chooses to act will the people of God find the hoped-for king reigning over them.

B. Daughter of Zion (10:32)

Biblical language is full of images to describe God's work with his people. Many of these are family images, showing God's intimacy with his people. The people of Judah and Jerusalem were called the daughter of Zion or even the virgin daughter of Zion (2 Kgs. 19:21; Lam. 2:13). Jerusalem and her residents are thus the protected, beloved children of God.

Zion was an ancient name for the oldest part of Jerusalem on its southeast ridge, a name apparently going back to times before David's conquest of Jerusalem (2 Sam. 5:7). Solomon enlarged the Zion area, extending the name to the new temple area (1 Kgs. 8:1). Zion thus became the residence or palace of Yahweh, the God of Israel, where people came to worship and sacrifice to him (Pss. 9:11; 76:2). There his name had its home (Isa. 18:7). There he chose Judah as his beloved people (Ps. 78:68), his inheritance (Ps. 74:2). Anyone who attacked Jerusalem was attacking God's beloved daughter (Isa. 10:32) and bringing judgment on God's people (Isa. 1:8; Mic. 4:10) and their violent wickedness (Mic. 3:10–12). Zion also housed Israel's future hopes. One day God will roar from Zion (Joel 3:16). The good news would be preached to Zion (Isa. 40:9; 52:7). God would bring his people back to Zion (Ps. 126:1). They would trust in Zion (Jer. 50:5). God would send his victorious king there (Isa. 62:11; see Matt. 21:5). There Messiah would reign (Ps. 2:6). From Zion would come a redeemer (Rom. 11:26), the cornerstone of Zion (Isa. 28:16; 1 Pet. 2:6). From Zion God would rule the world forever (Mic. 4:7). Foreign nations would come and worship in Zion (Isa. 16:1). The Lamb will stand there with his 144,000 faithful (Rev. 14:1).

VII. TEACHING OUTLINE

A. INTRODUCTION

1. Lead Story: No Hugs, No Home, No Hope
2. Context: Chapters 9–11 turn from biographical stories of the prophet to oracles of judgment and salvation, centering on two messianic promises in chapters 9 and 11.
3. Transition: Isaiah showed how his people had to experience God's judgment because they refused to depend on him. He also showed

that judgment was not the end of God's people or his plan for them. He would preserve a remnant and send to them his Messiah.

B. COMMENTARY

1. Sons of Salvation (9:1–7)
2. The Abiding Anger of the Almighty (9:8–10:4)
3. Rattling the Rod (10:5–19)
4. Rewarding the Remnant (10:20–27)
5. Marching to Murder (10:28–32)
6. Pruning the Powerful (10:33–34)
7. The Spirit's Stump of Salvation (11:1–9)
8. The Day of Decision (11:10–16)

C. CONCLUSION: GOD OF THE NEW BEGINNING

1. Wrap-up: God controls history, ancient and modern. He warns his people of judgment to come and calls them to repentance. When we refuse to repent, he chooses whatever instrument he pleases to discipline us. As he does so, he points forward to his continued plans to save us.

2. Personal Challenge: The church is the remnant God has chosen to represent him in our day and in our world. How are you representing him? In a way that calls for more discipline? Or in a way that shows the world that the Messiah has come, that good news is available, that whosoever believes in him should not perish but have everlasting life?

VIII. ISSUES FOR DISCUSSION

1. In what ways do you see God active in the affairs of world history and powerful nations today?
2. In what specific ways is God calling your church to work for justice and righteousness today?
3. Explain how Jesus is the fulfillment of the messianic prophecies in Isaiah 9 and 11.
4. Is remnant theology still one of God's ways of working with his church?

Isaiah 12

The Remnant's Response

"*T*he God who was angry is now acknowl-edged to be Israel's great friend, advocate, ally, support, and only hope. It is this Yahweh who can and will, in great authority and power, completely transpose historical conditions."

Walter Brueggemann

Isaiah 12

IN A NUTSHELL

*T*he prophetic disciples who collected Isaiah's preaching (see 8:16) marked the end of the first collection of sermons with a song which should be sung "in that day"—that is, when the prophecy found its fulfill-ment, when the remnant of God's people had returned to their land from foreign exile. The first twelve chapters were thus prepared for use in the worship of the post-exilic community.

The Remnant's Response

I. INTRODUCTION

Troublemaker, I Take You

A man adopted a troubled teenage girl. Everyone in town knew the girl's reputation. She lied. She cheated. She refused to obey any authority. She often turned destructive. Why would anyone want to adopt her? Still the man took her into his house, gave her a special room of her own, and treated her like his daughter. She treated him just like everyone expected. One day she ran home from school, raced into the house, and started looking everywhere for money. Finding none, she went on a rampage, disrupting and destroying everything in sight. When the man returned home from work, a horrendous sight greeted him. The entire house was turned topsy turvy. Many precious possessions lay shattered on the floor.

The neighbors watched to see the girl's expected expulsion. They came to him with advice: "Don't finalize the adoption papers. Send her back." The man steadfastly refused all such advice.

"Send her back," neighbors and friends repeated. "After all, she is really not your daughter."

"I know," the man admitted. "But I told her she was" (Lucado, *In the Grip of Grace*, p. 127).

Isaiah 1–11 describes us at our worst. Every sin we could imagine is laid out before us. In one way or another we have had to admit, yes, that is the way I am. I am a sinner. I deserve all the judgment God has described, all the punishment he has given me. Then we turn to look at the Father. "Are you going to exile us from your presence forever?" we ask plaintively.

"No, my child," he answers. "I told you, you are my child. I meant it. Come, see my salvation and celebrate with me."

Today we look at Isaiah 12 and learn how to celebrate God's salvation.

II. COMMENTARY

The Remnant's Response

MAIN IDEA: *The final day of the Lord will be a time of praise and thanksgiving as God's people see his anger pass and his salvation appear.*

A Praise for Salvation (12:1–6)

Song of thanksgiving (700 B.C.)

SUPPORTING IDEA: *Those who experience God's salvation want to praise God and make him known throughout the earth.*

12:1–2. The opening verse of the song startles the reader, reading literally, "I thank you, O Yahweh, because you were angry with me" (author's translation). This is modified to describe God's turning, his repentance of his anger, to console his people. The song was placed in the first person singular to make it personal. Reflecting upon his personal history, the believer praised God for the time of discipline and for the deliverance from that crisis period. He then turned to traditional language of praise to describe the greatness of God in his relationship to the individual believer (cp. Exod. 15; Ps. 118).

The theme of God's comfort and consolation will appear again in chapter 40. Experiencing God's discipline teaches us that **God is my salvation**. Isaiah could sing this boldly and invite his readers to do the same because his own name meant "Yahweh is salvation." We can give thanks and praise to the **angry** God, because we know his nature is love and his primary acts bring salvation, not wrath.

12:3. The song turns from the individual *you* of verse 1 to the plural **you** of the entire congregation. The great **salvation** of God was not confined to the individual but encompassed the entire congregation. The prophet invites the congregation to fill their buckets with salvation from God's ever-flowing **wells**.

12:4–6. Everybody must join the hymn of praise. The individual congregation is not large enough. Praise must echo throughout the entire earth. God's name must be **exalted** internationally. Such praise should resound to distant nations, inviting them to join the proclamation. Judgment spread Israel across the known world (11:11–12). News of his deliverance must spread just as far. The whole world must see that God has proved himself trustworthy and powerful, fulfilling his promise and saving his people. They must be invited to take up the song of salvation.

Dark overtones cloud Isaiah 1–12, but the remnant's rousing response rings it to a close. Salvation is God's final word for his people. The **Holy One of Israel** resides in his temple in **Zion**, the center of his praise.

> **MAIN IDEA REVIEW:** *The final day of the Lord will be a time of praise and thanksgiving as God's people see his anger pass and his salvation appear.*

III. CONCLUSION

Take a Drink

Isaiah 1–12 is a call to repentance (ch. 1) and to thankful praise (ch. 12). Between the two lies a history of God's disappointment, anger, rejection, and announcement of punishment for his people and for their conquerors. Gloom is broken only by occasional hints at salvation and by promises of Messiah, promises that bring hope for the future but pronounce judgment on the current regime. Gladly we hear chapter 12 ring out the praise of God the Savior and invite us to drink from his wells of salvation.

PRINCIPLES

- Thanksgiving is a central part of life with God.
- God is the source of all deliverance and salvation.
- God can be trusted.
- God's people witness to the world of God's saving acts in history.
- Singing praises to God is a major aspect of worshiping and living with him.

APPLICATIONS

- Compose your own song of thanksgiving to God for everything he has done for you.
- Tell a person who does not worship God about how God has saved you and wants to save him.
- Find specific worries in your life that you will turn over to God.
- List the actions God has taken in your life.
- Spend an hour in meditation and prayer, experiencing God's personal presence.

IV. LIFE APPLICATION

Daddy's Going to Sing

I did not make the fourth grade choir. Several years later the director of the youth choir would announce on Sunday morning that youth choir practice was that afternoon, and all the youth should plan to attend, but then he often added, "But Trent, you are excused." Many years later, my children beside me in church would whisper, "Please, Daddy, don't sing."

You get the picture. Here in this world, I have had few opportunities and no invitations to sing. Although I have never heard anyone sing off key, my friends and family assure me that I do. But God has a special song for me to sing when I get to heaven. I will not need any voice lessons or any special practice. I will just join the angelic voices praising God for all he has done for me and for all his people. That will be an exciting day.

The excitement begins when you accept salvation from God and receive his assurance that you will be part of his people in heaven. Give your heart to Jesus today and then begin singing his praises. When we all get to heaven, I will chorus in with you.

V. PRAYER

God, thank you for your anger. It shows me that you care and are determined to make me what I can be and what you created me to be. It shows me that you are still at work in this world, leading people and nations to participate in your plan of salvation. I raise my voice in praise to the God of my salvation and will invite people from all nations to join me in proclaiming the glory of your name. Amen.

VI. DEEPER DISCOVERIES

God's Anger (12:1)

Many people in the church today seek to extinguish this topic from the church's vocabulary, dismissing it as Old Testament religion replaced by the loving God of the New Testament. Such theological moves reduce the Old Testament to something less than the inspired Word of God and ignore much of the New Testament, especially the episodes of Jesus cleansing the temple, Jesus arguing heatedly with the Pharisees and other Jewish leaders, Jesus teaching on the end of the world in the parable of Lazarus and the rich man, and in the sermons in Matthew 23–25; Mark 13; and Luke 21. The Old Testament is rich in language describing divine anger.

The term in Isaiah 12:1 (Hb. *'anaph*) introduces us to several of the concepts associated with God's anger. Human sin rouses God's anger, leading him to discipline his people (1 Kgs. 8:46; 2 Chr. 6:36). The entire history of Israel can be described as a history of anger-inducing sin (Deut. 9:3–29). This applies to the individual as well as the people collectively (Deut. 1:37; 1 Kgs. 11:9–11). Human sin and divine anger do not shut off communication; prayer and repentance can actually call forth divine compassion, forgiveness, and restoration (1 Kgs. 8:47–53).

The psalms contain these kinds of prayers that seek renewed relationship with an angry God who seems to have forgotten his people and extended his anger forever (Ps. 85:4–7; cp. Ps. 60:1–5). Such prayers can ask God to protect his reputation and punish the guilty nations (Ps. 79:1–13). Israel knows God has a point of no return when anger becomes the final word (Ezra 9:14–15). After experiencing God's anger, his people turn to thanksgiving because God turns from his anger and comforts his people (Isa. 12:1).

VII. TEACHING OUTLINE

A. INTRODUCTION

1. Lead Story: Troublemaker, I Take You
2. Context: Judgment has ruled most of Isaiah's first eleven chapters—judgment on disobedient people, greedy rulers, luxury-loving women, and even on cruel enemy nations called to punish God's people. Sandwiched around most of the judgment speeches have been promises of hope beyond discipline. These centered particularly in a baby boy who would enter the world and be everything the present leadership was not.
3. Transition: Isaiah provided his people words to use when God turned from his anger and brought the promised salvation. These words form a brief hymn of thanksgiving, thanking God for his anger. They show us how to respond to and what to expect from an angry God.

B. COMMENTARY

1. Praise for Salvation (12:1–6)

C. CONCLUSION: DADDY'S GOING TO SING

1. Wrap-up: Our sin makes God angry. We need time to see what sins we have committed; then we must confess them to God and ask for his forgiveness and renewal. That is not the end of the story. We also need time to thank God for what he did in his anger that brought us

back to him and for what he is doing to help and comfort us after his time of anger has passed.

2. Personal Challenge: Think through the implications of God's anger for your life. When did you last experience the anger of God? How did you respond? What do you need to do now in relationship to God's anger and your life?

VIII. ISSUES FOR DISCUSSION

1. How would life be different if God never became angry?
2. In what ways can the history of your church be written in relationship to the anger of God?
3. Have you ever expressed thanks to God for his anger?
4. How does trust in God relieve your fears?
5. What are you and your church doing to make God's name known to all the nations of the world?

Isaiah 13–14

Banishing Babylon

Quote

"*Indeed,* I tremble for my country when I reflect that God is just."

Thomas   Jefferson

Isaiah 13–14

 IN A NUTSHELL

Isaiah begins a series of sermons against foreign enemies (13:1–23:18) by pointing to Babylonia, the nation that eventually destroyed Jerusalem and the Southern Kingdom. He warns that the day of the Lord is coming to Babylon because of their pride and because the Lord wants to restore his chosen people to the land he gave them.

Banishing Babylon

I. INTRODUCTION

A Surprising Source of Salvation

*L*ife's surprises may be our salvation. A moment from the life of President Theodore Roosevelt shows how this happens. Living before bifocals, the president had to carry two pairs of glasses wherever he went, one for reading and one for viewing the world. One day he visited Milwaukee. Suddenly, a man fired a gun and shot the president. A surgeon quickly worked on the president's wound. When he finished, the doctor handed the president a surprise gift—his steel spectacle case. The assassin's bullet had struck the glasses case instead of entering the president's heart. The president was saved by a case he hated to carry.

As he works his plan of salvation for the world, God is full of surprises. Babylonia thought they controlled the world and had no one to threaten them. Israel got so low and desperate that they decided God had forgotten them and no longer had the will or way to save them. God had surprises for both Babylonia and Israel. We may find that in our habit-driven life where we think we know how everything is going to turn out, God has a surprise for us, too (Patterson, p. 1).

The prophets of Israel often counseled the nation and its leaders in times of political crisis. In time of battle the prophet reassured the army with an oracle that promised victory against the enemy (see 1 Sam. 15:2–3). This was another custom that Israel shared with her neighbors (Num. 22–24). Preaching against the enemies was not limited to times of battle. Times of national weakness and crisis called the nation to the temple for services of national mourning and grief. Prophets rose to announce the divine answer to the nation's prayers.

Parts of such answers dealt with the enemies, who formed a large part of the cause of Israel's grief. Amos transformed the tradition of preaching against the nations into a literary art form by listing several such sermons together and then suddenly including his own people in the oracles against foreign nations (Amos 1:3–2:16). We have seen how Isaiah used a similar device in 9:7–10:11. Most of the other prophets included such oracles against the enemies.

Sermons against enemies dominate Isaiah 13:1–23:18, but there are also sermons against Judah (ch. 22), including her as an enemy of God. By this means a section that should bring hope to the people of God was transformed into a judgment against sinners in general, no matter what their national origin. The sermons are more. They were directed against nations seeking political alliances with Judah. For Judah, they served as warnings against political alliance. Judah's only ally was her God.

II. COMMENTARY

Banishing Babylon

> **MAIN IDEA:** *The day of the Lord will come upon Israel's major enemies as God punishes the world for its sinful pride and arrogance. This will result in new hope for his people.*

A A Message for Babylonia (13:1–22)

Call to battle (about 701 B.C.)

> **SUPPORTING IDEA:** *Babylon's glory days are over. God will punish the prideful nation and its arrogant king for their reign of terror. Then he may reunite his people and give them new life.*

13:1. The Hebrew word for **oracle** is a technical term for a prophetic sermon or pronouncement and usually occurs in headings introducing books or oracles (Nah. 1:1; Zech. 1:1; cp. Jer. 23:33–38). Otherwise, it occurs only in Proverbs 30:1; 31:1; 2 Kings 9:25; Lamentations 2:14; and 2 Chronicles 24:27.

Babylon, the capital of ancient Babylonia, was located between the Tigris and Euphrates rivers, south of modern Baghdad. In Isaiah's day it looked back to the glorious days of Hammurabi (1792–1750 B.C.) and a brief revival under Nebuchadnezzar I (1146–1123 B.C.), but it was suffering impatiently under Assyrian rule. Isaiah himself saw Babylonian secret diplomacy trying to overthrow Assyrian rule (see ch. 39), but he did not see Babylonia as the "jewel of kingdoms" (13:19). The historical context here is that of Babylonia after the rise of Nabopolassar in 626 B.C. and after Nebuchadnezzar's destruction of Jerusalem in 587 B.C., which established Babylonia as Judah's enemy number one.

13:2–5. As he had prepared the people for praise when they returned from exile in 538 B.C. (ch.12), so here the prophet mysteriously called an unnamed **army** to lift the battle insignia and prepare for **war**. The army was composed of Yahweh's specially consecrated **warriors**, highlighting the awesome atmosphere. Divine **wrath** dominated the scene. The commanding general was the divine warrior, the Lord of Hosts (NIV, LORD **Almighty**). He did not immediately reveal the nature of the army being summoned, indicating only that **they come from faraway lands, from the ends of the heavens**.

13:6–16. The prophet issued an invitation to a mourning ceremony: **Wail, for the day of the LORD is near** (see 2:12–22; see "Deeper Discoveries"). The **Almighty** (Hb. *Shaddai*; see "Deeper Discoveries") was primed to act in **destruction** and **anger** (for God's anger, see "Deeper Discoveries," ch. 12). This would strike terror in the enemy and throw the cosmos into confusion. What prompted such terror? Human sin! Babylon's **pride** stood in the center of the divine attention. The remnant (see "Deeper Discoveries," chs. 2–4) would be as rare as gold.

Note that **Ophir** was a location, apparently in Arabia near Yemen (or perhaps in eastern Africa), traced back to a Semitic descendant of Noah (1 Chr. 1:23). It was known for exporting fine gold (1 Kgs. 9:28; 2 Chr. 8:18; Ps. 45:9) and other precious commodities (2 Chr. 9:10). The nations in exile would be able to flee home in the confusion. Horrible atrocities of war would be commonplace (vv. 15–16).

13:17–22. Having created such a tense and gloomy atmosphere, the prophet finally introduced the cast of characters. The army summoned by God for his purposes was the **Medes**, from northwest Iran with their capital at Ecbatana. They had settled the area about 1400 B.C. They battled the Assyrians at least from 800 B.C. onward, but they had to pay tribute to Assyrian kings at least from about 720 B.C. until King Cyaxares (about 625–585 B.C.) joined Babylonia in defeating the Assyrians (612–610 B.C.). Cyrus, king of Persia, the son of a Median king, revolted against the Medes and destroyed their empire (553 B.C.). Isaiah 13 and 21 join Jeremiah 51 in picturing the Medes as God's historical agents used to bring the day of Yahweh against Babylonia in punishment for its treatment of Judah. Second Kings 17:6 and 18:11 show that some of the Israelite exiles went to Media.

God's agents could not be bribed. They would treat Babylonia just as she treated Judah with all the atrocities of war. Finally, the prophet named God's enemy facing destruction—mighty Babylonia.

Chaldeans (used in Hebrew text with **pride** in v. 19), is a synonym for Babylonia. It referred originally to tribal groups in southern Babylonia near the Persian Gulf. They gained political control of Babylonia under their kings Nabopolassar and Nebuchadnezzar II and were responsible for the destruction of Jerusalem in 587 B.C. Now, said the prophet, their time had come. Their city would become uninhabited wilderness like **Sodom and Gomorroh**, the Bible's prime example of evil being punished (Gen. 10:19; Deut. 32:32; Jer. 49:18; Lam. 4:6; Amos 4:11; Matt. 10:15; Luke 10:12; Rom. 9:29; Jude 7).

Arab (v. 20; see 2 Chr. 17:11; Neh. 6:1) names a race of people and should probably be translated as "nomad" or "homeless wanderer." Babylon's proud population would become like the class of people they snubbed and hated.

B Compassion for the Chosen (14:1–23)

Proclamation of salvation (701 B.C.)

SUPPORTING IDEA: *Judgment on the enemy means God is showing compassion on his chosen people and moving ahead with his plan of salvation for the world.*

14:1–2. Chapter 14 shows the effects of Babylon's destruction upon Israel. Israel would again know God's **compassion**. God's parental love for his children guaranteed the security of their lives. Through such love God forgave a repentant people and restored them to their land. Love is of a piece with divine anger that brought judgment. As such it represents the freedom of God in dealing with his people (Exod. 33:19). Such love belongs to the very nature of God himself. (For God's compassion, see "Deeper Discoveries.")

Such love brings God to **choose** Israel **once again**. This election theology is unique to Israel among their neighbors in the Near East. It is first expressed in Deuteronomy 7:6–7. The response to such loving election is also made clear in Deuteronomy 10:12–16. (For God chooses, and we are free, see "Deeper Discoveries," chs. 45–46.) Even though they were God's elect, Israel's refusal to obey brought the expected punishment (see Deut. 30). After punishment, God's love brought a renewed election, restoring Israel to **their own land** for a second chance with God (cp. Deut. 4:36–39). Now the definition of Israel was expanded, since the foreigners who lived in the land would join Israel. Israel's political power would again exert itself, turning the tables on her former captors.

14:3–8. Israel would again experience **relief** (the same Hebrew word occurs in Isa. 14:1,3,7), the goal of the original conquest (Deut. 12:10; Josh. 1:13,15; 23:1). Having received anew God's love, election, and rest, Israel would mock her enemies (vv. 4–20) as they were once mocked (see Ps. 137). They would be joined by the whole earth that Babylonia once ruled, but which now would have rest. Even the trees would join in.

14:9–10. A welcome-home party is being prepared. Babylon in the person of her king would be escorted to the eternal resting place to be greeted by former kings who had also lost their power (cp. Isa. 5:8–30). (For grave or Sheol, see "Deeper Discoveries," ch. 5.) Now they were almost too weak to rise and greet a newcomer. Their greeting joins the mockery begun by the nations and the trees. In Sheol Babylon was now as weak as the kings whom the Babylonian army had dispatched there.

As Oswalt describes it: "It is evident that the Hebrews conceived of the realm of the dead as a dusty, shadowy place where a dim reflection of the person lived on in inactivity. . . . This conception was not fully worked out, however, for the concept of an immortal and faithful God contrasted with it and prevented such a thorough working out. . . . there is no god or goddess of the underworld, who would be a central figure if this poem were written outside the Israelite milieu. Here the existence of only one God rules out such a possibility and makes the human figures the main actors" (Oswalt, p. 318, n. 15).

14:11–19. Glittering royal robes gave place to hungry **maggots** and **worms**. This was all because of Babylon's pride, trying to occupy the throne of God. The Babylonian king is mocked with a lament. The word **How** often introduces a statement of grief and bereavement. This lament is mockery, a song of joy. The evil king tried to portray himself as the **morning star**—that is, as the planet Venus understood by Israel's neighbors as a god. Now such delusions of grandeur disappear in the realism of Sheol. What a fall! Certainly he was not anything like **the Most High**. (For Almighty and Most High, see "Deeper Discoveries.")

This is not the fall of Satan, but the fall of a proud human being who tried to usurp divine authority and divine worship. One who wanted to join the **assembly** of the gods must content himself with a bed of worms. Even Sheol's occupants stand amazed at such a fall from world domination to worm food. The situation was the same on earth. Babylon's own people did not give him the normal honor of a common burial, much less a regal interment. He had to lie on the battlefield in the pile of battle casualties. Nor could he expect a king's normal heritage—a son left on the vacated throne. Instead, his sons would never receive mention; they would vanish from history. The only dynasty Babylonia would establish would be in the realm of the dead.

14:20–23. The prophet concluded with a curse on Babylon, seeking to prevent a repetition of such pride and destruction. Anyone with a claim to inherit the throne would be destroyed (cp. 2 Kgs. 10:17). No longer should captive peoples such as Judah have to suffer under royal building projects seeking to glorify the king of Babylon. God confirmed that he would answer the prayer and bring the curse to reality.

 Aiming at Assyria (14:24–27)

Divine oath against the enemy (701 B.C.)

> **SUPPORTING IDEA:** *Neither mighty Assyria nor any other peoples can thwart the sovereign plan of God when he decrees judgment against them.*

14:24. The LORD Almighty (Lord of Hosts), the divine commander, raised his hand to solemnly swear that Assyria, just as Babylonia, would not have the last word in history. As Assyria had once been the "rod of my anger" (10:5), now God will not spare the rod on her. He had considered all the options and worked out his plan. (For God's plan and purpose, see "Deeper Discoveries," chs. 42–44.)

14:25–27. His **hand**, once **stretched** over the people of God (5:25; 9:12,17,21; 10:4), would now extend over Assyria. The divine hand stretched against Assyria would have universal effects, because in Isaiah's day Assyria controlled virtually the entire region. Such a prophetic judgment went against all historical probability, for Assyria's King Sennacherib was already in the country on **my land; on my mountains**. The prophet was convinced that the Lord of Hosts had greater military might than any earthly general. His strength was not limited to Israel, but extended over all the universe. No one could push back his hand. No one could **thwart** his plan. No matter how human eyes see things, eyes of faith know God is in control in every situation. No human power stands a chance against him.

Ⓓ Panic Among the Philistines (14:28–32)

Invitation to mourning ceremony (725 B.C.)

SUPPORTING IDEA: *People easily misread history and think an event promises hope and victory when it is only the prelude to darker days.*

14:28–30. The **Philistines** were the first major threat to Israel's independence (Judg. 14:16; 1 Sam. 4:7; 13–14; 17; 27–31). David finally defeated them (2 Sam. 5:17–25), but after the division of the monarchy (1 Kgs. 12), the Philistines again gained their independence and repeatedly threatened Israel and Judah. The Assyrians subdued the Philistines in 734 B.C. and again in 733 B.C. under Tiglath-Pileser.

14:31–32. At Tiglath's death the Philistines had every right to rejoice and look for better days ahead. Isaiah called them to come to the house of worship not for thanksgiving but for mourning. The worst was yet to come. On the northern horizon Assyria was already coming again. The years ahead brought the downfall of Gaza (720 B.C.), Ashdod (711 B.C.), and Ekron (701 B.C.), the major Philistine cities. Isaiah's word was not simply a judgment on Israel's first major enemy. With it he warned Judah not to join the Philistine foolishness and revolt against Assyria.

As in chapter 7, the prophet claimed political action could not save God's people. The hope for God's people lay with her God, not with her neighbors. The prophet had an explicit message for Philistine **envoys** who encouraged Judah to join in revolt (v. 32). God's people had been **afflicted** both by outside enemies and by their own rulers. The faithful would no longer depend upon kings and military action. They would seek **refuge** and rest in God.

MAIN IDEA REVIEW: *The day of the Lord will come upon Israel's major enemies as God punishes the world for its sinful pride and arrogance. This will result in new hope for his people.*

III. CONCLUSION

In God We Trust

God's prophet had a message for the enemies of his people as well as for his own people. God controls all history and all nations. He may use a people to discipline his disobedient nation. He may allow a king to rule the world for a time, but that says nothing about the power, ability, or goodness of the human ruler. When such kings proudly assume divine powers, God quickly plots their fall. When they violate God's people, God comes to the rescue of his chosen. Such a word to their enemies brings two words to God's people. First, they cannot trust in political alliances, because God is the only one worthy of trust. And second, trusting in God, they can rejoice at his display of power against the enemies. This is also a display of his compassion for his people.

PRINCIPLES

- God controls even the most powerful nations on earth.
- God has a time of judgment for everyone who opposes him.
- God has a plan for all nations and all peoples and will carry his plan out.
- God chooses people to bless and to use in his universal plan of salvation.
- God's people will win the final victory.
- God's people face times of hurt, sorrow, and turmoil before victory comes.
- Proud, powerful leaders may suffer eternal punishment.
- Humans cannot scale the heights to become like God.
- God is the secure refuge for earth's needy, mistreated people.

APPLICATIONS

- Thank God that he has a plan to punish unjust rulers and nations.
- Ask God for patience as you wait for him to complete his plan for the world.

- Ask God for assurance that you are part of his people and do not face the kind of judgment described in these chapters.

- Ask God to have compassion on you and deliver you from difficult situations that you may face.

- Ask God to reveal to you any prideful ways that you have that would cause him to come in judgment and discipline.

IV. LIFE APPLICATION

The Perfect Plan for Prejudice and Pride

I have seen pride and prejudice from two viewpoints. Growing up as a youngster, I never could understand one part of my life. I could play Little League or Pony League baseball with some very good athletes who were black or who spoke Spanish instead of English most of the time, but they could not go to school with me. As I grew up, I saw the prejudice and hatred that forced separate school systems in a small West Texas town that did not have enough children for one good system, much less two. In my adult years, I have found those experiences coming back subconsciously to influence my perception of certain people and circumstances.

I had the tables turned, however, when I was a missionary in Europe. There I found myself treated often as poor white trash, uncouth because I did not have the European facility in several languages or know the customary ways of doing things that had been in operation for a thousand years or more. They had better clothes, more money, and (they thought) a distinctly better culture than I did. Now I understood to some extent the anger and frustration of the Blacks and Hispanics at home. It is no fun to be on the other end of the prejudice line.

Israel had to learn the prejudice lesson as they faced the people of Egypt, Assyria, and Babylonia. All these countries had much greater history, culture, and civilization than did Johnny-come-lately Israel. At times Israel would arrogantly point to their religion and the promises of their God and show how superior they were to all other nations. At other times they would cower under military oppression from the nations and blame God for letting the other nations be so superior and so powerful.

God had to show Israel its place among the nations. They occupied a place among the nations for only one reason: God had created them. They had hopes of maintaining a place among the nations for only one reason: God would exercise his supreme power over all the nations. Israel had to bury its prejudice as well as its sense of weakness and ineptitude. They had to trust in God and join him in his work among the nations.

V. PRAYER

Lord of Hosts, you are the divine general. You have power over all armies, all military power, all weapons systems. No one can face you and win. Thank you that just as you control political history, you also control personal history. You have a plan for our country and a plan for me. Let me see you working out that plan, and show me how to join you as you work. I trust you and you alone. Amen.

VI. DEEPER DISCOVERIES

A. Day of the Lord (13:6)

The day of the Lord is an Old Testament concept with complex history and meaning. Even in Isaiah's day and beyond, people debated its meaning and taught opposing viewpoints about it (Amos 5:18–20).

The day of the Lord will bring exaltation and praise to God and not to humans (Isa. 2:17). It is a day when God reveals his majestic power, causing people to fall on their knees in worship and a day when he reveals his terrifying power, causing people to fall on their faces in fear (Joel 1:15; 2:1). It is a day of decision when people show whether they are on God's side or not (Joel 3:14), a day of retribution for the deeds a people have done (Obad. 15). It is a day of God's wrath against sinners and those who have not trusted him (Zeph. 1:14–15). It is particularly a day when God defeats human pride (Isa. 2:12).

People, particularly those who participate in the worship of the one true God, may expect the day of the Lord to be a day of victory and reward, but they may well be surprised (see Amos 5:18; Matt. 25). Human strength cannot survive God's day (Joel 2:11). The day of the Lord is the day God has chosen in his universal plan to show the world that he is king of the universe and that no one has power to oppose him.

Such a day may be directed against one enemy such as Babylonia and appear to them cruel (Isa. 13; Ezek. 30:2–4) or even against God's own people (Isa. 22:5; Zech. 14:1–5). Such a day calls for mourning, not celebrating. It can also be a day when God takes his revenge on people who have mistreated his chosen nation (Isa. 34:8). Wealth and resources will not matter in that day (Zeph. 1:18). Only humble people seeking to worship God have a chance to escape (Zeph. 2:3).

The historical day of the Lord can occur many times against different enemies of God. Each instance points beyond itself to a final day of the Lord (Mal. 4:5) when God will reward his people and punish his enemies for the final time. This is what the Book of Revelation describes so vividly (cp. Matt. 23–25; Luke 21).

B. Almighty (13:6) and Most High (14:14)

Isaiah constantly used different names and titles for God. Each carried its own history and its own meaning. Almighty in 13:6 translates the Hebrew term *Shaddai*. The name is often combined with *El*, an ancient word for *God*, forming the name *El Shaddai* (Gen. 17:1; 35:11; 48:3; Exod. 6:3; Ruth 1:20–21; Job 5:17–40:2 [31 times]; Ps. 68:14; Isa. 13:6; Ezek. 1:24; Joel 1:15).

This name is clearly connected with Israel's patriarchs: Abraham (Gen. 17:1), Isaac (Gen. 28:3), Jacob (Gen. 35:11); and Jacob's twelve sons (Gen. 43:14) as well as Job, whose story is set in ancient times. It is also connected with Balaam, the prophet called upon to curse Israel (Num. 24:4,16, where *Most High* is also used), with Ruth, another figure in Israel's early history, and with the ancient hymn in Psalm 68. A key text is Exodus 6:3 that distinguishes between *Shaddai* as the name revealed to the patriarchs and Yahweh (LORD) as the name revealed to Moses. Otherwise, the term almost disappears from Israel's history, being resurrected in one psalm (91) and by three prophets (Isa. 13:6; Ezek. 10:5). Each of these gives a somber note to the power and majesty of God. The name itself is so ancient that its original meaning is lost to us, the translation *Almighty* coming from the Septuagint, the earliest Greek translation of the Old Testament.

Elyon (Most High) is another ancient poetic name for God, but note that the *El* portion of this name is not related in Hebrew to the word *El* for God (Gen. 14:18–20,22; Deut. 32:8; Pss. 7:17; 21:7; 50:14; 77:10; 91:1,9; 107:11; Lam. 3:35,38).

Elyon is connected with Melchizadek, the priest of Salem, probably Jerusalem, to whom Abraham gave his tithe (Gen. 14) and with Balaam as seen above and with God's ancient acts of separating the nations (Deut. 32:8). It is part of Israel's retelling of their salvation history (Ps. 78). It is part of the prayer life of the tabernacle and temple. People call for God to come to his people as in days of old (2 Sam. 22:14; Pss. 18:13; 77:10) and give thanks to him for deliverance (Ps. 9:2). He is the hope and refuge of his people (Ps. 91:1,9). They pray for the earthly king (Ps. 21:7) and to the heavenly King (Pss. 47:2; 97:9) who judges the nations (Ps. 82:6).

This may well be an ancient name used in Jerusalem worship before Israel conquered the city and adopted by Israel to express the universal, all-ruling nature of God. It shows God as the King and Creator of the universe with power and authority over all creation and all creatures, even kings who claim to have divine powers.

C. God's Compassion (14:1)

Isaiah used a verb (*racham*) to describe God's relationship to his people. This verb is related to the Hebrew word for "womb," and it describes the deep love parents have for a newborn child. Such love is usually not an abstract reality but an emotion that leads to a specific action. It is always used of a person in a superior position in their relationship to someone socially or economically inferior and is never used of a person's love for God except in Psalm 18:1. The person expressing love often restores the person loved to a relationship that has been interrupted or discontinued by disloyalty and anger (Deut. 30:3; Hos. 1:6; Jer. 12:15; Ezek. 39:25).

Thus loving compassion replaces wrath as the dominant emotion in the relationship (Deut. 13:18; Isa. 54:8; Lam. 3:32; Zech. 1:12). God's compassion leads to forgiveness of sins (1 Kgs. 8:50; Prov. 28:13; Lam. 3:32; Dan. 9:9).

The noun (*rechumim*) occurs in the language of prayer and confession and emphasizes God's gift of loving compassion to a person or people in need (Pss. 25:6; 51:1; 77:9; 103:4; 119:77; 145:9; Lam. 3:22; Neh. 9:19,27–28,31). Occasionally it appears in prophetic proclamation (Jer. 16:5; Zech. 1:16). Disobedient Israel lived under God's wrath. They pleaded and prayed for God's compassion to restore the relationship of love, reunite the family ties, and deliver Israel from enemy torture and oppression. When God promised and showed his compassion as in Isaiah 14:1, Israel knew the election continued and they could again count on their relationship to God as Creator, Covenant-maker, Redeemer, and Lord.

VII. TEACHING OUTLINE

A. INTRODUCTION

1. Lead Story: A Surprising Source of Salvation
2. Context: The first section of the Book of Isaiah ends with a hymn for Israel to sing once they have experienced God's wrath and are on the way home from exile. The second section of the book strings together a series of oracles against foreign nations. Such oracles show the supremacy of God over all participants in world history. They also call Israel to be ready for God's act of deliverance, to trust in God and not in foreign powers.
3. Transition: It is easy to listen to oracles against the enemy and feel good about the world, knowing God is in charge. It is easy to encourage God in his battle against the enemy. The prophet has other ideas for us. He wants us to take spiritual inventory and see if we are on God's side or the enemy's. Are we the people God is defending or the

ones he is attacking? What causes God to go on the offensive against the enemies of his people? Do we show the characteristics of people of God or of enemies of God?

B. COMMENTARY

1. A Message for Babylonia (13:1–22)

2. Compassion for the Chosen (14:1–23)

3. Aiming at Assyria (14:24–27)

4. Panic Among the Philistines (14:28–32)

C. CONCLUSION: THE PERFECT PLAN FOR PREJUDICE AND PRIDE

1. Wrap-up: God is sovereign over all powers and is adamantly opposed to all pride. A nation devoted to material resources and personal power and prestige must be on the lookout. Are we as a nation or as individuals on God's list of targets? Is the next oracle against an enemy nation directed to us?

2. Personal Challenge: List the sins of pride that beset you every day. What else in your life makes you an enemy of God? Ask God to forgive you of those sins, take them out of your life, and show you a way of life that avoids the temptation to those sins. Pray for his forgiving compassion.

VIII. ISSUES FOR DISCUSSION

1. How do you react to the picture of God as a warrior dressed for battle ready to lead his troops to victory over another army?

2. Describe your understanding of the day of the Lord. Do you want it to come tomorrow? Why? Why not?

3. Do you think it is possible that God could punish the United States and turn the entire country into a desert wilderness without inhabitants?

4. Is it fair of God to use a people for his purposes and then to punish them?

5. What does it mean when we claim that God has a purpose and a plan for the entire world?

Isaiah 15–17

Remember the Rock

I. INTRODUCTION
Right Actions and Wrong Accomplishments

II. COMMENTARY
A verse-by-verse explanation of these chapters.

III. CONCLUSION
Armies Human and Divine

An overview of the principles and applications from these chapters.

IV. LIFE APPLICATION
Fighting or Faithing

Melding these chapters to life.

V. PRAYER
Tying these chapters to life with God.

VI. DEEPER DISCOVERIES
Historical, geographical, and grammatical enrichment of the commentary.

VII. TEACHING OUTLINE
Suggested step-by-step group study of these chapters.

VIII. ISSUES FOR DISCUSSION
Zeroing these chapters in on daily life.

Quote

"*T*o one who has faith,

no explanation is necessary.

To one without faith,

no explanation is possible."

T h o m a s   A q u i n a s

Isaiah 15–17

IN A NUTSHELL

*O*racles against foreign nations continue with announcements of the end for Moab and Syria. The prophet also promises new hope for a Davidic king and new devotion to God instead of idols.

Remember the Rock

I. INTRODUCTION

Right Actions and Wrong Accomplishments

*E*ven the woman wearing the crown of Mrs. United States can tell you of a time when she did everything right and it turned out all wrong. As a teenager Sheri Rose Shepherd sensed that a friend was despondent and desperate. Trying to help in some way, she went to visit the friend. What a shock! The house was in the worst mess she had ever seen. No one had tried to clean up anything in months.

Cheery, helpful Sheri went to work. Soon the den was in as good a shape as a teenager could make it. Then the vacuum cleaner attacked the rugs and floors. The duster came next. She went so far as to clean the filthy bathrooms. Then came the worst—the kitchen. Dirty dishes growing green things everywhere—on the stove, on the counters, on the tables, even filling the refrigerator. Sheri went to work enthusiastically, cleaning, moving, and especially throwing away. Dishes seemed so filthy and mold-controlled that some of them went out with the filth. Finally everything seemed just about like Sheri wanted it. Just in time. She heard steps coming toward the kitchen. Turning to see the joyful smile lighting the face of her friend's mother, Sheri gasped. Thunder and lightning rolled from the woman's countenance. The loudest scream in the history of feminine screams rang out.

"What's wrong?" Sheri gasped.

"Someone just threw out my grandmother's china," shouted the angry woman (Shepherd, pp. 21–23).

Yes, doing our best sometimes leads to the worst possible results. Moab certainly thought they had done everything right as they carefully navigated the political waters of the Ancient Near East. Egypt, Assyria, Babylonia, Israel, Judah, and Syria all tendered offers for Moab's help. Carefully, they dealt with each one in the most astute way possible. Then suddenly a new voice entered the bargaining arena. This speaker offered no bargaining room, however. This was the Lord God of Hosts. He came calling the joyful land to lament. Destruction lay around the next corner with no way out.

Have you ever sat on top of the world singing songs of victory and joy, only to see the world collapse beneath you? How can this happen? Is there hope after collapse? Or even a way to prevent collapse? God has a word of warning and hope for you today.

II. COMMENTARY

Remember the Rock

> **MAIN IDEA:** *God turns joy and praise into weeping and mourning for a people, even his own, who depend on their wealth and political maneuvering. But he brings hope for a new king and a new future of justice and righteousness.*

A Mourning for Moab (15:1–16:14)

Mourning rituals and prophecy of judgment for Moab (728 B.C.)

> **SUPPORTING IDEA:** *Pride, joy, praise, and worship turn to humble weeping and mourning for Israel's wealth-worshiping neighbors, while God promises a new king of righteousness for his people.*

15:1–4. Moab blocked Israel's way as she entered eastern Jordan and prepared to cross the Jordan River (Num. 22:1–24:25). She also enticed Israel into false worship (Num. 25:1–5). The Moabites traced their ancestors back to Lot (Gen. 19:37). This is why Israel could not claim Moab as her own territory (Deut. 2:9). (For Moab and its cities, see "Deeper Discoveries.") Such Moabite opposition brought forth divine warning that forbade Israel from allowing the Moabites to participate in Israelite worship (Deut. 23:3–6). The two nations warred constantly.

On the other hand, Judah had close ties to Moab, since David's ancestors were Moabites (Ruth 1:4; 1 Sam. 22:3–4). In the final years of Tiglath-Pileser of Assyria, nomads on the border of Moab apparently crossed over and destroyed several of the major cities in northern Moab. The Moabites went to their **temple** for national rites of grief and mourning.

15:5–9. Fugitives fled as far south as possible. The prophet mimicked the Moabite mourning as he described their flight from disaster. Even nature added to their troubles, refusing to give rain. Moab took their money and ran. They could not escape. Waterways became **blood** ways. And the prophet's word promised more trouble to come. Even the remnant, **those who remain in the land**, would not escape.

16:1–5. The text of 16:1–5 has caused translators problems as far back as the earliest translation into Greek (cp. KJV, NEB, NRSV, TEV, NIV). The Hebrew text as it stands reads: "You all send a ram of the ruler of the land from Sela (or the rock) of the wilderness to the mountain of the daughter of Zion" (author's translation). Neither the **land** nor the **ruler** is named. Apparently, Moab is meant, since the king of Moab was famous for his flocks (2 Kgs. 3:4). The king was either in **Sela**, the capital of Edom, or in the rocky wilderness. The prophet advised the king to pay **tribute** to Jerusalem and ask for political refuge and asylum for himself and his fellow refugees.

Apparently, in verse 2 the prophet turned to his Jerusalem audience and described the plight of the Moabites, then gave advice about how Jerusalem should react in kindness to the **fugitives** (vv. 3–4a). The basis of such advice is outlined in verse 5. Isaiah's understanding of the role of the Judean king was expressed in 9:2–7 and 11:1–9 and repeated here. Isaiah advised Judah to take in the Moabite refugees and treat them with God's **justice** and **righteousness**. The king of Judah did not fill the role in Isaiah's day. Nor did any other king. The Christian church points to Jesus of Nazareth as the only fulfillment, yet we still must wait for the coming day of total fulfillment when Jesus returns to establish a kingdom of righteousness.

16:6–14. When the prophet pointed to Jerusalem's responsibility to help the fugitives, he did not neglect Moab's deserved punishment. **Pride** went before the fall (see 9:9; 14:11; 25:11). Moab's punishment brought drought and death for the fertile fields and vineyards. Instead of songs celebrating the **harvest**, Moab would hear the victory songs of enemy warriors. Moab's thanksgiving festival would become a service seeking deliverance from the enemy. Isaiah predicted that such prayers would not win the victory. Later (v. 13), a new situation presented new hopes for victory, but the prophet repeated the same song, second verse: the few scattered **survivors** could accomplish nothing.

For Isaiah, **Moab's** future was certain. Destruction awaited. Any intrigue that Moab started was doomed. Jerusalem must not depend on Moab's help in rebellion against Assyria. Rather, Jerusalem must remember the task of her own kingship and the promises God had given her. Later the prophet Jeremiah took up the same message in almost the same wording (see Jer. 48). Judah and her kings refused to learn God's lesson.

B Doom on Damascus (17:1–3)

Prophecy of disaster on a foreign nation (733 B.C.)

> **SUPPORTING IDEA:** *God does not just pick on his own disobedient people when his day of punishment comes. He has judgment in store for every nation that depends on its own power and resources instead of giving honor and glory to God.*

17:1–3. In the midst of the Syro-Ephraimitic War (see chs. 7–8), the prophet predicted total defeat for the invading Syrian army from **Damascus**, Syria's capital city, and its ally, Israel. **Aroer** was an Amorite city on the border with Moab. Later it was the southern border of King Hazael of Syria (2 Kgs. 10:33). Isaiah's prophecy was against an Aroer controlled by Syria. Jeremiah

48:19 and the Mesha Stele (see "Deeper Discoveries") show that Moab controlled the city about 850 B.C. It overlooked a deep canyon on the northern side of the Arnon River three miles southeast of Dibon and two and one-half miles east of the King's Highway. God gave it to Moses in victory over King Sihon (Deut. 2:36; Josh. 12:2) and to the tribe of Reuben (Josh. 13:16). The tribe of Gad reinforced the city (Num. 32:34).

Isaiah concluded ironically that the **remnant** of Syria (NIV, **Aram**) would be as great as the **glory** of Israel, which had lost all its defenses. Only pasture for flocks would remain. Thus Israel, the Northern Kingdom, was lined up as a foreign nation receiving God's judgment.

🄲 Journey's End for Jacob (17:4–14)

Prophecies of disaster against a foreign nation (733 B.C.)

SUPPORTING IDEA: *People who consider themselves people of God may find God has a different opinion and includes them among his enemies. As such they face discipline and judgment that seeks to turn them again to depend on their Creator.*

17:4–6. The emphasis of the chapter turns to Jacob, the Northern Kingdom. This part of the people of God had become just another foreign nation that God must destroy (see 9:8–10:4). The remnant of Israel could be numbered on one hand just as could the few grains of wheat left by poor people who gleaned the fields after the harvesters had finished (cp. Lev. 19:9–10; Ruth 2:2–23). **The Valley of Rephaim** was a fertile valley southwest of Jerusalem on the border between Judah and Benjamin (Josh. 18:16). The question remains, can God do anything with such a tiny remnant?

17:7–9. Such drastic action was required to turn Israel away from her own creations to her Creator. Her attention had been focused on the wrong worship places and the wrong kinds of worship. The **Asherah** was a Canaanite goddess of fertility taken over by Israel and worshiped. Trees or special wooden poles were an integral part of this worship. These symbols themselves were also called the Asherah. The unusual word used for **incense altars** appears to refer to a special type of altar used only in Canaanite worship. God would turn Israel's military fortresses into undergrowth (cp. other translations of vv. 9–11, where the Hebrew text is difficult).

17:10–11. The reason for punishment is clear. Israel's defense system was built around her **Rock**, but they had **forgotten God your Savior**. Israel had worshiped foreign gods, using worship practices involving planting special **plants** that could blossom forth in a day to show the power of the god. Such worship would not help when God destroyed the **harvest** and brought **incurable pain** on the people.

17:12–14. Finally, the prophet summarized his understanding of the foreign nations by pronouncing a woe oracle (**Oh** of v. 12 is the Hebrew "Woe"). The nations were sound and fury, signifying nothing. God would blow them away like the **chaff** separated from the grain. They would create a giant dust storm, vanishing in a day. This was applied directly to Isaiah's audience, the people of Judah. They were terrified (see 7:4) without cause. They needed to make no international alliances. They needed simply to trust God (see 7:9).

> **MAIN IDEA REVIEW:** *God turns joy and praise into weeping and mourning for a people, even his own, who depend on their wealth and political maneuvering. But he brings hope for a new king and a new future of justice and righteousness for his people.*

III. CONCLUSION

Armies Human and Divine

Whom do you trust? The right answer is often quite obvious from a worldly standpoint—you trust the guy with the biggest, "baddest" guns. Israel and Judah tried this. God sent the prophet to show that human armies are no match for God's forces. Human alliances will never prevail over God's plan. God has shown time and again that he controls history and can defeat all enemies. When will we believe him?

PRINCIPLES

- God's judgment often comes suddenly and unexpectedly.
- Stored-up wealth cannot buy escape from God's judgment.
- God's people should seek to establish justice and righteousness even in relationships with their enemies.
- Everything that boosts our pride can vanish in a moment.
- Worship and religious ritual do no good when they celebrate the wrong god.
- Proud tradition does not guarantee escape when God brings judgment.
- Judgment seeks to bring people back to proper worship of the true God.
- Neglecting God brings disaster in every area of life.
- God's people have no reason to fear, since God promises them protection and victory.

APPLICATIONS

- Trust God to keep you during the most horrible situations of life.
- Form a love relationship with God now so you will not face his judgment later.
- Take an inventory of your attitudes and actions with regard to wealth and riches; confess wrong attitudes to God and pledge to trust him instead of trusting your possessions.
- Be active as a part of God's people, not a part of his enemies.
- Ask forgiveness for wrong attitudes toward your enemies, and ask God to show you ways to bring justice and righteousness to them.
- Learn to mourn for your enemies rather than rejoicing over their misfortune.
- Determine whether you are relying on religious tradition and church promises rather than a real relationship with the true God.
- Engage regularly in heartfelt worship of the true God.
- Ask yourself what is functioning as a false god in your life and surrender this to the true God.

IV. LIFE APPLICATION

Fighting or Faithing

I will never forget Manuel and his little brother Rodrigo. Their father and mother were my students at the seminary. They lived in the married-student apartments next door to our house. The two young boys were confused and frightened in a foreign culture where no other kids spoke their language or lived out their parents' culture. The boys reacted in the only way they knew. They fought with every weapon they could find. My own boys were always coming home with new Manuel and Rodrigo stories. They threw rocks. They slipped knives out of the kitchen. They told the most improbable lies about what they had done and whom they had hurt. These two little boys wanted the whole world to be afraid of them.

Moab was quite similar. A very small nation, the people of Moab tried to hide among their tall, rocky cliffs and present a strong front to all the nations. They thought their defenses were impregnable and their cities were secure. They soon found a Rock much higher and stronger than any they possessed. God was the only defense system on which they could truly rely.

Much of our lives are filled with Rodrigo and Manuel—or Moab—stories. We batten down our fears, battle our confusion, and strike out against the world. Notice me. See how strong I am. See what I can accomplish. Dare you to fight! Too often we join Rodrigo and Manuel in scurrying back home to lick our wounds and find the safety of Mommy and Daddy. How many times must we suffer defeat before we accept the fact that God is our only hope? When will we give up on our powers and our abilities and trust him to fight our fights and win our wars?

V. PRAYER

God, you are our Rock. The only defense system that works in this world is one built around you and your promises. Forgive us when we trust our power. Forgive us when we see worldly powers and cower beneath their mighty arms rather than depending on the everlasting arms. Show us the way to righteousness and justice, and help us walk in it and lead others to it. Amen.

VI. DEEPER DISCOVERIES

Moab and Its Cities (15:1–16:9)

Moab was the country across the Dead Sea east of Palestine that stretches eastward to the Arabian desert. It measured only about sixty miles north to south and fifteen miles west to east. The region was basically a rolling plateau about three thousand feet above sea level. The Zered River (Wadi el-Hesa) formed the southern boundary of Moab, while the Arnon River (Wadi el-Muib) divided the country into northern and southern parts. Both rivers flowed into the Dead Sea.

The southern part of Moab was quite isolated, but the northern part formed an international battleground and was controlled at times by the tribe of Gad (see Num. 21:21–31; 32; Judg. 11:12–28), by Moab, by Syria, and eventually by Assyria and Babylonia. The Bible names the country for one of Lot's sons (Gen. 19:37). The country supported agriculture and pastures for sheep and goats except during drought periods as in the time of Naomi and Ruth (Ruth 1:1,6).

Egypt exercised influence over Moab from about 1500 B.C. The Israelites under Moses took northern Moab from the Amorite king Sihon. Settlement in the area gradually increased from about 1300 to 1100 B.C. One king of Moab, Mesha, is known from a stele found in archaelogical excavations. Mesha ruled from about 860 to about 835 B.C. He claims to have regained control of Moab from Israel and to have built a temple dedicated to the Moabite god Chemosh. King Salamanu of Moab paid tribute to Tiglath-Pileser of Assyria about 734 B.C. Sargon of Assyria charged that Moab joined Ashdod in revolt against Assyria in 713 B.C.

Ar is the Moabite word for "city" and apparently refers to a major city in the country located near the Arnon River, Moab's northern border (cp. Deut. 2:18). Ar can also refer to a wider region, perhaps even the country as a whole

(Deut. 2:9,29). *Kir* is Hebrew for "wall," but Moabite for "city." The term may mean "city" here or may refer to a town named Kir, apparently the same as Kir-Hareseth (Jer. 48:31,36; cp. 2 Kgs. 3:25–27). It is modern Kerak, seventeen miles south of the Arnon River and eleven miles east of the Dead Sea on the King's Highway. At one time it was the capital of Moab.

Dibon was a Moabite city first conquered by Sihon, king of the Amorites (Num. 21:26–30). Israel then took it (Num. 21:21–25,31) and assigned it to the tribe of Reuben (Josh. 13:15–23), but Gad soon controlled it (Num. 33:44–45). A Moabite inscription called the Mesha Stele also refers to Gad as being in control. Dibon was an important commercial city situated on the King's Highway (Num. 21:22) just north of the Arnon River near the village of Dhiban about thirty-eight miles south of Amman, Jordan. Mesha, king of Moab, made Dibon his capital city shortly before 850 B.C.

Nebo was a town in northwest Moab near Mount Nebo where Israel stopped on its way to the promised land (Num. 33:47). It may be modern Khirbet el-Mekhayyat. The name comes from a Babylonian god and may represent Babylonian settlement in Moab. The tribe of Reuben occupied the city (1 Chr. 5:8). Jeremiah also condemned it (Jer. 48:1,22).

Medeba was a Moabite city eighteen miles south of Amman, Jordan, on the King's Highway (see Num. 21:30; 1 Chr. 19:7).

Heshbon was a city in the mountains of northern Moab that served as the capital for King Sihon of the Ammonites (Num. 21:25–30,34; Judg. 11:12–28). It was fifteen miles east of the Jordan River, thirty-three miles east of Jerusalem, twelve miles south of Amman, Jordan, and four miles northeast of Mount Nebo. It changed hands frequently through history (Josh. 13:15–28; 1 Chr. 6:81; Jer. 48–49).

Elealeh was another northern Moabite city located at modern Khirbet et Al, about one and one-half miles northeast of Heshbon. The Reubenites controlled it (Num. 32:3,37) and Jeremiah condemned it (48:34).

Jahaz in northern Moab was the site of King Sihon's battle with Israel (Num. 21:23; Judg. 11:20). The city was apparently south of Heshbon on the eastern border of the Moabite plateau. It may be modern Khirbet Medeiniyeh. It was a Levitical city in the tribe of Reuben (Josh. 13:18). Jeremiah condemned it (Jer. 48:21,34). King Mesha claims to have taken Jahaz back from Israel about 850 B.C.

Zoar was a town two miles east of the Dead Sea, just south of the Zered River, apparently in Edom, to which Moabite refugees fled (see Gen. 13:10; Deut. 34:3). Jeremiah also preached against it (48:4,34).

Eglath Shelishiyah or the Third Eglath can mean a calf under three years old and thus not broken (Jer. 46:20; Hos. 10:11). It may mean that here and in Jeremiah 48:34, or it may refer to an otherwise unknown town probably in Edom.

Luhith was a town in southwest Moab, also condemned by Jeremiah (48:5). It may be at modern Katrabba.

Horonaim was a town in central or southern Moab between the Zered and Arnon rivers.

The waters of Nimrim are the modern Seil en Numera, a stream going through the cliffs on the southwest edge of the Moabite plateau to the Dead Sea.

The Ravine of the Poplars, also translated as the Brook of the Willows, is one of the many wadis or ravines that become full in the rainy season and flow into the Jordan River or Dead Sea. It is sometimes equated with the Brook of Zered.

Eglaim's location is uncertain, perhaps Mazra on the Lisan Peninsula that separates the Dead Sea into two parts.

Beer Elim may be the same place as Beer (Hb. for "well") in Numbers 21:16. It may be located on the Wadi et-Themed ("waterhole") north of the Arnon River, though others locate it south of the Arnon near Kerak.

Dimon may be mentioned because its first two consonants are the same form as the Hebrew word for blood. Some scholars think a scribe miscopied Dibon, since the Dead Sea Scrolls and the Latin Vulgate read Dibon here. If Dimon is the correct reading, it may be located at Khirbet Dimneh two and one-half miles northwest of Rabbah in Moab.

Moses allotted Sibmah to the tribe of Reuben (Josh. 13:19). Its location is not certain, some seeing it as a village on the outskirts of Heshbon or perhaps on the plain of Medeb near Beth Baal Meon.

Jazer was captured by Moses (Num 21:31–32), and it became a levitical city in the tribe of Gad (Num. 32:35; 1 Chr. 6:81). It marked the border of Ammonite territory (Num. 21:24; cp. Num. 32:1) and became part of David's empire (2 Sam. 24:5); cp. 1 Chr. 26:31). Both Isaiah and Jeremiah (48:32) condemned it. It is apparently located just northeast of the northern end of the Dead Sea at Khirbet Jazzir at the head of the Wadi Sueib that flows into the Jordan.

VII. TEACHING OUTLINE

A. INTRODUCTION

1. Lead Story: Right Actions and Wrong Accomplishments
2. Context: Isaiah's oracles against foreign nations begin with the major world powers—Babylonia and Assyria. Isaiah showed that these mighty military machines would have their day in the headlines of world history, but it would be brief, because God had a plan for world history—a plan to bring salvation to his people. The problem was one

of trust. Would God's people trust his plan more than their own political plans?

3. Transition: In chapters 15–17 the prophet shifted attention to the smaller nations around Judah—Philistia, Moab, Syria, and even Israel. The subject is a foreign nation, but the true audience is Judah, the Southern Kingdom. Can the prophet convince God's people that God is their Rock and a king on the throne of David is their hope? Or will Judah continue on a course of depending more on foreign alliances than on God?

B. COMMENTARY

1. Mourning for Moab (15:1–16:14)

2. Doom on Damascus (17:1–3)

3. Journey's End for Jacob (17:4–14)

C. CONCLUSION: FIGHTING OR FAITHING

1. Wrap-up: God's plan for saving his people revolves around his promised king on David's throne, not around alliances with proud pagan nations.

2. Personal Challenge: Does your life show in any way that you have forgotten God your Savior and are looking elsewhere for hope, meaning, and deliverance? Is it time for you to turn your eyes to your maker?

VIII. ISSUES FOR DISCUSSION

1. Why would God cry for the plight of a nation and then promise more disaster?

2. What king does Isaiah point to in Isaiah 16:5?

3. Do you see in your own life the kind of pride that God condemns?

4. What do church people look at today that take their eyes off God our maker?

5. What signs do you see in our world and especially in our churches that people have forgotten God our Savior and Rock?

Isaiah 18–20

God Beyond Politics

I. INTRODUCTION
The Fly That Moves the Horse

II. COMMENTARY
A verse-by-verse explanation of these chapters.

III. CONCLUSION
The One with True Power

An overview of the principles and applications from these chapters.

IV. LIFE APPLICATION
Finding the Fellow to Follow

Melding these chapters to life.

V. PRAYER
Tying these chapters to life with God.

VI. DEEPER DISCOVERIES
Historical, geographical, and grammatical enrichment of the commentary.

VII. TEACHING OUTLINE
Suggested step-by-step group study of these chapters.

VIII. ISSUES FOR DISCUSSION
Zeroing these chapters in on daily life.

Quote

"*If* Yahweh gives, Yahweh can take.

And when Yahweh takes back wisdom,

the erstwhile wise are reduced to foolishness,

stupidity, and delusion."

W a l t e r   B r u e g g e m a n n

Isaiah 18–20

 IN A NUTSHELL

*E*thiopia and Egypt are unreliable alliance partners. Nations like Ethiopia, that think they can manipulate nations as they will, must face the plans of God and pay him his due. Nations like Egypt, that depend on false gods and human wisdom, must face judgment, because God plans to bring all nations together to worship him.

God Beyond Politics

I. INTRODUCTION

The Fly That Moves the Horse

*A*braham Lincoln appointed a man to an important position as a presidential adviser. Soon everyone noticed that the adviser was usually the only one who opposed Lincoln's suggestions or plans. Finally, Lincoln's friends came to him and recommended that he gently move the argumentative adviser out of his influential position. As he did so often, Lincoln answered with a story.

He was walking down a country lane one day when he spied a farmer plowing his field with a horse. Drawing closer, Lincoln discovered a huge horsefly flitting around the strong animal and giving him fits. With his customary spirit of helpfulness, Lincoln raised his hand to swat the fly away and relieve the horse of his agony. The old farmer stopped him in mid swat. "Don't do that, friend," he said. "That horsefly is the only thing keeping this old horse moving" (Templeton, p. 72).

Isaiah must have felt like Lincoln's adviser much of his life. He was always against what the majority of the people and government thought. In a real sense he was the horsefly that kept biting away, making the people of God move even when they did not want to. Even when he preached a message they wanted to hear, he attached a kicker that upset the people. So the defeat of Egypt would seem to be just what Israel wanted, but with it came the promise that Egypt would join Israel in worship.

As you listen to God's word today, listen not only for what is familiar and what you want to hear, but listen also to God's kicker that may be calling you to obedient action and worship even though this may not be what you expect to hear or want to hear right now.

II. COMMENTARY

God Beyond Politics

MAIN IDEA: *Political supremacy does not indicate universal power, because God has plans to bring all peoples to bow in worship before him.*

Sacrifices from Strangers (18:1–7)

Woe oracle against foreign nations (712 B.C.)

SUPPORTING IDEA: *The most-feared world power will eventually pay tribute to the true God of the universe.*

Prophetic eyes turned south to the first enemy Israel had defeated. In the exodus from Egypt, Israel learned the personal name of her God—Yahweh (Exod. 3:13–16); experienced the power of her God among the nations (Exod. 14); learned how to worship her God (Exod. 12–13); and expressed her faith in Yahweh (Exod. 14:31–5:21). Centuries later historical fortunes had changed radically. Assyria, not Egypt, dominated world politics and military fortunes. Egypt had to resort to political maneuvers with potential allies to protect themselves. They tried to entice Judah to revolt against Assyria, promising Judah they could depend on Egypt for military and economic aid. Throughout the maneuvers, Isaiah spoke the word of God to his Judean leaders. Several pieces of his counsel are gathered together in chapters 18–20.

18:1–2. Egypt was a country divided against itself. Rival rulers reigned in Tanis, Leontopolis, Heracleopolis, Hermopolis, Sais, and Thebes. Finally, Ethiopian (Hb. **Cush** represents the land we call Ethiopia) rulers began to come north about 730 B.C. and by 715 B.C. controlled the entire country. (For Egypt and Ethiopia, see "Deeper Discoveries.") Israel tried to make political alliances with Egypt against Assyria in 725 B.C. (2 Kgs. 17:4), resulting in the final destruction of the Northern Kingdom. In 720 B.C. Egypt tried to help Gaza, without success. In 716 B.C. Sargon II of Assyria marched to the Egyptian border and received tribute from the king of Tanis. The Ashdod revolution of 712 B.C. brought Sargon back to Philistia, but the Egyptian king refused asylum for the Philistine ruler, handing him over to Sargon.

During Sennacherib's expedition to Palestine in 702–701 B.C. in which Judah was devastated and Jerusalem was besieged (see ch. 36), the new Egyptian king marched north to help but retreated quickly. The Ethiopian pharaohs who ruled Egypt sent a political delegation to Jerusalem either in 712 or 702 B.C. to conspire against Assyria. Isaiah responded with a woe oracle against them (18:1–7), calling on the leaders of Judah to trust in the word of God rather than the weak promises of Egypt. The nation that sent **swift messengers** seeking alliances faced God's judgment.

18:3–7. Ethiopia needed to join the **people of the world** in noticing the signs God had given. They were assured they would be able to **see it** and **hear it**. In his **quiet** way God will look down from his **dwelling place** and prepare the nations for his harvest. Egypt would soon send another delegation to Jerusalem with **gifts** for the Lord of Hosts. The people who sent messengers seeking military alliance would now bring tribute to God, the ultimate victor. They would be placed in the temple, where God's **Name** resides.

Egypt's Exodus Encore (19:1–10)

Oracle against a foreign nation (716 B.C.)

SUPPORTING IDEA: *As he once led his people in the exodus from Egypt, so God will again destroy Egypt's economy.*

19:1–3. Isaiah warned Judah against seeking Egyptian help. As in the exodus, God himself would go to **Egypt** to defeat Israel's enemies. His presence would send Egyptian gods into panic. Internal revolution would shake the land. Egypt, long noted for its wisdom, would find its **plans** confused and useless. They would forsake the gods for **mediums** and **spiritists** (see "Deeper Discoveries," chs. 6–8).

19:4–10. God himself would give victory to a **cruel** king who would rule Egypt harshly. It is not clear if Isaiah referred to a foreign king, such as an Assyrian, or to the new winner in the Egyptian revolution. The economic life of the land with its utter dependence upon the **Nile** River would be destroyed; the river would totally **dry up.** Agriculture, weaving, and fishing would vanish. The entire work force would go into mourning.

Zeroing in on Zoan (19:11–15)

Taunt song against a foreign nation (726 B.C.)

SUPPORTING IDEA: *God's plans make fools of Egypt's "wise counselors" and render the nation helpless before him.*

19:11. God took up a song, taunting proud but weak Egypt. **Zoan** (also known as Tanis), only twenty-nine miles south of the Mediterranean Sea, was the Egyptian political center nearest Palestine. Israel knew it had an ancient history (Num. 13:22). Zoan was Egypt's political capital in the Twenty-First Dynasty (1176–931 B.C.) and continued through the Twenty-Second Dynasty (931–725 B.C.). Even with the capital moved to Sais and Napata, Zoan remained important and prosperous. Temples to Amon, Mut, and Khonsu dominated the city. For centuries Egypt preserved the learning of its sages in literary collections. God had turned its counselors and rulers into **fools.**

19:12–15. God posed a rhetorical question: **Where are your wise men now?** Egypt had no answer. Only the prophet could proclaim the purposes of the Lord of Hosts, the God of Israel. **Memphis** was thirteen miles south of Cairo on the Nile River. Its history goes back at least to 3050 B.C. when Menes of the First Dynasty founded it. It served as capital city, burial ground for pharaohs, and center of the worship of Ptah and Hathor. Memphis was replaced as capital from 2200 to 1526 B.C. and again in 1300 B.C. Still it played an important political role until it declined from 1070 to 711 B.C. Neither Zoan's more recent wisdom nor Memphis' ancient wisdom tradition could save the country. Yahweh confused all Egypt's wise men. Egypt had a horrible drunken hangover and was incapable of action. God had the last bit of wise advice: **There is nothing Egypt can do.**

𝔻 Unity for the Universe (19:16–25)

Announcement of future events (712 B.C.)

SUPPORTING IDEA: *God will deplete Egypt's courage, create places to worship him in their midst, and heal them so they will join Assyria and Israel in worshiping him.*

19:16–17. The prophetic poetry turns to prose in verses 16–25, giving explicit interpretation to the poetic oracle of verses 1–15. Each section begins with the refrain **in that day,** pointing to God's threats against Egypt and thus promises for Judah in God's plans for the future. Egypt's military heroes will suddenly become effeminate when God **raises** his **hand.** The mere mention of **Judah** will bring terror to Egypt because of the reputation of her God.

19:18. Five Egyptian cities will go so far as to learn the language spoken in Palestine so they can communicate with the powerful Jews and worship the LORD. These cities included the **City of Destruction.** This may represent a copyist's change from "City of Righteousness" (as in the Septuagint), a play on Jerusalem where "righteousness used to dwell" (1:21). It may be a copyist's attempt not to mention an original Heliopolis, the "City of the Sun" (see REB, TEV, NLT, NRSV, NAB, NJB, GW, based on Dead Sea Scrolls and many Hebrew manuscripts; see NIV footnote).

19:19–22. An **altar to the LORD** would be built in Egypt. This went against the grain of all Judean thinking. An altar belonged in Jerusalem and only in Jerusalem. What is more, a pillar (Hb. *matstsebah;* **monument**) was to be constructed. In its earliest days Israel built memorial pillars at sacred places (Gen. 28:18; Exod. 24:4). The law prohibited such objects as part of worship since they were connected with Canaanite idol worship (Exod. 23:24; Deut. 7:5). Still Israel built them (1 Kgs. 14:23; cp. Hos. 3:4). Jeremiah 43:13 connected pillars with Egyptian worship at Heliopolis. Isaiah put a new face on the worship of Yahweh, permitting a temple in a foreign land.

Such worship would be a witness to the Egyptians. Yahweh did not have to be a holy "terror" for them (see v. 17), but could be their **savior,** as he was Israel's Savior from the land of Egypt so long ago (cp. Exod. 14:10–14). No longer must Israel escape Egypt to offer **sacrifices** to God (Exod. 5:1–3). The Egyptians would now sacrifice with them. God introduced himself to Moses (Exod. 6:3) and tried to introduce himself to Pharaoh in the time of the exodus

(Exod. 5:2; 8:10,22; 11:7). The prophet looked to the day when Egypt would truly know Yahweh. Egypt's defeat would be her victory, because it would bring her to God to be healed rather than be plagued as in the exodus.

19:23–25. The climax of the prophetic message promises the impossible. God would create a great triangle of nations serving him—**Egypt, Assyria,** and **Israel. Highways** would no longer echo the tramping of warriors but the trumpeting of worshipers. Finally, the promise to Abraham that his descendants will be a **blessing** to the nations will be fulfilled (see Gen. 12:1–7).

E Stripped as a Sign of Shame for the Southland (20:1–6)

Report of a prophetic symbolic act (712 B.C.)

SUPPORTING IDEA: *A shameful prophetic sign warned Egypt and all her allies of impending shame and doom.*

20:1–6. **Ashdod,** one of the five major Philistine cities, revolted in 712 B.C. Judah was tempted to join in, expecting Egyptian assistance. Isaiah went to the extreme to get the political leaders of Jerusalem to listen to him. Obeying God's command, he performed a symbolic act. (For prophetic symbolic acts, see "Deeper Discoveries.") The prophet took off his clothes to appear as a prisoner of war marching into exile, symbolizing what would happen to Egypt with its new Ethiopian rulers. Wall reliefs from Assyria and Babylonia show captives being marched into exile completely naked.

Isaiah's act would have had great effect in Judah, especially since it lasted **three years.** Judah hoped Egypt would support the revolt. Apparently, Isaiah won the day, for Judah did not become involved in the Ashdod revolt, or at least Judah withdrew in time to escape punishment from the Assyrian king. In so doing Isaiah finally got across to Judah for a brief time his message that trust in political alliances was futile. Only trust in God paid off. Neither Egypt nor Philistia made good allies. God is the perfect ally.

MAIN IDEA REVIEW: *Political supremacy does not indicate universal power, because God has plans to bring all peoples to bow in worship before him.*

III. CONCLUSION

The One with True Power

Looks are deceiving, especially in the arena of politics and international diplomacy. Unless one trusts the only One with true power, he will eventually guess wrong in the game of alliances and counter-alliances. No human partner can deliver you from all your troubles. God is always ready to hear people who call on him in trust. He wants to bring all people to worship him.

PRINCIPLES

- Neither international trade nor power politics guarantees protection from God's judgment.
- Secret means of revelation such as divination and astrology or horoscopes do not work, because only God knows the future.
- God cares even for the people he judges and will heal them when they call to him in faith, because God wants to bless all people.
- God seeks to bring all people together to worship him, overcoming all prejudices and animosity.

APPLICATIONS

- You have no reason to fear any person, group, or nation if you trust in God.
- Trust God even when you do not hear his voice or understand what he is doing.
- Give your gifts to God now freely and gladly before you are forced to do so by his act of judgment.
- Quit your secret use of ways to control your future such as Ouija boards, tarot cards, mediums, horoscopes, and astrology.
- Commit yourself to participate in a mission trip to help fulfill God's worldwide purpose.

IV. LIFE APPLICATION

Finding the Fellow to Follow

Ross taught me many lessons. He was the oldest boy on the block. One day he got angry and chased me home with rocks, one splitting the back of my head. I learned when and where not to pick fights. He was the first person I knew who used language I had never heard before. He was the first to talk about enjoying beer. Oh, yes, Ross taught me many lessons.

But Joe taught me some better ones. When we chose players for football, Ross always got the guys on his team whom he wanted, and the rest of us small guys were left to try to accomplish the impossible. Joe was the smallest of the small and the youngest of the crowd, four or five years younger than Ross. Ross or one of his big cronies would take the ball and start running through us little runts. Then Joe would deftly duck low under the stiff arms and move his head to the side away from churning knees. He would take his strong little arms and wrap them around a pair of ankles. Down would come the runner with a huff and a strong word for Joe. Joe would get up and go back for the next play.

If and when we got the ball, Joe would briefly tell everyone what to do, then take the ball, and rifle a pass into someone's waiting arms. Joe gave us a chance to win against the big boys. Ross dropped from sight, continued the profligate life, and died sadly at a very young age. Joe continues to enjoy a very successful career in one of the professions.

Quiet Joe showed me whom to trust and whom to follow—the one who can put achievements on the board, not brag about what he plans to do. God taught Israel the same lesson. Egypt clearly had the brawn among all the choices Israel had as an ally. Egypt also had the cultural history and the tradition of wise counselors. God made it clear that Egypt was a collection of fools, unable to understand the real nature of the world and how to live in it. We must learn to trust the quiet, invisible God rather than the blow-hard, self-confident ally who can never bring help when we need it.

V. PRAYER

Father, for too long we have lingered undecided, not knowing whom to trust, whom to follow. Today we confess our foolishness. We have depended on human help, on the wisdom of fools. No longer, Lord. We turn ourselves in complete trust to you. You are all-wise and all-powerful. We submit ourselves to be part of your plan for this world. We trust you and no one else. Amen.

VI. DEEPER DISCOVERIES

A. Egypt and Ethiopia (18:1; 19:1)

Egypt was one of the world's oldest civilizations. Its relationships with Israel reached back to Abraham (Gen. 12:10), Joseph (Gen. 37–50), and the exodus (Exod. 1–15). Egyptian evidence shows trade and military contacts as early as 3000 B.C. Egypt controlled Palestine for a few centuries before Joshua's conquest. During Israel's monarchy Egypt assisted their enemies (1 Kgs. 11:14–22,26–40), made treaties with Israel (1 Kgs. 9:16), invaded Judah (1 Kgs. 14:25–26; 2 Chr. 14:9–15), joined Judah against Assyria in the Battle of Qarqar in 853 B.C., and made alliances against Assyria (2 Kgs. 17:4; 19:9). Egypt's last stand in Palestine and Assyria came when it tried to aid Assyria against Babylonia but lost the battle of Carchemish in 605 B.C. (Jer. 46).

The Bible often mentions Egypt and Ethiopia (Cush) together (Ps. 68:31; Ezek. 29:10; Nah. 3:9). The Hebrew term *Cush* is usually translated as "Ethiopia," although it does not cover precisely what we refer to as Ethiopia today.

The ancient texts refer to a land south of Egypt inhabited by people unrelated to the Egyptians. Cush's ill-defined southern border reached deep into Africa. South of Ethiopia lay the land of Put.

Ethiopia's climate varied from the drought-ridden steppe of the north, to the southwest swamp, to the southeastern mountains reaching eight thousand feet above sea level. The Persian Empire eventually reached Ethiopia as its western extent. In New Testament times, the land was known as Nubia and included present-day Sudan and Ethiopia. It was known for its rivers (Gen. 2:13; Zeph. 3:10). Job 28:19 shows the commercial importance of Ethiopia, where traders went for ivory, rhinoceros horns, ebony, topaz, spices, incense, slaves, and other precious goods. The varied population was known for its dark skin and tall, slender stature (Isa. 18:2). Genesis 10:6–8 seems to trace the population to western Arabia (cp. Isa. 43:3; 2 Chr. 21:16–17).

Moses' wife was from Ethiopia (Num. 12:1). Some Ethiopians moved to Palestine (2 Sam. 18:21–32; Jer. 38:7–13). King Asa defeated a huge Ethiopian army (2 Chron. 14:9–13). Around 700 B.C., the latter years of Isaiah's ministry, Ethiopian rulers dominated Egypt. King So of 2 Kings 17:4 may have been an Ethiopian ruler of Egypt. Thus Isaiah saw Assyria attacking both Ethiopia and Egypt (Isa. 20:3–4). About 689 B.C. an Ethiopian general led the Egyptian army against Assyria in Palestine (2 Kgs. 19:9 = Isa. 37:9). Amos 9:7 shows God cares for the Ethiopians. Zephaniah warned of Ethiopia's destruction (Zeph. 2:12) and its worship of the true God (Zeph. 3:10).

B. Prophetic Symbolic Acts (20:1–6)

Isaiah's shocking behavior must be understood within the larger world of symbolic acts, one way the prophets communicated God's unexpected and shocking message to his people. Hosea married a prostitute and gave his children shameful names (Hos. 1–3). Jeremiah preached subjection to Babylonia with a yoke around his neck (Jer. 27–28). Ezekiel in exile ate God's scroll of judgment (ch. 3), created a clay replica of the city of Jerusalem under siege, and lay bound up for over a year, eating defiled food (ch. 4). He shaved himself bald and used his hair to demonstrate the city's fate (ch. 5), mimicked the way exiles leave a city (ch. 12), refused to mourn his wife's death (24:17–19).

By such dramatic actions, the prophets let their audience see as well as hear God's word. They showed that the message was more than just a spoken word. It was a reality embodied by the prophet's very life. God was willing to use the most dramatic means possible to catch his people's attention and make them at least think about the message. Isaiah's three-year naked trek around Jerusalem should have convinced the city that God truly meant to take its citizens into exile. But even this dramatic expression failed to touch the hard-hearted people.

VII. TEACHING OUTLINE

A. INTRODUCTION

1. Lead Story: The Fly That Moves the Horse
2. Context: Isaiah used a southern strategy in his oracles against the nations. Having pronounced doom on the northern superpowers and on the neighboring states, he turned to Egypt and Ethiopia, lands that promised trade riches and military alliances against the superpowers.
3. Transition: Do human promises woo us away from God? Do bright materialistic hopes dim our faith in God? What options do you really face when times get tight and hopes for a bright future fade?

B. COMMENTARY

1. Sacrifices from Strangers (18:1–7)
2. Egypt's Exodus Encore (19:1–10)
3. Zeroing in on Zoan (19:11–15)
4. Unity for the Universe (19:16–25)
5. Stripped as a Sign of Shame for the Southland (20:1–6)

C. CONCLUSION: FINDING THE FELLOW TO FOLLOW

1. Wrap-up: God calls us to join in his mission to bring all people to worship him. Too often he has to discipline and punish us before we get the message.
2. Personal Challenge: How do you respond in your most desperate moments? Do you turn to astrology or mediums? Or do you expect God to work out his purposes in your life and that of your country?

VIII. ISSUES FOR DISCUSSION

1. What causes us to fear other people? What does fear of earthly things reveal about our relationship to God?
2. Why do people in today's educated, sophisticated society turn to the same kinds of mediums, astrologers, and seers as did people in Bible times?
3. How does God use natural conditions to reveal himself and his plans to us today?
4. Is there a people group or a segment of our society whom you do not expect to worship the true God and you do not want them to do so? Why?

Isaiah 21–23

Real Power

"A response to divine grace has been flaunted that calls forth the full intensity of God's judgment."

Brevard Childs

Isaiah 21–23

IN A NUTSHELL

*I*saiah 21–23 shows that Jerusalem had become just another of the enemies of Yahweh and was destined for destruction. Other nations with military, economic, geographical, and political resources offered no hope for Jerusalem. Neither did her own religious tradition!

Real Power

I. INTRODUCTION

A Maniac of Ferocious Genius

*S*ir Winston Churchill described a solemn moment in world history as he wrote: "Mighty forces were adrift; the void was open, and into that void after a pause there strode a maniac of ferocious genius, the repository and expression of the most virulent hatreds that have ever corroded the human breast—Corporal Hitler." To those words Charles Swindoll adds: "Around the world today, men with similar traits direct their power-hungry dictatorships or uprisings with the same illogical sadism and cruel determination. What will happen next is anybody's guess, which only darkens the harsh clouds about us" (Swindoll, p. 74).

Hunger for power and control seems to confront us in every generation and in every sector of life. In government, at work, in the entertainment world, at home, and even at church we meet people seeking to exercise power and show they are in charge. Isaiah confronted this problem long ago. Jerusalem's proud leaders showed off their political savvy and spouted their religious platitudes as they defended their political positions and sought help from anyone who had military and economic resources.

God had to paint a clear picture of life's deeper realities. Power belonged to God and to him alone. No one could exercise any kind of power that would defeat God. You and I know this truth. Sadly, it does not always control our actions. We live as if everything depended on our maneuvering, our power, our resources. God's Word tries one more time to get through to your heart and soul and guide you to the real power source.

II. COMMENTARY

Real Power

MAIN IDEA: *No one can claim exemption from God's judgment day, no matter how great their military power, economic resources, religious tradition, geographical location, or political alliances.*

Blowing Away Babylonia (21:1–10)

Awesome vision against Babylonia (701 B.C.)

SUPPORTING IDEA: *God's judgment day will bring defeat and destruction for military powers that misuse their strength to decimate and humiliate other peoples.*

21:1. Babylonia led the intrigue against Assyria (see ch. 39). Later she destroyed Jerusalem in 586 B.C. (see 2 Kgs. 25). The title of this prophetic oracle is unusual. It does not describe the enemy, but the nature of the prophetic vision. The vision came from the wilderness or **Desert by the Sea** (cp. Exod. 13:18). God often came from the southern wilderness, from the holy mountain, to speak to his people (Deut. 33:2; 1 Kgs. 19:8).

21:2–5. The vision is **dire** or grim (REB), telling of the plunder and destruction of war. Elam and Media are the attackers, but who is attacked? A people who have brought **groaning** to the world! The prophet described his own reaction. Unlike false prophets who played to the audience and rejoiced over the defeat of the enemy, he suffered agony—**pangs** of **labor**—that such horrors must enter the world. He was **staggered** and **bewildered**, condemned to a sleepless night. The scene changed to the generals who were enjoying a great banquet when they were called to battle. But whose generals?

21:6–10. Next we hear God's command to set up a **lookout** for news of battle. The lookout takes his post much like Habakkuk (see Hab. 2:1). The report of battle comes! **Babylon has fallen.** Her grand **images** of her gods are ground to gravel. The prophet turned finally to his audience, addressing Judah as a people who had suffered enough of the horrors of war. He swore to tell the truth and the whole truth as God had shown it to him. He left his audience to draw the conclusions. Could Judah really depend upon Babylonia and her gods in the fight with Assyria? Or should she return to trust in her own God who can predict the future?

B Arrows over Arabia (21:11–17)

Prophetic announcement of judgment on foreign nations (695 B.C.)

SUPPORTING IDEA: *Economic might is no reason to think you can escape God's judgment day; it provides no example for others to follow your plan of escape.*

21:11–12. From 738 B.C. onward Assyria repeatedly forced the tribes and towns in the Arabian desert to pay taxes and recognize the authority of the Assyrian king. Again and again the tribes tried to regain their independence, but without success. Nabonidus, the last king of Babylonia, spent ten years in Tema, about 550–540 B.C. The nomadic tribes of Kedar finally established control over a large part of the Arabian desert around 500 B.C., reaching possibly to the border of Judah and perhaps to Egypt. Their economic power exceeded their military might. They controlled rich trade routes, delivering gold, precious stones, incense, and animals to their northern trading partners.

The Arab rebellions were an indicator of Judah's chances for success in similar ventures. Thus the prophet addressed three brief statements to the Arabians. The headings of the first two are difficult to understand. The first is against **Dumah** (see "Deeper Discoveries"). A wordplay on the meaning of "silence" is intended. The prophet took the role of a night **watchman** on military guard duty. He heard an inquiry from across the southern border in **Seir**, another name for Edom. The watchman had no news, telling the inquirer to call back later. Silence from Arabia meant there was no time for Judah to revolt against Assyria. But action could come at any time.

21:13–15. Action did come from Arabia. Verse 13 introduces a second oracle whose heading is not clear. The Hebrew term **Arabia** occurs twice in this verse. Words very similar in sound mean "desert" or "wilderness" (NRSV, NJB, JPS), and "evening." Both have been suggested for the meaning here.

Dedan and **Tema** were oases south of Dumah in the Arabian desert. The prophet called upon Tema to help her neighbors, stranded in the desert after an attack on their trading caravan. A people who cannot protect their own caravans certainly could offer no hope in a rebellion against a superpower.

21:16–17. The Arabian section ends with a prediction of disaster for the nomadic sons of **Kedar**. Arabs could not help Judah rebel against Assyria. Isaiah consistently told Judah to sit tight and wait for God's action.

Ⓒ Zion's Zero Hour (22:1–14)

Oracle against the foreign nation Judah (701 B.C.)

> **SUPPORTING IDEA:** *A great religious tradition and history as God's people could not protect a nation from paying the price for their sins on God's judgment day.*

22:1–3. Isaiah had experienced the desperate situation of 701 B.C. (see chs. 36–39) and found no one following his preaching. When God won the victory over Assyria, forcing her to withdraw from Jerusalem, the people went into exultant jubilation. Feasting took the place of fasting. Isaiah looked deeper into the people's situation. The time of trial had revealed treachery. Leaders had deserted their posts to save their own necks. God protected the city and those who remained faithfully at their post.

22:4–5. Assyria and her allies camped in the valleys surrounding Jerusalem. Particular emphasis is placed on **the Valley of Vision**, probably referring ironically to prophetic visions reported in the Valley of Hinnom outside Jerusalem (Josh. 15:8). Such prophets would speak in the name of dead sons offered in sacrifice to foreign gods (2 Kgs. 23:10; Jer. 19:2–6). Isaiah said the true vision belongs only to Yahweh and his prophets. Judah's lack of faith had produced the ominous **day** of Yahweh (cp. 2:12), when God used enemy armies to judge Judah.

22:6–11. Elam and **Kir** apparently represent small countries who were forced to contribute fighting men to Assyria's army in the attack on Jerusalem (see "Deeper Discoveries"). Judah did not look to God but to their special storehouse of **weapons** (cp. 1 Kgs. 10:17). The **Palace** (or House) **of the Forest**, also called the House of the Forest of Lebanon (1 Kgs. 7:2; 2 Chr. 9:16,20), was part of the storage facilities in the temple complex. It was apparently made of cedars from Lebanon. Judah sought to man the barricades and repair the defenses at the last minute. Hezekiah built an extension to the city walls to enclose the city's western expansion (2 Chr. 32:5). Stones for the new wall evidently came from the destruction of private **houses**. Hezekiah also built the famous Siloam tunnel to bring water into the city and created a supply system with two pools or cisterns (2 Kgs 20:20; see Isa. 7:3; 36:7).

Only divine effort could bring deliverance (Isa. 37:36–38). Israel's Creator certainly had power to protect and preserve, but Judah **did not look to the One who made it, or have regard for the One who planned it long ago**.

22:12–13. In the midst of Israel's victory celebrations, a new word came from God. Mourning and weeping, not **joy and revelry**, was the order of the day! Why? Because neither in the midst of crises nor in the moment of miracle did Judah learn her lesson. She refused to repent and trust her God. So the prophet took up the proverb to counsel the people to go blindly on with their celebration. Tomorrow others would mourn their death.

22:14. This verse summarizes the message dramatically and emphatically, with the divine oracle formula at its beginning and end. God swore an oath against Judah. The people who would not take his advice and thus had to face agony and destruction had been given a final chance to repent. Instead, they celebrated the success as if they had brought it about. The day of atonement was history for them. God had endured their sin of ignoring long enough. Forgiveness of their **sin** was no longer possible. Judgment was the only option. (For atoning for sin and guilt, see "Deeper Discoveries," chs. 6–8.)

🄳 The Famous Will Fall (22:15–25)

Prophetic report (701 B.C.)

SUPPORTING IDEA: *Fame and position cannot protect a person from God's judgment.*

22:15–19. Shebna, the chief official in charge of the king's house, used his office to gain glory and eternal fame for himself. He built himself a handsome **grave**, apparently one worthy of royalty, and accumulated **chariots** for his personal use. He brought **disgrace** on himself and on his boss. God moved in to **hurl** him into a distant land where he could not exercise the authority of his **office** or even use his burial chamber.

22:20–25. The prophet used the language of the ceremony of installation in **office** to announce Shebna's successor—**Eliakim** (see 2 Kgs. 19:2; Isa. 37:2). The prophet had high hopes, calling him the **servant** of God. The Old Testament seldom uses the phrase "servant of God" for a lower official. He was to be a **father** to those over whom he exercised **authority**. Sadly, Eliakim proved no better. He could not deal with his own family, who apparently demanded high positions at court for themselves. So Eliakim had to be taken down a peg . . . **in that day**.

⟨E⟩ Taps for Tyre (23:1–18)
Call to mourning (704 B.C.)

SUPPORTING IDEA: *A well-protected geographical location combined with economic success and power cannot protect a people from God's judgment day.*

23:1–6. The oracles against the nations do not end with Jerusalem. Israel had depended on Phoenicia for overseas trade since the beginning of the monarchy (2 Sam. 5:11). This was natural. The major political powers—Babylonia, Assyria, and particularly Egypt—depended on the Phoenician seamen to export their goods over the known world. The Phoenicians had become skilled sailors over a period of twenty-three hundred years. Dependence on the Phoenicians created economic problems for Israel (1 Kgs. 9:10–14). One way to solve such problems was marriage alliances (1 Kgs. 16:31), but this brought religious problems (1 Kgs. 16:32–33).

The major Phoenician city was **Tyre**, located on a rocky island off the coast forty-five miles southwest of Beirut and about thirty-five miles northeast of Haifa. Twenty-five miles to the north was **Sidon**. Racially the people were part of the Canaanites (v. 11), but their political ties were with **Egypt**. They carried on trade from Carthage on the African coast, to **Tarshish**, probably in Spain. In spite of their wealth and sea power, the Phoenicians could not remain politically independent. Isaiah pictured Phoenician sailors returning home from a trading expedition. They heard the news of defeat as they came to **Cyprus**, and the prophet called them to mourn. The sea complained that she was not productive. The mourning spread to the chief trading partner **Egypt**, as well as **Tarshish**, possibly representing the geographical extremities of the Phoenician shipping routes.

23:7–12. Tyre had become unrecognizable. The major question was, **Who planned this**? Could it be the king of Assyria? Of course not. Only the **Lord**

Almighty, Yahweh, the God of Israel, had such power. He acted in world history to **bring low the pride** of the rich and famous. The text, translation, and interpretation of verse 10 are very difficult (cp. TEV, NIV, REB, KJV, NASB, NAB, NJB). If the NIV is correct, God called on Tyre to return to farming like the people of Egypt who lived along the **Nile** River, because her harbor was destroyed. The only language which can describe the event is that of the act of God in the exodus (Exod. 15:12) with his hand **stretched out**. The king might escape to **Cyprus**, but it would do no good.

23:13–14. With verse 13 we again meet difficult problems of translation. The Hebrew says literally without any changes in the text: "Look! The land of the Kassidim (that is, the Babylonians)! This is the people. It was not. Assyria founded it for wild beasts (same word as in 13:21; 34:14, but which in 33:21; Num. 24:24; Ezek. 30:9; and Dan. 11:30 means ships). They caused its siege towers to stand. They stripped away its fortified palaces, making it a ruin" (author's translation, with clarifying notes in parentheses). The Kassidim or Chaldeans took over Babylon in 626 B.C. They besieged Tyre for thirteen years, beginning about 585 B.C., and sent the king of Tyre to Babylon in exile, marking the beginning of the end of Tyre as an international power. Long before that, the Assyrians under Sargon and then under Sennacherib had defeated Babylon. What Babylon had suffered, Tyre could, too. **Ships** docking as far away as **Tarshish** will mourn, for their home port is destroyed.

23:15–18. Tyre is pictured as an old **prostitute** who has lost her charms. She will **walk** in dejection through the city streets and **sing** her charming **song**, trying to attract attention to herself. Such punishment must last **seventy years**, a round number used to express the lifetime of a generation (cp. Ps. 90:10). Then Tyre would regain her **prostitute** charms and continue to **ply her trade** with strangers around the world. She would have a new master and bring her earnings to him at the Jerusalem temple. The people of God would benefit from the Phoenician trade (cp. 18:7; 49:22–23). The oracle against Tyre joined the other oracles against the nations in warning Judah of any political alliances. Not even the island stronghold of Tyre could help to Judah. Second, if Judah would wait, God would give her victory. Then she could enjoy the spoils of Tyre for herself. Alas, Tyre fell, but Judah would not listen to God and also fell, never enjoying the favors of Tyre. One can read this prophecy in two ways. Either this promise is conditional upon Judah's obedience and so does not come to pass for a disobedient nation, or this promise remains to be fulfilled for an Israel restored to glory in the last days.

MAIN IDEA REVIEW: *No one can claim exemption from God's judgment day, no matter how great their military power, economic resources, religious tradition, geographical location, or political alliances.*

III. CONCLUSION

The Futility of Political Alliances

We live in a day dominated by economic concerns. Politicians often hear: "People vote their pocketbook." The church stands heir to a strong and old religious tradition that sometimes lulls us into a false security. The United States, especially, along with other North, Central, and South American countries, tend to see ourselves as isolated from war and immune to threats of attack. We depend on political alliances to keep us free from the ravages of war. God warns us not to be so smug and secure. When his judgment day comes, nothing can protect us from the forces he unleashes against us. Are we ready to trust his word, lean on his power, and receive his blessings?

PRINCIPLES

- God demands constant faithfulness to the task he has given us, even when we see no visible results.
- An ungodly nation, even if it rules the entire world, will meet God's destructive judgment.
- In times of deepest need and hurt, God's people need to hear God's word.

APPLICATIONS

- Commit yourself to study God's Word so you will be able to speak it clearly to others.
- Ask yourself whom you have really trusted in your decision-making when you should be turning to God for advice and help.
- Determine to use any position of authority you may have to bring blessing to the people you work with.

IV. LIFE APPLICATION

The Ruins of Rome

I was awestruck as I entered Rome. The majesty and history of the city made me feel small and insignificant in face of what stood before me—huge buildings, magnificent sculptures, incomparable works of art. How could a people who lived so long ago without the wonders of modern technology achieve so much? Then the thought struck me. No one lives in these awe-inspiring walls. They are ruins! They are signs of what once was and what might have been if decadence and false worship had not turned one of the world's greatest civilization into ruins. Then I turned back to true awe—marveling at what God has done to maintain his church even against the gates of hell. Civilizations come, accomplish, and vanish. But God comes, stays, and saves.

Take a good look at a world not yet in ruins, a world hailed as the greatest creation ever, a creation credited to the power of modern technology. How will this world look two hundred years from now? Will it reflect God's judgment just as Egypt and Babylonia and Greece and Rome do today? Do you need to step back from your fascination with civilization's accomplishments and take another look at what God has done, is doing, and will do?

V. PRAYER

God Almighty, you command the forces of the universe. You can sound the attack any time you choose. Forgive us when we feel so secure in our religious traditions, in our geographical isolation, in our military power, and in our economic strength that we quit depending on you. Make us truly your people, and protect us in the day of judgment. Amen.

VI. DEEPER DISCOVERIES

A. Dumah

This has been variously interpreted as the land of Edom (TEV, NASB, NLT, NAB, NIV footnote, subhead), an Edomite city, an Arabian oasis, or simply as a common noun "silence." The whole section seems to point to the Arabian town at the northern fork of the trade routes (cp. Gen. 25:14 and 1 Chr. 1:30).

B. Elam and Kir

The location of Kir is disputed, so its history cannot be written. Elam appears frequently in Scripture (Ezra 4:9; Jer. 25:25; Ezek. 32:24; Acts 2:9). Elam is documented back to 3200 B.C. Control shifted back and forth from Elam to Sumeria and Babylonia. Around 2000 B.C. Elam represented a political coalition that controlled territory east and north of the Persian Gulf to the Caspian Sea. Several dynasties rose and fell, fighting wars with Mesopotamian kings and using sophisticated knowledge and techniques to build up the city of Susa. After 1000 B.C. Medes and Persians squeezed Elam into the area east of the Zagros Mountains and north of the Persian Gulf centered in its capital of Susa. It owned or had trade access to huge deposits of natural resources. Several Elamite kings aided Babylonian leaders such as Merodach-Baladan against Assyria, but Assyria finally defeated Elam shortly after 700 B.C. In 691

Elam joined Babylonia and Persia to defeat the Assyrians. Between 665 and 653 Ashurbanipal of Assyria once again defeated Elam. Rebellion in 647 B.C. led to another Assyrian victory in 640, resulting in the deportation of some inhabitants to Samaria (Ezra 4:9–10). Cyrus of Persia rose to power and conquered Elam in 539 B.C. Still, Susa served as an important administrative city until Alexander the Great conquered it.

C. The Phoenicians

As early as 858 B.C. the Phoenicians paid tribute to Shalmanezer III of Assyria. They were generally content to pay tribute, but occasionally, they rebelled. We know of Tyre's participation in revolts against Assyria in 734–723 B.C. (when Tyre was besieged for five years), 704–701 B.C. (when Tyre apparently lost most of her control over Phoenicia), 676 B.C. (when Sidon was destroyed), 671 B.C., and 663 B.C. Isaiah 23 apparently reports the participation of Tyre in the major revolt of 704 B.C. (see chs. 36–39), in which Tyre was defeated and its king was forced to flee to Cyprus.

VII. TEACHING OUTLINE

A. INTRODUCTION

1. Lead Story: A Maniac of Ferocious Genius
2. Context: The prophetic oracles against the foreign nations come to a conclusion with strong words against those powers whom Israel would depend on for any reason, even against Jerusalem itself and its security in its religious tradition.
3. Transition: As we complete the study of oracles against powers long passed from the world scene, let us hear them in light of our sources of security. In what ways can we see ourselves mirrored in these people who experienced God's judgment so long ago?

B. COMMENTARY

1. Blowing Away Babylonia (21:1–10)
2. Arrows over Arabia (21:11–17)
3. Zion's Zero Hour (22:1–14)
4. The Famous Will Fall (22:15–25)
5. Taps for Tyre (23:1–18)

C. CONCLUSION: THE RUINS OF ROME

1. Wrap-up: The last days will be days of judgment on people and nations who put more trust in material power and religious tradition

than they do in the living God. We must constantly check where our trust lies and on whom we depend for our security.

2. Personal Challenge: What activities in your life show you are trusting in military power, economic resources, religious tradition, geographical location, or political alliances for security? What activities show that you place great trust in these? Check your topics of conversation, your checkbook, and your use of time and energy.

VIII. ISSUES FOR DISCUSSION

1. In what way is our nation ripe for divine punishment? Do you believe God can and will punish a rebellious nation today?
2. What does it mean to look to God and have regard for him?
3. Does the church today hear a divine call to lament and mourn over the condition of our nation and our world? How is your church answering such a call?
4. What will happen to you if "tomorrow we die"?
5. What evidence do we have that economic resources are the number one priority and source of security in our country today? Do church people differ from the rest of the population in this matter?

Isaiah 24–27

Apocalyptic Announcements

I. INTRODUCTION
Lepers in Paradise

II. COMMENTARY
A verse-by-verse explanation of these chapters.

III. CONCLUSION
God's Final Plan

An overview of the principles and applications from these chapters.

IV. LIFE APPLICATION
Destroying Egypt

Melding these chapters to life.

V. PRAYER
Tying these chapters to life with God.

VI. DEEPER DISCOVERIES
Historical, geographical, and grammatical enrichment of the commentary.

VII. TEACHING OUTLINE
Suggested step-by-step group study of these chapters.

VIII. ISSUES FOR DISCUSSION
Zeroing these chapters in on daily life.

Quote

"*B*eing defeated is often a temporary condition. Giving up is what makes it permanent."

M a r l e n e   v o s   S a v a n t

Isaiah 24–27

IN A NUTSHELL

*O*racles against foreign nations show that God will bring universal judgment before establishing his kingdom.

Apocalyptic Announcements

I. INTRODUCTION

Lepers in Paradise

A leper colony in Hawaii may be the starkest example we can find to open our eyes to the real situation of our world. Mention Hawaii, and ooh's and aah's escape the lips of everyone. Eyes fill with stars as people reawaken their life's dream—a Hawaiian vacation. But Damien, the missionary, found a new dream in Hawaii. Amid the blue waters, erupting volcanoes, cloud-free skies, rustling palm trees, and sandy beaches, Damien discovered a leper colony. Yes, where everything appeared like Eden itself, Damien saw that the old snake had been there, too. Everywhere Damien looked in this corner of Molokai, he saw the stigma of death. Bodies literally were falling apart, knowing the only escape was to stop breathing forever (Miller, *The Empowered Leader,* p. 10).

Isaiah spoke to a people who had seen God defeat the enemies and promise that all the power blocs of the world would soon be decimated. One could easily think Israel stood on the threshold of final victory. At last, she would realize her God-given destiny and rule the world. Isaiah stopped them in their tracks. Yes, God had a plan to bring in his kingdom, but terror and horror would come first. The last days do not result from human military victory. They come only after God has brought his final judgment on the world.

Christians too often live with a naïve view of God's final plans for the world. We think we are on a Hawaiian vacation before we discover the leper colony in the middle of the island. What will we do? Missionary Damien went to work, devoting the rest of his life to helping those whom everyone else considered hopeless and helpless. Do you have a God-given mission while you wait for God's timing to bring the final judgment and victory?

Having described the weakness and hopelessness of the nations, the Book of Isaiah now draws theological conclusions. What will this mean for the world as a whole? What will it mean for the people of God? How does God want his people to respond? Has hope vanished for everyone?

II. COMMENTARY

Apocalyptic Announcements

> **MAIN IDEA:** *God's plan for the world leads to a day of universal judgment and terror. This will happen before the coming of God's eternal kingdom where death and terror no longer exist.*

Ⓐ Cosmic Convulsions (24:1–13)

Prophecy of disaster against the earth (695 B.C.)

> **SUPPORTING IDEA:** *No nation can escape when God brings his cosmic judgment on human sin.*

24:1–3. This section sets the stage for what follows and summarizes what has come before. Add up the message of chapters 13–23, and you get one answer: total disaster on the whole earth. No social or economic class is exempt. Why? Because the whole **earth** stands guilty before God.

24:4–13. The people broke God's **everlasting covenant**. God's everlasting covenant promised that God would not repeat the destruction of the days of Noah (Gen. 9:8–17). Isaiah 24 shows that the eternal covenant included **laws** and **statutes** that the whole world should understand and obey. When the whole world neglects the moral rules of the universe, God is bound to bring devastating punishment. A covenant **curse** must follow (cp. Deut. 27:11–26). Rejoicing was rejected; parties perished. Desolation dominated.

Ⓑ Reason to Rejoice? (24:14–23)

Prophetic argument and personal woe oracle (695 B.C.)

> **SUPPORTING IDEA:** *God's day of judgment will eventually reveal him as king over all the earth. But until that time comes, no nation has reason to rejoice.*

24:14–20. Hearing the prophecy of world disaster, God's people break into songs of praise. Exiles from all corners of the globe join in. Jerusalem's day had come. **Glory to the Righteous One!** Isaiah reacted violently. He returned to mourning—for himself! The time to rejoice had not yet come. Even the people of God had not learned their lessons. **Treachery**, not truthfulness, reigned. The announcement of judgment must be repeated (cp. Jer. 48:43); the earth **falls—never to rise again** because of **the guilt of its rebellion** against God.

24:21–23. Judgment is not the final word. **That day** is coming. (For day of the Lord, see "Deeper Discoveries," chs. 13–14.) Heavenly and earthly

powers will fall. The divine Warden will throw them in prison to serve their just sentence. The **moon** and **sun**, elements worshiped by Israel's neighbors as the high gods of the universe, must hide their faces in shame before the brilliance of King Yahweh. (For God as king, see "Deeper Discoveries".) He who has been worshiped as king in **Jerusalem** (Pss. 93; 95–99) will reveal his kingship with his dazzling glory. As at Sinai (Exod. 24), so now the **elders** of God's people would be present. The glory that Isaiah discovered in his call vision (Isa. 6) would become visible finally to the whole earth.

Sadly, total judgment had to bring the earth to its knees before they could see his majesty. Sad also that the people of God are so quick to leap into action with their songs of rejoicing while God is still punishing the earth for its stubborn sinfulness. The prophet told the people to mourn for the sad state of the world until that day when God chooses to reveal his glory.

C Sing to the Savior (25:1–12)

Hymn of thanksgiving (695 B.C.)

> **SUPPORTING IDEA:** *God's people can join in praise to God for his coming kingdom on earth, for his protection of the helpless, and for his victory over death.*

25:1–5. When God ascends his throne before all the earth, thanksgiving and rejoicing will be in order. The prophet even provided the right hymn. Thanksgiving is addressed to **my God**, being based on a personal relationship, not hearsay evidence. Normally God is praised for his wonderful deeds (Exod. 15:11; Ps. 77:11,14). Here the focus is moved into the future. The prophet praised God for planning deeds which could be compared to the great wonders of salvation history (cp. 9:5). God made such plans **long ago** and carried them out **in perfect faithfulness**. (For faithfulness see "Deeper Discoveries.") The deeds are described as the destruction of **the city**, that is, the capital of the great enemy, left unnamed. The results are astonishing; the defeated enemy turns to worship and **honor** Yahweh. (For honor or glorify God, see "Deeper Discoveries.") The result for God's people is peace. Certainly, this is an appropriate thanksgiving to follow the events of chapter 24.

25:6–8. Thanksgiving is also acted out in a **feast** celebrating God's kingship. This banquet is open to **all nations**. No longer will the nations veil themselves in mourning over the victims lost in the battle of the last days. God will invite all who are left to feasting and joy. **Death**, the last enemy, will be conquered. If the people can hold back their rejoicing (ch. 24) until the proper time, God will give them unprecedented reason for joy. Death will no longer threaten the world; mourning will vanish from human experience; joy and thanksgiving will last forever.

25:9–12. The people of God again break out in thanksgiving to **our God**. They will understand once and for all the nature of **salvation**. **We trusted in him, and he saved us**. Such personal experience and certainty of salvation is the perfect reason to **rejoice and be glad**. The chapter names Moab as the enemy and describes its fate (cp. chs. 15–16). All nations may be invited to the final victory feast, but those continuing the **pride** of Moab will face destruction in spite of their **cleverness**. The people who are giving thanks will be the people who surrendered their pride to trust in God's salvation.

🄳 Praise for the Promise of Peace (26:1–21)

Song of trust and lamentation (695 B.C.)

> **SUPPORTING IDEA:** *The final victory will bring joy and singing for God's people who have trusted in him and who have seen him reward the righteous and raise the dead.*

26:1–7. Again a proper response is given the people. **This song** should be sung in the victory procession into Jerusalem after God has given the final victory. Victory is reserved for the **righteous nation** that **keeps faith** (see 11:5; see "Deeper Discoveries"), the people who **trust** in God (see 12:2). Such trust must endure **forever**. God responds to such trust with victory for his **poor** ones. They can use familiar proverbs to repeat their confession of trust in their **upright** God who smoothes the **way** for the **righteous**.

26:8–11. The people of God should not remain content with singing about the victory to come. They should also bring the brutal facts of present reality to God. Here is the language of lamentation known so well from Psalms. They claim obedience, because they are **walking in the way of your laws** (more literally, your judgments or verdicts; for justice, see "Deeper Discoveries," ch. 1). Still they do not experience their deepest yearning—God's presence. The Hebrew text does not read **in the morning** (NIV follows an emended text) but "my spirit within me searches for you." God's people pleaded with him to act so the **wicked** would **learn** their lesson and see the need and value of acting with **righteousness**. But even in good times, they do not learn. (For righteousness, see "Deeper Discoveries," chs. 50–51.) Instead they ignored **the majesty of the** LORD. So they deserved **the fire reserved for your enemies**.

26:12–15. Alternating between trust and lament, God's people in that day were to confess their confidence that God would bring **peace**. They laid aside pride to admit that anything they had accomplished **you have done for us**. They claimed their innocence in spite of overwhelming temptations. Even under Assyrian rule they refused the temptation to worship anyone but God **alone**. They called to mind the great deeds God performed for them in the past. He totally **wiped out** their enemies who would never again **rise** to threaten God's people. God had **extended** Israel's **borders**, again fulfilling the promises to David and to Abraham. This brought **glory** to God, not Israel. This is the song of victory for God's people when God signals it is time to sing.

26:16–18. Victory came only after suffering. Israel's victory song looked back and described their previous distress and helplessness. Verse 16 almost defies translation. A literal reading is: "LORD, in distress they visited you; they restricted (or distressed) with an incantation (or charm); your discipline (or instruction) was for them" (author's translation). The people knew they had experienced God's discipline. Apparently it came after they tried magical incantations or charms to escape a distressful situation. They cried out in **pain** like a woman in labor. This time they did not turn to other gods or magical incantations. They cried in God's **presence**. The last line of verse 18 reads literally "salvation we have not done (for) earth, and the residents of the dry land have not fallen" (author's translation). The REB probably comes close to the original meaning with its translation: "We have achieved no victories for the land, given birth to no one to inhabit the world."

All human effort is vain until God puts his plan into action. The world will not get better and better because of human invention and technology. The world continues to serve satanic values and materialistic goals. Only a people disciplined by God and obedient to him can expect to see **salvation**— salvation created by God, not by human effort or intelligence. (For salvation, see "Deeper Discoveries," chs. 47–49.)

26:19–21. God heard and answered. Many interpretations of his answer have been given. The Hebrew text reads, "Your (singular) dead ones will live; my corpse they will rise. Awake and rejoice you dwellers in the dust, for the dew of the lights is your (singular) dew, but the land of the Rephaim will cause to fall" (author's translation).

The early interpreters from the Dead Sea Scrolls on had trouble interpreting this verse and translating it. Before studying the text, you will do well to read several modern translations. The verse repeats in some way the promise of victory over death given in 25:8. It stands in stark contrast to the fate of Israel's former enemies (v. 14). This verse may mean simply that in contrast to their enemies, the nation of Israel will live again, being able to produce children instead of being barren, as she was pictured in verse 18.

Note the agricultural image of the last half of the verse referring to the dew which was all-important for Israel's agricultural economy. This may be a promise of renewed growth of crops in a dead land. However, the context apparently demands something more than this. The horrible, barren situation of God's people in the last days (cp. 24:16–23) can be changed only by something radically new. John Oswalt concludes that this verse along with 25:8 "represents the highest conception of resurrection in the Old Testament"

(Commentary, p. 485) and then reminds us in a footnote that God's revelation is not subject to an evolutionary scheme.

This means that one cannot deny such a statement to Isaiah and force it into the post-exilic age just because it goes beyond what other pre-exilic and even post-exilic literature says. Israel mourns her dead, lost in the armed conflict that God brought to discipline his people. Through the prophet God promises their **dead will live**. Those buried in the **dust** of the earth will rise out of the dust and hear God's call to **shout for joy**. The **dew** on their graves will vanish like the dew in the **morning** sunlight. The earth has swallowed the dead, but only for a moment. Israel could not repopulate the land because of God's discipline, but the **earth will give birth to her dead**.

Here, for Isaiah, resurrection hope is not immediate, however. God's people must wait. For the period of waiting, God gives directions: **hide yourselves for a little while**. Why? Because God's uplifted hand will no longer be hidden. Indeed, **the Lord is coming out of his dwelling to punish the people of the earth for their sins**. Murder can no longer be concealed. God will vindicate his innocent followers. But until he does, his people must hide and wait, preparing to join in the victory procession of peace and to shout for joy when **his wrath has passed** by and the resurrection hope is realized.

▣ Ready for Renewal and Revenge (27:1–13)

Promise of God's final salvation (695 B.C.)

SUPPORTING IDEA: *God's final day of judgment and victory calls on his people to destroy all signs of worship of false gods so they can join together from around the world to worship him in his chosen place.*

27:1. The judgment against the nations and the view toward the last days climaxes in a statement ranging from creation to the final day of salvation. It begins by taking up ancient language of a battle at creation between God and **Leviathan**, the chaos monster (see Job 3:8; Ps. 74:14). This imagery of sailing into the deep sea and confronting the horrible **monster of the sea** represented the most frightening language ancient people could hear. God has plans to calm all such fears eternally. The day is coming when the powers of darkness and chaos will hold no fear for God's people. God has been in control since the world began, and he will prove this once and for all **in that day**.

27:2–6. The new day will be a day of total transformation. Even the prophetic message will be transformed. The "Song of the Vineyard" in Isaiah 5:1–7 can no longer be sung in judgment of Israel. Rather, God invites his audience to sing the song of praise for his **vineyard**. He describes how he continues to care for it, not destroying it as in chapter 5. His anger has disappeared. He is ready to **march against** any enemy to defend his beloved vineyard. He prefers that everyone, even the enemy, **come** to him for **peace** and protection, just as people had at one time run to his temple and grasped the horns of the altar for safety (1 Kgs. 1:50; 2:28).

Verse 5 begins literally, "or let him grasp hold of my stronghold (or place of refuge)." In God's plan of salvation, **Israel**—the vineyard of God—will one day prosper and provide good **fruit** for the entire world (cp. 5:7).

27:7–11. Such hope for God's people is not automatic. God lays requirements on his people. This is the message of verses 7–11, although the precise translation and interpretation is difficult, especially in verse 8 (TEV is probably right here). God has punished his people, but not as severely as he has punished their enemies. Atonement that brings **removal of his sin** requires something from Israel before God acts. (For atoning for sin and guilt, see "Deeper Discoveries," chs. 6–8.) If Israel wants God's final blessing and peace, she must respond to the punishment of God by demolishing the **altars** and other paraphernalia she has used to worship false gods. Otherwise, Israel would be forced to remain content with what she had, a deserted city with a great past and no future. Even in an apocalyptic promise of the final salvation for God's people, demands are made on God's people. No salvation of God is automatic. A people **without understanding**, no thought for God, cannot simply wait until God decides to exercise his great **compassion** and grace. (For God's compassion, see "Deeper Discoveries," chs. 13–14; for God's grace, see "Deeper Discoveries," chs. 28–33.) The **Creator** looks to the day when he can destroy the powers of evil and chaos forever, but he waits for the day when his people are discerning and trusting so they reject the sins that have caused their punishment.

27:12–13. When **that day** comes, God will sound his **trumpet** to call all his people back from their exile in the east and west. The **Euphrates** is the ideal border between Palestine and Assyria/Babylonia, while the **Wadi of Egypt** is the Wadi el-'arish which ideally separates Palestine from Egypt (Josh. 15:4,47). God will reach beyond both these boundary lines to snatch his people from exile and bring them home. God's people will no longer worship other gods. They will join together in God's chosen place to **worship** the Holy One of Israel on his **holy mountain**. This is God's ultimate goal for his people—to be separated from all other gods and united in worshiping him.

MAIN IDEA REVIEW: *God's plan for the world leads to a day of universal judgment and terror. This will happen before the coming of God's eternal kingdom where death and terror no longer exist.*

III. CONCLUSION

God's Final Plan

God's final plan for his people includes both judgment on sin and redemption of an obedient people. The greatest reward is victory over death as well as victory over the worship of all false gods. Neither horrible monsters of the sea nor heavily armed peoples can prevent God from establishing his plan. The question is, Who will trust him by rejecting false gods and false political alliances? These people will see the salvation of our God.

PRINCIPLES

- Neither social class, profession, economic worth, nor religious work will make any difference when judgment comes.
- God's final judgment leaves no escape route.
- Even heavenly powers will face punishment on the day of judgment.
- Judgment will lead to God's final glorious reign.
- God's final victory will be over death itself.
- God's judgment seeks to teach people righteousness.

APPLICATIONS

- Trust in God to save you from the final judgment.
- Wait patiently, trustingly, and faithfully for God to complete his work of judgment and salvation.
- Examine your life and get rid of everything that may be a false god that you worship above the one true God.

IV. LIFE APPLICATION

Destroying Egypt

I destroyed Egypt one Thursday night. I joined my family in going to College Heights Baptist Church, where they were just finishing Vacation Bible School. The theme was built around the Ten Commandments and Egypt. Oases, palm trees, camels, blue skies, and sand dunes dotted each of the rooms where children had been given a realistic setting to learn about God's truth for their lives. In a couple of hours, however, we had destroyed Egypt. The classrooms were back to normal without sand, camels, trees, skies, or any of the other decorations.

The next Thursday night I recreated Egypt. Yes, I took Egypt out of College Heights Baptist Church and recreated it in Gallatin Baptist Church, where we once again had Vacation Bible School. The new creation was augmented by some special flourishes provided by a couple of professional artists in our church. Egypt looked better than ever.

Isaiah said this world will look better than ever some day. God will create a new heaven and a new earth. The old heaven and earth will be destroyed. All things will be new. Tears will vanish. Banquets will abound. Life will never have been so good.

Are you ready for this new world that God is creating? Have you shifted your trust from economic and political powers to God's power? Have you let God be your Savior? Only then will you be part of God's new world. Only then can you join in singing the songs of salvation he has planned for the heavenly chorus. Only then will you be able to survive the horrors of destruction and participate in the glory of a new creation.

V. PRAYER

Father God, you are our Savior. You have planned salvation for us your people. We want to be part of your marvelous plan of salvation. We forsake our sinful ways, turn away from our false gods, leave behind our trust in materialistic powers, and rely wholly on you. Come, Lord Jesus, come. Amen.

VI. DEEPER DISCOVERIES

A. God as King (24:23)

In its hymns and poetry, the Old Testament often celebrates God as the king of the world (Exod. 15:18; Isa. 24:23; Pss. 29:10; 93:1; 97:1; 99:1,4; 145:1; 149:2). The king is Yahweh, the king of glory, who enters Jerusalem and the temple (Ps. 68:24) and wins victories for his people (Ps. 44:4). He rules over all gods and nations (1 Chr. 29:11; Pss. 22:28; 103:19; Dan. 4:34). Israel's king owes all he is and has to the divine King (Ps. 89:18), since God's kingdom is everlasting (Dan. 4:3).

Early in their history, however, Israel rejected Yahweh as king, wanting a king of their own (cp. Judg. 8:22–23 with 1 Sam. 8:7; 12:12). Still God asserted his position as king over his people and over the world (Isa. 43:15; Ezek. 20:33). He showed his superiority to false gods who would claim to rule the world because of an earthly king who won a battle (Isa. 41:21). Thus the Heavenly King comes to earth to deliver his people (Zeph. 3:15). His subjects cry to him for help and relief from danger (Pss. 5:3; 74:12).

Isaiah fell to his knees in awesome fear and repentance because his eyes saw the divine King (6:5). The presence of this God puts the heavenly bodies to shame. His glory puts out their light (24:23). All the evidence would call Israel to obedient service to their king, but the historical evidence paints a picture of Israel constantly searching for another king.

B. Faith, Faithfulness, Belief, Trust (25:1)

The Hebrew root 'mn forms nouns, verbs, and adjectives which encompass the meanings "to be faithful, to be enduring, to have faith, to believe, to trust, to rely on—faithful, faithfulness, trustworthy." Isaiah could use the verbal adjective to describe a firm place in the wall where a nail could be securely implanted (22:23,25). The same term applied to reliable witnesses (8:2). Isaiah described God as faithful (Isa. 25:1; cp. Deut. 7:9) because he faithfully carried out his plans for salvation that he had made long before he created the world. Thus the promised messianic king is also faithful (Isa. 11:5).

Faithfulness is not just an abstract description of God. It is testimony to the way God acts. God can be counted on to fulfill his promises, in contrast to human unfaithfulness and disloyalty (Deut. 32:4; Pss. 33:4; 40:10; 89:1–50; 98:3; Lam. 3:23). His faithfulness means people can trust him. He will answer prayer (Ps. 143:1). He will show that he has truly chosen Israel as his people (Isa. 49:7) and David as his royal house (2 Sam. 7:16; 23:5). He will judge correctly and fairly at the last judgment (Ps. 96:13).

God's faithfulness calls people to be trustworthy in relation to others (Prov. 11:13; 25:13) and in relationship to God and his covenant demands (Pss. 78:8,37; 101:6). But Isaiah lamented Jerusalem's lack of faithfulness and looked forward to the day of renewed faithfulness (1:21,26).

People can exhibit such faithfulness and show they are trustworthy only because they faithfully hold on to God in belief and trust (see Gen. 15:6; Hab. 2:2–4). With the plagues God challenged the Egyptians to trust his word and believe in who he is (Exod. 4:5,9). So Isaiah challenged King Ahaz to believe God's word (7:9). He called people to trust the cornerstone God was laying (28:16). The time came when no one believed and trusted the message God sent (Isa. 53:1). Such belief in God may be the only hope a person has (Ps. 27:13). God chooses his people as his servant to know him and witness to what he has done for them among the nations (Isa. 43:10).

C. Honor or Glorify God (26:15)

The Hebrew term for "honor" or "glorify" carries the basic meaning "to be heavy," "to carry weight." Isaiah uses the verb twenty times and the noun thirty-eight times. The large army of Isaiah 36:2 is literally a "heavy army." Battle exerts pressure, weighing in on those in conflict (Isa. 21:15). In judgment God makes the yoke heavy (47:6). Sin becomes heavy on a person (24:20). God's unhearing ear is also heavy or dull (59:1). To harden the heart is to make it heavy (6:10). Wealth and respect are heavy burdens to bear (10:3; 66:12).

The verb comes to mean to acknowledge the weight or importance that one carries, so that children honor their parents (Exod. 20:12). Nations earn respect and show their power and wealth as glory (Isa. 8:7; 16:14). Israel, too, has its own kind of glory (Isa. 62:2), as do its leaders (Isa. 22:23). Even nature shines with honor and glory (Isa. 10:18; 60:13). Human products such as chariots may be glorious (Isa. 22:18). God has promised his messianic king a glorious place (Isa. 11:10; cp. 4:2).

Proverbs gives interesting ways to gain honor (Prov. 27:18). Such honor is recognition of one's status in a community but does not necessarily point to a social hierarchy of one person being innately better than another. Human honor and glory ultimately rest on God's protection and blessing (Pss. 3:3; 84:11). At times one receives glory he may not want (Isa. 22:24).

Nothing on earth carries as much weight or significance as does God. He has his own glory which humans can only recognize and acknowledge (Exod. 24:16–17). Such glory can be seen by viewing creation (Ps. 19:1). Still, God's glory resides in the temple (1 Kgs. 8:11; cp. Exod. 40:34–35), but leaves the temple and city as God's punishment (Ezek. 10:4,18–19; 11:22–23). To recognize the weight God carries, the significance he has leads a person to praise him, to give him honor and glory. Thus the verb becomes a part of the vocabulary of worship (Pss. 22:23; 66:2).

Deliverance from trouble leads to praise of God (Judg. 13:17; see also 1 Sam. 6:5). People in trouble ask for help so God's glory will be seen (Ps.79:9). Righteous living and cultic worship both give glory to God (Ps. 50:23). Tithing brings honor to God (Prov. 3:9). But some praise is fake and dishonest (Isa. 3:8; 43:23; Mal. 2:2). The day is coming when God will reveal his glory to all nations in the beauty and power of Jerusalem (Isa. 4:5; 62:2). They will recognize who he is and honor and glorify him (Ps. 86:9; Isa. 25:3).

VII. TEACHING OUTLINE

A. INTRODUCTION

1. Lead Story: Lepers in Paradise
2. Context: Isaiah has pictured God's sovereign control of world history by picturing God's promised fate for the nations around Israel. Every nation, even Israel and Judah, must face God's punishment. These oracles against the nations cast glimmers of hope beyond punishment but leave one wondering if judgment is God's final word.

3. Transition: Isaiah 24–27 points to a new type of prophecy and literature in Israel as it uses image-filled language to describe the end of time. Such language will eventually lead to the apocalyptic writings of Daniel and Revelation. Isaiah focuses upon God's eternal purpose for his people and his world and shows how God is faithful in carrying out his plan of salvation. That salvation will be so complete that all nations will be affected, all peoples will be judged, and the last enemy—death—will be defeated. In these chapters Isaiah gives the Old Testament's strongest statements about victory over the grave.

B. COMMENTARY

1. Cosmic Convulsions (24:1–13)
2. Reason to Rejoice? (24:14–23)
3. Sing to the Savior (25:1–12)
4. Praise for the Promise of Peace (26:1–21)
5. Ready for Renewal and Revenge (27:1–13)

C. CONCLUSION: DESTROYING EGYPT

1. Wrap-up: God has a plan for the earth's last days. In that time God will show once and for all that he is sovereign over all nations and that he will be faithful to give his people victory over their enemies as well as death.

2. Personal Challenge: Are you prepared to die? Do you truly believe that God will be the winner in the last days and that death itself will be defeated?

VIII. ISSUES FOR DISCUSSION

1. What do you think will cause the destruction of the earth? Why do you believe this?
2. What reasons do you have to give glory to God? In what ways do you glorify him?
3. Describe marvelous things God has done in your life and ways you have honored him by telling others about his great deeds for you.
4. In what ways are you preparing to die? What role do you think God will play in your death and beyond?
5. What activities in your life show the world that you trust in God's eternal plan of salvation?

Isaiah 28–33

Mandate Against Military Might

I. INTRODUCTION
A Scar-Faced Savior

II. COMMENTARY
A verse-by-verse explanation of these chapters.

III. CONCLUSION
God's Ultimatum

An overview of the principles and applications from these chapters.

IV. LIFE APPLICATION
Angry and Hopeless

Melding these chapters to life.

V. PRAYER
Tying these chapters to life with God.

VI. DEEPER DISCOVERIES
Historical, geographical, and grammatical enrichment of the commentary.

VII. TEACHING OUTLINE
Suggested step-by-step group study of these chapters.

VIII. ISSUES FOR DISCUSSION
Zeroing these chapters in on daily life.

Quote

"An army of sheep led by a lion would defeat an army of lions led by a sheep."

Arab proverb

Isaiah 28–33

IN A NUTSHELL

Isaiah pronounced a woe on drunken Israel for looking to military powers rather than to God. He added a woe on the city of Jerusalem for hypocrisy and on Judah for ignoring God, rejecting his prophets, and looking to Egypt for help. Still God had a word of hope.

Mandate Against Military Might

I. INTRODUCTION

A Scar-Faced Savior

Calvin Miller reminds us of the fable of the little girl whose mother's face was hideously scarred from an early injury. As the little girl grew, made friends, and gained her own identity, she became more and more ashamed of her mother's horrid appearance. As she walked down the street with her mother, she noticed people moving over to the far side of the walk or even crossing the street to avoid them. Gradually, the girl found ways to avoid being with her mother in public. Eventually, the girl became an adult, married, and moved to another town. Her lonely mother suffered financial setbacks and faced basic hunger. Her daughter continued to ignore her, even in such destitute circumstances.

One day the daughter discovered an old diary of her mother's. It described a horrible fire that swept through their home. The mother rushed into the burning house, scooped her daughter into her arms, and ran back out, burning herself beyond belief. The truth dawned on the girl. Her mother's horrific scars came from saving the daughter's life. A new kind of shame raced through her heart and soul. She went to her mother and threw her arms around what now appeared to be a beautiful face. In tears she expressed her gratitude for all her mother had done. A new love relationship controlled their lives from then on (Miller, *Until He Comes*, p. 139).

So often we depend on outward appearances as we choose our leaders and friends. We do not look behind appearances to find the truth about a person, a program, or an organization and their abilities to help us. Israel kept looking beyond her boundaries to find a strong ally to deliver her from enemies. Time and again God sent word to trust him and let him be the only ally they needed. What does it take to reveal the truth to us about who can really help us and meet our needs? Who has proved true and faithful in our times of deepest distress? Are we ready to turn to the Faithful One, or will we seek yet another earthly ally?

II. COMMENTARY

Mandate Against Military Might

> **MAIN IDEA:** *God will reveal his kingdom and his salvation to his people, but they must repent and trust him rather than trust in political alliances and military powers.*

Doom for Ephraim's Drunkards (28:1–13)

Woe oracle (724 B.C.)

> **SUPPORTING IDEA:** *Leaders intoxicated with their own power and with wine will find that God sends them reeling to defeat and dishonor.*

The Assyrian section of the Book of Isaiah (chs. 1–33) concludes with a series of prophetic sermons and narratives calling Judah to trust in her God for deliverance in times of crisis rather than to expect the military might of her government or her allies to help her. This structure shows us that the apocalyptic hope for the last days when all the national enemies are defeated (chs. 24–27) is not the last word of the prophet. Such hope is the reason for God's people to trust him and his ways in the midst of the present crisis.

28:1–4. The Northern Kingdom lost most of its property and its hope for independence in 732 B.C., but hope sprang eternal among the leaders. King Hoshea refused to pay tribute (2 Kgs. 17:4). Isaiah showed the stupidity of such a proud act by describing the drunken parties celebrated in Samaria, the capital of the Northern Kingdom. Such parties may have taken place at the temple in Bethel (cp. Ezek. 23:36–45). Isaiah turned the woe against the partygoers into a description of Assyria's reaction. Samaria with her ramparts sat like a proud crown on a hill overlooking the **valley** below. She would become nothing more than the **fading flower** worn like a crown by the partygoers. Ripe for the picking, they would soon be swallowed by the Assyrian enemy, a prediction that came true in 721 B.C.

28:5–8. The true **crown** bearer was the only hope; he would crown his people with beauty. Sadly, only a **remnant** would remain to receive the crown. They would receive a new ruler who would be controlled by the **spirit of justice** rather than the spirits that flowed through the veins of the ruler of Isaiah's day. (For justice, see "Deeper Discoveries," ch. 1.) This new ruler would win any **battle**, even if the enemy had already entered the city **gate**.

The royal party was not the only culprit. Religious leaders who were supposed to seek the word of God and give it to the people could not blame an ecstatic experience of the Spirit for their condition. They drank of other spirits. Religious parties rather than prophecies ruled their lives (cp. Lev. 10:8–9). Here we see that the temple staff included both **priests** and **prophets**. Their job was to teach the people of God and to interpret messages that God sent to his people (see Deut. 17:8–12). In such festive conditions, they could not accomplish the assigned task. God was left with babies—or with adults whose action was no better than babies—to instruct and direct his people.

28:9–13. The priests and prophets shouted back, trying to mimic Isaiah and accuse him of saying one thing on one occasion and another at a different time—one time judgment, another time hope. They saw themselves as consistently promising hope for God's people. The precise translation and explanation of verse 10 is not clear (cp. NRSV, REB, TEV, and especially NIV and its note). Perhaps JPS helps us hear it best, "That same mutter upon mutter, murmur upon murmur, now here, now there." Brevard Childs calls the words here "incomprehensible nonsense." Isaiah's opponents try to mock him but find they cannot even form an intelligible sentence. God could no longer use the professional ministers. He had to call on people with **foreign lips** who could **speak** the only language God's people understood—the language of military power. God had tried to give his people **rest**, but they turned deaf ears to him. So he would speak their incomprehensible language to them and fulfill his threat of judgment given in 8:15 and quoted here. All this would happen because God's ministers mixed drinks with their messages, turning festivals of faith into foolish observances. The wrong spirit ruled.

🅱 A Stone for the Scoffers (28:14–22)
Prophecy of disaster (733 B.C.)

> **SUPPORTING IDEA:** *Political alliances are never strong enough to overcome God's decrees of destruction for a sinful people.*

28:14–20. The dating and interpretation of this oracle are difficult. After Ahaz refused to take Isaiah's advice (see 7:1–9), the prophet turned to the king's political advisers and warned them of the consequences of their new political alliance with Assyria. Isaiah addressed these wise counselors with their own wisdom language, making plays on each Hebrew word. Those **who rule** also can mean "maker of proverbs." **Covenant with death** could be a ritual with a foreign god of the underworld, an alliance to fight to the death, or a treaty with a foreign power. The **lie** and **falsehood** could refer to the politicians' clever ability to make a treaty when it was useful with the clear intention to break it when it was no longer to their advantage. They could also refer to the worship of false gods. The **cornerstone** appears to refer to the temple, to a new king, to a new building project which would ensure the defenses of the city, or to a new community of faith. For the prophet, it is a **tested stone** or a stone of testing, unless recent scholars are correct in seeing Egyptian influence so the meaning is "strong fortress."

Isaiah subtly accuses the leaders of Jerusalem with being **scoffers** who rule by playing with words. They entered into political and military agreements with foreign governments apart from God's leadership; indeed, they did it in the name of false gods through deadly rituals. What they consider ingenious political maneuvering, God sees as participating with foreign governments in deals dedicated to false gods. God is building a new beginning for his people, with new people of faith, a new worship center, and a new messianic king.

The current rulers will find God's building simply a stone of testing, and they will fail the test. They fooled themselves into thinking they could escape approaching danger in the form of the Assyrian army. The false covenants they entered into had two parties, neither of which intended to keep their side of the bargain. When crunch time comes, Egypt's army will not help Judah. Her leaders will have no place to hide. The prophet called the politicians away from rejoicing over their latest political achievement to remind them of God's call for faith (7:9). Only those who trusted him and not foreign governments would escape the fray and be part of God's new beginnings.

Meanwhile, the Master Carpenter was coming to the city. He was not in a building mood. Rather, he wanted to check out the security of the city. Had it been built straight and **plumb**? The tools of the Carpenter are **justice** and **righteousness**. The proper response is faith, not fast action or false treaties. Everything was out of plumb. The Master Builder would **hail** down stones from heaven to destroy what they had built. Their treaty partner would bring **death** and destruction. They could not hope to survive one raid and be done with it. Over and again the foreign army would flood their land. Finally, they would understand Isaiah's **message**, but it would be too late.

The only reaction they could make would be sheer terror as they faced the reality Isaiah had described and they had ignored. So Isaiah quoted a familiar proverb. The politicians would have to live with the **bed** they had made, but it was too small to do the job right. In the fullness of God's time a carpenter appeared in Galilee, calling men to follow his way instead of the paths of the political and religious leaders of his day. He became God's foundation stone by which even Gentiles gained righteousness through faith. He also became a stumbling stone by which the unbelieving people of God were tested and found wanting (Rom. 9:30–33; 1 Pet. 2:6).

28:21–22. God was using Assyria to do his work, just like when he gave David his first victory over the Philistines in **Mount Perazim** (2 Sam. 5:18–20) and when Joshua defeated the Canaanites in the **Valley of Gibeon** (Josh. 10). This would be a strange, foreign work of Yahweh, defeating his own people rather than giving them victory. The politicians continued to mock the prophet. As Isaiah warned, Sennacherib came and destroyed the land (see chs. 36–39).

 Facts from the Farmer (28:23–29)

Prophetic instruction (701 B.C.[?])

SUPPORTING IDEA: *God's ways are beyond understanding, but he is wise and constantly at work, doing exactly what is needed to achieve his purpose with his people.*

28:23–29. In forty years of prophetic ministry, Isaiah faced many situations and found God's specific word for each situation. The people of Jerusalem, and even his own disciples, did not always understand what the prophet was up to. How could he proclaim oracles of judgment against Judah's enemies, and then turn around and say those enemies would be used to punish Judah? How could he proclaim that God was using Assyria to punish Judah, and then proclaim salvation for Jerusalem even when the Assyrian armies surrounded the city? Was God constantly changing his mind? Was God inconsistent in his actions? At some point in his ministry, Isaiah took time to teach his disciples what he meant. He borrowed the style and vocabulary of the wise men of Judah, using one of their parables and giving his own explanation. God could be compared to a **farmer** who engaged in many activities to prepare the **soil**, sow the seed, harvest, and thresh the crop. The farmer did not spend all his time doing the same thing. He did not act the same way with the small spices and seasonings as he did with the larger grain crops. Yes, the farmer could be charged with inconsistency. The fact could not be denied. But he successfully produced his crops. Why? Because **God instructs him and teaches him the right way.**

How much more wonderful was God's **wisdom** in working to produce the proper fruit in his own people. God did everything necessary at the proper time to bring forth the proper results. The ways of God were not determined once and for all in such a way that men could expect the same type of treatment all the time. Just as a farmer carefully watched his crops and did what was needed at each stage of growth, so God carefully watched his people and brought his people to be what he had created them to be. God is not programmable; he is personal. His works are not to be predicted, but to be praised!

 Agony for Ariel (29:1–8)

Woe oracle and promise of salvation (701 B.C.)

SUPPORTING IDEA: *God's people must respect the divine freedom and respond appropriately to each historical situation, trusting God to be at work fulfilling his purposes for them.*

29:1–4. As the Assyrian army approached Jerusalem (see chs. 36–39), the people continued life as usual with their annual religious **festivals** (see Exod. 23:14–17). Isaiah used the language of festival to pronounce **woe** on such activities and attitudes. **Ariel** is the top of the altar on which sacrifices were burned (Ezek. 43:15–16). Note the same word occurs at the end of verse 2, translated in the NIV as **altar hearth**. Jerusalem, the **city** taken by **David** (2 Sam. 5:7), could be compared only to the smoking altar, which did not burn itself but which caused everything around it to burn.

The city with the proud past and perverse present faced a fearful future filled with mourning. The enemy would soon surround her walls. The boastful people who thought God could never give his people into the hand of the enemy would hide themselves in the **ground** and pretend to be dead to escape the enemy. They would be so scared they could only speak **ghostlike** (see 19:3). The enemy's teeming hordes would make the outlook hopeless.

29:5–8. Suddenly, the prophet changed the mood. Beyond all expectations, in the midst of despair, God would intervene **in an instant**. But what would God do? God's coming is usually for judgment and punishment. The language of **windstorm** and **fire** sounds ominous. What would the **hordes of all the nations** do? They would vanish as a **dream** or **vision in the night**! A specific historical example has proved the teaching of the preceding section correct. God is free to respond to his people as he chooses. He can attack and punish his own people. He can also turn the tables on his agent of discipline. God's people must respect the freedom of God and act in a way that is appropriate to the situation and is consistent with the word of God.

E The Ruin of Religion by Rote (29:9–16)

Prophecy of disaster combined with woe oracle (701 B.C.)

SUPPORTING IDEA: *Neither human reason nor religious practices can help God's people escape divine judgment when they no longer have a personal relationship with him.*

29:9–12. In his call vision, Isaiah learned that his message would be ignored (6:9–10). He reacted by pleading for his people, "How long?" (6:11). Long years of ministry proved the truth of his first vision. In the crisis of 701 B.C., Judah's politicians refused to listen to God's word, electing instead to depend on Egypt and other allies in an attempt to gain independence from Assyria. Isaiah told them to go ahead and continue in their retreat from reality. The TEV puts it accurately and bluntly: "Go ahead and be stupid!" (v. 9). The hardening of the people's hearts was related to a specific historical situation and began with the stupid actions and attitudes of the people. This was followed by God's action. Instead of pouring out his spirit on the **prophets**, God poured out a **deep sleep**, so deep the prophets no longer had visions.

The people did not seek God's word from God's proper spokesman in God's proper time, so God would no longer provide even the opportunity to hear his word. The living word to the prophets was closed. The written word in God's book was also **sealed**, with no one able to open or read it.

29:13–16. The people had an entirely different picture of things. They continued going to **worship**, singing hymns, and saying prayers. The temple was flourishing. But they were doing only what the priest **taught** them! They did not know God through personal experience. They expected nothing from him. Religion had become routine rather than real. God promised to make it real. He would again **astound** them with **wonder upon wonder**. These miracles would not deliver Judah from political crisis. They would deliver the politicians from their burden of human **wisdom** that prevented them from seeking divine wisdom. Human **intelligence** would **vanish**.

Facing new wonders of God, the prophet again turned to his cry of **Woe**! Human wisdom had climbed upon the divine throne. Instead of asking God's advice, Judah's political counselors decided among themselves and then tried to **hide** their decision from God. They thought no one would know, so no one could blame them if their **plans** failed. They might fool men, but they could not hide from God. Their whole understanding was turned **upside down**. Mere creatures could not tell the Creator what to do. They could not claim greater wisdom or power than God, even though they tried.

F Holy Help for the Humble (29:17–24)
Promise of salvation (725 B.C. [?])

SUPPORTING IDEA: *God gives hope when his people quit mistreating the unfortunate, start listening to his word, recognize their own spiritual poverty, and give God all the honor and glory.*

29:17–24. Stupidity and stupor were not the prophet's final expectations. It may be that the coronation of Hezekiah brought new hope (cp. 11:1–9). Even nature would mirror the hope. The cedar forests of **Lebanon** would be transformed into dense forests of fruit trees. The **scroll** (see v. 11) would be open, and the **deaf** could **hear** it read. The **blind** (see v. 9) would see. God's wonders would once more heal instead of wound his people.

The people would have a new image. No longer would proud politicians get rich off the weakness of the poor. No longer would the legal processes of the **court** be turned to political and economic profit at the expense of the poor. In that day Yahweh would be the joy of the **humble** and the **needy**. When God's people accepted their identity as the poor ones who depended on God rather than on human wisdom, then he would remove their shame. The people then would react naturally by making the **name** of God **holy**. Israel at last would trust God and the word of God's true prophet. They would give glory to God for all his wonderful deeds rather than try to gain credit for their own political wisdom. This is the foundation of the opening statement of the Lord's Prayer. Such an attitude represents a total reversal of the situation in 29:13–16. The people would finally accept prophetic **instruction**.

G The Emptiness of Egyptian Embassies (30:1–7)

Woe oracle (701 B.C.)

> **SUPPORTING IDEA:** *Human alliances cannot help a people who will not trust God.*

30:1–5. Chapters 18–20 did not complete Isaiah's message about the Egyptian problem. Isaiah had more to say. In a society that placed supreme value on **children** obeying their parents (Deut. 21:18–20), Judah had rebelled against their Heavenly Father. The rebellion was clearly defined. They trusted in a political alliance with Egypt (**Egypt's shade**) rather than depending upon the word of God from his prophet. As always before, Egyptian aid proved too little too late. Pharaoh Shabaka of the Twenty-Fifth Dynasty gave no more help than any of Egypt's other pharaohs, even though he controlled both Upper and Lower Egypt. All Judah received was **shame** and **disgrace**.

Judah learned neither from her history nor her prophets. She continued to trust her political savvy. She continued to send political emissaries to the Egyptian cities of **Zoan** and **Hanes** seeking advice and military help. (For Zoan, see commentary on Isa. 19:11.) No one profited. **Hanes** was the home of the Twenty-Second Dynasty (about 935 to 735 B.C.) and was also known by the Greek name of Heracleopolis. It was sixty miles south of Cairo.

30:6–7. Egypt's help was **useless**, because Egypt was an **unprofitable nation**. Judah wasted all her effort and resources seeking to carry treasures through the wilderness to entice Egypt to help her. Ironically, it was through that wilderness that Israel had escaped from Egypt under Moses. Egypt was as helpless as **Rahab**, the chaos monster that Yahweh crushed and cut into pieces at the creation of the world (cp. Job 9:13; Ps. 87:4; Isa. 51:9). God has the power even when foreign allies do not.

H The Book That Brings Banishment (30:8–17)

Prophecy of disaster (701 B.C.)

> **SUPPORTING IDEA:** *A holy God takes his word away from an unholy people but preserves it so new generations may learn lessons that previous generations rejected.*

30:8–11. God had seen enough. He had done all he could to prevent Hezekiah from rebelling against Assyria. Nothing he did worked. Finally, he told

Isaiah to **write** his message down. Then coming generations could interpret the inevitable disaster in light of what God had done. God could not be blamed for the destruction that Judah had to suffer. God's people had rebelled not only against Assyria but against God as well. They were **unwilling to listen to the LORD's instruction.** God had sent **seers** and visionaries (the normal Hebrew word for **prophets** is consciously avoided). They had refused to listen. Their preachers entertained them with **pleasant things** and gave them hope, even deceitful hope (Hebrew word for **illusions** is literally *deceptions*). They did not want to hear of a **Holy** God, who demanded that his followers be a holy people (cp. ch. 6). The people found the kind of prophets they wanted (Isa. 9:15; Mic. 3:5–8), but the words of such prophets did not prove true. They could not pass the test of time (Jer. 28:9).

30:12–14. God spelled out their sin in concrete terms: they **rejected** Isaiah's **message**; they oppressed the poor and needy, **and depended on deceit** from their prophets and in their political dealings. The sin of the people was like a small crack in a wall, unnoticed at first, but one day **bulging** out and collapsing **suddenly.** The resulting destruction would be so complete that it could be compared only to a potter so angry with his work that he smashes it to bits and then grinds them into the ground so no usable piece remains. All is dust. In Isaiah's day, broken pots could be used as a tablet for messages or they could be used to stir the **coals** of a fire or to dip **water.** Judah's destruction would leave the nation so weak that it would be good for nothing.

30:15–17. Isaiah consistently called Judah to **trust** God in the most difficult political and military situations (cp. ch. 7). Judah consistently trusted her political alliances and her political savvy. Isaiah trusted in the God who had proved his military might in the exodus and the conquest. He called Judah to **repentance and rest** in this God who would give them **strength** for victory.

Judah wanted military cavalry like Egypt's and Assyria's. Isaiah countered with the claim that such troops could not be trusted in the moment of crisis. They would **flee** at the first sign of trouble and leave Judah defenseless.

Judah refused to listen to Isaiah's word. He had to write it in a book to remind future generations that God banished those who believed in their own power instead of in God's strength. Isaiah's hardened generation rejected him and God's word; a new generation would return to that word, hear its call to repent and trust, and would obey.

▐ Waiting to Wipe Away Weeping (30:18–26)

Promise of salvation for a future generation (about 695 B.C.)

SUPPORTING IDEA: *Weeping is not the last act for God's people, and destruction is not God's final word for them. In his grace God plans a new future for a people who will pray and obey.*

30:18–22. Drastic judgment was not God's final word. The prophet knew God's nature. He was just and **gracious** with **compassion** for his people. As **a God of justice**, he would restore the just order of the universe. This would come only after the guilty had been justly punished. God's people must become a people **who wait for him**. The time for lamentation over the destruction of the temple, such as appears in the Book of Lamentations, would pass. God is a God who hears the complaints of his people and will **answer** them with love and grace. Verse 19 provides all the reason necessary for God's people to **cry for help**, to pray to him in all honesty as well as in total confidence and expectation of his answer.

God punished his people to teach them the necessity of following him, but after the punishment God appeared again to direct his people along every step of life. Previously, they had mocked and rejected his teaching. Now they would listen to their **teachers**, the prophets. They would know both the Holy God and the holy **way** in which God was teaching them to **walk**.

This meant that God's people would respond to the gracious guidance of God by removing from their midst anything which would lure them away from God. The horrid nature of such things is shown in the Hebrew language, which describes them as **a menstrual cloth** and then by making a wordplay using a term which means both **Away with you** and "excrement" (see REB, *filth*). Valuable gold idols would be trashed, because God's people would finally realize such things are powerless.

30:23–26. God reacts to human obedience by showering his blessings. He promised that even the work animals would feast daily. Palestine, plagued constantly by drought, would see **water flow** from every **hill**. Such a paradise was tempered by the thought that not everyone would share in such blessings. The day of God's grace for his people would, at the same time, be a **day of great slaughter** for God's enemies. Those of his own people who were injured by God's punishment would find that God had become their great physician who bound up all their **wounds**. Weeping must come for God's disobedient people, but this cannot be God's last word to his world. God has a new word of deliverance and grace for a people who pray and obey.

Furious Festival of Fire (30:27–33)

Divine theophany (701 B.C.)

> **SUPPORTING IDEA:** *God's gracious deliverance brings judgment upon those whom he uses as agents to punish his people, but judgment may return if God's people do not learn their lesson.*

30:27–33. Judah had experienced the great catastrophe of Sennacherib's destructive march through all her cities (see chs. 36–39). Only Jerusalem remained. The prophet used traditional language to describe God's action in the moment of extreme crisis. The people thought God was **afar** off and had forgotten them, but God would come from his holy residence to punish the **nations** that were afflicting his people. God controlled the nations just as a farmer controlled his beast of burden. Yahweh would lead these unruly beasts in the wrong direction as they tried to harm his people.

Israel's lamentation would turn into a celebration of the **holy festival** (contrast 24:14–16). Joy and rejoicing would be the agenda of the day. Finally, in verse 31 we learn the cause of God's anger. **Assyria**, once the rod of God's anger (10:5), would now feel the brunt of his wrath.

The translation and interpretation of verses 32–33 are quite difficult. **Topheth** (v. 33) involves a wordplay on the "burning place" or "oven" (see TEV, NRSV, NAB). As a proper noun it indicates the place in the Valley of Hinnom south of Jerusalem where child sacrifice to pagan gods was practiced (2 Kgs. 23:10; 19:6,11–14). The reference to the king again involves a wordplay that promises judgment not only upon the **king** (Hb. *melech*) of Assyria but also upon Molech, the deity to whom child sacrifices were given.

Now, said the prophet, God has prepared the sacrificial fire for the enemy and will set it **ablaze** himself. The fiery visit of God has burned the enemy but brought festive celebration to the people of God. Yet the people of God must remember that God's action can be understood only as an action of his grace (v. 18) upon a people whom he has had to punish severely. The people of Jerusalem forgot this. So they eventually called forth God's judgment of 22:12–14 upon themselves.

K Human Helpers Humbled (31:1–3)

Woe oracle (701 B.C.)

> **SUPPORTING IDEA:** *God helps his people to victory when they depend on him, but he humbles them and their allies when they depend on military power and strategy rather than on God.*

31:1–3. Assyria responded to the rebellions of 701 B.C. by entering Syria-Palestine with all her military power. She defeated the Philistines, even when

Egypt tried to help by sending troops to Eltekeh. Then Assyria turned on Judah. In spite of Isaiah's warnings, Hezekiah and his political advisers continued to depend upon **Egypt**. In desperation, the prophet declared **woe** upon Egypt and those who sought help from her. He could not understand why God's leaders did not do the obvious thing and **seek help** from the **Holy One of Israel**. Certainly, the wisdom of King Hezekiah's counselors could not be compared to God's wisdom. Yet the king followed their foolishness rather than divine wisdom which the prophet proclaimed. Like Ahaz before him (ch. 7), Hezekiah could not believe and **trust** in God. The result was easy to predict. God would be faithful to his word of warning and defeat the plans of Hezekiah and his counselors.

The basic sin was a false perspective. Judah placed **the Egyptians** in the place of **God** as the one who was all-powerful. Egypt claimed that her pharaoh had divine powers. Isaiah claimed that only God had such powers. The outstretched divine **hand** still controlled Judah's security. God's **spirit** and not human or animal flesh controlled the world. The military power of Egypt and the wise counselors of Judah would perish together.

L Aid Against Assyria (31:4–9)

Promise of salvation (701 B.C.)

SUPPORTING IDEA: *No matter how his people act, God remains faithful to them and to his saving purposes as he calls them to repent.*

31:4–5. Isaiah warned against all alliances with other nations. He condemned the political actions of Jerusalem's rulers. Still, when everything appeared hopeless, he had yet another surprise for his audience. In spite of the faithlessness of the people of God, the Lord of Hosts would prove himself faithful to his people. He would protect their capital city. **Band of shepherds** is an appropriate wordplay, since kings were often called shepherds. God is pictured as a **lion** with his **prey** in his paws. The shepherds sought to scare him away from the prey. God remained strong and faithful to **Jerusalem** and would not forsake her. **Pass over** is a verb form from which the noun Passover comes, making a wordplay on God's death angel passing over Israel in the exodus and God's promised action for Jerusalem.

31:6–9. Such divine action should bring forth human repentance. Repentance, in turn, should express itself concretely in the destruction of false gods and thus the total dependence of the people upon Yahweh, the Lord of Hosts. Politically, this meant that the Divine Warrior would raise his **sword** to strike down **Assyria**. God had a **fire** ready in Jerusalem to sacrifice the enemy who would attack the city (see 30:33).

Ⓜ Renovating Royalty (32:1–8)

Messianic promise (700 B.C.)

> **SUPPORTING IDEA:** *In the worst of times, God continues to promise a way of salvation for his people through his righteous Messiah.*

32:1–2. The aged prophet looked back on a career filled with rejection. His high hopes for Hezekiah (see 9:2–7) lay broken in history. His country was in shambles; only the capital remained. Once more the prophet turned to God. Again a surprising word came forth. A new **king** remained the source of hope, one who would reign in **righteousness** (see "Deeper Discoveries"), who would surround himself with princely advisers whose joy was **justice**. A **storm**, whether military or natural, would pose no threat.

32:3–8. This king would set such an example that God's prophet would no longer face the deaf, blind audience among whom Isaiah had labored so long (see 6:10; 29:9–10). Society would no longer be turned upside down (v. 5; cp. 3:1–12). The land would no longer have foolish leaders who brought iniquity (see 31:2) and misinterpreted the word of God (see 30:9–11) while ignoring their social responsibilities and misusing their legal powers in the courtroom (see 29:21). The new king would be truly **noble** (which in Hebrew implies generous) in what he planned and in what he rose to defend.

Here is Isaiah's mature definition of kingship for Judah. Neither he nor his successors saw the ideal realized. In fact, Hezekiah's successor, Manasseh, proved to be just the opposite (2 Kgs. 21:1–16). In the fullness of time, God sent his Son to fill the role that the kings before him refused to fulfill. Even he had to call upon those who had ears to hear to listen. Yes, even the Messiah found the same deaf ears that confronted the prophet Isaiah.

Ⓝ Lazy Ladies, Lament! (32:9–14)

Call to lamentation (701 B.C.)

> **SUPPORTING IDEA:** *God expects his people to know the signs of the time. They should rejoice at the proper moment and weep at the proper moment as they observe what God is doing in his world.*

32:9–14. The prophet stood up as a teacher in front of his classroom and saw the girls acting silly. He called them to attention and warned them to take seriously the political situation of the day. It was no time for frivolity. Danger loomed. It was time to cry and mourn before God in hopes that he would not let disaster happen. **Complacent** and **feel secure** are not necessarily negative terms. The same Hebrew terms are used in verse 18 to refer to God's promise of a day when his people would live "in secure homes" and "in undisturbed places of rest." The basic meaning of the terms is "security" and "trust." The issue was the people's source of security and the time for trust. Jerusalem had come to the point of seeing her own political measures as the source of her security and "for ever" as the time for trust. The prophet had to teach the people that only God and his measures provided a source for security and that God brought his moment of discipline as well as the time for trust.

In little more than a year is an idiom whose meaning is not absolutely clear. It may mean simply wait until next year, "at the turn of the year" (REB), pointing ahead to the end of the **harvest** period when the new year was celebrated. The new year celebration would turn to mourning. Instead of harvest, the prophet predicted that God would bring destruction on a disobedient people. Only the beasts of the field would find **delight** in what would happen. God's people must learn that they have "a time to weep and a time to laugh; a time to mourn, and a time to dance" (Eccl. 3:4).

The Spirit Sows Salvation (32:15–20)

Promise of salvation (701 B.C.)

> **SUPPORTING IDEA:** *Peace, security, and trust can be achieved only when the Spirit of God rules to bring justice and righteousness.*

32:15–17. The chapter ends by reflecting back to the opening verses. It promises salvation after the gruesome destruction of Jerusalem. God's gracious activity can rebuild what people have torn down. This picture of salvation uses the language and images of verses 9–14 to show how God reverses things for his people. The passage also gives a climax to the hope expressed in chapters 9 and 11. Here is Isaiah's hope in a nutshell. Such hope began with the **Spirit** given by God. God was acting from **on high** to change the people below. God's act would change life in both the physical and ethical realms. Fertility destroyed by the enemy (v. 10) would be multiplied so that fruit trees would grow as close together in the uninhabitable **desert** as trees in the natural **forest**. The wilderness (a more appropriate description than desert for southern Judea), dominated by the law of the jungle, would be transformed into a human dwelling ruled by **justice** and **righteousness**.

When conditions of justice and righteousness prevail among people, **peace** comes. Here is the prophet's major point that must not be missed. Peace, security (life in **quietness**), and trust (or **confidence**) among people can be achieved only when the Spirit of God rules to bring justice and righteousness.

32:18–20. Only then will wars and rumors of wars cease. Only then can **My people** be "at ease in Zion" (Amos 6:1). The meaning of verse 19 is hidden from us because the Hebrew text has not been well-preserved (cp. KJV,

TEV, NRSV, REB). The REB reads, "it will be cool on the slopes of the forest then, and cities will lie peaceful in the plain," but this uses Arabic to find new, unique meanings for familiar Hebrew terms. The text may describe the opposite pole of God's salvation—his judgment on the enemy city. Or it may describe the destruction of all urban life with its complex confusion and temptation, leaving only the idyllic rural life where "every man will sit under his own vine and under his own fig tree, and no one will make them afraid" (Mic. 4:4). In light of this, verse 20 turns to congratulate those who proved to be part of the people of God by pronouncing a blessing upon them. Both man and beast would be able to carry out their normal activities anywhere they desired without any fear. Human powers and pacts cannot produce this peace. This comes only by God's Spirit.

Ⓟ Festival Against Foreign Foes (33:1–24)

Eschatological order of worship (695 B.C.)

SUPPORTING IDEA: *After all the terror and despair of God's punishment, he will bring in his kingdom. This will offer his people the perfect atmosphere for worship and praise rather than lamentation and complaint.*

33:1–6. As in chapters 12, 25, and 26, so here in this chapter the prophet provides an order of worship for the people of God who experience God's salvation. This section is remarkable for the fact that the people of God do not recognize immediately that they are experiencing divine salvation. The section begins with a woe oracle against the unnamed enemy (v. 1). This is followed by the proper response of the people in lamentation (vv. 2–9), a prophetic oracle announcing divine judgment, again on an unnamed enemy (vv. 10–13), and a list of the requirements for those who want to be on God's side (vv. 14–16). The chapter ends with the prophetic promise that God's people will experience the kingdom of God (vv. 17–24).

The **woe** oracle says it will be done unto you as you have done unto others. The proper response to such a warning is not gleeful celebration that the enemy has received what he deserves. Rather, the people of God should pray for divine grace and help in light of the international confusion. Everyone hated the ruling nation and its treacherous, destructive practices. Still, the enemy preserved some type of international order. The fall of the great world power could bring even worse chaos.

Every morning God's people must seek God's **strength** and **salvation**. His was the only **voice** that could gain immediate obedience and thus maintain order. The attacking nation, fleeing at God's voice, must leave its **plunder** behind. Those who were plundered now **swarm** over the plunder to recover it. Such promises call the people to worship and praise their **exalted** God. Kings have failed in the past to meet the prophet's and the LORD's expectations. Now God himself will **fill Zion with justice and righteousness**.

Verse 6 is filled with important terms for Isaiah, but the exact meaning of their combination remains unclear. A literal reading is: "He will be the faithfulness of your times, a treasure vault of salvations, wisdom, and knowledge. The fear of the LORD—that is his treasure" (author's translation). This apparently continues the praise of the previous verse and indicates that everything people need is available only through reverence and worship of God. But woe to those who seek their treasures elsewhere.

33:7–9. Even with such a picture of God, the people delved into further lamentation. The real-life situation was not like their hymn of praise. The translation and meaning of verse 7—especially the first word—is uncertain. **Brave men** or "heroes" is related in Hebrew to the "Ariel" of 29:1–2. Apparently the verse describes the political and military insecurity of the times, while verse 8 pictures the economic problems. Political **envoys** were unsuccessful; trade routes could not be traveled; and an economic **treaty** meant nothing. The Hebrew word for **treaty** or "covenant" may be used in a double sense to refer both to the economic agreements among nations or individuals and to the covenant of Israel with God. Everyone had lost respect for everyone else. Such turmoil in every sphere of life resulted in judgment even on the natural order, where fertility would fade.

Sharon is the fertile Plain of Sharon stretching thirty-two miles north and south and eleven miles east to west along the Mediterranean Sea from the Yarkon River north to the Tanninim River (cp. 1 Chr. 27:29; Isa. 35:2). The **Arabah** in its widest meaning refers to the geological rift which housed the Sea of Galilee, the Jordan River Valley, the Dead Sea, and the territory southward to the Gulf of Aqaba. In the larger picture the rift runs from Turkey to Mozambique. The reference in Isaiah, however, represents the more popular and narrower meaning of the very dry territory between the Dead Sea and the Gulf of Aqaba, a complete contrast to Sharon.

Bashan is the lush, fertile land east of the Jordan River and north of the Yarmuk River below Mount Hermon. **Carmel** is a fertile mountain range that juts into the Mediterranean Sea at the northern tip of the Plain of Sharon and the southern tip of the Jezreel Valley near modern Haifa (Song 7:5; Jer. 46:18; cp. Amos 1:2). The range is 13 miles long and 8 miles wide and varies from about 556 feet to 1800 feet above sea level.

33:10–12. God would not ignore the lament of his people. He promised to act. His actions came for one reason—to gain the proper exaltation and honor that he deserved. The enemies have no chance. All they can produce is useless **straw**. The threats they breathe out will come back on them, and they will self-destruct. They will not even receive proper burial, only a public burning of the corpses scattered on the battlefield.

33:13–16. God's people would get the message! War separated them, sending some far away. God called all to **hear** and respond. God acted so people would recognize him in action and acknowledge his **power**. Panic associated with the enemies of God in holy war would grip even the inhabitants of **Zion**. Even they would join the classification—**sinners**, **godless**. The latter means they are hypocrites who appear pious to the outward world but actually ignore God in their daily lives. The prophet showed such people the only way to act in the moment of God's judgment.

Fire and **burning** involve a wordplay on fire's role in the temple sacrifices and its role as an instrument in God's judgment on the world. To escape judgment and remain under God's protection, God's people had to remember what God required of anyone who would enter his temple to worship. The godly person does not participate in activities which result in cheating the poor, avoiding the proper processes of the court, injuring innocent people, or becoming involved in any type of **evil** plots or activities. To a godly person, God promised true security and provision.

33:17–19. For those who responded properly in the moment of crisis, the prophet offered a promise. They would **see** the divine **King** in all his royal splendor. He would rule a **land** that stretched far beyond the narrow confines of Israel under the Assyrian and Babylonian empires. The **terror** of foreign oppression and the agitation of paying out tribute to foreign rulers, who carefully controlled Israel's military defenses, would recede into the past, entering the mind only in moments of historical reflection. No longer would the rulers confuse and annoy them with their foreign language and unfamiliar customs.

33:20–24. In God's time the worshipers **look upon Zion** without seeing foreign officials. They could again enter Jerusalem with joy for the annual worship **festivals**. Never again would Israel have to worship in a movable sanctuary that might be destroyed or carried away by enemies. The people would not envy Egypt and her Nile River or Assyria and the mighty Euphrates River. God would provide all the beauty, comfort, convenience, and transportation they needed without opening the country up to a **mighty ship** from an enemy navy. Yes, God would be personally present, ruling over his people and delivering them from all enemies. They would no longer need to fear the whims and fancies of earthly kings, who refused to accept the kingly role defined by God and his prophets (see chs. 1; 11). The present might look like a huge ship unable to sail. But God would provide all the **plunder** and provisions they needed without ships to plunder the enemy or to carry goods from afar. Sickness would vanish and no longer be understood as the result of sin, because God would forgive the **sins** of the people.

MAIN IDEA REVIEW: *God will reveal his kingdom and his salvation to his people, but they must repent and trust him rather than trust in political alliances and military powers.*

III. CONCLUSION

God's Ultimatum

This long stretch of Isaiah's prophecies hammers home a few key issues. God is faithful. He is the sovereign ruler of the universe. He has plans to establish his kingdom and his messianic king on earth. But people are a different lot. We cannot be trusted. We are not faithful. We go off seeking the highest bid for our services or the lowest bid to bail us out of our problems. We vacillate between trusting and tricking people. God places an ultimatum before us. Trust him. Be faithful to him. Wait on his kingdom, or become like the foreign nations who face his absolute judgment. So what will we do? Repent or retreat? Trust God or be terrified of his judgment? He is King, Savior, Lawgiver, Hope. Are we on his side?

PRINCIPLES

- Salvation is God's proper work, but to accomplish it he has to do his work of judgment.
- God delivers his people after he has disciplined and judged them.
- God knows everything we think and do. It is futile to try to hide things from him and think we can evade judgment.
- God is trying to teach his people the way to walk each day.
- True safety and security come only from God.
- God's judgment will climax with a life free from evil and full of forgiveness.

APPLICATIONS

- Trust in God to bring you salvation.
- Become an agent of justice and righteousness in God's world.
- Cry out to God with your troubles, expecting him to hear and act.
- Study God's moral expectations and commit yourself to walk in his ways.

IV. LIFE APPLICATION

Angry and Hopeless

Once in my life I spent time in a pulpit speaking directly to one man. In the midst of my sermon in a small German Baptist church, a man swung open the back doors and staggered down the aisle yelling at me: "Don't talk about that Jehovah of yours. I have had enough of him. Look what he's done to me." One look or one sniff quickly let you know what he meant. This man from a Christian home and background now stumbled down the streets looking in trash cans for food and using any money he found or begged to satisfy his insatiable thirst. He was ashamed of himself, angry at people who made fun of his plight, and unable to find a way out of his misery. All he knew how to do was cry over his situation and yell at anyone who would listen about how bad he was being treated.

I tried to reason with the man, but in his condition, he was beyond reason. The deacons quietly escorted him out of the building and tried to find a way to help him.

Too many church people find themselves in that man's shoes. They come to church, hear the beautiful promises, and then go home and complain about the pain, poverty, and powerlessness of their lives. They see no way out. They have no hope. They are angry because others seem to have what they lack. The word of the Lord promises eventual hope for them.

V. PRAYER

Almighty and faithful Father, we have heard too many woes. We have lamented our plight long enough. Raise our eyes from earth's horrors to your kingdom. We trust you. We know you will bring your kingdom. O Lord, your kingdom come, your will be done on earth as it is in heaven. Amen.

VI. DEEPER DISCOVERIES

A. Word of the Lord (28:13)

Twelve times Isaiah says, "the LORD spoke." Ezekiel uses the same formula eighteen times. "Word of the Lord" occurs 242 times in the Old Testament, first coming to Abraham (Gen. 15:1) but mostly (225 times) appearing in the prophets. Ezekiel uses the term sixty times, and Jeremiah, fifty-two. Isaiah, however, uses the term only nine times. The word of the Lord is God's way of making his will known to his people.

God does not play games with his people, expecting them to obey commands they have never heard. God tells them precisely what his will for them is and then expects them to obey. Thus Isaiah can point to Moab and say with authority: "this is the word that the LORD spoke to Moab from that time" (16:13; author's translation). Isaiah can also use the word of the Lord in a sarcastic contest when mimicking false prophets (28:13) before announcing the authoritative word to them (28:14). Interestingly, *word of the Lord* seldom refers to the law of Exodus through Deuteronomy. Rather, it most often refers to a specific demand or promise presented to a specific audience by a prophet of God under specific historical conditions.

Thus the word of God is much more the revealed will of God for a person or people than it is the law of God. Isaiah did place the word of the Lord parallel to "the law of our God" (1:10) as he called Israel's leaders to repent and as he described God's promised time of salvation (2:3). Isaiah also used the term to refer to God's promise in response to Hezekiah's obedience (38:4). But the word of the Lord can also pronounce judgment on Hezekiah's disobedience (66:5).

This word is more than empty sounds. It is a personal force that creates change in the human heart and brings to pass what God desires. "It will not return to me empty, but will accomplish what I desire" (Isa. 55:11). Pharaoh's servants illustrated the correct response to the word of the Lord. They "feared the word of the LORD and hurried" to act (Exod. 9:20). At Sinai the people correctly answered, "We will do everything the LORD has said" (Exod. 19:8).

B. God's Grace (30:18–19)

Hebrew has a strong group of words that speak of God's goodness, love, mercy, compassion, and grace. One of these is *chanan* which means "to show favor to someone, to be gracious to them" (Gen. 33:5,11; Exod. 33:19; 2 Kgs. 13:23; Pss. 9:14; 26:11; 30:11; 41:5,11; 56:1; 59:5; 77:19; 102:13; 123:2–3; Isa. 27:11; 33:2; Amos 5:15). As can easily be seen from the list of passages in which it occurs, the term is at home in the psalms where people praise God for his grace and beg him to be gracious and show favor to them in their need. The meaning is seen in the use of the related noun *chen* in Genesis 6:8, where Noah found favor in God's eyes and so was not destroyed in the flood and in Genesis 19:19 where God shows Lot favor.

Such favor or grace is undeserved, unearned, and cannot be expected on demand. It comes freely from God because being gracious and favorable is part of his nature (Exod. 33:19). It is always possible, however, that God will not show favor (2 Sam. 15:25–26). Those who do find favor with God pray to know him better and find even more favor (Exod. 33:12–14). A sinful, defeated people still have hope because God is gracious (2 Kgs. 13:23; Isa. 30:18–19). The problem lies in a people who refuse to learn from God's grace

(Isa. 26:10). Still "the LORD longs to be gracious to you" (Isa. 30:18), and people longing for him pray, "Be gracious to us" (Isa. 33:2).

C. Righteousness (28:17)

The Hebrew term *tsedeqah* is a complex term that describes human relationships. It occurs 157 times in the Old Testament. Words related to the same stem or root bring the total to 523 occurrences, with *tsedeqah* occurring 36 times in Isaiah and the words related to the root 81 times. The term relates to the creation of an order in the community based on faithfulness and loyalty. The legal system is set up to restore order to the community, restore full rights to the innocent or righteous, and rid the community of the guilty and the effects that such guilt brings on the community (2 Sam. 15:4).

Righteousness goes beyond the legal system to include norms of what is righteous, moral behavior in the particular community. Righteousness thus involves a concept of society in which actions carry built-in consequences. The proper consequences must be carried out for the righteous order to prevail. When people, especially leaders, are not punished for actions that destroy the community's right order, then chaos breaks loose until the order is restored. The question is: Must both righteous and wicked be punished to restore that order? (Gen. 18:22–33).

When a person shows loyalty to the community, obeys the laws of the community, and lives a moral life according to the standards of the community, that person is righteous (Gen. 6:9). A righteous person does what is proper in a specific situation in contrast to the wicked who does the improper thing (1 Sam. 24:17). Such a person is recognized by God and rewarded accordingly (2 Sam. 22:21–25).

The ultimate standard of righteousness is God himself, because the Lord is a righteous person (Exod. 9:27; 2 Chr. 12:6; Neh. 9:8). He exhibits this righteousness by right actions—actions that are loyal and faithful to his relationship with his people. Interestingly, the Bible does not usually connect such right action to the covenant. Rather, it is the assumed personal relationship between God and worshiper. God recognizes a person's loyal action as appropriate and righteous (Deut. 6:25). Abraham's faith is recognized as such a loyal action (Gen. 15:6). Only the person recognized by God as righteous may enter his place of worship (Ps. 24:3–4). For such a person or nation of people, God does righteousness—he intervenes in their life to create the order and quality of life he wants them to have.

Isaiah speaks of righteousness more than any other prophet. "Isaiah insists on relating *tsdq* to the sphere of social justice and to the needs of the oppressed" (Reimer, NIDOTTE, 3, p. 765). For Isaiah justice and righteousness "encapsulate the idea of a social order solicitous for the rights of individuals, especially of the most vulnerable and marginal" (Blenkinsopp, AB,

p. 187). God's redemption of Israel and the world depends not on Israel's actions and loyalties, but ultimately on divine justice and righteousness (1:27; 59:16–17), a righteousness (or righteous order of peace) that "will never fail" (51:6,8). This is guaranteed by God's integrity, the "righteousness that went forth from my mouth" (45:23 author's translation), but is a threat to an unrighteous people (46:12–13).

God's righteousness had led to the destruction of his sinful people (10:22), since he expects his people to be righteous (48:18). By mistreating the poor, they had failed the test of righteousness and justice and destroyed God's order of peace and salvation (5:7,23; 48:1). The creator, king, and judge of all the earth will do right in the end, establishing the order of life that he desires, an order based on justice and righteousness (32:16–17; 45:8; 60:17). In such a new order, righteousness will prevail, while terror, tyranny, and fear will disappear (54:14,17). He will establish justice and righteousness through his Messiah (9:7; 62:1–2) so that faithful, loyal, righteous people will not endure the fire of judgment (33:14–15).

God's righteous acts that bring salvation come to those who recognize and repent of their sin and lack of righteousness (59:9,14). God will reveal his holiness through the right acts that he performs for his people (5:16). Meanwhile, as God's people wait for his righteous acts, they are to "maintain justice and do what is right" (56:1). But this must be true righteousness, not deeds done for the sake of appearances (57:12).

VII. TEACHING OUTLINE

A. INTRODUCTION

1. Lead Story: A Scar-Faced Savior

2. Context: Isaiah's picture of God's glorious future for his people (chs. 24–27) seems to form a fitting end for the book. What else could be said? The prophet had thirty-nine more chapters. God's word spelled out carefully who would participate in the final salvation and who would not. The kingdom is coming, but what must we do to be a part of it?

3. Transition: The long section embracing chapters 28–33 paints a radical portrait of reality. While talking theology exhilarates and excites, such discussions often are disconnected from the day-to-day decisions that determine everything about your future. What good are theological promises in a world of oppression, injustice, war, poverty, and death? Can you trust God's Word in such intimidating circumstances? Or is human reason and foolishness a better resource?

B. COMMENTARY
1. Doom for Ephraim's Drunkards (28:1–13)
2. A Stone for the Scoffers (28:14–22)
3. Facts from the Farmer (28:23–29)
4. Agony for Ariel (29:1–8)
5. The Ruin of Religion by Rote (29:9–16)
6. Holy Help for the Humble (29:17–24)
7. The Emptiness of Egyptian Embassies (30:1–7)
8. The Book That Brings Banishment (30:8–17)
9. Waiting to Wipe Away Weeping (30:18–26)
10. Furious Festival of Fire (30:27–33)
11. Human Helpers Humbled (31:1–3)
12. Aid Against Assyria (31:4–9)
13. Renovating Royalty (32:1–8)
14. Lazy Ladies, Lament! (32:9–14)
15. The Spirit Sows Salvation (32:15–20)
16. Festival Against Foreign Foes (33:1–24)

C. CONCLUSION: ANGRY AND HOPELESS
1. Wrap-up: God has promised his kingdom. He will act in his righteousness for a people who are loyal to him and thus righteous. People who trust in God's faithfulness must repent of their sins and trust God completely, refusing to trust in military or political resources that earth provides.
2. Personal Challenge: List all the alliances you are involved in. What trust factors are involved in each of those alliances—with doctors, mechanics, friends, community leaders, family, etc.? In what way do these trust alliances relate to your trust in and dependence on God? Do they prevent you from trusting God as fully as he wants you to? What can you do about it?

VIII. ISSUES FOR DISCUSSION
1. Why does Isaiah talk so much about a remnant or the rest of God's people? In what way is the church a remnant? Is there a remnant in the church?
2. What does the Bible teach about the use of alcoholic beverages? What is your own personal practice in regard to their use? Why?
3. In what concrete ways is the Word of God the authority for your life?
4. List the characteristics that make a person righteous.
5. In what way is your worship made up of rules taught by men (29:13)? What other sources give content and form to your worship?

Isaiah 34–35

In God's Time

"Within the movement of events is the Designer, who plans and arranges the times and the seasons, including the minutest detail of life."

Charles R. Swindoll

Isaiah 34–35

IN A NUTSHELL

God has a final day of judgment on the whole universe and especially on those who mistreat his people, but he comes to save his people and meet their needs.

In God's Time

I. INTRODUCTION

Judy's Wonderful Mother

*I*njustice prevails in so much of life. Convicted criminals seem to get preferential treatment and not suffer for their crimes. Some businessmen and politicians ignore all moral laws as they climb to the top of the heap. Bias and prejudice stall people from achieving success in their chosen fields simply because of color or gender.

Then there are people like Judy's wonderful mother. She greeted everyone with a smile. People received notes of encouragement from her just as their hopes seemed to melt. She worked her way down church halls and into friends' homes on her canes and crutches. For several decades we watched strength ebb from her body as crippling arthritis took control. We knew this was not fair. The wicked should get punished. People like this dear lady should enjoy life without suffering and grief. At least, that is the way things would happen if we ruled the world.

God has a longer view on things and works them out in his ways on his time schedules. Chapters 34–35 show the two sides of this issue. The evil people of the world will eventually get what is coming to them. The righteous will find redemption from life's troubles and enter the halls of eternal joy.

II. COMMENTARY

In God's Time

> **MAIN IDEA:** *God will heal all human hurts and restore justice to his world on his time schedule and in his ways.*

🄰 Call to Condemnation (34:1–17)

Oracle against foreign nation (695 B.C.)

> **SUPPORTING IDEA:** *God's Word promises that God is on schedule to restore justice to his world even if human eyes cannot discern what he is doing in history.*

34:1–4. Israel pictured Edom as her closest relation among the nations. Edom came from Israel's brother Esau (Gen. 25:30). Edom received special privileges from God (Deut. 2:4–5). Edom, identified with the hill country of Seir (Gen. 36:8–9), was Yahweh's mountain residence from which he came to help Israel (Judg. 5:4). Yet Israel continually battled Edom, from the wilderness wanderings onward. Judah's anger against Edom reached its height when Edom joined Babylonia in the conquest of Jerusalem (Obad. 11). Edom became the chief target of Judah's prophetic oracles against her enemies, becoming almost the symbol of God's anger and hatred. The chapter is filled with rare Hebrew words that often defy precise definition. Anyone studying this chapter should consult several translations. Isaiah 34 joins the chorus of condemnation by calling the **nations** of the world, the **earth**, and the **world** as witnesses to the Lord's oath against **all nations**. He will execute his anger. (For God's anger, see "Deeper Discoveries," ch. 12.) Edom's punishment would come as part of God's universal judgment upon his enemies, a punishment that would not even allow honorable burial for **their dead**. The judgment reaches into the heavenly bodies so that **stars** and **sky** disappear. Such language points beyond mere military victory over an enemy to the last days and final judgment. We must read chapters 34–35 as more than a temporary stage in human history. This is the final stage of God's eternal plan for his universe and his people.

34:5–8. The chapter pictures in gruesome detail the extent of God's wrath and judgment against his enemies. He is a warrior stained with **blood** marching forth to battle on his **day of vengeance**. (For the day of the Lord, see "Deeper Discoveries," chs. 13–14.) Having won the victories in the **heavens**, he comes to earth to deal with his enemies here. It is based on a theology of history stated in verse 8. God's control of history may not always be visible. His enemies may appear to have the upper hand. But God is on schedule. He will intervene to bring his opponents to justice. **Bozrah**, the capital of Edom, was located about twenty-seven miles north of Petra in the modern village of Buseirah (Gen. 36:33; Jer. 49:13,22). It served as a major transportation center with north-south and east-west routes crossing there.

34:9–17. In this case, justice is so complete that the land is left to the wild beasts, the **night creatures** (vv. 11–15). (For various understandings of the exact nature of these creatures, cp. KJV, NRSV, NIV, REB, NKJV, JPS, NASB.) The authority for such prophecy comes from its being part of the Bible, found in the **scroll of the LORD**. The prophet claimed authority for his own word and reminded readers that when the fulfillment came, they could come back to the book and check it out. God would do precisely what the prophet said. Here is another indication of the spoken prophetic word becoming written Scripture (30:8). The certainty of the prophecy is underlined (v. 17) by taking up the legal process of dividing property with the sacred lot (Josh. 18:6). This time the territory of Edom would be allotted to wild beasts rather than to people. God's **Spirit** would bring all this to pass.

B The Return of the Redeemed (35:1–10)

Prophecy of salvation (695 B.C.)

SUPPORTING IDEA: *God reveals his plan to redeem his holy people and his world and to heal all human weaknesses.*

This section gives the final prophetic sermon before the narratives of chapters 36–39. The sermon serves to prepare for the prophetic message of chapters 40–55, bridging the gap between the dark days of Judah's humiliation by Assyria and Babylonia and the hope for a new day after the return from captivity. The chapter shines even brighter against the dark background of chapter 34. It forms the climax of the hope for Judah given in chapters 1–39, and, in a way, summarizes the message of the Book of Isaiah as a whole.

35:1–2. Israel's hope includes the natural as well as the human order. Even the most barren **desert** or wilderness will **blossom** with flowers in the day of salvation (contrast 33:9). The only comparison for the newly budding wilderness would be the fertile plain of **Sharon** and the fruitful apex of Mount **Carmel**. The land can have its glory because God reveals his glory (Exod. 33:18–23). (For glory of God, see "Deeper Discoveries," chs. 6–8.)

35:3–7. The revelation of God's glory provided the background for a new prophetic commission (vv. 3–4; cp. ch. 6). If God could change the dry wasteland so radically, how much more he could do so for humanity! The prophet was called to encourage the weak and **feeble**. Their reason for fear would vanish. God would come in **vengeance**. The divine appearance would destroy the enemy (34:8) but bring salvation to the people of God. Such salvation is not limited to a spiritual realm. The sick and disabled would find all their reasons for having an inferiority complex destroyed.

35:8–10. The best was yet to come. God's people would no longer face isolation in a foreign land. God's purified people would pass over his **highway—the Way of Holiness**—and enter **Zion**. God would provide total safety for the joyous journey. Only the persons whom God had **redeemed** from captivity would be allowed on the road. Unholy **fools** cannot enter God's holy way. Life would become a festival of **singing** to Yahweh. Half of human life would be removed in the day of redemption, because **sorrow and sighing will flee away. Gladness and joy** will be **everlasting**.

MAIN IDEA REVIEW: *God will heal all human hurts and restore justice to his world on his time schedule and in his ways.*

III. CONCLUSION

A Long-Term Perspective

If we judged by things as they are in the present, we could claim that life is unfair and the world is ruled by injustice. But this is the short-term look. God provides a longer perspective. He promises that he has a time schedule by which he will restore justice and fairness to the world. The wicked will receive all the punishment they deserve. The righteous will have reason to sing and dance and celebrate with joy and gladness.

PRINCIPLES

- God will express his anger at sin in a universal judgment.
- God is on schedule to carry out his plan for the world.
- God does what he has recorded in his Word.
- God saves his people to reveal his glory.
- God expects his people to be holy.
- God's plan is to bring everlasting joy to his people.

APPLICATIONS

- Trust God to know your desperate plight and to have a plan to deliver you.
- Give your fears to God.
- Quit complaining about your weaknesses and feeling sorry for yourself.
- Praise God for every sign of his saving work in your life.

IV. LIFE APPLICATION

The True Source of Justice

Infuriating! That is the only word to describe life sometimes. Every time I visit my friend, frustration rises in my heart. A childhood bout with polio leaves her on two walking canes. She struggles to take every step. To watch her courageously lift one leg and then the other into her car and drive away is a lesson in persistent devotion to life and a reminder of how evil rules in the world. This happens on a larger scale. Both persons and nations who have committed crimes go unpunished. Some of them have the appearance of prosperity. Will justice ever prevail? The study of Isaiah 34–35 lets you put your true feelings on the table. Are you disappointed because you feel you have not been treated fairly? Do you think justice has not prevailed for you?

Do you have an enemy against whom you want to say, "Sic 'em, God"? Lay these feelings before God as you study these chapters. Let him show you the true source and hope for fairness and justice.

V. PRAYER

Loving Lord, I am so impatient. I want to see the world changed right now. I want justice done today, and I want to be able to define what justice is. Help me to trust you more and to know that you are a God of justice. Help me patiently wait for you to restore justice and fairness to the world on your timetable. I trust you. I love you. I repent of my impatience and my desire to see results now. Thank you for your promise to defeat the wicked and redeem your people. Amen.

VI. DEEPER DISCOVERIES

The Scroll of the Lord (34:16)

Scholars have filled pages of commentaries, journals, and notebooks trying to explain what this phrase means. John Oswalt says the phrase "is problematic because it is not clear to what book the author is referring" (Oswalt, p. 617). The earliest translators had trouble understanding the meaning. The Septuagint, the earliest Greek translation, reads, "By number they pass by and not one of them is destroyed."

Bible students have four solutions to the problem: (1) a reference back to Isaiah 13:21–22; (2) a later editor's stamp of authority on Isaiah's message; (3) God's heavenly book containing the roll of the people to be saved; (4) a reference for people to remember when the prophecy comes true.

The first solution would prove little except that the prophet can use the same figurative language twice. Nothing in chapter 34 would automatically make one refer back to chapter 13 except the trouble one has in interpreting this phrase. The second solution is the easy way out for those scholars who are always ready to use later editorial work as the solution to a problem they cannot easily solve from the prophet's own perspective. The heavenly book solution is immediately attractive except for the fact that Isaiah calls the reader to look in the book, something no human can do with regard to the heavenly records. Thus this must be another instance of the prophet staking his claim to authority on the power of God's Word even when that Word cannot be immediately verified.

The scroll of the Lord is a part if not all of the prophet's writings preserved for future generations to read. The message is that God is true to his promises and that they had better follow the prophet's advice, because it also comes from God himself. Thus the prophet turns his sermons into written form and hands them over to his disciples while God hides his timetable for fulfillment (8:16–17).

VII. TEACHING OUTLINE

A. INTRODUCTION
1. Lead Story: Judy's Wonderful Mother
2. Context: Isaiah has presented to his disciples God's call for repentance (chs. 1–11), a song of victory when God's day comes (ch. 12), promises of victory over the foreign nations with Israel and Judah included on the list of foreigners (chs. 13–23), a final apocalyptic hope with appropriate hymns of celebration (chs. 24–27), and finally strong prophetic oracles showing that military and political power do not suffice when God is the enemy (chs. 28–33). Isaiah summarizes this first section of his book in chapters 34–35 by dealing with the hot question of the day: Is God just? What proof do you have of his justice? When will we receive justice?
3. Transition: If we cannot trust in military and political power, where are we to turn for justice in an unjust world? All around us are evidences of injustice and lack of fairness. We could write a long list of examples and evidence in a few minutes. Isaiah 34–35 shows us the value of the list and the way to turn to find hope for justice in a world dominated by injustice.

B. COMMENTARY
1. Call to Condemnation (34:1–17)
2. The Return of the Redeemed (35:1–10)

C. CONCLUSION: THE TRUE SOURCE OF JUSTICE
1. Wrap-up: God will bring justice to this earth, but it comes according to his plan and on his timetable. We must trust him and wait to see how he will bring justice in situations we think are unfair.
2. Personal Challenge: List the top five complaints you make repeatedly about life. Lift each one to God in prayer, asking him to give you patience until he shows you his way of dealing with your problems.

VIII. ISSUES FOR DISCUSSION

1. Can people expect justice in this world? Why? Why not?
2. In what ways have you witnessed God bringing justice into your life?

3. Do you really want justice in life, or do you depend more heavily on grace? What is the difference?
4. Is it a true answer to a friend's problem when you tell him that God will bring justice in his way and on his time schedule?
5. How is God's vengeance connected to his plan for bringing justice?

Isaiah 36–39

Proof of the Power of Prayer and Prophecy

I. **INTRODUCTION**
Florence Nightingale

II. **COMMENTARY**
A verse-by-verse explanation of these chapters.

III. **CONCLUSION**
Our Prayers and God's Sovereignty
An overview of the principles and applications from these chapters.

IV. **LIFE APPLICATION**
In Life's Darkest Moment
Melding these chapters to life.

V. **PRAYER**
Tying these chapters to life with God.

VI. **DEEPER DISCOVERIES**
Historical, geographical, and grammatical enrichment of the commentary.

VII. **TEACHING OUTLINE**
Suggested step-by-step group study of these chapters.

VIII. **ISSUES FOR DISCUSSION**
Zeroing these chapters in on daily life.

"*A*doration of God, like the Law of God, acts as a mirror to show us the blemishes of our character and drive us to a posture of contrition."

R .   C .   S p r o u l

Isaiah 36–39

IN A NUTSHELL

*I*n a national and personal crisis, King Hezekiah had to choose whether to trust political allies like Egypt, the words of the representatives of the invading Assyrian army, or God. Prayer and trust in God brought deliverance from the enemy and healing from sickness, but reversion to politics-as-usual brought God's announcement of future judgment.

Proof of the Power of Prayer and Prophecy

I. INTRODUCTION

Florence Nightingale

*T*ough times either separate us from God or bring us closer to him. Florence Nightingale's family was wealthy, and she lived among the social elite of London, England. At age thirty-one, however, Florence wrote in her diary: "I see nothing that I desire today, other than death." This unhappy young lady then took inventory of her life. She found one thing she wanted. She wanted to be a nurse and to help people. Her parents disowned her for such a socially reprehensible undertaking. Her mother wrote, "We are two ducks, my husband and I, and we've given birth to a wild swan."

In spite of her mother's opinion, Florence's life took on a swan's beauty and grace as she volunteered as a nurse to help the wounded in the Crimean War. Her mother saw her as either possessed by demons or victim of a nervous breakdown. After three years of heroic war duty, she returned home with a dream for a new type of nursing care in a new type of hospital. A God-given dream and a consuming faith led a suicidal socialite to become the mother of modern nursing and health care (Schuller, pp. 178–179).

In a similar fashion, King Hezekiah of Judah found himself in an impossible situation. Death stared him in the eye in the person of Sennacherib, king of Assyria. People assumed Hezekiah would have to surrender and in so doing accept exile or death. Instead, Hezekiah went to the prophet Isaiah and then at his word to God in prayer. A transformed kingdom resulted, at least for a while.

II. COMMENTARY

Proof of the Power of Prayer and Prophecy

The last four chapters (36–39) of the first division of Isaiah's book repeat almost word for word the report of 2 Kings 18:13–20:19. A similar report appears in 2 Chronicles 32:1–31. Interestingly enough, we also have an Assyrian record of the events in the Annals of Sennacherib (translated in Pritchard, ed., *Ancient Near Eastern Texts Relating to the Old Testament*, 2nd ed., pp. 287–288; translated by Cogan, *The Context of Scripture*, vol. 2: *Monumental*

Inscriptions from the Biblical World, eds. Hallo, Younger, Leiden, pp. 202–203).

The fact that we have four accounts of the events—three of them in the Bible, and each different in its own way—should teach us something about the way we study the Bible. God's preservation of the three biblical accounts should underline the importance of these narratives. They deserve our close attention. The distinctiveness of the various accounts reminds us that each serves its own function and purpose within the Bible, so that we must examine the materials closely to determine what each of the narratives is trying to say in its own literary context. One helpful way of doing this is to look precisely at those points where the materials diverge from one another. Often, it is here that the perspective and purpose of the narrative can be found, because it is here that the author is underlining his own point of emphasis. Our task is to see what the narrative says in the context of the Book of Isaiah.

We learn from Sennacherib's report that he forced the king of Sidon to escape to Cyprus and set up a new "puppet king." Sennacherib received tribute from the kings of Byblos, Ashdod, Beth-Ammon, Moab, and Edom. He exiled the king of Ashkelon to Assyria, replacing him with a former king who paid tribute to Sennacherib. Ekron rebelled against their king, handing him over to Hezekiah and trusting Egypt to help them. Sennacherib faced the Ethiopian king of Egypt at Eltekeh and won, then restored the king of Ekron. He conquered forty-six cities of Judah and countless small villages, capturing over two hundred thousand people. He made Hezekiah "like a bird in a cage" in Jerusalem and then forced him to send heavy tribute to Nineveh, since Hezekiah's army had deserted.

The biblical account shows that Hezekiah surrendered to Sennacherib, paying heavy tribute (2 Kgs. 18:14–16), but it is more interested in other developments. The account in Isaiah contains only these other matters. This shows us its center of interest. It seeks to illustrate the authority and power of God and his prophet in the midst of extreme political crisis.

MAIN IDEA: *God displays his authority and power by protecting and delivering his loyal, praying leader in the face of disaster.*

Assyria Asserts Authority (36:1–22)

Historical narrative (701 B.C.)

SUPPORTING IDEA: *God's people must choose whom they trust: those with political and military power or the God who has promised to deliver them.*

36:1–3. The central theme of the narrative complex is that of authority. Thus the opening episode shows the Assyrian claim to total power in face of

King Hezekiah and his God, Yahweh. **In the fourteenth year of King Hezekiah's reign** would mean that Hezekiah began to reign in 715 B.C. This stands in some tension to the note in 1 Kings 18:1 which indicates that he began to reign in the third year of King Hoshea of Israel, which would be 729 or 728 B.C. It may be that Hezekiah was named crown prince or began to share royal duties with his father at the earlier date.

The **field commander** is called "Rabshakeh" in Hebrew, apparently a transliteration of the Akkadian term that means "chief cup-bearer." The exact duties of this officer are not known to us, but he was certainly one of the highest-ranking diplomats in the Assyrian court. The Assyrian official was a diplomat, not a military officer. The accompanying military force was to protect him, not to begin the battle against Jerusalem. The meeting place was where Isaiah confronted Ahaz earlier (7:3). Hezekiah sent his chief officials (ch. 22). This shows us that these opening verses represent a summary of all that Sennacherib did rather than the chronological starting point from which the remainder of the narrative follows.

Lachish would have been one of the first stops on Sennacherib's tour of destruction in Judah. Lachish is modern Tell ed-Duweir, a large thirty-acre site thirty miles southwest of Jerusalem and fifteen miles west of Hebron.

36:4–12. The central word of the narrative is "trust" or "faith" or "confidence" or "depend on," all translations of the same Hebrew word appearing in various forms eight times in 36:4–7,9; 37:10. Rabshakeh listed the various possibilities open to Hezekiah: (1) trust wise battle **strategy** in spite of lack of a powerful army (v. 5); (2) trust **Egypt**, in spite of the repeated proof that **Pharaoh** bites the **hand** that feeds him (v. 6); (3) trust Yahweh, your **God**, in spite of the fact that **Hezekiah** had destroyed all his **altars** (2 Kgs. 18:4)—an argument which would appeal to the people who loved to use the ancient worship places outside Jerusalem, even when God's messengers condemned such practices (v. 7).

In such a situation, the Assyrian was willing to supply weapons for Judah, because she did not even have the soldiers to use them. Sennacherib did not fear Yahweh, because he had a copy of a treaty with Hezekiah that was sworn in the name of the God of Israel as well as the gods of Assyria. Hezekiah had broken the treaty, so Assyria could claim to **march** against Jerusalem in the name of the God of the treaty (v. 10).

Assyria was not the only nation with protective soldiers. Judah's soldiers sat on the city **wall** protecting their envoys. The envoys were in such a delicate situation that they did not want the loyal soldiers to **understand** the bargaining process, so they pled for use of **Aramaic**, the official diplomatic language, rather than **Hebrew**, the local vernacular. This encouraged Rabshakeh to shout louder, including the soldiers in the conversations.

36:13–20. The soldiers faced a choice—**trust** King **Hezekiah** and his theological promises or trust **the king of Assyria** to provide food rather than starvation in the present moment and a permanent home just like this one in the exotic and powerful land of Assyria for the future. History proved that theological promises were empty, claimed Rabshakeh. Even **Samaria**, also a city of Yahweh, fell.

36:21–22. Hezekiah's messengers had been commissioned to listen, not talk, so they returned to their master, but in a state of mourning. Assyrian authority had been asserted, Hezekiah's and Yahweh's denied. The struggle over who to trust was on.

B A Ruler's Righteousness Rewarded (37:1–38)
Historical narrative (701 B.C.)

SUPPORTING IDEA: *People can trust the creator God to answer their prayers by fulfilling his promises to David and by protecting his own reputation, thus revealing that he is the only God.*

37:1–4. **King Hezekiah** joined the mourning rites, but he did so in the proper manner and place. He went to God's house with his complaints and sent to God's **prophet** for advice (contrast ch. 7). Hezekiah wanted God to take revenge on those who would dare to mock the true God. He recognized that he had already suffered great military losses against Sennacherib, so hope remained only for **the remnant that still survives**.

37:5–13. Isaiah replied with an oracle of salvation, telling Hezekiah not to trust or fear the blasphemer from **Assyria**. God already had a plan to defeat him and his forces. The triumphal procession of Sennacherib drew nearer, moving six miles north of Lachish to **Libnah**, apparently modern Tell el-Bornat. **Tirhakah** was not as undependable as the Assyrians thought. The Egyptian pharaoh came to help. (For historical problems in the narratives of Isaiah 36–39, see "Deeper Discoveries.")

Sennacherib tried to hurry the bargaining process. The Assyrian king took up another argument often used by his enemies: Yahweh would protect his capital city where his holy dwelling stood. The Assyrian king claimed that the evidence of history had proved this wrong. The question thus rested again on the element of trust: should one rely on God's history or on Sennacherib's history?

37:14–16. **Hezekiah** again displayed his trust in Yahweh. Again he went to the **temple** with the **letter** from the Assyrians and **spread it out before the** LORD. He based his trust on the theological confession of Yahweh as the universal Creator who continues to control creation. (For God the creator, see "Deeper Discoveries," chs. 40–41.) Hezekiah took seriously the Assyrian arguments, but he drew a sharp distinction between the gods that were the creations of human hands defeated by Assyria in the past and the Creator who held the world in his hands and who now confronted the Assyrians.

Hezekiah prayed to the LORD Almighty. (For Lord Almighty/Lord of Hosts, see "Deeper Discoveries," ch. 1.) He was the God of Israel, a divine title reaching clear back to Jacob and used in some of the key turning points in Israel's history (Gen. 33:20; Josh. 24:23; 2 Sam. 12:7; 1 Kgs 1:48; Isa. 21:10; 29:23; 37:16,21; 45:3,15; 52:12). He was "enthroned between the cherubim," a description of God based on the ark of the covenant (1 Sam. 4:4; 2 Kgs. 19:15; Ps. 80:1) where God met his people (Exod. 25:22).

This God had proved himself in Israel's history. Thus Hezekiah could claim against Sennacherib that Yahweh alone was **God over all the kingdoms of the earth**. Hezekiah made such a brash statement in what appeared to be the darkest moments of Israel's history when the world's leading military power stood before their gates and threatened to wipe them out.

37:17–20. On such a theological basis, Hezekiah cried to Yahweh to prove himself among the nations. Victory itself had a theological purpose, not just a selfish reason for the king alone. Sennahcerib's words were an **insult** to God himself. Sennacherib was right in one thing he reported. No other gods had been able to deliver their people from Sennacherib's attacks. God could prove his power by defeating Sennacherib. Then **all kingdoms on earth may know that you alone, O LORD, are God**.

37:21–29. God again used the prophet to communicate his response. **God** responded because **Hezekiah prayed** about the decision he faced. **Sennacherib** was pictured as a lover who was trying to court the young **virgin** Jerusalem, but the girl showed her spirit by refusing all advances. God rose to protect his daughter and rebuke the insolence of Sennacherib, who dared insult **the Holy One of Israel** (see "Deeper Discoveries," ch. 1).

Sennacherib listed all his mighty achievements in defeating the nations. But God, not Sennacherib, was in charge of human history. God had **planned** the course of events. Yes, even the victories of Assyria's king came because the God of Israel planned them. Sennacherib had no future in Judah. God told him to **return** to where he came from. Just as he had forced so many people into exile, so God would send him back home.

37:30–32. Isaiah had a message for Sennacherib as well as a word for **Hezekiah**. The Assyrian siege had destroyed the crops. God would provide enough food through what came up wild for two years. Then the normal agricultural activities could resume. This would be a symbol of growth for **Judah**, even though the nation appeared as dead as the farm crops. What grew was only a **remnant**, because God had punished Judah so that many of her people died in battle or were taken captive. (For survivors/remnant, see "Deeper Discoveries," chs. 2–4.) How could Hezekiah be sure God's promise would come true? God's jealous **zeal** would spur him to action. (For zeal of the Lord, see "Deeper Discoveries," chs. 9–11.)

37:33–35. Isaiah's message is summarized in these verses. Jerusalem would not see fighting. God would defend his city to protect his own reputation and to protect the promises he had made to David (2 Sam. 7). The Northern Kingdom was destroyed. Many in Judah would say that Sennacherib had a death grip on Judah. All appeared hopeless from a human standpoint. Still, God stood by his promise. He had to defend his own reputation, and he had to show that he was true to his promise that David would always have a king on the throne of his people. Yes, God would prove to Judah that he could be trusted.

37:36–38. God proved as good as his word. He attacked the Assyrian camp, forcing Sennacherib to give up on his siege and go back to Assyria with an army in disarray even though no human battle had been fought. Twenty years later in 681 B.C., a brief period in God's timetable, Sennacherib died in political revolt. Assyrian annals report that he was smashed over the head with the images of protective deities.

The divine name Nisroch is not known in any other ancient document. Ararat is known as Urartu in Assyrian records and centered in Lake Van in Armenia. Assyrian sources apparently refer to Adrammelech as Arda-Mulishi. Assyrian records that we have recovered do not refer to Sharezer, but the Assyrian form of the name would be Sharra Utsur, "may the god protect." (For historical problems in the narratives of Isaiah 36–39, see "Deeper Discoveries.")

Prayer, the Proper Prescription (38:1–22)

Historical narrative (701 B.C.)

SUPPORTING IDEA: *God maintains a personal relationship with his people by answering their prayers for deliverance and healing.*

38:1–3. The narrative shifts its attention from national welfare to the personal health of the king. The central issues remain trust and prayer. We learn how ancient Israel understood one part of the prophetic office and how it understood the prayer relationship between people and God. Here is the first time in the narrative (chs. 36–39) that **Isaiah** faced **Hezekiah** personally. The **prophet** had a stern prognosis: death. Hezekiah, however, found the proper prescription: prayer.

The content of Hezekiah's prayer is interesting. As so often in the psalms (Pss. 7; 26), a confession of innocence appears. The Israelite did not take his struggles sitting down. He was not ready immediately to accept the total blame for the situation. When he did not think he deserved the fate he received, he went straight to God with his complaint. Hezekiah did not show a self-righteous attitude. He engaged in bitter wrestling to understand the personal relationship with God. He wanted to know where he had gone so drastically wrong as to deserve the sentence of death. The experience caused Hezekiah to weep **bitterly**.

38:4–8. God **heard** such a sincere **prayer** marked with **tears** and sent his prophet back with a new **word**. Here we must note the understanding of prophecy that these verses show. The prophet had to contradict his earlier message. God remained free to respond to prayer even when it involved changing what he had previously proclaimed. Personal relationship with his people, not a predetermined divine plan, predominated for God. The prophet understood this and was willing to be God's instrument, even if his own reputation might be called into question as one who said first one thing, then another.

The prophetic promise answered not only the personal problem of the king, but it also extended hope to the nation. God underscored his determination to answer prayer by giving a spectacular **sign** to Hezekiah. The exact nature of the sign is hard to understand because the Hebrew text is not clear at this point (cp. several translations). A **stairway** of some type is probably meant. Such a stairway may have been used to keep track of time, or it may have been a simple staircase in which shadows appeared regularly. The important point is that God reversed the normal direction of the shadows. He did something humans could not do to show his presence in the situation.

38:9–20. Hezekiah prayed not only in time of trouble. He returned to God with a prayer of thanksgiving formed like many in the psalms (e.g., Pss. 9; 34; 118). This prayer does not appear in the account in 2 Kings 20 and is thus significant for understanding Isaiah's interpretation of these events. It puts further emphasis on the importance of prayer in the relationship between God and his people. Hezekiah revealed his inner emotions in the time of trouble (vv. 10–12), related how he turned to God (vv. 13–16), and concluded with his response of praise and thanksgiving to the mighty miracle (vv. 17–20).

The prayer reveals the Hebrew understanding of **death**—that the dead live in Sheol (v. 18; NIV, grave; for grave or Sheol, see "Deeper Discoveries," ch. 5). They could **not again** see the LORD or **mankind**. They were without **house** or work, and could no longer sing **praise** to God. They had no more **hope**. They were in **the pit of destruction**. Such an understanding shows how good the gospel of resurrection really is. The poem separates the final two verses from the position they occupied in 2 Kings 20:7–8, the Isaiah text underlining Hezekiah's righteousness by concluding with his desire to go to the **temple** to worship.

With all this experience of approaching death, Hezekiah could still confess that it was God who **restored me to health and let me live**, and that **it was for my benefit that I suffered such anguish**. Hezekiah also confessed that his **sin** was involved in his suffering and that healing came because God "tossed behind your back my sins" (author's translation). This phrase occurs nowhere else in the Hebrew Bible. The expression "to toss behind one's back" refers to the human sin of neglecting God or his law (1 Kgs. 14:9; Ezek. 23:35). Hezekiah knew that God had reversed human action, placing his sin where he often placed God. This was language of faith, trust, and prayer. The nature of Hezekiah's sin and his repentance is made clear in 2 Chronicles 32:25.

38:21–22. These verses are out of chronological order in Isaiah's account, while 2 Kings 20 places them after the parallel to Isaiah 38:6. Many interpreters try to explain this as the work of a later editor who tried to include in Isaiah all that was in Kings (see for instance the conservative commentary of Oswalt). However, it appears more likely that Isaiah reserved these verses for the end because he wanted to show the place of prayer in God's working with Hezekiah rather than to emphasize the manner in which God healed. He included this material of the Kings account as an integral part of the tradition but only after he had demonstrated how prayer was the central element in all that happened. The use of such an element as a **poultice of figs** in healing was secondary to the element of prayer. Healing came when Hezekiah prayed boldly and honestly.

🄓 Frightful Future Foreshadowed (39:1–8)

Historical narrative (701 B.C.)

> **SUPPORTING IDEA:** *Human pride and selfishness bring God's judgment even on those whom he has previously healed.*

39:1–2. The final narrative points back to the beginning of the oracles against the nations (ch. 13) and forward to the announcement of deliverance from Babylonian captivity in chapters 40–55. **Merodach-Baladan** was a Babylonian prince who rebelled against Assyria and gained independence that lasted from 721 until 710 B.C., when Sargon defeated him and took over the Babylonian throne for himself. Merodach-baladan was exiled but continued to stir up trouble, regaining his independence briefly in 703 B.C. In this latter period he sent his messengers to Jerusalem. They claimed they were coming on a political courtesy call to acknowledge Hezekiah's illness and give him a **gift**. But they actually came on a political mission to encourage Hezekiah to join in revolt against Assyria in the west, so that Assyria would have to fight on two fronts. **Hezekiah showed** the messengers all his resources that could be used in the revolt.

39:3–8. Isaiah was furious. He had attempted to persuade the kings of Judah that they had to lean on God, not on foreign alliances, for help against Assyria (see chs. 7–8). The **prophet** had ominous news. **Babylon** was the next major enemy for Judah. Judah's treasures would be **carried off** by Babylon, not Assyria. This refers to the first major defeat of Jerusalem in 597 B.C. (2 Kgs. 24:10–17).

Hezekiah's response surprises us. He told Isaiah that everything was well and **good**. Here the king reverted to selfish thinking. All he was concerned about was his **lifetime**. The prophet was concerned about Judah's entire history which rested on the king's trust in God rather than in their own welfare. Our narrative says that defeat in 597 B.C. and the final defeat in 586 B.C. had their origins in a king who became proud and selfish, ignoring the prophetic warning, and accepting prophetic judgment as long as it did not affect him personally. A righteous king could save Jerusalem (chs. 37–38), but a selfish king paved the way for its downfall (ch. 39).

On this note, the first section of the Book of Isaiah ends, preparing for the second, a word of hope in the hour of horror.

> **MAIN IDEA REVIEW:** *God displays his authority and power by protecting and delivering his loyal, praying leader in the face of disaster.*

III. CONCLUSION

Our Prayers and God's Sovereignty

Our prayer life shows our relationship with God. When troubled times come, the person of faith takes his personal and emotional thoughts and feelings to God. Faith calls on God to show what is happening and why. But faith acknowledges that all that is happening will fit into God's plan. Today's prayer for deliverance may be answered, but that does not set a pattern that God must follow. If we choose to revert to self-centered ways and attitudes, God's healing may revert to announcements of judgment.

PRINCIPLES

- Desperate situations call God's people to prayer.
- God wants the entire world to know he is the only God.
- God keeps his promises to his people.

APPLICATIONS

- Ignore worldly promises that guide you away from God.
- Pray to God for help when you see no hope.
- Ask God to help you understand the benefit you should see in your suffering.
- Ask God to deliver you from selfishness and give you commitment to his ways and plans.

IV. LIFE APPLICATION

In Life's Darkest Moment

Sheri Rose Shepherd, a former Mrs. United States, illustrates the importance of prayer for us in dramatic fashion. On a plane to a speaking engagement she shifted around until she found a comfortable position and nodded off in sleep. God would not let her sleep. He told her gently, "The man next to you has a daughter in trouble. Talk to him." Sheri refused, convincing herself she was making the voice up because "God doesn't speak to me in this way." Much like Samuel of old (1 Sam. 3), she heard the voice again and again.

Finally, she surrendered, telling God: "Okay, if this is really God nudging me, I am going to take a chance on totally humiliating myself and ask this perfect stranger about his daughter." She looked at the man and blurted out, "Excuse me, is your daughter in trouble?" A shocked look quickly gave way to sobs. Finally, he said, "How could you possibly know that? I have a daughter who is away at college, and she is in trouble. She was a virgin, and she was raped by one of her employers. Now she is pregnant."

Sheri responded, "The best thing I know to do, sir, is to pray. I don't know what I can say to lighten your burden. But I know that when I don't have words, God does." So they prayed for the daughter, the baby, the employer, the man, and his family. As soon as they left the plane, the man called home and told his wife they had to commit their lives to God, start praying for their daughter, and go back to church. Six months later the man told Sheri how prayer had changed the daughter's life. She did not have an abortion. She decided to put the baby up for adoption. She was going to church. So were the man and his wife. Prayer turned life's darkest moment into a pathway to God (adapted from Sheri Rose Shephard, *Life Is Not a Dress Rehearsal*).

Hezekiah found that true in the nation's darkest moment and in his own confrontation with death. You, too, can find that God has something to say to you and do for you, no matter how bleak life appears. He calls on you to trust him and talk to him honestly and openly about your darkness.

V. PRAYER

God, too often I pray only in moments of convenience. I treat you like a convenience store where I can get what I want whenever I want it. Teach me to pray. Teach me to take my darkest moments and turn them over to you. Help me trust you with my biggest problems and expect you to be there with your answer on your schedule. Amen.

VI. DEEPER DISCOVERIES

Historical Problems in the Narratives of Isaiah 36–39

Critical scholars raise many questions about the historicity of these chapters because of certain apparent anachronisms in the narrative.

The first of these concerns Tirhakah of Egypt in 37:9. Originally from Sudan, Tirhakah was part of the Twenty-Fifth Egyptian Dynasty and ruled from 690 to 664 B.C. He renewed Egyptian building efforts comparable only to building campaigns of 500 years earlier. He lived in Memphis, but spent capital funds on the worship centers of the god Amun at Thebes and Napata. He led military expeditions into Palestine from 683 to 680 B.C. and signed treaties with Tyre and Sidon. Eventually, he repelled Essarhaddon of Assyria's attack on Egypt in 674. But in 671 Essarhaddon caught Tirhakah by surprise and captured Memphis. Again in 666 Assyria under Ashurbanipal defeated Tirhakah. To all appearances, Tirhakah was not ruling Egypt in 701 when Sennacherib attacked Hezekiah.

Two solutions to this problem have been suggested. S. H. Widyapranawa (ITC, p. 241) represents the more critical approach: "In 701 he (Tirhakah) would have been too young to be commander of the Egyptian army. Presumably the narrator mixed up this campaign with another (unknown) military campaign by Egypt to oppose the Assyrian power in the south. Because he was the most famous pharaoh of the 25th Dynasty, Tirhakah's name may have been employed uncritically in this narrative."

John N. Oswalt argues that "the majority of modern commentators admit the possibility that Tirhaqah is here identified by a position which he held later in life" (NICOT, p. 649). He cites Kenneth A. Kitchen (*The Third Intermediate Period in Egypt,* pp. 154–172, 387–393). Walter Kaiser also cites Kitchen (*A History of Israel,* p. 381, n. 14) in concluding, "The claim that Tirhakah was a teenager in 701 B.C. rests on a miscalculation of the chronology of the Twenty-Fifth Dynasty of Egypt and stelae 4 and 5 from Kawa. Kenneth Kitchen has shown that Tirhakah was twenty or twenty-one in 701 B.C. and was able to be at the very least the 'titular head of the expedition,' who was probably called 'the Cushite king' in 2 Kings 19:9 in proleptic anticipation of his kingship that began in 690 B.C."

Neither side can prove their position here, for it is not a matter of evidence but of one's understanding of the nature of Scripture. Those who believe in Scripture as the trustworthy record of God's actions certainly expect that the Egyptian named led the army as they marched against the Assyrians. That the writer used a title or office familiar to his audience from a slightly later date is simply a way of keeping the record up-to-date and assuring that the original readers knew exactly who was intended. Similarly today we speak of President Truman or President Eisenhower for actions they took long before they became president and at a time when they no longer held the title of president.

The concluding verses of Isaiah 37 picture God coming in the person of his messenger or angel to defeat the Assyrian army, massacring 185,000 of them, without human effort on Israel's part. Many commentators have seen great problems here, even though the account sounds much like the great miracle of the Old Testament—the exodus account in Exodus 13–15.

Ronald Clements argues, for instance, against the historicity of the account because of the kind of faith it teaches: "We may argue that the belief that Isaiah did affirm such a remarkable degree of assurance and protection for Jerusalem in a moment of exceptional crisis raises as many problems as it solves. . . . It leaves us with an interpretation of Isaiah's message which cannot altogether escape the label of being 'Utopian' and unrealistic. . . . Little more than a century later, Jerusalem was twice, in just over a decade, faced with a threat from the Babylonians closely comparable to that posed earlier by Sennacherib. We know that on both occasions the city was ultimately forced into submission and no 'angel of Yahweh' appeared from the skies to kill off the attacking forces. It is also clear that the faith that is reflected in the narrative of Jerusalem's deliverance in 701, and such psalms as 46 and 48, may well have contributed in no little measure to the false expectations that Jerusalem would be secure from such defeat. . . . Even if we conclude, therefore, irrespective of how events actually turned out, that Isaiah had summoned Hezekiah and his kingdom to a bold and exceptional act of faith in defying Sennacherib in 701, would this not in the end lead us to a picture of Isaiah as an exceedingly dangerous and misleading kind of prophet? . . . It merely leaves us with the notion of a kind of ideal faith which can subdue kingdoms and defeat armies, but which is of so rare a kind as to be impossible for ordinary people. *Our knowledge of history and of the workings of divine providence shows us unmistakably that angels do not come from heaven to slay the enemy.*"

Thus Clements concludes that a tension exists between two kinds of faith: "the faith that finds its object in security and deliverance and the faith that recognises, and can embrace, tragedy and judgement. For those who ultimately see the centre of all biblical history in the death and crucifixion of the one who came as the deliverer of Israel there is no question as to which type of faith can penetrate to a more profound level of human existence" (Clements, *Isaiah and the Deliverance of Jerusalem,* pp. 25–27).

Over against this, John N. Oswalt contends: "Isaiah insists that the Assyrian monarch did not go home because he was satisfied with Hezekiah's surrender, or because his objective in the West had been reached, or because of some crisis elsewhere in the empire. He went home, says the prophet, because of the upshot of two issues: Sennarcherib had asserted that human glory was superior to God's, and that Hezekiah had dared to trust God. Because of these God intervened in natural events and decimated a significant number of the Assyrian army. Cut out this event as a historical fact, as all too many commentators wish to do, and the whole theological content of the passage falls to the ground. God did not deliver Hezekiah anymore than he did Menaham (2 Kgs. 15:19–20), and he did not punish Sennacherib any more than he did Tiglath-Pileser III. The unknown redactors have built a lofty theological edifice, insisting either innocently or fraudulently that it was true because it was historically validated. If we now asert that the validation is false, then the theology is equally false. Only if there was indeed a significant difference between the experience of Menahem and the experience of Hezekiah is there any satisfactory explanation for Isaiah's moving theology of God's sovereignty and his trustworthiness" (Oswalt, NICOT, pp. 668–669).

Brevard Childs makes the important point that this writing is "confessional history" in which "the confrontation is now posed completely as a theological contest. . . . God's action is portrayed apart from all natural causes, without reference to human agencies. . . . Sheer evil is smashed by the direct hand of God in the conventional idiom of the *malak YHWH,* his divine personification. God himself thus slew the enemy, and when the army awoke, there were a hundred eight-five thousand corpses around them. . . . [This] is a confession: God indeed brought victory to his people as he had promised." (author's italics; Childs, OTL, pp. 277–278).

One other point must be made against Clements. This is a contest between good and evil, not a contest between two kinds of faith. Faith leaves God free to act in each situation as God chooses. Faith does not preclude one course of action and limit God to bringing one type of result every time. Just because a people may have used one action of God to stereotype God and expect that same action every time does not mean that the first act of God was in some way wrong or that the type of faith it expected and it aroused was somehow false.

God promised judgment on a guilty people and fulfilled that promise. People of faith formed the remnant with whom God worked to bring future deliverance and salvation. In other instances God promised and delivered victory for his people, expecting them to sit quietly and wait for that victory. This is the tension in Isaiah's own message, the tension between when to repent in face of judgment and when to quietly believe in face of promises of victory. The Christ came and suffered, but the New Testament message is that the suffering itself was the prelude and the medium leading to victory.

Mention of Merodach-Baladan (39:1) leads to a question of the chronological order of Isaiah's narrative. If the Babylonians came in 701 or slightly later as the straightforward reading of chapters 36–39 would suggest, they would have found something much more important than Hezekiah's illness to discuss. They would have had to deal with the strength of Sennacherib, the tribute he forced Hezekiah to pay, and how to gain new resources for Judah. Instead, they focus strictly on the illness, and Hezekiah is able to show them storehouses full of treasures. This makes it likely that the events of chapter 39, and probably chapter 38 also, took place before those of the preceding two chapters. The narrative order is not determined by chronology but by historical theology.

Chapter 39 ends the Assyrian section of Isaiah's book and points forward to the Babylonian section beginning with chapter 40. Hezekiah may have escaped the Assyrian threat and not faced exile or death, but he did not end all threats to Israel forever. He was not the final Messiah bringing final victory for Israel. Instead, Hezekiah was a man of strong faith and strong political dreams. At times he let the dreams overcome the faith. The last story of his life in Isaiah's book emphasizes the latter to show the strength and danger a later generation would face not from Assyria but from Babylonia.

VII. TEACHING OUTLINE

A. INTRODUCTION

1. Lead Story: Florence Nightingale
2. Context: Chapters 36–39 complete the first major section of Isaiah's book that were devoted to the Assyrian crisis of Judah and Israel and their royal leaders. They underline again a major theme introduced in the first chapter of the book—the call to trust in God rather than in political alliances. Here we find Isaiah's strongest emphasis on prayer. A person who trusts God takes both good and bad times to God in prayer to find God's ways, God's plans, and God's timetable. The problem remains—the person of faith may also be a person of strong ego and personal dreams who forgets God at crucial moments and reverts to political maneuvering. This section shows how God can deliver his people in times of personal and international trouble, but also how God reacts when his faithful follower suddenly reverts to

worldly ways of dealing with crises. In so doing, the section points us beyond the Assyrian period of history to the one dominated by Babylonia.

3. Transition: What can we expect from God? Do prayers uttered in deep trust and expectation really make a difference? What happens when we neglect our prayer life and return to a worldly routine and outlook? This lesson leads us to deal with the depth of our trust in God and the need to commit ourselves to ongoing trust not interrupted by political maneuvering and trust in worldly powers rather than in God.

B. COMMENTARY

1. Assyria Asserts Authority (36:1–22)

2. A Ruler's Righteousness Rewarded (37:1–38)

3. Prayer, the Proper Prescription (38:1–22)

4. Frightful Future Foreshadowed (39:1–8)

C. CONCLUSION: IN LIFE'S DARKEST MOMENT

1. Wrap-up: God calls on his people, and especially on his leaders, to trust him in every situation, even the darkest ones, and to show that trust by open, honest prayer, committing oneself to God's ways, God's plans, and God's timetables.

2. Personal Challenge: Take the most serious problems you face and spread them out before God, honestly telling God how you feel about him, yourself, and your future. Ask him to give you a sign that he is working to solve your problems and meet your needs even if you cannot see evidence of him at work right now.

VIII. ISSUES FOR DISCUSSION

1. What do you expect to accomplish by praying to God in time of desperation and hopelessness?

2. How do you show God, the church, and the world that you trust fully in God?

3. What do you see in your future with God? Why?

Isaiah 40–41

The Comforter and Creator Comes to Court

Isaiah 40–41

Q u o t e

"*W*hen belief in God becomes difficult, the tendency is to turn away from Him; but in heaven's name to what?"

G . K . Chesterton

I N A N U T S H E L L

*J*udgment was not God's last word for his people. Having laid out the reason for judgment and exile, he came to them with a word of comfort, calling them to prepare to leave exile in Babylon, march with him on a highway through the wilderness back to Jerusalem. To convince them to make the journey, he set up a court trial against the gods of Babylon and showed they were false, mere creations of human craftsmen, unable to predict anything about history or do anything in history. The true God announced the coming of Cyrus to defeat Babylonia and send exiled Judah home.

The Comforter and
Creator Comes to Court

I. INTRODUCTION

What Does History Prove?

*D*avid Hume, the Scottish skeptic, defended his skepticism quite dramatically. He wrote: "Were a stranger to drop suddenly into this world, I would show him a specimen of its ills—a hospital full of diseases, a prison crowded with malefactors and debtors, a field strewn with carcasses, a fleet floundering in the ocean, a nation languishing under tyranny, famine, or pestilence. Honestly, I don't see how you can possibly square [that] with an ultimate purpose of love" (quoted by Zacharias, p. 63).

Israel stood on Hume's side. Jerusalem was destroyed. The majority of the Jewish population lived in exile in Babylon. Yahweh, the God of Israel, appeared to have gone down to defeat by the Babylonian army and their gods. What hope did Jews have? Time to forget God and get on with life the best they could. But God was not finished. He had a message for exiled Babylon, a message from the prophet of old. This message featured a courtroom confrontation between Yahweh of Israel and the images of Babylon. Who was the true God? Yahweh set the agenda—show what you are doing in history and what is going to happen in history. Or at least show that you control history because you created the universe. Babylon's gods remained silent. They had no power of speech, much less power to control history.

You can list with David Hume the problems you face and the insurmountable difficulties that blight your life. You need a word from God to show that he is still your God and that he will lead you to a new life with new hope. This lesson should help you learn to wait in hope for God the comforter.

II. COMMENTARY

The Comforter and Creator Comes to Court

The historical focus changes dramatically with chapter 40. We begin to breathe the air of 545 B.C. Cyrus of Persia occupies center stage politically (41:2; 45:1,13; 48:14–15). Israel was living in Babylon, not Jerusalem (42:24; 47:1). The prophet's declarations of disaster disappear. Only hope from heaven appears. The whole section is a call of comfort to the captives, joined with arguments trying to convince them to accept the comfort that God has offered. The prophet had spent the first thirty-nine chapters of the book preparing for life in Babylonian exile. Now he turned the corner to show the way of escape from such exile. Unlike many of the oracles in chapters 1–39, these messages of hope and comfort do not give us clues about the time and place where the prophet delivered them.

> **MAIN IDEA:** *Israel's Shepherd, the only God and Creator, cares for, comforts, and acts to save his people.*

The Call to Comfort (40:1–11)
Military chain of command

> **SUPPORTING IDEA:** *The divine Shepherd reveals his glory by fulfilling the promises of his eternal word and comforting his people.*

Isaiah's call to condemn his people appears in chapter 6. By contrast, chapter 40 is a call to **comfort**. This call appears like a military order passed through the troops, occurring in four stages:

1. The command apparently began in the heavenly council (see ch. 6) with a call to its members to go to the aid of **my people**. As in chapter 6, so here, the prophet was present in the council.
2. The prophet reported to the people in verse 3, relaying the call to action from **our God**.
3. The prophet continued to report in verse 6, but then realized that the new command was no longer in the plural to the people but in the singular, addressing him personally. He reacted with a question, expressing his inability to fulfill the assignment, as occurred so frequently in the prophetic experiences (6:5). His complaint received a blunt answer (v. 8).
4. The prophet relayed the message to **Jerusalem**—that is, to the people of Judah now in exile in Babylon but claiming Jerusalem as their hometown. Jerusalem was to become an army messenger bringing the news of victory back to the **towns of Judah** (v. 9).

40:1–2. The prophetic task has changed from the hardening of God's people (ch. 6) to comforting them. Such comfort was God's reaction to the lamentations of his people, who had cried that they had no comforter (Lam. 2:13). Human strength could provide no comfort. The people were reminded that **your God**—not Babylon's god, but Yahweh, the God of Israel—could provide comfort. The content of such comfort became clear. Her "period of service" (NJB), **hard service** (NIV), "warfare" (NASB), "term of bondage" (REB) had ended. The captivity in Babylon was interpreted as work that a prisoner of war had to do for his captor. God announced unexpectedly that the prisoner had been pardoned. Outwardly, Judah appeared to be a captive of

Babylonia because she was the weaker party militarily. Seen from a higher perspective, she was Yahweh's prisoner because she had sinned against him.

Yahweh was ready to release Judah. Babylonia was not. Yahweh proclaimed that Judah had taken **double** punishment from the hand of Yahweh. This was in line with the Israelite law that required reimbursement plus payment for damages in certain crimes (Exod. 22:1,7,9).

40:3–5. As Israel first experienced salvation by escape into the **wilderness**, God planned a new wilderness experience. To prepare for this, he called for a **highway** to be built. This imitated Babylonian practices in which a highway was built for the great religious festivals so the images of the gods could be paraded before the people. Yahweh's highway was not to show off his beautiful artwork and clothing. It was to deliver his people in a moment of historical crisis. Such a highway was to be **level** so God's people would have no trouble crossing it as they followed their God to freedom. This historical act would reveal the true **glory** of God to the entire world, because God would accomplish what Babylonia was not ready to do. (For glory of God, see "Deeper Discoveries," chs. 6–8.)

God would show his historical power over the majestic kingdom of Babylonia. Such news seemed unbelievable to a people so far from home. The prophet said it was certain to happen, because its source was God himself.

40:6–9. Even with such assurance, Isaiah was taken by surprise. He sounded the common complaint of his people. Humanity had lost its meaning, being no more significant than **grass**, which springs up only to be mowed down. The sense of the Hebrew of verse 6 is not conveyed by "beauty" (NLT, NJB) or "constancy" (NRSV) or **glory** (NIV) or "goodliness" (KJV), or "loveliness" (NKJV, NASB), but no other English word is better. The original expression (Hb. *chesed*) is often used for the grace or steadfast love of God to human beings (e.g., Exod. 20:6) and of the devotion people should show to God and to one another (Hos. 2:19; 6:4). In this text, the term apparently indicates all the grace and graces of humanity. It is that for which people may be trusted and relied upon. God's **breath** (which could also be translated "wind" or "spirit") had destroyed all that humanity had to offer. So the prophet complained, Why preach to people whose reactions are meaningless?

God answered! Comfort comes not from mankind but from God. His **word** is reliable, and he promised comfort. The prophet finally fulfilled his mission, calling upon Jerusalem to take up her **high mountain** watchpost and relay the news of victory. Victory was won because **Here is your God**. The coming of God is the content of comfort!

40:10–11. God is coming with **power**. No one can stand against **his arm**. He comes not in vengeance (34:8) but with a reward for his people, probably reflecting the practice of bringing spoils of war and tribute back to the people.

Israel does not have to rely on their military trophies. God brings all they need. But he comes to his people not as a military warrior but as a caring shepherd, often an image for a king. He knows those with special needs and treats them as a new mother and her baby. He **gathers the lambs in his arms and carries them close to his heart; he gently leads those that have young.** This is the comfort we need.

B The Creator Comes to Comfort (40:12–31)

Legal dispute

> **SUPPORTING IDEA:** *The holy, eternal Creator is the one, unique God who brings renewed strength to his people.*

40:12–17. The prophet took his audience to court and brought legal arguments to prove the incomparable nature of the God of Israel over against the claims of all other gods, especially those of Babylonia. Only the Creator knows the earth's measurements. His Spirit (NIV translates **mind** but Hebrew is clearly "Spirit"), not the **counselor** of the Babylonian king, has all wisdom and **knowledge.** In his measuring **scales,** the heavyweights among the **nations** weigh no more than the **dust** that collects on scales. He deserves sacrifices and offerings beyond measure. The famous forests and grazing hills of Lebanon could not provide enough firewood or enough sacrificial animals to give God what he deserves.

40:18–26. Isaiah declared that **God** is beyond **compare.** The other gods are images, only creations of human hands; they did not create the universe. Exactly how Isaiah described this is questionable, since the Hebrew text of 19b–20a is almost impossible to read. The main concern of the builder of an idol is not whether it is a god who can deliver on promises but whether the image will **topple.** The god does not have power even to stand on his own two feet.

News about God's power is not new. It has been available **since the earth was founded.** Earthly **rulers** and kings are **grasshoppers** when viewed from God's heavenly throne. They are weak plants which God's **whirlwind** blows away. Yes, he is beyond **compare.** He has no **equal.** God is so powerful that he created the **hosts** of heaven and so intelligent that he knows **each by name.** (For God the creator, see "Deeper Discoveries.")

40:27–31. The prophet addressed Judah with a series of questions that showed them the weakness of their faith and the ridiculous nature of their complaints—complaints which he himself had shared (v. 6). The **Creator** who knew the names of all the stars certainly knew the problems of his own chosen people. He would certainly give **strength** to his people even in a time so trying that the youngest and strongest warriors were totally exhausted.

Winning international conflicts by political and military means led to total exhaustion and the need to fight again. Escape from exhaustion comes only from God.

Those who place their **hope in the LORD** find new strength they did not know they had. They will be able to soar like eagles to new heights of achievement. They will be able to run the race and have energy left to run again. They can walk through the toughest situations without giving up or fainting. This was the comfort the Creator conceived for his confused and concerned creatures. The way was opening for Israel to run home to her fatherland and to her Father. God would build the highway, lead the way, and give strength to endure on the way.

Conquerors Called to Court (41:1–7)

Concluding legal summary

> **SUPPORTING IDEA:** *The eternal God proves his power through surprising acts in history.*

41:1–4. The prophet pictured God addressing the international court-room and summarizing his case against the foreign gods. Afterwards, the **nations** would have a chance to summarize their case. God pointed to history and asked, Who is responsible for the unexpected victories of Cyrus, the ruler **from the east**? God did it, and did it in **righteousness**—in a way that would establish justice among the nations and show the steadfast dedication of God to be fair and just to all peoples. The description probably points to Cyrus's victories over the Medes and Lydians.

To answer the question of verses 2–3, God raised another question (v. 4a): **Who has** always **done this**? Who has directed history from the beginning? The answer is blunt: Yahweh, who was there directing the **first** act of history (Gen. 1–3) and who will be there directing the **last** act of history (see Revelation). The God of Israel had proved through his surprising historical actions that he and only he is God, the world's Creator and history's director.

41:5–7. The **islands** called to prepare their case in verse 1 could not respond. They simply trembled in **fear** and tried to encourage their neighbor. They had **come forward** as told to do in verse 1, but that was all they could do. With ironic genius, the prophet pictured the reaction of the craftsmen who made the idols. They told one another how good their work was, so good it could sit on its pedestal without falling. The idol makers had lost both their religion and their business. This, too, was comfort for God's people.

The Savior Soothes His Servant (41:8–20)

Oracle of salvation

SUPPORTING IDEA: *The holy Redeemer shows his care for his chosen servant people through his work in nature.*

41:8–10. The prophet moved from courtroom to temple to announce salvation for his people. He began by using **Abraham** to remind God's people of all that God had done for them—a surprisingly rare reference to the patriarch in prophecy. The purpose was to show Israel that she was defined by God's acts and purposes, not by her own power and accomplishments. Israel was the servant of God. (For the servant of Yahweh, see "Deeper Discoveries," chs. 52–53.) This expression includes two meanings. First, Israel was the political vassal who served King Yahweh and was dependent upon him for all her political power. Second, Israel in her laments to Yahweh had confessed his authority by referring to itself as servant of the divine Master. In Isaiah 40–66 *servant* becomes a major theological theme. Israel was servant of God because God chose her. (For God chooses, and we are free, see "Deeper Discoveries," chs. 45–46.) God sought in love one people from among all the nations to worship him and him alone. The destruction of Jerusalem in 587 B.C. did not cancel God's election, but rather confirmed that election included responsibility and mission. God had not **rejected** his people. He had simply renewed and reaffirmed their mission for him.

God's choice involved seeking Abraham in the eastern end **of the earth** and later bringing Israel up from Egypt in the western end. Finally, God returned to Babylonia and to Egypt to bring the exiles back to the place he had chosen for them. The word of election was thus a word of comfort and not a reason for **fear**. In spite of all the odd twists of history and personal experience, God is still **with you**. He is still **your God** (40:1). He knew their weakness. He would **strengthen** them because he still held them with his **righteous right hand**.

41:11–16. God's choice of Israel resulted not only in help and victory for Israel but also in destruction and shame for her enemies. God's help would enable Israel to overcome all obstacles in her path back to her land (40:3–4). The purpose was that Israel might quit complaining and lamenting and return to **rejoice** in the great acts God accomplished for her.

41:17–20. God would provide all the needs on the way. As he had provided quail and manna on the road through the wilderness from Egypt under Moses, so he would bring water and food for the journey through the wilderness from Babylon. God would never **forsake them** on the way. Again, God had a purpose in this. He wanted people to know that he was still active in history. The defeat of Jerusalem was not the end of the line for the Holy One of Israel (see "Deeper Discoveries," ch. 1). God's saving work for Israel was his testimony of his power to the nations.

Ⓔ Indictment Against Idols (41:21–29)
Courtroom trial

SUPPORTING IDEA: *God alone can predict history because all other gods are weak and helpless.*

41:21–24. God called the gods of Babylonia to court (40:12–31) to **present your case**. Man-made images had to face **Jacob's King**—that is, the One who had ruled Israel since the days of the great patriarch. One issue was decisive: Who could predict history and carry out the predictions? The gods could not **tell us what is going to happen**. They could not even describe past happenings and point to their **final outcome**. They could do nothing at all, good or bad, and so were proved to be nothing. A god's actions should fill mere mortals with awe and **fear**. But these gods' inactivity brought disgust on themselves and on all who worshiped them.

41:25–29. The contrast between these inactive gods and Yahweh is striking. Yahweh had called Cyrus, **one from the north**, to take over world rule. The Hebrew text of verses 25–27 has not been well preserved, so the precise meaning and translation is often difficult. The Dead Sea Scrolls in verse 25 read, "He called by his name," which may mean that God called Cyrus by name (45:1). In verse 26 God continued to question the gods without success. Yahweh had spoken the **first** word to **Jerusalem** through his **messenger of good tidings** (cp. 40:9). No other god had an **answer** for Yahweh's cross examination. In fact, they could not even say one word. The court decision was clear. Only Yahweh stood the test. The gods were **false**—created images, just a bunch of hot air doing **nothing**. Yahweh alone directed and interpreted world history. Thus Yahweh alone is God. Yahweh alone deserves our worship.

MAIN IDEA REVIEW: *Israel's Shepherd, the only God and Creator, cares for, comforts, and acts to save his people.*

III. CONCLUSION

The God of Comfort

Darkness enters every person's life. We see no way out of the situation we face. God seems a distant reality from another lifetime with no connection to what is happening now. When that time comes, Isaiah has a word for all of us. God is more than one who brings punishment and judgment. He is also the one who brings comfort and shepherds you through the valley of the shadow of death. You have no reason to fear evil, because in the darkest moments God is still your God and is still with you. Trust in your Comforter to shepherd your life, but allow him to do it in the way he chooses.

PRINCIPLES

- God does not punish a person too harshly for his sins.
- God controls the destiny of all peoples and nations.
- God can use any person he chooses to accomplish his purposes.
- God alone can know the future, since he alone controls history.

APPLICATIONS

- Trust God's promise to save you even when you are suffering.
- When you are tired of doing good, ask God for strength to continue serving him.
- Turn every fear you have over to God.

IV. LIFE APPLICATION

Searching for Love

Little Kathy came to the home for homeless kids dressed in dirty rags. She brought only one possession with her—an old aluminum paint can. She never let the can go. Queries about the can's contents brought a brief shrug and "can't tell you today" answer. Often, she sat alone in a dorm room, hugging the can to her chest, sometimes talking to it. One day a counselor invited Kathy to eat breakfast with her. They talked together over the roar of 150 homeless kids eating breakfast in the dining hall. Finally, the counselor drew up her courage and said to Kathy: "That's a really nice can. What's in it?"

Seconds passed. Then minutes of silence. Tears welled in Kathy's eyes. At last she spoke. "It's my mother. I went and got her ashes from the funeral home." Hugging the can closer, she continued, "I never really knew my mother. She threw me in the garbage two days after I was born. I moved from one foster home to another, madder and madder at my mother. Then I decided to find her. I was lucky. Someone told me where she lived. But she was not there. She was in the hospital, dying from AIDS. I got to meet her the day before she died. She said, 'I love you!' My mother said she loved me."

Israel was much like Kathy, searching for someone to love them. They considered themselves a hopeless case with a God who had forsaken them and lost the battle to a stronger god. Then they heard God's message: "I love you, am preparing a future for you, and will shepherd you home." Israel could hardly believe it, much as Kathy could hardly believe her ears when her mother said, "I love you" (adapted from Zacharias, pp. 165–167). Are you looking for that someone to love you? Has life cast you to and fro? Listen. God has a word for you. He still loves you and wants to bring love, comfort, hope, and salvation to your life. Will you listen to him and follow where he leads?

V. PRAYER

Shepherd of life, speak to me. In the darkness of my loneliness and loss, I have somehow lost contact with you. I sometimes wonder if you really exist. Give me your word of hope and comfort in a way so clear that I know it comes from you. Show me the highway you have for me to travel. Help me trust and follow you in ways I have never done before. Amen.

VI. DEEPER DISCOVERIES

God the Creator

More than any other prophet, Isaiah speaks of God's creative acts. He uses many types of language to describe God as the Creator or Maker of the universe and its people. He uses creation language, however, not to teach creation, per se, but to show the greatness of God in comparison to other gods and to remind Israel of God's power to perform his promises.

- As Creator, God makes things (Hb. *'asah*) (see Gen. 2:4; 2 Kgs. 19:15; Job 4:17; 35:10; Pss. 104:19; 118:24; 124:8; 136:7–9; Isa. 22:11; 44:24; 66:22; Jer. 27:5; Hos. 8:14; Jon. 1:9).
- He forms things like a potter (Hb. *yatsar*) (see 2 Kgs. 19:25; Pss. 33:15; 74:17; 104:26; Isa. 22:11; 37:26; 44:2,21,24; 46:11; Jer. 1:5; 18:11; 51:19; Amos 4:13).
- He buys or acquires things by creating them (Hb. *qanah*) (see Gen. 4:1; Deut. 32:6; Pss. 74:2; 104:24; Prov. 8:22; Isa. 11:11; Mal. 2:10).
- God stretches things out to bring them into being (Hb. *natah*) (see Job 9:8; Isa. 40:22; 44:24; 51:13; Jer. 10:12; Zech. 12:1).
- God spreads out something to create it (Hb. *tippach*) (see Isa. 48:13).
- God lays the foundations (Hb. *yasad*) (see Job 38:4; Pss. 24:2; 89:11; 104:5; Prov. 3:19; Isa. 48:13; Amos 9:6).

- God establishes (Hb. *cun*) (see Exod. 15:17; 2 Sam. 7:13,24; Job 31:15; Pss. 8:3; 48:8; 119:73,90; Prov. 3:19; Isa. 45:18; cp. Pss. 9:7; 87:5).
- God builds like a carpenter (Hb. *banah*) (see Gen. 2:22; Amos 9:6; cp. Jer. 31:4).
- God gives birth (Hb. *yalad*) (see Deut. 32:18; Pss. 2:7; 90:2; cp. Job 38:8).
- God brings forth with labor pains (Hb. *chil*) (see Ps. 90:2; Prov. 8:24–25).
- God brings things out (Heb *yatsa'*) (see Gen. 1:24; Isa. 40:26).
- God defeats the deep or Rahab or Leviathan, a theme belonging to the creation stories of Israel's neighbors but made a part of history in Israel's faith (see Gen. 7:11; Job 3:8; 9:8,13; 38:9–11,16,30; Pss. 33:7; 74:12–17; 89:9–13; 104:5–9,26; Isa. 51:9; Jer. 5:22; cp. Ps. 87:4; Isa. 30:7; Ezek. 31:15; Amos 7:4).
- God speaks things into existence by his word (see Gen. 1:3,6,9,11,14,20,24,26; Ps. 33:6; Isa. 41:4; Amos 9:6).
- God creates, a special Hebrew word (*bara'*) for which God is always the subject (see Gen. 5:1–2; 6:7; Exod. 15:11; Num. 16:30; Deut. 4:32; Pss. 51:10; 102:18; 148:5; Eccl. 12:1; Isa. 4:5; 41:20; 43:1,7,15; 48:7; 57:19; Jer. 31:22; Amos 4:13).

Isaiah, especially in chapters 40–55, picks up the various ways of talking about creation and molds them into a logical argument: God is the one and only God of the universe. He is the Creator; all other gods are created by human plans and human hands (45:16–21). He is the first and the last, who poured the earth's foundations and spread out the heavens and can foretell all historical events (48:12–14).

Remembering God's great creative victories of the past gives hope for the future (51:9–10). You take your troubles to the maker of heaven and earth, proclaim him as the only God, and wait for him to answer your prayers (37:16; 64:8–9). You know he will be by your side in all times of trouble and danger (43:2). You can resist the arrogant claims of the enemy, knowing God has planned all historical happenings, even the rise to power of enemy rulers (37:26; 44:28).

Since he is the only God, the Lord creates light and darkness, prosperity and disaster (45:7). You may not always understand God's plans and ways (40:27–28). Still, you can detect false prophets and ignore foolish diviners, depending instead on the salvation promises of the One who stretched out the heavens and made all things (44:24–28; 51:14–16). You can look with trust to the heavens and be reassured of his strength and faithfulness (40:26). You can depend on God for the breath you breathe (42:5).

You can see past judgment and rejoice in being part of the surviving remnant because you focus on your Maker, the Holy One of Israel, and not on altars and divine symbols created by human fingers (17:7–8). You know the God who created you will also redeem you and know you intimately (43:1). He created salvation and righteousness (45:8). So you can return to him (44:22). You have no reason to fear, for he comforts you (51:12–13). Fear and terror come only when you forget God (51:13).

God will never forget the people he made as his servants (44:21). He will gather his children from afar because he made you, creating you for his glory (11:11; 43:6–7,14–15). He will supply the needs of his people so that they can fulfill his purpose and proclaim his praise (4:5; 43:20–21; 57:18–19). He will do what he has promised (40:28).

You look to God's creation of new heavens and a new earth, because there your name and descendents will endure as all people come to worship the one true God (66:22–23). Then all the ends of the earth will be saved (45:22). All enemies, even the horrible monsters of the sea, will face defeat (27:1).

Not all people accept the argument of God as Creator. They want to argue with their maker, and so they hear God's deadly "woe" (45:9). They raise questions about God's future plans and try to order him to do things their way (45:11). Refusal to look to the planner and Creator of all things brings judgment and disaster (22:11). A people devoted to foreign altars and Asherah poles finds their maker has no compassion (27:11). But as Creator of the universe and all its parts, he has the right to plan history the way he wants, even if it means raising up a Persian king as his agent for freeing his people and rebuilding his city (45:13). God also has the right to reduce the world's rulers to nothing (40:15,17,22–23). Foreigners will understand the truth that God is the only God, so Israel should easily understand it (45:14). God has no equal (40:18,25); all other contenders are pretenders—images formed by human hands (40:19–20).

VII. TEACHING OUTLINE

A. INTRODUCTION

1. Lead Story: What Does History Prove?
2. Context: Chapter 40 marks a sharp break in the content of Isaiah's book. Up to this point Assyria and Syria have controlled center stage as Israel's enemies. Judgment has been the word for the current generation with hope deferred to the future. In chapter 40 we turn to a new historical era. Babylon dominates Israel in exile. Hope lies just around the corner in the person of Cyrus of Persia. Thus we have turned from 700 B.C. and King Hezekiah to 538 B.C. and King Cyrus

of Persia. Israel appears to have lost all hope and all identity. They have become a footnote in world history, apparently never to be mentioned again. But God has something to say about that. He is the one who plans history. He is ready to announce his plans.

3. Transition: Are the skeptics right? Do the horrible realities of life mean God does not exist, love will not conquer, and hope is only a dream? The Bible will not let us give in to such dark pessimism. The Bible paints a picture of hope. In the darkest moments of existence, God's Word comes to say, "I will be your Comforter, your Shepherd, your Redeemer, because I am God and there is no other." As you read these chapters, you must decide who is right: the skeptical pessimist or the God of the Bible.

B. COMMENTARY

1. The Call to Comfort (40:1–11)
2. The Creator Comes to Comfort (40:12–31)
3. Conquerors Called to Court (41:1–7)
4. The Savior Soothes His Servant (41:8–20)
5. Indictment Against Idols (41:21–29)

C. CONCLUSION: SEARCHING FOR LOVE

1. Wrap-up: Life may seem miserable and hopeless, but God will not let it stay that way. He is your Shepherd who comes to comfort you and gather you in his arms. He is the Creator who has better plans for you than you have for yourself.

2. Personal Challenge: You can give in to circumstances and give up on life, or you can accept the Bible's challenge to faith in the Creator who wants to comfort you and redeem you. The choice is yours—futility or faith. Which will you choose?

VIII. ISSUES FOR DISCUSSION

1. What evidence does a skeptic have that leads to the denial of God's love?
2. What evidence do you have that provides an answer for a skeptic's arguments?
3. How has God revealed his glory to you?
4. What can you say to a person lost in the darkness of depression, pessimism, and skepticism?

Isaiah 42–44

Redemption for Righteousness

"*T*he people we admire most are those who

have suffered most and yet endured with grace."

Kay Arthur

Isaiah 42–44

IN A NUTSHELL

*G*od announces his way of salvation and deliverance for Israel: he will send his servant, who will be empowered and guided by his Spirit. He will establish justice on earth and bring salvation even to the Gentiles. Only the one true and powerful God can announce something as remarkable as this and then do it. So God's people should respond in praise, but they have become blind servants unable to respond. God thus turns them over to their enemies. Not for long, however, for God in his love comes to redeem his people and bring them safely home. Israel is God's witness that he is the only true God because he does what no other god can do. They will now have a new act of salvation to which they can bear witness. Israel must forsake the idols she has worshiped and become God's faithful servant and witness to God's act of salvation through Cyrus of Persia.

Redemption for Righteousness

I. INTRODUCTION

Responding to Grief

I prayed for God to bring new hope and new life after my wife's death. I agonized in prayer, devoted myself to Bible study, and sought every way I knew how to get hope and direction for life. I almost gave up. I decided I was to be lonely for the rest of my life with no way to understand what God was up to with me or with the death of my beloved companion. Finally, I went to a grief group because I knew that was what a person in grief is supposed to do. There I found people with the same emotions, complaints, sorrows, and questions that I had. I thanked God that at least he had shown me I was not crazy. I was responding to grief just like everyone else did.

Then God surprised me. He led my employer to begin a program of mission trips. I joined the first one to Kenya. There I found new involvement in God's work and discovered God was still using me to minister to others and lead them to know him as Savior. All this when I had just about given up on myself.

God surprised me again. He led me closer and closer to a member of the grief group until he led us to new marriage commitments. This one came with a ten-year-old daughter attached. Through a new wife, a new daughter, and a new mission field, God brought me back to life. In a real sense he redeemed my life and made me his servant.

Similarly, Israel felt near death. In exile under foreign rulers surrounded by foreign worship, Israel felt alone, deserted, forsaken, worthless, and hopeless. Despair hovered over everything. Then they heard the promise God had given his prophet long ago. Now the prophetic word had a new ring and a new reality. God was calling Israel to a new mission, new worship, and a new experience of salvation.

II. COMMENTARY

Redemption for Righteousness

> **MAIN IDEA:** *God acts to redeem his servant people and create a righteous community through his Spirit.*

Servant Sent in the Spirit (42:1–4)

Formal introduction

> **SUPPORTING IDEA:** *God's servant, empowered by the divine Spirit, comes to make justice prevail for the nations.*

42:1. This is the first of four "Servant Songs" in Isaiah 40–55 (49:1–6; 50:4–9; 52:13–53:12). Here God formally presented the servant to an audience, although both the name of the servant and the nature of the audience remain mysteriously unclear. (For servant of Yahweh, see "Deeper Discoveries," chs. 52–53.) We do not have to find answers to all our questions about the servant. We need to understand that he is God's **chosen** one, God takes great **delight** in him, and God **upholds** or supports him.

The servant's mission surprised Israel and it surprises us. His mission was not to deliver Israel from captivity and exile. The mission was for **the nations**. The servant gained power for his mission from the divine Spirit just as earlier rulers and prophets had. (For Spirit of God, see "Deeper Discoveries," chs. 62–64.) The servant's task was to **bring justice to the nations**. (For justice, see "Deeper Discoveries," ch. 1.) Justice involves a much broader meaning than the English term. In verse 4 it stands parallel to Torah, law or teaching. It is the verdict handed down by a judge (2 Kgs. 25:6); the whole court process (Isa. 3:14); the gracious and merciful judgment of God (Isa. 30:18); or the natural right and order claimed by a person or group of persons (Exod. 23:6).

In our text, the term for the servant's mission apparently encompasses a broad meaning. It refers to the natural world order and the rights expected by the nations of the earth within that order. God restores that order with its natural rights through his gracious and merciful judgment on the basis of his law or teaching.

42:2–4. The way the servant was to accomplish his task is also surprising. He would not be a street preacher or political rebel inciting the population, nor a royal messenger reading the king's proclamations. The servant had been given royal power by the divine King. Yet he would exercise that power in such a way that he would not damage anything—not even a broken **reed** that appears useless or a wick so used up it could no longer produce fire.

Still, the servant would succeed. The word for **faithfulness** should be translated "he will bring to reality" with an undertone of "lasting, enduring," implied. Justice would prevail! The servant would not suffer the fate of the useless utensils of verse 3. He would report to his King, "Mission accomplished." Matthew saw the fulfillment of the first servant song in the healing ministry of Jesus (Matt. 12:17–21). The meek and mild Savior showed the world the meaning and hope of world justice even as he suffered under the injustice of his own people and a foreign government.

B A Covenant for the Countries (42:5–9)

Oracle of installation

SUPPORTING IDEA: *The Creator God who controls history has sent his servant to create a righteous community that cares for the feeble and forgotten.*

42:5. Having introduced the servant to the audience, God spoke directly to the servant through a prophetic oracle. He began by quoting a familiar hymn that praised him as Creator of the **heavens** and the **earth** as well as the only source for **breath** and **life** among earth's inhabitants. This confirmed the servant's power and importance for all people everywhere.

42:6–7. God then confirmed his servant in the high office. This was done in **righteousness**. Such a statement does not repeat the obvious—that God is righteous. Rather, it defines the power given to the new official. God gave him the power to restore the right in the world—that is, to bring salvation. He could do this because God **will take hold of your hand**. The translation and meaning of **keep you** remains uncertain. It may mean "I have formed you" (NAB, REB), "shaped you" (NJB), or "created you" (JPS). Or more likely it may simply mean "will watch over you" (NASB). God's purpose for the newly installed servant was clear. He represented God's **covenant**, God's promise to the nations to bring **light** into their darkness. This is help for the helpless—sight for the blind, freedom for the prisoner.

42:8–9. The tone changes suddenly. God reminded the newly installed servant that he had limits. Yahweh alone must receive proper honor and **praise**. Worship of other gods or their images was forbidden. Why? Because God had proven himself to be God through his acts in history and he would do so again through the servant. He had done **former things**, including the exodus from Egypt, and he would do **new things**, such as the delivery from exile. The **you** of verse 9 is plural, not singular, so that God's announcement and warning (v. 8) are applied not just to the servant but to a larger audience—the people of God who have sung the hymn of verse 5 in their worship for many years.

The major question remains unanswered: Who was this servant commissioned by Yahweh? At one time, it may have had a definite historical reference. Commentators have often thought of Cyrus (44:28) and of the nation Israel or a remnant within the nation. But within the written Scripture it became a promise of God's future actions through a people or an individual who would accept the commission of God. Jesus of Nazareth is the God-man who has taken such a commission seriously and brought it into reality. For Christ's followers, the Servant Songs are challenges again to be the people of God, using Jesus as the model servant whom we are to follow.

Thanksgiving for Triumph (42:10–13)

Hymn

> **SUPPORTING IDEA:** *The world should rejoice over God's saving acts for his people.*

42:10–13. This passage functions almost as the closing hymn for the preceding verses (cp. the function of ch. 12). It is a call to the world and its most distant, isolated inhabitants to celebrate God's new action. It resembles Psalms 96, 98, and 149. (For Kedar, see Isa. 21:16–17; for Sela, which may simply mean "rock," see 16:1.) The new act is seen as holy war led by Yahweh (see Exod. 15:3). The enemy will fall. Let all the world rejoice.

The Moment to March (42:14–17)

Promise of salvation

> **SUPPORTING IDEA:** *God has a time when he will break his silence and deliver his people from their troubles while punishing those who trust in other gods.*

42:14. Israel, exiled in Babylon, tended to think God had lost his power or had totally forgotten his people. The prophet rose to say that God was aware that he had not acted for them in a long time. Now God had seen enough. He could stand the pain of separation from his people no longer. He would cry out like a **woman** giving birth and spring into action for his people.

42:15–17. God would destroy all natural obstacles and prepare **paths** through the wilderness for his **blind** people. He would **light** the way home. Then they could be sure God would not **forsake them.** Deliverance of God's people has a theological consequence. People who give up on God and give glory to **gods** must face the consequences. It is all a matter of **trust** in God or in the man-made **idols.**

Here Isaiah uses the Hebrew term *batach* rather than a form of *'aman*. *Batach* means "to feel strong and secure" and often appears in prayers of the Psalter (cp. Isa. 12:2; 26:4). It points to strong reliance on something for security. Isaiah uses it for false military reliance (31:1; 36:4) and false trust in worthless idols or personal powers (30:12; 47:10), when such confident assurance should come only from a life of righteousness (32:17). Thus Isaiah called on Israel to find security only in God (26:4; 30:15).

E Salvation for the Sightless Servant (42:18–43:13)

Oracle of salvation following a dispute

SUPPORTING IDEA: *The only God and Savior created his people, punished his people, and plans to redeem and protect them because he loves them and plans to gain glory through their witness.*

42:18–20. The prophet of salvation met as much opposition as did those who prophesied doom. Here we see clearly the hot debate that ensued between prophet and unbelieving audience. Finally, the prophet resorted to name-calling to get the audience's attention. Israel saw themselves as the servants of God, but they did not see their role in the same way as did the prophet (cp. 42:1–9). So the prophet declared they were **blind** and **deaf**! Israel did not understand what God was doing in their history, so they were **blind**. Israel paid no attention to God's prophets and the words he gave them, so they were **deaf**.

42:21–23. God was righteous and wanted to restore the right (42:6), so he chose to glorify his Torah, his **law** or instruction which could lead his people to become righteous. The people had not listened to God's instructions and so faced God's righteous punishment. Blind and deaf, they marched into exile and found themselves imprisoned, at the mercy of their captors, with no one powerful enough **to rescue them**.

Apparently the people used this situation to mock the prophet and claim their hopelessness. Verse 22 represents the language of lament they used as they told the prophet his words of salvation were only pipe dreams that would never come true. No one could possibly issue the order, **Send them back**. The prophet took up their mocking words and threw them back in their faces, concluding with the bitter question of verse 23, a strong echo of verse 19. What would it take for this people to quit feeling sorry for themselves and **pay close attention** to what God was trying to tell them?

42:24–25. Would anyone really assume the role of the servant of Yahweh as pictured by the prophet? Or would they remain blind? They had every reason to answer the prophetic call. After all, God caused the present situation in reaction to their sins. Sin is specifically defined as **not** following **his ways, not obeying his law.** Sin is always **against the LORD** and brings forth his punishment. The people thought Babylonia and their gods deserved the credit for victory in battle and exile of the people from Judah. The prophet argued that Babylonia could have done nothing if God had not **poured out on them his burning anger.** If the people would simply see that God had caused their problem, then they could believe he was going to act again. At that moment he was calling his people to accept the new role he had for them as his servants, who would respond and witness to his salvation.

43:1–3. The basis of such a call was the oracle of salvation (43:1–7) that promised God's people that even in exile they had no reason for **fear.** The God who had **created** Israel would redeem her from captivity. (For God as creator, see "Deeper Discoveries," chs. 40–41; for God's redemption, see "Deeper Discoveries," chs. 60–61.) Redemption was not a grandiose act for a huge mob. It was a very personal act by a God who could call each redeemed individual by **name.** Having been redeemed, they belonged to him: **you are mine.**

God would overcome all obstacles (43:2). Notice that this promise was put in a specific historical situation. God was about to open a path through the desert wilderness over which Israel had to walk to get home. God listed the most dangerous hindrances they would face on their journey and promised to overcome them. One of these was walking through fire without being burned. This did not, however, become an open-ended promise for anyone to test God by seeing if he would deliver them from burning fire.

Israel could count on the **LORD, the Holy One of Israel,** their **Savior.** Once God had delivered Israel from **Egypt.** (For Cush [Ethiopia], see commentary on 18:1–2.) **Seba** (cp. Gen. 10:7; Ps. 72:10) was apparently a country in northeast Africa near Egypt and Ethiopia whose people were known for their unusual height (see 45:14). It may have been Abyssiania and could have been settled by people from Sheba, modern Yemen.

God was ready to give Egypt to the new world ruler, to Cyrus of Persia, in exchange for the freedom of his people. What a huge **ransom** for such a little nation!

43:4–7. How God did **love** his people! Even living in exile, Israel had no reason to be **afraid.** God was ready to do whatever was necessary to bring all his people from their places of exile around the globe. They were his **sons** and **daughters.** He had placed his **name** on them, because they were the people of Yahweh. He had created them for his **glory** (cp. v. 1) and now would restore them for his glory.

43:8–9. Having given the promise of salvation, the prophet returned to his dispute with his audience. Taking up again the language of the courtroom, he resumed his name-calling (see 42:18) as he assembled the people of

God as both jury and witnesses at the same time. Then he called the other **nations** to join the process. He directed the first question to the nations. Could they defend the rights of their gods? What evidence did they have that another god had faithfully predicted what would happen in history? Who **proclaimed to us the former things** before they happened? Only Yahweh had done that. The gods of the nations were guilty of making false claims to deity, claims Yahweh alone could substantiate with proof. No one could say of the nations' testimony, **It is true**.

43:10–13. Turning to his own people, God swore them in as his **witnesses** and proclaimed that they were his servants, thus reinstalling them in assignment that they had refused to carry out (see 42:19). They had not earned the right to be his servants. God had **chosen** them for the role. As servants of Yahweh, the people of God had one mission. They must **understand** and **believe** in the nature of their God as the Creator, the **savior**, the only God. There never has been and never will be another God. He is the only one. They must be totally loyal to him and to no other. They could look at their own past history. It proved the validity of the claim God made for himself.

From the exodus onward, God had delivered Israel and proclaimed his word to her. Now was the time for the blind servants to open their eyes to God's actions and for the deaf servants to open their ears to his words. Then they could open their mouths as **witnesses** to the claim of Yahweh to be the one true God.

The translation and interpretation of verse 12 is difficult. **Not some foreign god among you** reads literally, "and not among you all a strange one" (author's translation). It can be present or past tense. The "strange one" may mean (1) strange god; (2) that Yahweh was not a stranger; (3) there were no foreigners; or (4) that there were no outsiders among them who had not heard the news. This last sense may well be correct. The prophet qualified his audience as witnesses by saying that they knew all that God had said and done and could testify to it.

The conclusion is that God will continue to be what he has always been—the God and Savior of Israel. The promise of deliverance from Babylonian captivity was not impossible. It simply fitted the pattern of how God had always acted with his people. No one had power to stop God from acting as he chose. Would Israel wake up, believe, and witness to this God?

◼F◼ Breaking the Bars of Babylonia (43:14–21)

Promise of salvation

SUPPORTING IDEA: *God, the holy Redeemer, plans surprises for his beleaguered people and expects them to follow him and sing his praises.*

43:14–15. The prophet had one concrete word of promise to give to the exiles in Babylon. God would defeat **Babylon**! The basis of such a promise lay in the nature of God, the **Holy One**, who is utterly faithful to his covenant. Notice that the Hebrew in the second half of verse 14 is so obscure that translation is almost impossible. Note the ASV reading: "And I will bring down all of them as fugitives, even the Chaldeans, in the ships of their rejoicing" compared with that of NRSV: "For your sake I will send to Babylon and break down all the bars, and the shouting of the Chaldeans will be turned to lamentation."

Again God confirms his promise by introducing himself again to his people: **I am the LORD, your Holy One, Israel's Creator, your King.** God has to pile up all his titles to make his own people stop and realize who he is and how much power he has. Surely they will believe his promise and be ready to go back home when he defeats the Babylonians.

43:16–21. On the basis of God's new word of promise and hope and on the strength of his consistent character, the prophet drew the consequences. The God of the exodus had something new for them. They must **forget** the **past** and its problems. They must surrender thoughts that Yahweh was only the god of the good old days. They must look forward to God's **new thing**. Be ready to be surprised by God! God had a new exodus through a new wilderness across new **streams** that were ready for his people so the people he **formed** might sing a new hymn to God. Note that various translations interpret the animals in widely different ways.

ⓖ The Spirit to Save Sinful Servants (43:22–28)

Oracle of salvation following a legal appeal

> **SUPPORTING IDEA:** *If they want forgiveness, God's people must become his servants instead of trying to be his master.*

43:22–24. God's problems with his people appear again. He had to answer accusations that they made against him. He began with a counter accusation. **Israel** forgot God. They quit praying to him. They were tired of him and did not wear themselves out to serve him. (For burnt offerings, see Lev. 1; for sacrifices, see Lev. 3.) In Babylon such offerings were impossible, but even before the exile the people went through the motions of worship without making contact with God because their hearts and attitudes were wrong. Certainly, when she had a temple, Israel loved to bring sacrifices (see Isa. 1:11). Such sacrifices did not express devotion or bring honor to Yahweh. They simply added to the nation's sense of pride and self-accomplishment. They thought they had done everything God had demanded and had done it quite well, thank you!

Indeed, the situation was quite different. God, the divine King, had not caused Israel to serve like a vassal king or slave by demanding hard-to-prepare **grain offerings** (cp. Lev. 2) nor had he worn them out with expensive and hard-to-get frankincense, which might be seen as tribute brought to a king. The other side of the picture was that Israel had not gone the extra mile and paid out her hard-earned money for a special present for Yahweh. Nor had she been able with her sacrifices to meet a physical need for Yahweh.

The problem was that Israel had tried to turn Yahweh into a servant rather than recognize that he was master. **Burdened me** reads literally, "you made a servant out of me" or "you made me serve you." Instead of being the servant of Yahweh, Israel tried to be the master of Yahweh. God became **weary** from trying to deal with Israel and their **sins**. Israel, not Yahweh, was guilty and deserved to be brought to court.

43:25. Israel had to be reminded again who their God really was. He was not an unreasonable taskmaster or a hungry weakling, panting longingly until Israel came to put a pittance at his door. Yahweh, the God of Israel, was the one who had repeatedly forgiven and forgotten Israel's sin. He blotted out their **transgressions** not because they deserved it or because they took the initiative to ask him to. He forgave a nation who did not even call on him. Why? **For my own sake**! To accomplish his own purposes. Israel was God's servant whom he was going to use to bless the nations (Gen. 12) so that all nations would come and worship him. He cleansed them so they would become his witnesses and he could fulfill his purposes. Certainly God was not guilty. He was gracious.

43:26–28. God challenged Israel to come to court and **argue the matter** with him. He reminded them that since the time of their father Jacob (see v. 22), Israel's history had been a history of sin, exemplified in their **spokesmen**, that is, in their political leaders. This sin will have consequences. God will disgrace Israel's religious leaders and bring the entire nation to ruin. They will be the laughingstock of their enemies.

H The Spirit for the Servant (44:1–5)

Oracle of salvation

SUPPORTING IDEA: *God will revive his sinful people by giving them his Spirit and renewing the blessing of Abraham with them.*

44:1–5. God's judgment was not his final word. He remained free even when his people tried to enslave him. In spite of the events of 586 B.C., **Israel** remained God's **servant**, his **chosen** people. He called to them even when they did not call to him. He would revive his lifeless people with the life-giving **Spirit** and with a renewal of the **blessing** to Abraham (Gen. 12:2;

13:16). Everyone would be proud to be an Israelite, a worshiper of the LORD. Yes, God's people, not God, were guilty. God was free to punish them, but he also was free to forgive them and promise them a new future. Could the people of God believe such a promise or would they continue to accuse God and try to make him serve their purposes?

▓ Ours Is the Only One! (44:6–8)
Oracle of salvation

SUPPORTING IDEA: *Israel's eternal king and redeemer has no competition; he alone is eternal and he alone controls history.*

44:6–8. Isaiah repeated his central message. God has proved that he is the only **God** (40:12–31; 42:8,17). No one else had dared to reveal his historical plans to his people as Yahweh had. No god could **foretell what will come**. Israel had no reason to **be afraid**. She could trust Yahweh to keep his word even in the lowest point of her history, the Babylonian exile. They were **witnesses** to the history of prophecy, the history of God proving his claim to be the only God, the only **Rock**, the only one worthy of trust. On the brink of God's great new act in salvation history, would they believe what he promised and be ready to march with him across the wilderness?

▓ Idolaters Are Idiots (44:9–20)
Song of mocking

SUPPORTING IDEA: *Idolaters don't see how ridiculous it is to worship what their own hands have made.*

44:9–11. Israel despised the mocking she received from her enemies. Here we see clearly the prophet's expertise in mocking as he described carefully and sarcastically the process involved in making idols. What resulted from the skilled craftsmen's hard work was what had existed when God began to create the earth—**nothing**, the same word translated "formless" in Genesis 1:2, perhaps better translated as "chaos." Although Israel had trouble witnessing for the Creator God, her enemies readily witnessed on behalf of their **worthless** gods. In so doing they proved themselves **blind** and **ignorant** and filled with **shame**. Why shape **a god** with a carving knife and then cast metal to adorn him when it **can profit him nothing**? Nor will it profit the craftsmen in the end, although they may receive good wages for their work. They should **take their stand** now in court and witness to their god, because they would soon face **terror and infamy** or shame.

44:12–17. Skilled workers wear themselves out creating a god. They become **hungry** and **faint**. They lose their **strength**. Such people deserved their fate—being put to shame, producing only the beauty and **glory** of a human image rather than the power and glory of deity. They are robbed of the remainder of their kindling wood with which they **warm** themselves. They display their ignorance as they bow down and worship something made from the same material they burn in the **fire**. They pray, expecting deliverance out of trouble from something their own hands have produced. By imitating and following the Babylonian worship style, Israel had lost all powers of reason and had become blind (cp. 42:18).

44:18–20. Both Israel and Babylonia **know nothing, they understand nothing . . . they cannot see . . . they cannot understand**. With all their wearying labor, they have ended up with **a detestable thing . . . a block of wood . . . ashes . . . a deluded heart . . . in my right hand a lie**. This description may have been of the Babylonian craftsmen and idol makers, but the sad undertone of the passage is that Israel wanted to accuse Yahweh (see 43:22) and worship the images that the Babylonians created (see 42:8,17).

K Remember Your Redeemer (44:21–28)

Call to repentance

> **SUPPORTING IDEA:** *God calls his servant Israel to repent and to praise their Redeemer, who is using Cyrus to start his rebuilding program in Jerusalem.*

44:21–23. God reminded his audience once more of their true identity. They were **Israel**, the **servant** of Yahweh, the nation that God created and never forgot. God promised to redeem them through the activities of Cyrus of Persia. He had forgiven their **sins**. Israel must do their part in response to God's actions. They must remember what God had done and was doing and must **return to me**. That meant to turn away from their sins and the gods of Babylonia to their Redeemer. They must join in the hymns of praise to their Redeemer and **sing for joy**. Why? Because as God redeems his people, he **displays his glory in Israel**.

44:24–28. Still another task awaited Israel. They had to listen to the royal proclamation of the divine King as he announced his new political platform. God first laid the basis for his program by explaining precisely who he is: the Creator, the source of true prophecy, and the enemy of all Babylon's **false prophets** and **wise** men. Then God described his program as he promised to rebuild **Jerusalem** and **Judah** for his people: to destroy the chaotic world ruler Babylon, so proud of her position on the mighty Euphrates River, to use **Cyrus**, king of Persia, as his **shepherd**. This was a term often used for kings.

God did all this to fulfill his purpose of rebuilding Jerusalem with its temple. What a program! When the exiles in Babylon heard the political program of Yahweh, they had to be shocked that he would use a foreign king rather than someone from the line of David. What kind of heresy could this be? Dare they believe the prophet, lay aside their fasting and mourning rites along with their Babylonian gods, and take up the mighty hymn offered them by the prophet?

MAIN IDEA REVIEW: *God acts to redeem his servant people and create a righteous community through his Spirit.*

III. CONCLUSION

A God of Surprises

God's ways are not our ways. He constantly surprises us by the way he chooses to operate in our world for his purposes. How could a "defeated" God whose people controlled no land and no temple dare claim to be the world's only true God? Why would anyone believe the promises of such a God? Yet Israel's hope lay in believing that this God would use a Persian ruler to redeem his people, repopulate his nation, and restore his temple. Would they receive the Spirit he was pouring on them? Would they volunteer for the march through the wilderness? Or were they so comfortable in Babylon that they did not want to be bothered with such religious propaganda?

Christians face an even greater task. We expect people to believe that a Galilean carpenter knew more about God than any other person who ever lived. We expect people to pay homage to a man who died over two thousand years ago—and was raised from the dead. We expect people to believe the carpenter-turned-resurrected-Lord was God himself in human flesh and now lives in heaven. We expect people to believe that this Jesus is coming again to this earth and that the destiny of every human depends on how they respond to Jesus.

Israel saw Cyrus bring Persia to a place of power, allow the exiled Israel to return home, and make the rebuilding of the temple possible. God is the only one who could predict and bring to pass something like that. All his predictions about Messiah are true, too. We have every reason to believe Jesus is Lord and is coming again.

PRINCIPLES

- God's goal is to establish justice on the earth.
- God works by telling his people what is going to happen before he makes it happen.
- God creates people to bring glory and praise to himself.
- God never forgets his people.
- God accomplishes everything he plans and promises.

APPLICATIONS

- Praise God with his people for all he has done for you.
- Quit living in the past and complaining about the present by trusting God to deliver you in the future.
- Thank God for forgiving your sins.

IV. LIFE APPLICATION

The Greatest Moment

Marian Anderson had one of the greatest singing voices ever heard. Arturo Toscanini, the greatest symphony orchestra conductor of his time, said of her, "A voice like hers comes once in a century." That voice carried her to great moments in life that few people dare dream of, much less experience. In 1955 she became the first black person to sing with the New York Metropolitan Opera Company. The next year her autobiography, *My Lord, What a Morning*, became a national bestseller.

In 1958 President Dwight D. Eisenhower named Anderson a delegate from the United States to the United Nations. She gave a private concert for the president and his guests—the king and queen of England. In 1963 she received the Presidential Medal of Freedom. And one Easter Sunday Marion Anderson stood under the statue of Abraham Lincoln in Washington, D.C., and sang for seventy-five thousand people, including most of the government's leaders.

After all this, she faced a reporter one day. Among the many questions, one stopped her for a moment. "What is the greatest moment of your life?" But she did not wait long to reply. She chose none of the moments we have listed and would expect to be on top of the list. Rather, she pointed to the day she went back home to her mother and said, "Mother, you do not have to take in washing any more. I have enough money to support both of us" (Swindoll, p. 390).

Israel had many great moments in their history. They could look back to Moses, Joshua, David, Solomon, Hezekiah, Josiah, and many more heroes who had taken the country to great heights in international politics. But Israel's greatest moment may have come when they had no political leader, no territory to rule, and no temple where they could worship. In exile in Babylon, Israel heard God's call to be his servant. That was totally different from what Israel expected or how Israel perceived themselves. God continues to call his people to identify themselves not by their moments of triumph and accomplishment but by their moments of service to God and to others.

V. PRAYER

Dear Master, Give me a new identity. I am tired of chasing after worldly fame and fortune. I am tired of having to score another major triumph today so I can be remembered, because yesterday's victories are so soon forgotten. Make me your servant. Make me totally dependent on your redemption. Yes, Master, show me the first item on my to-do list in your service today. Amen.

VI. DEEPER DISCOVERIES

God's Plan and Purpose

The Bible has one basic message: God has a plan of salvation for his world and is working among his people to bring that plan to reality. The basic Hebrew term that describes this plan is *'etsah,* which means both "advice" and "plan." In reference to God's plans, the word occurs in Job 38:2; 42:3; Psalms 33:11; 73:24; 106:13,43; 107:11; Proverbs 19:21; Isaiah 5:19; 7:5–7; 14:26; 25:1; 28:29; 44:26; 46:11; Jeremiah 32:19; 49:20; 50:45; Micah 4:12. The verb *ya'ats* speaks of God's giving advice or making plans in 2 Chronicles 25:16; Psalms 16:7; 32:8; Isaiah 14:24; 19:12,17; 23:8–9; Jeremiah 49:20; 50:45.

The theme of God's plan, counsel, and advice is more important for Isaiah than any other biblical writer. Human leaders make plans and try to hide them from God (29:15). They "carry out plans that are not mine" (30:1). Wise men offer counsel, not knowing what God has planned (19:12), but God says: "It will not take place, it will not happen," for God expects faith in him and in his plans, not in human plans (Isa. 7:5–9). Thus human leaders may devise plans and strategy, "but it will be thwarted; . . . it will not stand, for God is with us" (8:10). God is "wonderful in counsel and magnificent in wisdom" (28:29).

God remains in control of his plans. Humans cannot force him to reveal those plans or to hurry up in executing them (5:19). Still, God's plans determine the future of nations such as Tyre (23:7–9), Egypt (19:14–17), and Assyria. He has a "plan determined for the whole world" (14:26) so that God can claim, "Surely, as I have planned, so it will be, and as I have purposed, so it will stand" (14:24). No one can thwart them or turn them back (14:27). His worshipers thus sing praise: "In perfect faithfulness you have done marvelous things, things planned long ago." (25:1).

God does not keep his plans secret and to himself. In his own time he reveals them to his prophetic messengers who tell them to the people. Then God carries them out (44:26). "I make known the end from the beginning, from ancient times, what is still to come. I say: My purpose will stand, and I will do all that I please. From the east I summon a bird of prey; from a far-off land, a man to fulfill my purpose. What I have said, that will I bring about; what I have planned, that will I do" (46:10–11).

God's counsel and planning do not end with the Old Testament period, for he has plans for a messianic deliverer who will be "Wonderful Counselor" (9:6) with "the Spirit of counsel and of power" (11:2).

VII. TEACHING OUTLINE

A. INTRODUCTION

1. Lead Story: Responding to Grief
2. Context: Chapters 42–44 introduce God's message to a people who were lost in self-pity, forgetful of history, depressed by present conditions, and resigned to life that would never get any better. A full generation of Israelites had lived in Babylon. The Jewish population there, for the most part, had never experienced Jerusalem and could not see any hope of returning there. They had settled down to life in a foreign land with the intention of making themselves at home. God had another plan. He called his people to forget Babylon and to look forward to Jerusalem. He wanted them to become his servants, witnessing to the mighty new act of salvation he was planning for them. He was about to give new meaning to the term *redemption*. Could Israel hear this word as a word of hope and good news? Or would they dismiss it as a pipe dream of the good old days with no connection to present reality? Could they believe that the God of Israel truly was the only God who controlled history and that he would make Jerusalem, rather than Babylon, the city that lived on? Sight said this was impossible. Faith said that God would do what he planned and announced through his prophets. Which do you follow? Faith or sight?
3. Transition: The Israelites in Babylon lived in two worlds—the old world of faith in the God of the exodus and of the promise to David and the new world of exile in Babylon where new gods seemed to control the world and where economic and political necessity called them to forget the dreams of the old world. We know the same tensions. Sunday brings the world of faith. Monday brings the world of economic and social reality. How can the words of Sunday impact our harsh reality of Monday through Saturday? These chapters of Isaiah should help us learn how to be a servant of God not only on Sunday but through the rest of the week as well.

B. COMMENTARY

1. Servant Sent in the Spirit (42:1–4)
2. A Covenant for the Countries (42:5–9)
3. Thanksgiving for Triumph (42:10–13)
4. The Moment to March (42:14–17)
5. Salvation for the Sightless Servant (42:18–43:13)
6. Breaking the Bars of Babylonia (43:14–21)
7. The Spirit to Save Sinful Servants (43:22–28)
8. The Spirit for the Servant (44:1–5)
9. Ours Is the Only One! (44:6–8)
10. Idolaters Are Idiots (44:9–20)
11. Remember Your Redeemer (44:21–28)

C. CONCLUSION: THE GREATEST MOMENT

1. Wrap-up: The case is plain. God is the only God. Everything and everyone who would take his place are shams and fakes. God has announced a plan for his people. We are to be his servants, witnessing to his plan of salvation for the world.

2. Personal Challenge: The time for decision is now. Do you believe the God of Israel, who revealed himself most fully in Jesus of Nazareth, is the only God? If you do, will you dedicate yourself to be his servant? Or do you have to maintain control as master?

VIII. ISSUES FOR DISCUSSION

1. What does it mean to live life as a servant of God?
2. Is it possible to live as a servant of God and succeed in the real world today?
3. What is the greatest moment of your life? Why?
4. Are you facing depression and thinking of giving up on life? What causes such feelings? In what way does God offer you a way of escape from such feelings? Has he shown you a first step to take? Have you taken it?

Isaiah 45–46

Working in Wonderful Ways

I. INTRODUCTION
Depending on the Wrong Source for Knowing God

II. COMMENTARY
A verse-by-verse explanation of these chapters.

III. CONCLUSION
God Knows Best
An overview of the principles and applications from these chapters.

IV. LIFE APPLICATION
Thank God for Problems?
Melding these chapters to life.

V. PRAYER
Tying these chapters to life with God.

VI. DEEPER DISCOVERIES
Historical, geographical, and grammatical enrichment of the commentary.

VII. TEACHING OUTLINE
Suggested step-by-step group study of these chapters.

VIII. ISSUES FOR DISCUSSION
Zeroing these chapters in on daily life.

"*W*hat to man is laughable is nevertheless true, for God's ways are not our ways."

Geoffrey W. Grogan

Isaiah 45–46

 IN A NUTSHELL

*G*od will call Cyrus of Persia to deliver his people Israel from Babylonian captivity. God pronounces woes on those who question his plans and his ways, claiming the right as Creator to act as he sees best. He challenges all other gods to gather and prove their deity by predicting history and repeats his claim to be the world's only God and Creator. When none can, he invites all the earth's residents to turn to him and be saved. He especially invites Israel to hear his promises, believe them, and be ready for his salvation.

Working in Wonderful Ways

I. INTRODUCTION

Depending on the Wrong Source for Knowing God

Author Henry Blackaby confessed, "When I was first learning how to walk with God, I depended too much on other people. I would run to other people and say, 'Do you think this is really God? Here is what I think. What do you think?' I would unconsciously or consciously, depend on them rather than on the relationship I had with God.

"Finally, I had to say, 'I am going to go to the Lord and clarify what I am absolutely convinced He is saying to me. Then, I am going to proceed and watch to see how God affirms it.' I began that process over a period of time in many areas of my life. My love relationship with God became all-important. I began to discover a clear personal way in which God was making known His ways. God revealed His ways through His Word. . . . God wants us to come to know and follow Him. As He speaks to us, He reveals Himself so we can have faith to trust Him in the assignment He calls us to. He reveals His purposes so we will be involved in His work and not just things we dreamed up to do for God. God reveals His ways so that He can accomplish His work through us in a way that He gets all the glory" (Blackaby, pp. 159–160).

Long ago, Israel had the same problem that Henry Blackaby confessed. They could not understand what God was saying, and they were not sure he was speaking to them. They realized that if the message was from God, then they surely did not understand his ways. How could the true God of the universe allow his people to lose their nation, their homeland, and their temple? How could he stand silently by while his people went into foreign exile? How could his promise of salvation and deliverance include a foreign king like Cyrus of Persia as his anointed rather than a king from David's line?

How could a God from a small nation like Israel claim to be Creator of all the universe and the only true God? How could this God think he could introduce himself to Cyrus in such a way to make Cyrus acknowledge him? How dare the God of Israel invite all the nations of the earth to share in his salvation! God is God, and he does not do things the way we might. Can we believe in a God who works so far outside the rules of human logic and the expectations of his chosen people?

II. COMMENTARY

Working in Wonderful Ways

MAIN IDEA: *The one and only true God works in unexpected ways as he keeps his promises to save his people and bless his world.*

A Calling Cyrus to Conquest and Construction (45:1–7)

Installation ceremony

SUPPORTING IDEA: *God anoints unexpected people to accomplish his saving purposes for his people and to introduce the world to the one true God.*

45:1–3. Here is the center of the political message of Isaiah 40–55. The prophet pictured the installation of **Cyrus**, king of Persia, in the office as Yahweh's **anointed** one. Yahweh took Cyrus by the **hand** (see 42:6) and described the mission he had for him. He was to **subdue nations**, particularly Babylonia, as Israel's God led the way. He was to receive the nations' treasures in their **secret** store **places** as his deserved tribute. God did this to introduce himself to Cyrus and to show Cyrus that he was only a vassal king under the divine King, the **God of Israel**. Cyrus must know that God had called him to conquer the world so he could help Israel. Cyrus had not earned the power and position by his own strength.

45:4–7. Yahweh acted **for the sake of my servant Israel**. Yes, to do his will and help his people, God could use someone who did not even **acknowledge** his existence. Yahweh could do this because he had no competition: **Apart from me there is no God**. Cyrus could not give credit for his **honor** and strength to Ahura Mazda, the god of the Zoroastrian religion of Persia. Nor could he give such honor to Marduk, the high god of Babylonia, even though he did so in the famous Cyrus Cylinder from Babylon. (For the view from the other side: the Cyrus Cylinder, see "Deeper Discoveries.")

The true picture is that the God of Israel would use Cyrus to spread the news around the world that only one God ruled the universe. God stepped outside the confines of Israel to use another world power to accomplish his purposes. Why? Because he wanted to widen the arena in which his purposes were recognized and honored. This meant, however, that God was responsible for all of world history, creating both the good and the bad. He brought destruction to his people when they refused to hear the prophetic call to repent. He brought return from exile when it would bring honor to his name.

Israel had to learn to honor and worship him in good times and bad. (For God the creator, see "Deeper Discoveries," chs. 40–41.)

B Rain Down Righteousness (45:8–13)

Hymnic introduction to woe oracles

SUPPORTING IDEA: *God's human creatures have no right to question God's ways and purposes as he works to create a righteous world.*

45:8–10. Once Cyrus is installed, God will be ready to get things moving. He commanded the heavenly powers to join the earthly powers in bringing forth **righteousness**, the proper world order, and salvation—the proper status for humanity in relationship to God and in relationship to the world order. (For righteousness, see "Deeper Discoveries," chs. 50–51; for salvation, see "Deeper Discoveries," chs. 47–49.) This would show that God not only **created** the darkness of the exile but could also create the light of a new day of salvation and right.

In spite of his assurances, God had to argue further with his people, and he did so by using prophetic woe oracles against those who disagreed with him (see Isa. 5:8,11,18,20–22; 29:15; 33:1; with 1:4; 10:5; 28:1; 30:1). God first set them in their place as creatures who were powerless to argue in court against the Creator, the heavenly Father. They were mere clay **potsherds** in his hands, waiting to be remolded into whatever he chose. Until then, they were useless, broken pieces of pottery.

45:11–13. Then he became specific. Could anyone accuse God of misusing his own **children**, who were created with his **hands**? Could he not treat his children as he desired? Did anyone know a better way than that of their Father? Could anyone claim that God was misusing the world and its inhabitants by installing Cyrus as his anointed? After all, God is the One who **made the earth and created mankind upon it**. The maker knows better than anyone what is best for his creatures.

So God concluded with the simple explanation of what he was doing with the works of his own hands. He would call **Cyrus** to restore the right order in the universe (see 42:6; 45:8). This would center on the right order for God's **exiles** in their own land with their own **city**. God would not hire Cyrus for such work as a king might hire a professional warrior or a vassal king. Rather, God would install Cyrus as his shepherd to perform the task he would give him. Cyrus would be God's official, not God's hireling.

ⓒ Evangelizing the Enemy (45:14–25)

Courtroom speeches

SUPPORTING IDEA: *God, the eternal Savior, often works in hidden ways to accomplish his purpose of bringing the world to recognize and serve him.*

45:14–17. This is a complex unit that has been interpreted in many different ways. Yet it is a very important section, containing some of the central theological points of the Book of Isaiah. It begins with an announcement of salvation for Israel, which is then defended against arguments which God's opponents brought against him.

The action of Cyrus (45:1–13) will bring **Egypt** and her African allies to their knees (43:3–4), but they will not pay tribute to Cyrus. Rather, they will follow a feminine singular "you," which dominates this section. This must be Zion/Jerusalem. Their reason will not be political but theological. These African nations will recognize that the work of Cyrus is made possible by the power of Israel's **God** (45:6). This will lead them to one of the great theological insights of the Bible. The God of Israel is not a God of pompous show and procession, tooting his own horn at every corner. He does not always act openly and clearly through the normal means expected in the Ancient Near East.

Rather, God often acts quietly, where people have to be very perceptive and attentive to see and understand what he is doing. From their perspective **you are a God who hides himself**. Even his own people remained blind to many of his activities (43:8). He did not even have to work with his own people. He could work through a foreign ruler like Cyrus (see 10:5). Yet when a person finally understood what God was doing, the appropriate reaction was a cry of praise, **O God and Savior of Israel**.

The prophetic proclamation had another side. It recognized how worthless the claims of other gods to the divine throne were (44:9–20) and how significant this was for God's people. The idols and their human **makers** would be **put to shame and disgraced**. Israel would be **saved**. This is a central biblical theme, and certainly an important emphasis of the Book of Isaiah. For Israel, salvation was a very concrete term that meant help in time of trouble, particularly deliverance in war from the enemy and deliverance in the courtroom from the accuser.

The exact opposite is to **be put to shame**, that is, to lose the case or the battle, to let the enemy win. The prophet thus looked to the day when Israel would no longer have to call on God to win her battles or to restore her social order. He would have done it once and for all with **an everlasting salvation**. The New Testament shows us this salvation was not won on the battlefield or in the courtroom. Everlasting salvation came through the death of the Lamb of God, Jesus Christ, on the cross.

45:18–19. The problem was that the prophet's audience did not believe him. They claimed that God had returned everything to chaos. Using language from Genesis 1 (particularly the special Hebrew words *bara'* for create and *tohu* for **empty**, formless, chaos), the prophet answered, "Oh, no! Look back to the beginning. God did not create chaos. He changed chaos into a world where people could live." Chaos is the world of the Babylonian gods whose diviners and prophets have to go into **darkness**, even into the world of the dead, to find the word of their god. God did not call his people to seek him **in vain** (Hb. *tohu*). Instead, God speaks **the truth** (Hb. *tsedeq*, righteousness; see 42:6). But God gave his word through his prophet out in the open just like he always has.

45:20–21. The dispute was not only with God's people, who would not believe God's new word of promise. God also sought to work with the nations, at least those parts of the nations who survived after losing the battle to the God of Israel. Therefore, he called them to court. He charged them with serving worthless gods, **idols of wood that cannot save**. Again God's evidence was simple. He is sovereign over history and can thus predict the future.

45:22–25. God's control of history involved a radically new manner of behaving with the defeated enemies. He did not demand harsh payments and slave service. He wanted recognition and worship (vv. 14–15; see 42:10–13). He offered salvation not only to Israel (v. 17), but to all nations, **all the ends of the earth**. His ultimate purpose was not victory in war. Rather, he wanted all the world to know him and to bow to the divine King. They should see that only in Yahweh "are victory and strength to be found" (v. 24, TEV; cp. REB, JPS; NJB reads, "In Yahweh alone are saving justice and strength"). Those who do not recognize this and continue to fight against God must face him **and be put to shame**.

Isaiah added a final note to his argument. Israel had looked forward to their day of military might and supremacy. The prophet said such might belonged only to Yahweh. Israel must be content to let God prove that they were in the right. God did not call them to boast of their military victories. They could praise and boast only in God's victory of convincing the nations that **there is no God apart from me**.

Thus this "poem is about Yahweh's massive authority, capacity, and readiness to do right. . . . Yahweh's righteousness is engaged in the work of well-being. Israel has benefited from this gift of Yahweh's righteousness, and the nations are invited to participate in the same. But neither Israel nor the nations can receive such transformative activity unless they are among those who bend the knee and sear with the tongue to the sovereignty of Yahweh" (Brueggemann, *Theology of the Old Testament,* p. 306).

Ⓓ Bearing Your Burdens (46:1–13)

Legal dispute

SUPPORTING IDEA: *The weakness of other gods demonstrates that God will fulfill his saving purposes for his people.*

46:1–2. God had to argue repeatedly with Israel. Exiled Israel had gone so deep in self-pity at the thought of losing their homeland, their temple, and their political power that they could not believe that God had any power to save. The prophet turned to bitter sarcasm, picturing the fate of Babylon. It, like Judah, would go into exile. Before it could go, it would have to load up its gods—**Bel,** the chief god, and his son **Nebo**—on donkeys so the deities could join their people in riding away into **captivity.** The only thing the Babylonian gods were good for was to **burden** down the poor **beasts.** People could not bow down to such gods! The gods themselves had to **bow down,** and donkeys had to bow down under their weight.

46:3–7. Yahweh was just the opposite. He had **carried** Israel's burden from their **birth** and would continue to do so throughout their lives. He **carried** what he **made** and saved what he shaped. No one had to shape him or carry him. Unlike any other thing that claimed to be god, Yahweh could hear and respond to the burdens of his people rather than burdening them to carry him. Yahweh had moved from heaven to earth, from Jerusalem to Babylon to deliver his people, but the idol created by human craftsmen—**from that spot it cannot move.**

46:8–10. If only Israel would look up from her self-pity, which was her sin of the moment, and **remember** her history with God. Then she would understand that just as in the past, so in the present and future, **My purpose will stand, and I will do all that I please.**

46:11–13. Yes, even if God chose to call his ruler from a far eastern country rather than from Israel, he would still accomplish his **purpose.** Israel must quit being **stubborn** and get ready for God's great new action in their history. They could get ready only though **righteousness.** Even though he was using a foreign king, his purpose was to provide for the **salvation** of his people Israel.

MAIN IDEA REVIEW: *The one and only true God works in unexpected ways as he keeps his promises to save his people and bless his world.*

III. CONCLUSION

God Knows Best

God is faithful. He does what he promises. The problem is that we sometimes place limits on the way God should fulfill his promises. If he does not do things our way, then something is wrong with the world. The Creator of the universe knows better than we do what is right, good, and just, because he himself is right, good, and just. He can choose to use a Cyrus of Persia or a Martin Luther King or a Mother Teresa or even a Mahatma Gandhi to do his will and help bring his purposes to pass. He can also use you if you are willing to let him do things his way rather than insisting on your own way.

PRINCIPLES

- Nothing happens on earth outside God's control and purpose.
- God's plan is to create a new world of righteousness and salvation.
- God offers salvation to every one who will trust him.
- God will work out his plan so that all nations will eventually acknowledge him as God.

APPLICATIONS

- Talk with God person to person and tell him all the wonderful things you have learned about him.
- Ask God to forgive you for quarreling with and questioning him.
- Thank God for his everlasting salvation.
- Praise God for being with you every day of your life.

IV. LIFE APPLICATION

Thank God for Problems?

A woman was quite upset. Her "friend" had just asked her to thank God for the problems she was experiencing. She turned to Dr. Norman Wright for counsel and asked, "How can I thank God for this loss? It's disrupted my whole life."

Dr. Wright spoke from experience as he counseled the lady, because he and his wife had lost their twenty-two-year-old mentally retarded son Matthew. Wisely, Dr. Wright asked, "Did your friend mean for you to thank God for this specific loss as though it were good in and of itself, or to thank God for using this so you have an opportunity to change and grow?"

The woman pondered several moments, so Dr. Wright continued: "I know it hurts, and you and your family wish it had never occurred, but it did. The past can't be changed, and you feel out of control. Perhaps you can't change what happens in the future, but you can control your response to whatever occurs."

The woman took that home to think about. Finally, after some time, she thanked God for being with her and allowing her this time of growth. She said, "I thought about the choices I had. I could depend on God, thank him, praise him, and allow him to work through me. Or I could remain bitter and angry. Praising God didn't seem so bad when I considered the alternative."

The Book of Lamentations shows us how hard Israel grieved over the loss of Jerusalem. They were upset with God, and they demanded that he change his ways or admit he was not really God after all. God did not take their accusations sitting still. He came back at them to say, "I am in charge of all history, the good and the bad. I brought punishment on you to help you repent and come back to me. Now I have a new plan of salvation for you. It contains as many surprises as did my destruction of your beloved Jerusalem. Are you going to quit blowing off angry steam and listen to me, or will you let anger and bitterness control the rest of your life?"

Life brings each of us situations that arouse anger and frustration. We question where God is and why he let this happen. But questioning must not become the normal life mode. The time comes when we must face the same alternatives the bitter woman faced and decide for ourselves: will we go with God in his ways, or will we go on in our self-centered bitterness and anger? Do we want to grow? Or do we want to shrivel up into an isolated, angry, old man or woman?

V. PRAYER

All-wise and knowing God, forgive me when I play Job and decide I am wiser and smarter than you are. Forgive me when I let life's valleys so encompass me that I do not look up to the snow-capped peaks and the brilliant sunlight or the gorgeous moonlit night. Forgive me when I am content to complain in anger and grow bitter. Forgive me when I demand to understand your ways before I will believe your promises. Lord, I do trust you. I will follow your way. Let me see the open door you have for me. I will step through it, no matter who else is going with me or who is leading your people through this door. I am yours. Amen.

VI. DEEPER DISCOVERIES

A. The View from the Other Side: The Cyrus Cylinder (45:1–7)

The Bible clearly teaches that Yahweh, the God of Israel and the Father of our Lord Jesus Christ, called Cyrus of Persia by name, commissioned him, installed him as his anointed servant/messenger, and led him to victory over Babylon so Israel's exiles could go back home. Archaeologists discovered a document in Babylon called by modern scholars the Cyrus Cylinder. It gives the Babylonian viewpoint of Cyrus's capture of Babylon and quotes Cyrus himself as crediting Marduk, the high god of Babylonia, for his success.

The Cyrus Cylinder says: Marduk "surveyed and looked throughout all the lands, searching for a righteous king whom he could support. He called out his name: Cyrus, king of Anshan; he pronounced his name to be king over all (the world). He (Marduk) made the land of Gutium and all the Umman-manda (that is the Medes) bow in submission at his feet. And he (Cyrus) shepherded with justice and righteousness all the black-headed people over whom he (Marduk) had given him victory. Marduk, the great lord, guardian (?) of his people, looked with gladness upon his good deeds and upright heart. He ordered him to march to his city Babylon. He set him on the road to Babylon, and like a companion and friend, he went at his side. His vast army, whose number, like the water of the river, cannot be known, marched at his side fully armed. He made him enter his city Babylon without fighting or battle; he saved Babylon from hardship. He delivered Nabonidus, the king who did not revere him, into his hands. All the people of Babylon, all the land of Sumer and Akkad, princes and governors, bowed to him and kissed his feet. They rejoiced at his kingship and their faces shone."

Later lines on the cylinder quote Cyrus: "When I entered Babylon in a peaceful manner, I took up my lordly reign in the royal palace amidst rejoicing and happiness. Marduk, the great lord, caused the magnanimous people of Babylon (to . . .) me, (and) I daily attended to his worship. . . . I sought the welfare of the city of Babylon and all its sacred centers. . . . Marduk, the great lord, rejoiced over my (good) deeds. He sent gracious blessings upon me, Cyrus, the king who worships him. . . . I returned the (images of) the gods to the sacred centers (on the other side of) the Tigris whose sanctuaries had been abandoned for a long time, and I let them dwell in eternal abodes. I gathered all their inhabitants and returned (to them) their dwellings. In addition, at the command of Marduk, the great lord, I settled in their habitations, in pleasing abodes, the gods of Sumer and Akkad, whom Nabonidus, to the anger of the gods, had brought into Babylon. May all the gods whom I settled in their sacred centers ask daily of Bel and Nabu that my days be long and may they intercede for my welfare. May they say to Marduk, my lord: 'As for Cyrus, the king who reveres you, and Cambyses, his son, ( ) a reign.' I settled all the lands in peaceful abodes" (Cogan, trans., in Hallo and Younger, eds., *The Context of Scripture,* vol. 2: *Monumental Inscriptions from the Biblical World,* pp. 314–316).

B. God Chooses, and We Are Free (45:4)

The sovereign God who controls history does so through special people and especially a special group of people. The Bible maintains that these people have never earned the right to be the human instruments through whom God works. Rather, God has in his wisdom and grace chosen, selected, and elected these people. The major Hebrew vocabulary for this includes:

Chosen, pious ones (Hb. *bachir*) (see 1 Chr. 16:13; Pss. 89:3; 106:5,23; Isa. 42:1; 45:4).

God chooses (Hb. *bachar*) (see Num. 16:7; Deut. 14:2,23–25; 16:2,6–7,11,15–16; 26:2; Josh. 9:27; 1 Kgs. 3:8; 14:21; 2 Kgs. 21:7; 23:27; 1 Chr. 15:2; 29:1; 2 Chr. 7:12,16; 29:11; Neh. 1:9; Pss. 78:68,70; 135:4; Hag. 2:23).

As we study this special word, we must remember that word study is only a small part of the picture. Israel told much of her theology in story form rather than by use of specific vocabulary. The books of Genesis and Exodus speak quite loudly in their absence from the list above. There God called Abraham and the succeeding patriarchs, sent Joseph to Egypt, called Moses out of Egypt, and led Israel to Sinai, all acts of calling and election without using the terminology.

The Old Testament focuses the word "choose" on God's relationship to Israel's king (Deut. 17:15) and especially to David (2 Sam. 16:18). God rejected Saul and chose David (2 Sam. 6:21; cp. 1 Sam. 10:24; 16:8–13; Ps. 78:68). Note that the choice of David was by God's mysterious standards, not by human criteria. The rejection of Saul came on grounds of relationship to God, not on political or military grounds. This rejection of one previously chosen shows the tension the Bible holds in the doctrine of election. God chooses people for his service but holds them accountable and responsible to obey him.

As Hans Wildberger expresses it: "The king's failure explains the rejection. Just as the question arises as to how one chosen by Yahweh can fail, it expresses the recognition that election by Yahweh must find response in the proper behavior of the elect" (TLOT, 1, p. 214).

Thus the Southern Kingdom held fast to the line of Davidic kings because God had chosen David and his line (Pss. 78:67–72; 132:10–12). But even the Davidic line was taken away from Jerusalem (Ps. 89:38–51), yet still Israel held to the prophetic hope for the stump of the house of Jesse (Isa. 9; 11).

Israel's neighbors also considered their king to be the elected, chosen one of their god. What marked Israel as unique in this sphere was their insistence that God chose a people from among all the people of the earth for a universal mission (Deut. 7:6–7; 1 Kgs. 3:8; Ps. 135:4). Again Exodus 3; 6; 19–24 are crucial here, although they do not use technical election language. God chose a people to be a holy nation, a kingdom of priests. God's choice came not from human criteria or human merits (Deut. 9:4–6) but because of divine love (Deut. 4:37; 7:6–8; 10:15; Ps. 47:4). That Israel was elected and loved found its proof in the promise to the patriarchs and in the exodus from Egypt (Deut. 7:6–8). But from the first, Israel faced the fact that election brought responsibility to obey, to choose God (Josh. 24:15) or to face disaster (Deut. 7:9–11; 2 Kgs. 17:19–20; Amos 3:2). Still, disaster had a note of eternal election and expectation (2 Kgs. 21:7).

Wildberger summarizes in strongest fashion: Israel's election is "grounded only in Yahweh's love for Israel which cannot be further explained. . . . it attests to Yahweh's love and demands obedience in faithfulness on the part of God's people" (Wildberger, p. 217).

Having chosen a people and a king, God also chose a place where they could worship him, namely Jerusalem or Zion (e.g., Deut. 12:5–26; 16:2–16; Ps. 132). There an elect priesthood also served (Deut. 18:5). An elect people thus bore the responsibility to worship where and how God directed.

Israel's election is not an exclusive election that shuts out all other peoples. It is a missionary election to be a blessing to the nations (Gen. 12). Thus Amos can even extend election language to Israel's neighbors and enemies (Amos 9:7). This prevented the danger of election language: "It too easily gave rise to the dangerous illusion that Israel's salvation may be assured through the execution of the cult at holy places or that Israel is immune to disaster because it is chosen" (Wildberger, p. 218).

Such election and rejection as Israel experienced might seem to be a closed book with the story complete, but Isaiah would not let election die. The people in exile were called to listen to a new word of salvation from God, who chose them when he chose Abraham (41:8–13). "'You are my servant'; I have chosen you and have not rejected you" (Isa. 41:9). So Israel is not to fear but to trust God to deal with their enemies. The everlasting covenant with David remains in place even for an exiled people (Jer. 49:19; Zech. 6:9–15). God's plans for Israel go back even further than David, Moses, or Abraham. They go back to creation. (For God the creator, see "Deeper Discoveries," chs. 40–41.) So Israel must seek God and forsake evil (Isa. 55:6–7). God will again choose Israel, and settle them in their own land, then strangers will join them and attach themselves to the house of Jacob (see 14:1; 65:9,15–25).

Still, God's people retain responsibility for obedience (66:3–4). They must become God's servants and look for his suffering servant (for servant of

Yahweh, see "Deeper Discoveries," chs. 52–53), who will "justify many . . . and bear their iniquities" (53:11). "All previous interpretations of election are transcended, however, by the fact that the election of the servant of God is fulfilled in representative suffering. . . . Here, too, election means being placed under obligation, but now as Yahweh's servant among the nations, not only for obedience but even for a witness in apparent failure, in suffering, and in death" (Wildberger, p. 221).

For Israel, then, election was not a guarantee of security and safety. It was a call to obedience and service. Election was God's call that gave the people an opportunity to become part of God's eternal plan for the nations. Election is God's way of doing missions.

VII. TEACHING OUTLINE

A. INTRODUCTION

1. Lead Story: Depending on the Wrong Source for Knowing God
2. Context: Chapters 40–41 begin the second half of Isaiah's book with a call to comfort God's exiled people. The world's Creator is coming to be their Shepherd and give them renewed strength. Now God is calling a servant from the east to implement his plan and return his people to their home. He is also calling Israel to be his faithful, fearless servant, and challenging the nations and their gods to prove their power by predicting history. Chapters 42–44 continued the emphasis on the Creator God and his superiority to all others who claim to be God. God introduces his mild and meek servant who is empowered by the Spirit and makes his servant people Israel a covenant to the nations. Thus God can achieve his eternal plan of bringing salvation to the world. His plan has been interrupted by Israel's blindness and the necessity to punish them—an event that further proves the greatness and power of God. Punishment past, God is redeeming Israel because he loves them. Israel will become God's witness to the nations. First, Israel must join God as he does his new thing of leading them through the wilderness out of Babylon. Still, Israel must confess God's righteousness for punishing them for their sins. With this back-and-forth movement between the call to servant Israel and the condemnation of sinner Israel, Isaiah prepares us for a new chapter in God's dealing with his world.
3. Transition: The new section begins with a new divine call to servant Israel, a new promise of his Spirit, a new challenge to the nations and their gods to prove themselves or shut up, and an explicit installation of Cyrus of Persia as his servant. Israel stands befuddled. How will

God use a foreign king to deliver his people? What has happened to his promise to David? How can they be God's servant if Cyrus has that role?

B. COMMENTARY

1. Calling Cyrus to Conquest and Construction (45:1–7)

2. Rain Down Righteousness (45:8–13)

3. Evangelizing the Enemy (45:14–25)

4. Bearing Your Burdens (46:1–13)

C. CONCLUSION: THANK GOD FOR PROBLEMS?

1. Wrap-up: From eternity before creation God has known his plan for saving the world from the consequence of their sin and converting them into his servants. His way of accomplishing his plan involved both punishing his own sinful people and using Cyrus, the pagan king of Persia, as his anointed servant. God's ways confused his people and called them to a new kind of faith—faith in God's ways rather than human ways.

2. Personal Challenge: Life does not always follow the blueprint we draw. Rather, life throws us curves and forces us to endure many things that we would choose to evade. As you face the dark side of life, will you trust God and let him show you that even this is included in his way of salvation for you and his world?

VIII. ISSUES FOR DISCUSSION

1. What events and circumstances have proven to you that the God of Israel is the only true God?

2. What has happened in your life that has caused you to question the ways of God? What answers have you received that have helped you to greater faith in God?

3. In what ways have you experienced God as a God who hides himself? What have you learned from these experiences?

4. What testimony can you give of ways God has sustained, carried, and rescued you? Are you truly a witness for God?

Isaiah 47–49

Perfecting the Plan

Quote

"*The* almost-too-good-to-be-true fact is that God has made conscious, sovereign choice to let a weak, weary, and worn-down man like me share his power."

Bill Hybels

Isaiah 47–49

 IN A NUTSHELL

*G*od calls Babylonia to lament because they have trusted in magic and astrology. God gives Israel new promises for their deliverance. Then God gives the marching orders: Leave Babylon. Suddenly God's servant gives his testimony. God expands Israel's commission from witnessing to being a light for the nations. God will bring his people back to their homeland. As with a mother and her baby, God never forgets his people and their needs. All this will lead Israel and all nations to know that the Lord is God, the Redeemer and Savior of Israel.

Perfecting the Plan

I. INTRODUCTION

Power to Deliver

*B*illy Graham tells of his friend facing an impossible situation. The man stood on the top of a mountain looking down into the beautiful valley below. As he viewed the terrain, a frightening reality grabbed him. A car was coming around the mountain on his left. Another was coming on his right. Not able to see or sense each other's presence, they were on a collision course. Then with horror he saw a third car enter the picture, passing the car on his left as they both entered a blind curve. Dr. Graham's friend shouted a warning from his perch high above the traffic scene, but of course, no one could hear him. The ensuing crash was fatal; several people died. His friend knew what was coming but had no power to deliver the people from their danger (Graham, p. 21).

Isaiah tells of two nations on a crash course with disaster—Babylonia and Israel. God has a word for each of them. He calls one to lamentation, the other to salvation. The words are different, because the recipients are different. We listen to these words to see which message applies to us. Which nation are you most like? Which word from God applies to you?

II. COMMENTARY

Perfecting the Plan

> **MAIN IDEA:** *God calls his people to trust him as he works through them to bring salvation to the nations.*

Calling the Chaldeans to Complain (47:1–15)
Call to lamentation

> **SUPPORTING IDEA:** *God's people must trust his word and follow it rather than imitating the pagan world's way of determining the future and of knowing the best way to face the future.*

47:1–3. God's people spent years in Babylonian captivity complaining of all that had befallen them (see the Book of Lamentations). God turned the tables. He announced it was time for the captors to complain. He described precisely how they were to carry out the lamentation rites (vv. 1–3). They would be taken captive, thus losing their **throne** and all their power over other peoples. They would suffer what they had caused others to suffer and experience the **shame** they had brought to others. How could this happen? God would **take vengeance**.

47:4. Power lay not with Babylonia but with the **Redeemer**, the Lord of Hosts (NIV, LORD **Almighty**), the **Holy One of Israel**. The relationship of verse 4 to what precedes and follows is not obvious. The REB sees it as a quotation formula and so reads, "says our Redeemer, the Holy One of Israel, whose name is the LORD of Hosts." The NJB goes the other direction and sees verse 4 as a quote formula introducing verse 5: "Our redeemer, Yahweh Sabaoth is his name, the Holy One of Israel, says." Without adding words to the Hebrew text, the verse appears to be another brief hymn provided for the readers of the book to respond to the situation. Hearing what God is doing to their enemy, they confess their faith in God, using a string of divine titles to emphasize how great he is.

47:5–7. God, while he was **angry** with his people, had used Babylonia for his purpose—to punish Israel. But Babylonia had gone too far. They **showed them no mercy**, not even for the **aged**. Now he would use Cyrus to punish Babylonia and rescue his people. He would take away Babylonia's claim to be **queen of kingdoms**. The queen would be banished to the **silence** of a dark dungeon. Secure in her power and glory, Babylonia thought they would **continue forever—the eternal queen**. They needed to **reflect** a bit more and take God into the picture.

47:8–11. Babylonia had become proud and secure, claiming to be the only world power. This title, however, belonged to God alone (45:14). Babylonia forgot that only God dare say **never**. Babylonia thought she had the secret to success. She had developed a complex and comprehensive system of finding the will of the gods through various kinds of priests, prophets, astrologers, diviners, and sorcerers. They thought they could determine the future from the stars, the livers of animals, contact with the dead—almost every way imaginable. God brought them up short. They had forgotten the one way to the future. They trusted **wickedness** rather than the way of the one true God. In spite of the great reputation of their various kinds of prophets and of their great, wise counselors, they had to prepare for lamentation and mourning. The God of Israel, not the wise men of Babylonia, controlled the destiny of history. God promised **disaster**. Babylonia had no countermeasure.

47:12–15. The divine speech became caustic. **Keep on** keeping on with your **magic spells and with your many sorceries**! Listen to the **counsel** of your wise men! Ask your **astrologers** for their monthly predictions. Which of them can find a way to **save you**? The truth is that all their ways of seeking the future had **worn** them **out** without giving any real help. They had no Savior.

The word of Isaiah was directed to the exiles. They should not be tempted by Babylonia's useless systems of predicting the future, no matter how intricate and intriguing they might be. Israel must trust the prophetic word and look for the day of deliverance—the day of new destiny for God's people.

B Revelation and Release for the Rebels (48:1–22)

Legal dispute

> **SUPPORTING IDEA:** *The way to peace is to trust God's act of grace to save his people and to punish the wicked.*

48:1–5. God argued with his audience, who continued to doubt that he could be acting as the prophet said. God began by identifying his audience as physically descended from **Jacob** and **Judah** and known to the world as **Israel**, the people who made all their international agreements and public proclamations **in the name of** Yahweh, **the God of Israel**. But they did not do it "with honesty and sincerity" (REB). Rather, the people glibly recited religious clichés. God had been faithful to bring about what he promised, but Israel had not. They had relied upon **idols** just like Babylonia and the other nations, claiming for their idols powers that God claimed as unique to himself. Israel had refused to accept the evidence that God put forth.

48:6–11. God had offered the evidence. Now Israel must respond. Would they **admit** that God's testimony was true and fulfill their role as witnesses to what God was doing? God had even more evidence. Israel could not claim to be an expert on God, because he had something **new** in store. God stopped to emphasize that what he was about to do was brand new, freshly **created**, something never revealed before. This would not have been necessary if Israel had been faithful to their calling. But they were not. They were **treacherous**, a **rebel from birth**, so God had stored up this new act until now.

The something new was an act of pure grace. God would not totally destroy his people. This new act continued the purpose that God had always had, that of bringing **praise** and honor to his great name. This was the only reason he had not totally cut them off. Instead, God had preserved a remnant and **refined** them **in the furnace of affliction**. Note instead of **tested**, the Hebrew text reads "I have chosen you," showing that God's election takes place in the arena of world history and world suffering. It involves suffering as well as security and hope. (For God chooses, and we are free, see "Deeper Discoveries," chs. 45–46.) They could still fulfill their function among the nations, who must not be able to ridicule God and glorify another god instead of him.

48:12–15. God called Israel to court again and repeated the evidence for his unique claim to deity from history (**have called**), creation (**first . . . last . . . laid the foundations . . . spread out the heavens**), and from prophecy (**foretold these things**). He then revealed the basic reason why he astounded Israel and used Cyrus as his **chosen ally** (literally, "his love"; cp. NJB, REB, JPS, KJV, NKJV, NASB, NRSV). Could anything be more heretical! How could God love an enemy king? Certainly he loved Israel but, of all Israel's kings, only Solomon was said to be loved by Yahweh (2 Sam. 12:24). The only other individual in the Old Testament said to be loved by God is Cyrus.

Israel could hardly believe her ears at such a pronouncement! No wonder they debated with God. But God stuck to his word. God loved the Persian king and would use him to fulfill the divine purpose. God had called him just as surely as he had called the prophet (Isa. 6; 40).

48:16–19. Such a startling word is not a human invention or fantasy dream. From God's first actions with Israel through Abraham and Moses, he had made his will known through public **announcement**. When the time came to act on that announcement, God stated, **I am there**. Now he was doing the same. God had sent the word about Cyrus through his prophet by means of his **Spirit**. (For Spirit of God, see "Deeper Discoveries," chs. 62–64.)

God's people were reluctant to hear such a word about a beloved foreign anointed one. God tried to reassure them. He remained **your Redeemer, the Holy One of Israel . . . the LORD your God**. The new act with Cyrus was not aimed against Israel. It should teach Israel, showing them **what is best** for Israel. Israel should remain confident that their God would direct them in the **way you should go**. God had intended all along to bless Israel (Gen. 12:1–3), but Israel would not cooperate. Now Israel had one more chance.

48:20–22. God gave new marching orders: **Leave Babylon!** But Israel could not simply march. She was to be God's witness, to bring glory to his name to the **ends of the earth**. The joyous message was simple: **The LORD has redeemed his servant Jacob**. (For God's redemption, see "Deeper Discoveries," chs. 60–61; for servant of Yahweh, see "Deeper Discoveries," chs. 52–53.)

A word of comfort accompanied the word of command. God had helped Israel escape from Egypt. That served as an example of what would happen if they should decide to leave Babylon at his new command. In the wilderness from Egypt, God had supplied every need, especially water (Exod. 17:6). But would Israel quit arguing with God long enough to believe his new word and act upon it?

From all this, a final lesson is drawn, a lesson repeated in 57:21. The **wicked** will not find **peace**, wholeness, the good and full life. Did Israel belong to this group? Do you?

Sending the Servant for Salvation (49:1–6)

Report of commissioning

SUPPORTING IDEA: *God commissions his people as his royal representatives to share the light of his good news with the nations and with the faithless Israelites.*

49:1–4. This is the second of Isaiah's "Servant Songs" (42:1–4). The servant of God spoke to the **nations** in the language often used to describe prophetic calls (Jer. 1:5). He acted as if he were an ambassador or messenger from the court of Yahweh to the royal courts of the nations, presenting his credentials. He was God's secret weapon who was protected by the Lord. God had installed him in the office of the royal **servant**. The last part of verse 3 must have astounded the prophet's audience. The prophetic commissioning narrative was not talking about a single person's experience with God. This testimony was meant to be Israel's witness. **Israel**, who was pining away in exile, complaining about her fate, was supposed to be presenting her credentials as God's royal representative to the far-off lands. She was supposed to be glorifying God and showing off his royal **splendor** to the nations.

As often in prophetic narratives (Isa. 6:5), the called one complained to God that the task was too great and his power was too small. The exiles saw the whole history of Israel as adding up to nothing. **I have spent my strength in vain** (Hb. *tohu*, formlessness) **and for nothing** (Hb. *hebel*, meaningless, vanity, emptiness) combines the Genesis term for the formless chaos God formed into a world and Ecclesiastes' word for life's lack of meaning, result, and purpose. The exiles could only resign themselves to this: "Yet in truth my cause is with the LORD and my reward [or compensation] with my God" (REB, NAB, NJB, JPS). God wanted more than resignation. He wanted action: "Flee from the Babylonians" (48:20).

49:5–6. As usual, God had an answer to the complaint. The servant reported God's answer in first-person testimony. The servant idea was nothing new to God. He had planned for this since before there was an Israel.

God sought to use the servant to **bring Jacob back to him**. What? How could servant Israel bring Israel back to him? The prophet used mysterious language to arouse his audience's curiosity. He also implied a scandalous theology. Maintaining the personal language of the prophetic call, he said God had used the servant to turn Israel away from her sins. But if the servant was Israel (v. 3), then the prophet has divided Israel into two groups—the servant and the sinner. Here the implications of 48:1–5 are carried forward. Not all Israel was Israel, the people of God. Israel by birth was not the Israel of God. Israel the servant had a mission to Israel the sinner. The commission as royal representative of God was not automatic for every Israelite. It came to those who were willing to quit complaining and to accept the assignment.

Accepting the assignment meant not only bringing glory (42:8,12; 48:11) to Yahweh but also to be **honored in the eyes of the LORD**—to receive glory and **strength** from him. The divine King promised to share his power and glory with his royal servant.

The astonishing element of the servant's commission remained to be revealed. The exile had not narrowed the scope of servant Israel's commission. Rather, it presented opportunity for widening that scope. It should have been evident in exile that the major task of servant Israel was to revive Israel, but this was **too small a thing** for God's servant. He needed new responsibilities. What a shock when the prophet revealed what the new responsibilities meant! Israel was to be **a light for the Gentiles**. She was to get out of her mourning clothes, dress in royal regalia, and present herself as God's ambassador with full credentials at the foreign courts.

The desperate situation of God's people was no cause for complaint. It presented a chance to carry out a calling. God wanted to save **the ends of the earth**. He had commissioned Israel to be the servant who would carry out the commission. Would Israel rise to the task or remain in self-pity in her mourning?

Ⅾ Prosperity for the Prisoners (49:7–26)

Legal dispute

> **SUPPORTING IDEA:** *God's redemptive act for his people will reveal to the nations that he is Savior, Redeemer, Holy One, and God.*

49:7–12. Israel was not satisfied. She continued to argue. God continued to answer. It might seem like the impossible dream for an exiled people so **abhorred and despised** to achieve the position described for **servant** Israel. But the **Holy One** was also the **Redeemer**, faithful to his promises and purposes. He had **chosen** Israel. She could not fail. (For God chooses, and we are free, see "Deeper Discoveries," chs. 45–46.)

The interpretation of verse 8 is difficult. The reading probably should be, "In a favorable time I answered you, and in a day of salvation I helped you so I might form you and give you for a covenant to the people to establish the land and to give as an inherited possession the decimated inheritance" (author's translation; cp. NASB, REB, NRSV, JPS, NJB).

The prophetic proclamation of salvation was God's answer in the day he chose to recreate his people and give them a new task. But they could not brag about their covenant relationship with God. Indeed, God had made them a **covenant** (42:6) for the nations so they could gain God's salvation.

Only in this way could Israel hope to inherit again their land. This was a new style of conquest! Would Israel march obediently to these orders as they had under Joshua?

God spelled out his marching orders. Get out of hiding from the nations and march through the wilderness where God will protect you and provide. All of this is due to the Lord's **compassion**. Israel included not simply the Babylonian exiles, but the exiles around the world, even in southern Egypt. (**Aswan** or Syene is the southernmost town in Egypt at the first cataract just north of Ethiopia; cp. Ezek. 29:10. It was a flourishing trading and mining center. Many Israelite exiles lived on a nearby island called Elephantine.)

49:13–21. Along the march, Israel had a hymn to sing (v. 13), praising God for his comfort and compassion (ch. 40). But the people could not get caught up in the prophet's exciting good news. They preferred to argue. They wanted more than the word of a prophet. They wanted to stick to the facts: **The LORD has forsaken me, the Lord has forgotten me**. Note that this is placed in the mouth of Zion, the city of Jerusalem, which lay in ruins. Israel in exile wanted God to explain Zion's miserable fate.

Again, God had the answer. God had more love for **Zion** than the most deeply devoted **mother**. He was the divine architect, who had written the plans for his city on his own **hands** where he could never lose them. The vision of the destroyed walls of the city confronted God every time he glanced at his own hands. Verse 17 offers a word of assurance that the city will be rebuilt without difficulty, but the translation is difficult (cp. NRSV, NIV, REB, KJV, JPS). A literal translation reads, "Your sons (or your builders) hurry; your harrassers and hurters (those who dry you up) depart from you" (author's translation). The word **sons** includes a play on the word "builders" (REB, TEB, NASB, NJB, NAB) which is spelled quite similarly. In fact, the traditional Hebrew text has "sons," while the Dead Sea Scroll and earliest Greek translation text (the Septuagint) read "builders."

With sons, the image is of exiles rushing home to Jerusalem. With builders, it becomes carpenters hurrying to finish their work reconstructing the city. The wordplay continues in that *hurry* and *harrassers* begin with the same three letters in Hebrew, while *hurters* (NIV does not translate this word) has the same first and third letter with a similar letter in the middle. The prophet used unusual verbal skills to underline the promise: God will never **forget you** because **your walls are ever before** him. In fact, Isaiah implied, the work of salvation is hurrying to completion before you ever see it. All Zion must do is **lift up your eyes and look around**. Watch your children coming. These returning exiles are so beautiful they are forming the jewelry or **ornaments** that adorn Zion's bridal gown.

God renewed his promise of a rapid population growth for Jerusalem. This surprised the bereaved mother city (cp. 48:19). Suddenly she had children whose origins she could not remember.

49:22–26. The Gentiles would become the beasts of burden who would bring the population back to Jerusalem. The rulers of the earth would again pay homage to Jerusalem. All of this was to reintroduce Israel to the LORD their God. The lesson to be learned is spelled out in proverbial style: **those who hope in me will not be disappointed** or ashamed (KJV, JPS, NRSV, NASB).

The persistent people continued their argument. No one was strong enough to take battle spoils or **plunder** back from the victorious army. God patiently answered, because he had a purpose in what he was doing. He would do what the people considered impossible. He would **contend** with their enemies. He would **save** their **children**. The **oppressors** would suffer the fate Israel suffered in the 587–586 siege of Jerusalem. God wanted the entire world—**all mankind**—to see what he did for Israel and thus come to truly **know** him as Israel's **Savior . . . Redeemer, the Mighty One of Jacob**— all old, traditional names associated with Yahweh's choice and deliverance of his people.

Yes, God put up with the pitiful complaints of his people to perfect his plan. He wanted to reveal his person and his nature not just to Israel, but to the whole world. Israel was content to continue questioning. God would never forget Israel, but Israel so quickly forgot what God had done for them. They no longer trusted him to fulfill his promises. They no longer believed he is the only God. They no longer expected God's deliverance and salvation.

> **MAIN IDEA REVIEW:** *God calls his people to trust him as he works through them to bring salvation to the nations.*

III. CONCLUSION

Life's Basic Question

Who is God? That is the basic question life comes down to. The answer comes from experience and trust. Have you become hardened like Israel until you have come to believe that God has forsaken and forgotten you? Or will you listen as he proclaims his love and care for you? Do you believe God is still your Lord, your Savior, your Redeemer? Do you believe he still has a plan to defeat your enemies and bring you back to himself? Yes, God has a plan— and a mission—for you. He loves you too much to forget you. He waits for you to come back to him and again be his witness, his light to the nations. Do you have the faith to come back? Or are you too busy questioning God?

PRINCIPLES

- Anger at his people's sin causes God to discipline and judge his people.
- Suffering and affliction are often God's ways of refining and purifying the lives of his people.
- God's mission for his people is to extend his salvation to every person on earth.

APPLICATIONS

- Promise God you will never resort to sorcery, magic, horoscopes, or astrology. Instead, seek his will in prayer and the reading of his Word.
- Tell God that you have confidence that every command he issues is the best thing for you.
- Ask God to forgive you and to give you his peace and righteousness.

IV. LIFE APPLICATION

Untangling the Strings

Ruth Bell Graham remembers the evening her husband, Billy Graham, came home from a trip with another surprise toy for the children—a small puppet on the end of a stick. The children took the puppet and did everything with it except use it as a puppet. They kicked it, threw it, and played ball with it. Soon the poor puppet was tied in knots and no longer fit to play with. Ruth Graham had to hang it up by its hook to a nail in the fireplace mantel. Slowly, painstakingly, she untangled one knot and then the next. Finally, the strings were in order again, and the puppet was ready for the children to play with.

Israel thought they were a lot like that puppet. Life had battered and bruised them. As God's chosen people, they were supposed to stay safe and secure. Instead, they found themselves all tangled in knots, living away from their chosen homeland and forsaken by their God. They needed someone with patience to straighten them out so they could be useful again. God reached down to do just what they needed. Israel cried, "Oh, no! You can't do that. You don't know how. You let us down in the first place. Don't try to come back and take over now."

Patiently, God looked down and said, "But I created you; I am your parent. I am the only one who can help you. I have a plan to restore you, renew you, save you."

Do you share Israel's feelings of being abused and forgotten? Do you think you are a puppet that is being misused by the world? Are you willing to let God untangle your strings, put you back together, and then pull your strings so you can accomplish what he has planned for you? God wants to save you, restore you. He wants to use you meaningfully in his mission. He waits for you to quit complaining, stop your questioning, and start listening for his instructions.

V. PRAYER

God, I have spent enough time and energy complaining. I have accused you of everything and trusted you very little. Let me believe you are at work on your plan to deliver me and to use me. Here am I. Send me. Amen.

VI. DEEPER DISCOVERIES

Salvation (Hb. *yasha'*)

Hubbard notes, "In general, the root *ysh'* implies bringing help to people in the midst of their trouble rather than in rescuing them from it. It is almost exclusively a theological term with Yahweh as its subject and his people as its object" (Hubbard, NIDOTTE, 2, p. 556). The primary saving event in the Old Testament was the exodus from Egypt. Pharaoh with his army closed in on the fleeing Israelites. "They were terrified and cried out to the LORD" (Exod. 14:10). Moses' calm answer called the Israelites to "stand firm and you will see the deliverance (*yeshu'ah*) the LORD will bring you today" (Exod. 14:13). "That day the LORD saved Israel from the hands of the Egyptians" (Exod. 14:30). So Israel could sing: "The LORD is my strength and my song; he has become my salvation" (Exod. 15:2).

Similarly the period of the judges can be described as a time when the Israelites "were in great distress. Then the LORD raised up judges, who saved them out of the hands of these raiders" (Judg. 2:15–16). The same scenario occurs in the Book of Psalms with individuals rather than with the nation. Psalm 18:3 is typical: "I call to the LORD, who is worthy of praise, and I am saved from my enemies." God brings salvation in his own way, not through human resources that would give people reason for pride (Job 40:14). "It is not by sword or spear that the LORD saves; for the battle is the LORD's" (1 Sam. 17:47). Thus the nouns formed from the root *ysh'* are often translated "deliverance, help, victory, safety, welfare." Israel thus learns, "Do not say, 'I'll pay you back for this wrong!' Wait for the LORD, and he will deliver (*yasha'*) you" (Prov. 20:22).

Isaiah used *ysh'* fifty-six times in his book. His goal was for Israel to sing: "Surely God is my salvation; I will trust and not be afraid" as they live by drawing "water from the wells of salvation" (12:2–3). The reality is, "You have forgotten God your Savior" (17:10). The book operates in this tension between a people who have forgotten and a God who wants to be their salvation. He points to the day when Israel will once again call to the Lord and once again "he will send them a savior and defender, and he will rescue them" (19:20).

Why is salvation needed? Not because of any shortcomings in God (59:1) but because "your iniquities have separated you from your God; your sins have hidden his face from you, so that he will not hear" (59:2; see also vv. 11–12). God was angry at the people's sins. They experienced the anger and asked, "How then can we be saved?" (64:5). This question comes at the end of the Book of Isaiah but controls the book's picture of salvation. Because of their sins and their refusal to heed and obey God, they appeared to be in a hopeless situation. They had lost their homeland and their worship place. They lived in a foreign country in exile. They had no Moses, or Samson, or David, or Hezekiah. How could they be saved?

How does salvation come? "In repentance and rest is your salvation, in quietness and trust is your strength." The problem for Israel was, "you would have none of it" (30:15). God has the pattern for salvation. People must turn away from foreign gods and to him (45:22). He gave the invitation to salvation, but to experience salvation, Israel had to trust him rather than seeking actions of their own. They must lament as the psalmists did and ask for God's grace, strength, and salvation "in time of distress" (33:2) as exemplified by Hezekiah (37:20). Then God will be "a rich store of salvation" (33:6) and save his city (37:35). He will "contend with those who contend with you, and your children I will save" (49:25). Israel would then join Hezekiah in proclaiming: "The LORD will save me" (38:20).

What does salvation include? For Israel after judgment, salvation meant to see Jerusalem again and celebrate God's festivals there with God ruling as "our Mighty One . . . judge. . . lawgiver . . . king," the one "who will save us" (33:21–22). He will come to strengthen the weak and encourage the faithful, meting out "divine retribution" as he comes to save (35:2–4). He will establish peace and righteousness to replace violence (60:18; 62:1). Salvation also includes a mission for saved servant Israel, to be a "covenant for the people" (49:8). It is a call to "maintain justice and do what is right" (56:1).

Why does salvation come? It comes because God is angry with the nations and the ways they have treated his exiled people whom he punished (63:3–6). It comes because God identifies himself as "your Savior" who is intent on redeeming his people (43:3). It comes because of God's "compassion and many kindnesses," "his love and mercy" (63:7–9). It comes because of God's commitment to his people, his sons, whose distress he shares

(63:8–9). It comes because the time has come for his plan to be worked out: "The year of my redemption has come" (63:4).

God is "mighty to save" (63:1). He sees that no one else can bring justice and salvation for his people (59:15–17; 63:3). "Apart from me there is no savior"; for God has "saved. . . and not some foreign god among you" (43:11–12; cp. 45:15–22; 47:13–15). God creates salvation (45:8). Salvation comes because God has a purpose: "All mankind will know that I, the LORD, am your Savior" (49:26; cp. 52:10).

Who can be saved? Isaiah's central focus was salvation for Zion/Jerusalem/Israel (46:13; 62:1,11). But this is also where Isaiah stunned Israel. Through him God issued a universal invitation: "Turn to me and be saved, all you ends of the earth" (45:22).

When does salvation come? God promised Israel that "my salvation will not be delayed" (46:13); it is "on the way" (51:5). He announced to Jerusalem: "See, your Savior comes!" (62:11). Salvation is, then, first of all for Isaiah, an immediate, present action of God to bring help to an exiled people and bring them back to Jerusalem in righteousness, justice, and peace.

But an immediate salvation from Babylonian exile is not the only time of salvation Isaiah pointed to. The final days were coming when Israel would proclaim: "Surely this is our God; we trusted in him, and he saved us. This is the LORD, we trusted in him; let us rejoice and be glad in his salvation" (25:9). They would confess their own inability to bring salvation and would experience the resurrection of the dead (26:18–19). Then the tension would be resolved. The people would no longer forget their Savior; they would trust in him and experience his salvation from all sources of trouble. Then "Israel will be saved by the LORD with an everlasting salvation" (45:17).

VII. TEACHING OUTLINE

A. INTRODUCTION

1. Lead Story: Power to Deliver
2. Context: God has announced his plan to use Cyrus of Persia as his instrument to save Israel from Babylonian captivity. Israel cannot believe such a message. They want their own king, not a Persian king. God has to listen to their arguments and show them that his way may be mysterious but is best for them as he calls them to trust him, become his servant, and join his mission.
3. Transition: Chapters 47–49 introduce three parties to the scene. Babylon sits in dust and ashes, lamenting as Cyrus's army approaches and Israel's God announces their doom. None of their traditional means of help and rescue can deliver them.

Israel stands before God demanding an explanation for what God is doing. He points to his history with them, a history of fulfilled promises for a stubborn people. Will they just one time trust him to do what is best for them? Get up. Leave Babylon. Obey! God's servant Israel testifies to God's commission to bring Israel back to him and to be a light to the nations.

Reading these chapters, you can pick out which group you most resemble: lamenting Babylonia, combative Israel, or servant Israel. Are you willing to set out on God's mission to the nations? Or will you sit and scream, "God has forgotten me"?

B. COMMENTARY

1. Calling the Chaldeans to Complain (47:1–15)

2. Revelation and Release for the Rebels (48:1–22)

3. Sending the Servant for Salvation (49:1–6)

4. Prosperity for the Prisoners (49:7–26)

C. CONCLUSION: UNTANGLING THE STRINGS

1. Wrap-up: God has not forgotten you. He is the willing source of salvation. He knows your trouble and wants to help you. He alone has the power and a plan to help. It may not be the plan you would develop, but it is best for you.

2. Personal Challenge: God has the plan. God is willing to act. The situation now depends on your attitude. Are you too busy complaining and arguing to hear his call to action? Do you want to hold on to your way of doing things rather than let God do it his way, the best way? Ask God to give you a willing heart. Ask him to show you the first step you need to take to turn to him and experience his salvation.

VIII. ISSUES FOR DISCUSSION

1. What makes a person think that God has forgotten him? How do you try to show people that he has not?

2. In what ways have you seen God provide salvation in times of trouble?

3. What are you and your church doing to serve as a light to the nations?

Isaiah 50–51

Turning the Tables

Quote

"*In* their heart of hearts all men, even in the chaos and turmoil of their short and brutish lives, desire above all else the revelation of the living God."

George A. E. Knight

IN A NUTSHELL

*G*od questions his people, explains that they suffer because of their sins, and reminds them of his past saving acts. Then the servant testifies that he is strengthened in suffering because he knows God is near to help. He invites people in darkness to trust God and to walk in God's light. Otherwise they face torment.

Then God calls his people to trust him like their ancestors Sarah and Abraham. His justice will be a light to the nations, and his eternal salvation is on the way. So the people should choose God's righteousness and salvation instead of fearing human insults.

Suddenly the call comes for God to bring salvation to the ransomed people of God who will return to Zion in triumphant singing and praising. God reminds his people that he is their only comforter, so they must not forget him. The call comes for Jerusalem to wake up. They have suffered double for their sins and are filled with God's wrath. Now God will take suffering away from Jerusalem and give it to her tormentors.

Turning the Tables

I. INTRODUCTION

Losers Forever?

*S*ports fans come in all shapes and sizes. But they are alike in at least one way: They want their team to win. If they had their way, their team would go undefeated every year and always win the league championship. They forget that losses are inevitable in the competitive world of team sports.

But there is a difference between a loss every now and then and a perpetual habit of losing. Occasionally a team slips so far that it goes through an entire season or several seasons without winning a single game. The fans begin to wonder: Can we ever win? Must we resign ourselves to being losers? Or is this the year we will turn the tables and beat all those teams who have so soundly beaten us these past seasons?

Israel in exile knew about the experience of losing. Forty years in exile and no sign of relief. What did they have to do to escape their suffering and punishment? Had God truly forgotten them? When should a people decide they are lost, never to be remembered or rescued? What does it take for God to come to his people and turn the tables for them? Isaiah 50–51 helps us see God's ways in helping a "loser."

II. COMMENTARY

Turning the Tables

> **MAIN IDEA:** *God's people suffer for their sins, but one day God will turn the tables on their enemies. Then they will suffer as they made God's people suffer.*

A Examining the Exiles (50:1–3)

Courtroom trial

> **SUPPORTING IDEA:** *God's people must be ready to welcome him when he comes to redeem and reclaim them.*

50:1. God found himself once more in the role of a defendant in a trial. He came out questioning Israel. He used Israelite family law to defend himself. If he had divorced his wife Israel, he would have given her a **certificate of divorce** and could not remarry her, since she was now married to Babylon or the gods of Babylon (Deut. 24:1–4). If he sold his children into slavery to pay his debts, he would have no further claims on them (Exod. 21:7–11). Yahweh denied both charges. Israel, not Yahweh, was the guilty party and she deserved the fate she received. She still belonged legally to Yahweh, because she had neither divorce certificate nor bill of sale. **Sins** led to her exile, but God still loved his bride.

50:2–3. Yahweh then looked at the court and asked where his accusers were. Here is a wordplay on customs of hospitality. Yahweh **came**, but no one welcomed him at the door. Was he an unexpected guest? Had his own people not learned from their history that he was their redeemer and deliverer, as shown by his bringing Israel out of Egypt and giving them the promised land. God was at the door to bring an end to the captivity of his people. The **darkness** of nature was a symbol of God's joining Israel in mourning because of their captivity. However, the people saw neither God's sadness nor his readiness to deliver them. God's people continued their mourning and their accusations against God for not acting on their behalf.

B The Servant's Sermon (50:4–11)

Prophetic song of confidence

SUPPORTING IDEA: *Daily communion with God helps one maintain confidence in him during life's most difficult times.*

50:4–5. This is the third of the "Servant Songs" of Isaiah (42:1–4). The servant again spoke in first person (see 49:1–6). In contrast to the complaints of his audience, he testified to his trust in God in spite of all the persecution and mocking he had faced. He was confident because he had found his God-given mission. The servant had a **word** of comfort for his **weary**, complaining companions. He had such a word because each **morning** he listened to his God for a new word. He had such a word because he was not **rebellious**. He listened obediently to what God had to say.

50:6–9. Such communion with God led to confidence even in the most difficult situations. Persecutors tortured him. They inflicted the most embarrassing and shameful punishment on him—pulling out his **beard** and **spitting** on his face. But he did not **hide**. Why did he not turn the tables and fight back? Because God helped him. In the end God would not let him be **disgraced**.

He could be taken into court, but his attorney would vindicate him. No judge could possibly **condemn** him or pronounce him guilty. The servant's Babylonian accusers stood helpless. They would gradually wear out or be destroyed like a good suit of clothes, but his God would sustain him.

50:10–11. Suddenly, the servant changed his tune and faced his audience. He confronted them with the question: **Who among you fears the LORD and obeys the word of his servant?** The test to prove you are on God's side has one question—do you obey the voice of the servant commissioned by God? The servant, like the rest of the exiles, had no **special** light that showed him the way. He had simple **trust** in God day by day, morning by morning (cp. v. 4). Israel in the darkness of exile must trust God for their salvation. Trusting God meant believing the word of God's servant messenger.

Not all Israel were fearers of Yahweh. They could not believe that a **servant** who submitted to suffering and disgrace could be God's chosen. God pronounced the sentence upon them. They would be caught in their own firetrap. They would suffer the worst kind of **torment**.

Look and Listen to the Lord (51:1–8)
Legal dispute

SUPPORTING IDEA: *Remembering past history with God and paying attention to his word gives confidence that his eternal salvation is near.*

51:1–3. The people continued pouting and pleading with God. They had a simple case: We are pious people, direct descendants of Abraham and Sarah, but few in number and helpless. God had a direct answer for these God-seekers: Take a close look at history. Go back to your beginnings. Look at the meaning of your family tree rather than its many branches. God started with only **Abraham** and **Sarah**. It seemed physically impossible that they would have children. Yet God **blessed him and made him many.** If the hallowed ancestors could accept God's promise and begin his work with the nations, how much more should you believe the new message of hope? God will indeed **comfort Zion.** Indeed, he will transform the wilderness of rocks and dry riverbeds that surrounded Jerusalem into a paradise, a new garden of **Eden.** This would bring a new atmosphere dominated by **joy, gladness, thanksgiving,** and **singing.**

51:4–6. God commanded his people to quit listening to their own feeble frustrations and to heed his new edict. The divine King had proclaimed throughout the world that his time of salvation for his people had arrived. This **salvation** (see "Deeper Discoveries," chs. 47–49) would be unlike any previous deliverance from enemies that Israel had experienced. It would include all **nations.** Indeed, the nations were to **wait in hope** for the new day. This would be a day of **justice** and **righteousness.** (For justice, see "Deeper Discoveries," ch. 1; for righteousness, see "Deeper Discoveries.") This salvation would transcend all time, even after the natural order had disappeared. This **salvation will last forever.**

51:7–8. Still the people grumbled. They knew the **law** of God and kept it, but it did not help their situation. (For law, see "Deeper Discoveries," chs. 2–4.) They remained the object of **reproach** and **insults** from their captors. God reminded them of his previous promise. Such men would die, but God's promised **salvation** would last **through all generations**.

D A Road for the Redeemed (51:9–16)

Lament and oracle of salvation

SUPPORTING IDEA: *Security comes only from the Creator/ Redeemer, so people should fear him and never fear other people.*

51:9–11. The people responded with a traditional lamentation. They tried to wake God up (Ps. 80). He had talked so much about the creation and the exodus proving his power. They asked, Was it really you who did all this? (For Rahab, see 30:7.) The implication is, If you are so powerful, why are we in such a state here in Babylonian exile and why don't you show your power again? The prophet answered with a verse of a hymn (35:10) that promised deliverance: **The ransomed of the LORD will return**. (For God's redemption, see "Deeper Discoveries," chs. 60–61.) There was no cause for **sorrow and sighing**. **Gladness and joy** would be the theme from now through eternity.

51:12–16. God introduced an oracle of salvation. You have no reason to **fear**, he declared, because God **comforts you**. This comfort is not pie in the sky. It makes sense. The people you fear are simply mortals who will die as quickly as **grass**. Contrast them with the eternal Creator, whom you seem to have forgotten in your great concern over these mighty mortals. **Constant terror** only shows lack of faith, a vision fixed on humans and not on God. What evidence do you have of the power of this mighty **oppressor**?

The people retorted: "But we are bowed down in slave labor, because the Babylonians are so angry at us." God answered: "The oppressors, not you, are going to die. I am setting you **free**. Remember who I am, not who they are. Let me introduce you once more to the **LORD Almighty** (Hb. LORD of Hosts). You are safe in the palm of the **hand** that **laid the foundations of the earth. You are my people**. That should be comfort enough, no matter what your situation."

E A Cup for the Captors (51:17–23)

Oracle of salvation

SUPPORTING IDEA: *God's anger and punishment give way to comfort and rescue for his people as he turns the tables on their captors.*

51:17–23. This section begins with something of a parody of the people's lament in verse 9 (52:1). They asked God to wake up. Now he rouses the people to action. God acknowledged the situation of the people and confessed that he had been the cause. **Jerusalem** had **drunk from the hand of the LORD the cup of his wrath**. He had left her without leadership politically and religiously. They had no one to comfort them (40:1). God had the answer. He would turn the tables. After all he is **your God, who defends his people**. Israel's captors would have to drink the cup that God had first given to Israel!

> **MAIN IDEA REVIEW:** *God's people suffer for their sins, but one day God will turn the tables on their enemies. Then they will suffer as they made God's people suffer.*

III. CONCLUSION

A Perspective on Suffering

God's people suffer. Belonging to God is no guarantee of a safe, serene passage through life. Often our suffering comes because of our sins. God's people must confess those sins and admit they deserve what they are receiving. God's people can also turn to God and trust him. He has a plan of salvation and deliverance for his people. The enemy may seem strong, but our eyes should be focused on God, waiting for our Creator to act as our Savior.

PRINCIPLES

- Discipline comes because of sin.
- God's history with his people gives sufficient reason to trust him and expect his salvation.
- God will finally redeem his people and bring judgment on their enemies.

APPLICATIONS

- Trust God even when you cannot see what he is doing.
- Express your joy and gratitude to God.
- Let God be your source of hope even when life is at its worst.

IV. LIFE APPLICATION

Useful in the Dark Times

Marxist guerrillas captured missionary Bruce Olson and dragged him through South American jungles to an isolated camp in Colombia. Day after day, month after month he had no idea what the next day would bring except more suffering from malaria and more rain soaking his body. Each hour he faced a new, fresh guard. Every few days or weeks he faced a new trek through the jungle to a new hideout. Dislocated joints—no matter how painful—were no excuse not to walk on through the jungle. He taught himself a pain-ignoring technique. He told himself, "I'm in pain, yes, but this pain exists only in my body. I am not my body. My mind and spirit are above this, not part of it."

Olson wrote: "It may seem bizarre to some people, but the truth is that it never once occurred to me that it was God's responsibility to rescue me miraculously from this situation. Instead, I believed it was my responsibility to serve God right where I was." So each day he prayed, "Father, I'm alive, and I want to use this time constructively. How can I be useful to you today?" This was nothing new for Bruce Olson. "It was how I approached every day of my life," he wrote. "Why should my prayers or my outlook change now, just because I was in the hands of guerrillas? I knew it was God—not my captors—who would control the outcome of the situation" (quoted by Kay Arthur, pp. 137–139).

God used Isaiah's message to teach this lesson to the exiles in Babylon. They did not endure pain and discouragement, as did Bruce Olson. Rather, they lamented and groaned over their situation. Life brings such pain and disappointment to each of us. We must decide before it comes how we will live. Do we have to have a special plan for trying times, or can we pray each day the same way no matter what our outward situation and conditions may be? Can you pray to God to use you in a constructive way even when you face the darkest times of your life? You can if you begin praying that prayer daily before dark days come. Get in the habit of expecting God to use you rather than waiting for troubled times when you will only know how to cry to God to deliver you.

V. PRAYER

Lord of the universe and of my days, teach me to trust you no matter what the circumstances. Teach me to be so faithful in prayer and service for you that when disaster seems to control my life, I can still pray calmly to you to use me as you have been doing every day. I commit myself to love, serve, and obey you in the tough times as well as the good times. Amen.

VI. DEEPER DISCOVERIES

Righteousness (51:1)

The Hebrew term *tsedeq* with its related terms *tsadiq* and *tsedeqah* refer to loyalty and faithfulness that bring benefit to a community of people. Righteousness "indicates right behavior or status in relation to some standard of behavior accepted in the community.... Nowhere, however, is this standard made explicit" (Reimer, NIDOTTE, 3, p. 750). The standard is more like natural law, something assumed to be known and accepted by the whole community. The standard can refer to God or to humans. "When righteousness refers to God's righteousness, it is in some way related to His saving acts through grace. When it refers to human righteousness, it is related either to one's standing in the covenant with God and/or how one has treated other people ethically" (Smith, *Old Testament Theology,* p. 221).

These related terms appear 523 times in the Old Testament, eighty-one times in Isaiah. They are also strongly represented in Psalms and Proverbs. The term gets its basic definition from God, who is the supreme example of righteousness. He does everything possible for the benefit of his covenant people and the world he created (Isa. 5:16). "Yahweh's righteousness is perhaps the largest, most comprehensive category for Old Testament theology. . . . Yahweh's righteousness entails the governance of the world according to Yahweh's purposes, which are decreed at Sinai and which are assumed in the very fabric of creation. The substance of that righteousness is the well-being of the world, so that when Yahweh's righteousness is fully established in the world, the results are fruitfulness, prosperity, freedom, justice, peace, security, and well-being (*shalom*)" (Bruggemann, *Theology of the Old Testament,* p. 303).

When human righteousness disappears, God puts on his righteousness like battle armor and comes to defend his people and establish his righteous rule among the nations (59:16–18; 63:1). Thus righteousness is often translated "victory" or "triumph," as God intervenes in history to save his people (Isa. 45:8,21,25; 51:1,5–6,8).

The Hebrew terms for "righteousness" often refer to a servant's relationship to his king or master, but they can also describe the good citizen of a community (Gen. 18:24–25; 2 Sam. 4:11). "Isaiah insists on relating *tsdq* to the sphere of social justice and the needs of the oppressed" (Reimer, NIDOTTE, 3, p. 763). Thus in chapters 1–39 Isaiah often combines righteousness with *mishpat* or justice, so that righteousness is what humans are expected to do in connection with an assumed norm for human action under God. In chapters 40–55 righteousness is most often connected with a form of *ysh'* or salvation. This is God's promised gift to his people, a gift of victory that will restore the nation to righteousness.

God established his people in righteousness, but their sin destroyed the righteous order, giving way to murderers (1:21). They continued their regular worship practices without recognizing their sin and their unrighteousness (58:1–5). The people were no longer faithful to God, preferring their idols, and so had no righteousness (64:5–7). Thus God has to deal with a people who were "far from righteousness" (46:12) because they did not tell the truth (48:1). Their disloyalty and unfaithfulness deprived the people of the blessings of peace and righteousness that God wanted to give them (48:18–19; 32:16–17; 60:17).

Some people do not devote themselves to sin; instead, they "gladly do right" (64:5). That means they "remember your ways" (64:5). This is the kind of worship and fasting that God wants, the kind that brings protection to God's people (58:6–8). To establish his righteousness on earth, God has made "his law great and glorious" (42:21). God promises such righteous people that for them life will go well and they will "enjoy the fruit of their deeds" (3:10; see also 28:16–17). He calls them to be his servants and promises to protect them with his righteous right hand (41:10). He will vindicate his servant—that is, prove that he is righteous (50:8). Yes, God's righteousness is on the way and in a hurry (46:13). He will establish a people in righteousness so they have nothing to fear (54:14). He will use Cyrus of Persia to reveal his divine righteousness and to establish this new righteous order in Israel (45:13).

God's ultimate goal for Israel was to establish a social order dominated by righteous relationships rather than selfish manipulation among people (1:26–27; 33:5; 60:17). His righteous people will display God's splendor to the nations (61:3,11). God will achieve this by sending forth his messenger "in a robe of righteousness" (61:10), pouring out his Spirit (11:2; 32:14–17; 61:1–3), and establishing his messiah as the righteous king (11:1–9; 32:1). His people will seek him and pursue righteousness (45:25).

God will make righteousness appear among his people so that all nations may see it and praise him (45:8). All their enemies will recognize God's righteousness and bow before him (45:23–24). God's plan for righteousness extends beyond Israel to the nations (51:4–5). In righteousness God will make his servant a "covenant for the people and a light for the Gentiles" (42:6). God's righteous servant will suffer and die for the sins of the world (53:11). God will establish an eternal righteousness (51:6).

VII. TEACHING OUTLINE

A. INTRODUCTION

1. Lead Story: Losers Forever?
2. Context: God has called Babylon to lament the loss of their captives and has ordered Israel to leave Babylon for home. He has expanded servant Israel's role to that of witness to the nations. He will never forget them but will introduce himself to them and to the nations as the Redeemer and Savior. But how will Israel respond to God's call to leave Babylon and to be a universal witness?
3. Transition: Discouraged, suffering Israel is not up to the task. God has to remind them why they are in the plight they are complaining about and how he has delivered them in the past. The servant of the Lord has to testify to the motives behind his faithful service to God in spite of horrible treatment. He continues to be faithful because he knows God helps him. Israel faces the choice: trust God or continue in idol worship and face torment. God promises to bring salvation to his people just as he did for Abraham and Sarah. He calls Israel to believe in his eternal righteousness, his total commitment to bring salvation to his people. Will they trust him or continue to fear those who have them in exile? In spite of the doubts of the people expressed in scornful repetition of God's claims for himself, God still promises to comfort his people. He will turn the tables on their enemies.

Again Israel faces a decision: do they believe the alluring words of God or the bleak reality of the present situation? We face similar choices in our generation. Do we think history is simply an ongoing struggle between human powers—may the strongest person win? Or do we believe God controls history and can turn the tables so we do not have to be frozen by our fears?

B. COMMENTARY

1. Examining the Exiles (50:1–3)
2. The Servant's Sermon (50:4–11)
3. Look and Listen to the Lord (51:1–8)
4. A Road for the Redeemed (51:9–16)
5. A Cup for the Captors (51:17–23)

C. CONCLUSION: USEFUL IN THE DARK TIMES

1. Wrap-up: Israel maintained dialogue with God about their suffering. Israel faced the troublesome question: Did they trust their Babylonian

captors and their threats, or did they trust the claims and promises of God? Should they leave Babylon in obedience to God, or must they fear the consequences from their Babylonian masters? Had they paid all the price of their sin that God expected? Was the time of suffering past?

2. Personal Challenge: Sin brings suffering. You may suffer for your sin. You may suffer for the sin of an unknown bully. You may suffer because of what sinful acts have created in our environment. The question you face is not "Will I suffer? but "How will I respond to suffering?" Will I use it as an opportunity to vent my complaints and anger, or will I trust God to turn the tables on my life and bring things back to the way he wants them to be. Is God righteous? Or not? You must decide how to answer this question—and then act accordingly.

VIII. ISSUES FOR DISCUSSION

1. What part does God play in causing suffering and troubled times?
2. Does listening to the stories of what God did to help his people long ago help you make decisions about how you will react to suffering and hard times today?
3. What testimony can you give about God's work in times of desperation? Have such times increased your faith or your doubts?
4. What does it mean to say that God is righteous and expects you to be righteous?
5. In what ways have you experienced God's comfort? Does comfort always mean the absence of suffering?

Isaiah 52–53

The Suffering Servant Saves

I. INTRODUCTION
The Transforming Power of Sacrificial Love

II. COMMENTARY
A verse-by-verse explanation of these chapters.

III. CONCLUSION
The Role of the Suffering Servant
An overview of the principles and applications from these chapters.

IV. LIFE APPLICATION
Jesus Our Substitute
Melding these chapters to life.

V. PRAYER
Tying these chapters to life with God.

VI. DEEPER DISCOVERIES
Historical, geographical, and grammatical enrichment of the commentary.

VII. TEACHING OUTLINE
Suggested step-by-step group study of these chapters.

VIII. ISSUES FOR DISCUSSION
Zeroing these chapters in on daily life.

"*T*he thing that was new and revolutionary for the present speakers was the fact that in this case suffering which gave power to be a substitute and to atone was found residing in a quite ordinary, feeble and inconsiderable person whose suffering, disfiguring as it was, had brought him into contempt and abhorrence."

Claus Westermann

Isaiah 52–53

IN A NUTSHELL

*I*saiah 52–53 brings to a climax the teaching about God's servant. God calls Jerusalem to wake up and be ready for his redemption. No longer will peoples and nations blaspheme his name. Instead, they will know that he is the only one who foretells historical events. The messengers of good news, peace, and salvation are praised as they come to proclaim God's victory over the nations. He calls Israel to leave exile and return home under God's protection. Then God introduces anew his servant who was so scarred and ugly that his appearance was appalling. God promises to exalt him. The insignificant, rejected servant knew human sorrow and suffering. But his suffering had purpose, because he bore punishment for our sins to bring us peace. Every one of us strayed off like sheep, but God put our punishment on him. He endured it all without complaint. He endured the death penalty even though he was innocent. All of this fulfilled God's purpose, making the servant an offering to cover our guilt. Death and burial do not complete the story. He will live anew and receive a magnificent portion from God. Why? Because he bore the sins of many and made intercession for transgressors.

The Suffering Servant Saves

I. INTRODUCTION

The Transforming Power of Sacrificial Love

*E*rnest Gordon tells a story in *Miracle on the River Kwai* about Scottish soldiers forced by their Japanese captors to labor on a jungle railroad. Under the strain of captivity they had degenerated to barbarous behavior, but one afternoon something happened.

"A shovel was missing. The officer in charge became enraged. He demanded that the missing shovel be produced, or else. When nobody in the squadron budged, the officer got his gun and threatened to kill them all on the spot . . . It was obvious the officer meant what he said. Then, finally, one man stepped forward. The officer put away his gun, picked up a shovel, and beat the man to death. When it was over, the survivors picked up the bloody corpse and carried it with them to the second tool check. This time, no shovel was missing. Indeed, there had been a miscount at the first check point.

"The word spread like wildfire through the whole camp. An innocent man had been willing to die to save the others! . . . The incident had a profound effect. . . . The men began to treat each other like brothers.

"When the victorious Allies swept in, the survivors, human skeletons, lined up in front of their captors . . . (and instead of attacking their captors) insisted: 'No more hatred. No more killing. Now what we need is forgiveness.'" Sacrificial love has transforming power (adapted by Don Ratzlaff, *Christian Leader*).

Isaiah climaxes his prophecy by describing the servant of the Lord. His description has sent Bible students scurrying to discover exactly who the prophet had in mind. The question has been asked at least from the time of Philip and the Ethiopian eunuch (Acts 8:31–34). Among the multitude of Old Testament figures nominated as Isaiah's Suffering Servant are Moses, Joshua, David, Hezekiah, Uzziah, Jehoiachin, Zerubbabel, Sheshbazzar, Cyrus of Persia, Isaiah, Jeremiah, or a person among the exiles unknown to modern readers.

Others look back at earlier Servant Songs in Isaiah 40–55 (42:1–9; 49:1–13; 50:4–11) and decide that Isaiah consistently refers to Israel, or at least a remnant within Israel as the servant. More traditionally, conservative scholars have seen Isaiah 52:13–53:12 as a special piece of literature giving the most explicit prophecy of the coming of Jesus Christ in the Old Testament. As we wind our way through the most exquisite of Old Testament passages, we will have to see how mysterious the prophet wants to be in describing the Suffering Servant.

II. COMMENTARY

The Suffering Servant Saves

MAIN IDEA: *God's zeal for his people is revealed as he sends his servant to suffer and die for their sins.*

A. Zealous for Zion (52:1–12)

Marching orders

SUPPORTING IDEA: *The Divine King will rescue, redeem, and restore his people to show his salvation to all nations.*

52:1–2. The prophet became a commander ordering his troops into action. First, he had to wake them up and get them in parade uniforms ready for the great festival procession. God's people could junk their mourning clothes forever and put on their Sabbath-go-to-meeting clothes. On this holy day they must march to the **holy city**. No longer would they be bothered with the torments from their unclean, **uncircumcised and defiled** captors. They could rise from the **dust** of mourning, sit instead on Jerusalem's throne, and **free** themselves from the captive **chains**. God had commanded his people to "leave Babylon" (48:20). Now they should be on their way back to the **holy city** to again assume God's calling.

52:3–6. How could a captive people leave, throw away exile chains, and claim their freedom? God was going to redeem his people, but not ransom them. He got **nothing** for them when he gave them to Babylonia and would give no **money** in exchange now that he was about to redeem them from captivity (43:3).

God then gave a brief résumé of the history of Israel's oppression. It began in **Egypt** (Exod. 1–15) and had its climax in **Assyria** (Isa. 7–8). God asked a rhetorical question: literally, "what belongs to me here?" God had empowered the foreign rulers to capture and discipline his people, but God was getting no gain or glory from Israel's captivity and oppression, so he promised he would not let his name be **blasphemed** or defiled by his enemies any longer. Instead, he would restore his people and their worship.

Verse 6 is written in condensed, cryptic Hebrew, so translators render it in various ways. Westermann goes so far as to say, "The text of vv. 5b and 6 is so corrupt that the original meaning cannot now be made out" (OTL, p. 248). A literal reading of the verse is: "Therefore my people will know my name. Therefore (a word not in the Dead Sea Scroll and earliest translations) in that day that I am he speaking. Look at me" (or Here I am). The NIV's mention of history being **foretold** may go beyond the meaning of this text, although it is true to the larger message of Isaiah.

As in the exodus (Exod. 3:14–15), God would introduce himself to his people with his personal **name**—Yahweh. Once again his people would pay attention to his voice and believe in him as the only God. Note the use of the phrase "I am he" to declare God's uniqueness among all deities (Deut. 32:39; Isa. 41:4; 46:4; the only other Old Testament use appears in the mouth of David in 1 Chr. 21:17).

52:7–10. The prophet provided the proper hymn for such a joyous, festive return march. This enabled Jerusalem to praise the messenger who announced the **good news**. God had again shown that he was the Divine King of the universe (Pss. 47; 93). The chorus increased as the **watchmen** took up the song and watched the Lord parade in royal procession into his Holy City. Finally, all the destroyed **ruins** of the city were included in the mighty choir celebrating the fulfillment of Yahweh's mission to comfort his people (40:1) and redeem them (41:14; 44:6,22–24; 48:17,20; 54:5,8; 63:9,16).

The climax of the hymn turns beyond Israel again to the **nations**. God worked among his people to bring hope to the world. Yet even the word of **salvation** had an undertone of threat, because the holy arm of God brought judgment to those who stood against him (Ps. 98:1).

52:11–12. Finally, the words came for which Israel had waited many years in Babylon—the orders to march forth from captivity. The marching orders had specific conditions. They must go as the holy people of God, touching and carrying nothing but the temple **vessels** of worship which the Babylonians had taken into captivity as booty of battle (see 2 Kgs. 25:13–17). God promised Israel time to collect all her holy treasures. They were to march in orderly ranks from captivity. They would not be escapees, fleeing for their lives. They would be the army of God, who would march protectively at the **rear**.

God had given the marching dress, the marching hymn, and the marching order. The only question that remained was who would join in. History proved that the people of the captivity were slow to accept the divine invitation to leave the security of Babylon and march into a new day in the city they would have to restore.

B. Satisfaction for the Suffering Servant (52:13–53:12)

Testimony service

> **SUPPORTING IDEA:** *The inconspicuous, unappreciated servant of the Lord will suffer and die for the sins of the people.*

52:13–15. The fourth and final "servant song" (42:1–4) presents a service of testimony in which both God and the congregation lend their voices to praise the servant of Yahweh. This may be the best-known text in the Old Testament. It is in many ways the most difficult to translate, interpret, and understand.

As shown in the introduction above, the center of interest in this passage is usually the attempt to identify the historical personality behind the servant. This task is basically impossible, for the prophet intentionally wrote in mysterious language. He wanted to do much more than send us on a mystery chase. He wanted us to seek the message that the text seeks to bring to his audience with his poem and to see how that message can continue to speak to us in light of our experiences with God. The prophetic poet has already given us Cyrus, Israel, and a remnant in Israel as those called to be the servant of Yahweh. Now he shows us that this is to be a truly remarkable person representing his people Israel to the nations.

As we read, we have to ask, was Isaiah personifying Israel and all the nation's sufferings? Was he pointing to a specific leader among his own people? Was he describing his own mission as he did in chapter 40 and elsewhere? Was he pointing to the future to a person whom God would ultimately send? Or was he leaving a portrait in front of us and inviting us to place our own picture in the center of the portrait? Could it be that God intended the prophet's portrait of the Suffering Servant to be a combination of several or even all of the above alternatives? We will have to study the text closely to see what it teaches us and how we are supposed to respond to it.

To begin the study, the student should use as many translations as possible, giving particular attention to 52:14–15 and 53:7–11.

God opened the service by predicting the fortune of his servant: **act wisely, be raised and lifted up and highly exalted.** "Act wisely" involves a word with a double meaning—act wisely and be successful. "Raised up" can mean placed in a high position, have strength and victory, or be praised and exalted as God is. "Lifted up" means to be carried, to be raised on high, to be elevated to a high position. It too can be used to praise God on high. To be "highly exalted" is to be tall, to be high and exalted as God is. This description of the servant's future colors everything that follows. The picture of exaltation, praise, and success must remain in our mind as we read everything else about the servant. Fame and fortune should come his way. He would receive accolades otherwise reserved for God himself.

The prophet contrasted this positive portrait from God with the expectation of the multitudes. The Hebrew text describes this in testimony form: "Just as many shuddered (or were appalled) because of you, so disfigured from (meaning beyond) man; his appearance and his form from (meaning beyond) the sons of man" (author's translation). They were horrified at the physical appearance of the servant and told him so to his face. He no longer looked like a human being. What could have caused this? How could such a person expect exaltation and success? How is this related to the servant's portrait in 50:4–6?

Verse 15 begins with a statement that is difficult to understand in the context. The Hebrew apparently reads, "just so he will sprinkle many nations" (author's translation; see KJV). The earliest Greek translators understood the text to mean "he shall astonish many nations." Normally, we should interpret a line of Hebrew poetry as synonymous with or contrasting to the line that follows. In this case, the following line reads, "kings shall shut their mouths." This still does not tell us if the reaction is positive or negative. Is it a literal comparison or a military metaphor? Are the nations horrified at his physical appearance, or are they stunned to silence by the military might that he brings against them? Or has the servant attained such a high position that all other international dignitaries must wait to be spoken to before they can speak (Job 29:8–9)? As is true with so much of the Servant Songs, the text is mysteriously ambiguous.

The first verses set a mood of astonishment and expectation without allowing one to interpret the specific results. The conclusion completes the mysterious tone. It ties to 48:4–8, where an Israel that has refused to hear is promised they will now hear new things never before revealed. Here in 52:15b we find the group surrounding the servant **will see, and what they have not heard, they will understand**. Just as the servant's future is different from all expectations, so is that of the group testifying to and surrounding the servant. But are these a remnant from Israel, or is it the **nations** and **kings** of 15a?

53:1–3. The scene shifts dramatically. A group takes center stage to give its testimony. Are these the kings of 52:15 or the audience to whom the prophet normally spoke—the exiles in Babylon? They echo the note of astonishment—they had seen the unbelievable. They had seen **the arm of the LORD** revealed to the most unexpected person (people)! Then they turn to describe the event and again surprise us. They did not tell an event at all. They pictured the life of a most unlikely individual. The person **grew up** in the presence of God without receiving the blessings of God. Instead, he appeared to be cursed, having no physical attributes that would attract a second glance. People would, in fact, have nothing to do with him.

Verse 3 again presents translation problems, a literal reading going something like: "He was despised and abandoned by men—a man of pain and experienced in sickness. Like a person from whom faces should be veiled (hidden), he was despised and not respected by anyone" (author's translation). He was physically sick and either hideous to look at or dangerous to be around because of his sickness. His fellow citizens avoided him and saw no worth in him.

53:4–6. Now the astonishing revelation! The group must confess: "He carried our suffering and bore the load of our pain" (author's translation). All the time we thought **God** was punishing him (cp. the friends of Job). The problem could not be limited to the physical plane of life. The theological was also involved. He suffered because of our sins, so that we might be **healed** and find the life of **peace**. What's more, every one of us was involved as we went merrily along our own paths like dumb **sheep**, while God made the servant suffer with the load of sin and guilt that belonged to all of us.

53:7–9. Although he was **oppressed and afflicted**, he endured without a sound. He faced the death squad, still silent. He even had to go to trial and prison (the meanings of v. 8 are probably concrete judicial terms in KJV, REB, NKJV, TEV, NLT, NJB, rather than abstract as ASV, NRSV, NASB, JPS, NAB, and NIV). Not even one member of his generation (not the **descendants** of NIV) bothered to see what was going on. He was totally **cut off** from humanity, sick unto death. And all because of the sin of **my people**!

It got even worse. They buried him with the **wicked**, who do not even get last rites and ceremonies. They even put him out with the rich enemies instead of with his own people. He had done nothing to deserve such horrible treatment. What can all this mean? What is the purpose of it all? How could it have happened?

53:10. Why, Yahweh did it! It is all part of God's **will**. He chose to make his servant **suffer**. Note that the Hebrew text of verse 10 is difficult to interpret. It seems to read, "But Yahweh delighted in his crushing; he made him sick. If his soul would set up a guilt offering, he will see seed; he will prolong days, and the delight of Yahweh will prosper in his hand" (author's translation). The suffering of God's servant was a guilt offering (Lev. 5:14–19) when in the exile with the temple destroyed there was no chance for such offerings. What he did would help Yahweh's plan come to pass.

The guilt offering was not for the servant's sins, but for those of the people. Still God made the servant **prosper**. A part of that prosperity was new life after burial, life in which he would **see his offspring and prolong his days**. God's people in exile thought Yahweh was silent and had forgotten them, but he had been working in his servant! What a revelation!

53:11–12. That revelation was confirmed. Yahweh gave his own word to the congregation again (see 52:13–15). The understanding of the text again rests on translation problems—problems recognized as early as the Dead Sea Scrolls and the Septuagint, both of which add **light** to a difficult Hebrew text that does not give a direct object for **he will see.** A literal translation of verse 11 reads: "From the suffering of his soul, he will see; he will be sated. By his knowledge the righteous one, my servant, will bring righteousness for many. He will bear the burden of their guilt (or punishments or unjust actions)" (author's translation).

God acknowledged the **suffering** of the servant's **soul** or life. This suffering would not bind him to the darkness of death. He would again see. He would be **satisfied** or satiated with all he has done with his life. He would especially be satisfied because his knowledge—the experience of suffering and sacrificing for others—would bring justice to multitudes. They would be righteous before God and in their relationship with others because of his death for them. He would carry their burdensome sins. He would be numbered among the mighty heroes because he was willing to die among the sinners. He would receive God's victory **spoils** because he chose to obey God and die.

The servant was willing to sacrifice his reputation, be **numbered with the transgressors**, and even intercede on behalf of the **transgressors**. He took what appeared to be the wrong side of the battle and won! Why? Because he took God's side. Thus God reaffirmed the judgment of the group. The servant was the bearer of sins for the group. They owed their lives to him. And they had never suspected what he was doing.

We have finished, but we have just begun. Here we see as clearly as anywhere in the Bible why it is necessary to try to understand the historical setting in which a passage is first composed. The Book of Isaiah is set in the eighth century B.C. as a nation gradually descended from an economic wonder amid Middle Eastern powers to a nation paying heavy tribute to Assyria and having to depend on a divine miracle to escape the siege tactics of Sennacherib's army. To this people the Suffering Servant would be a scary specter forcing Israel to see that her role in international politics involved suffering and death before any sense of victory could be achieved.

The central section (chs. 40–55) of the Book of Isaiah centers on Israel's Babylonian period as the nation struggled to find new identity as exiles in a foreign nation with their own homeland a fading memory. These people would read the prophet's book as a dialogue. They could hear their own voices lifting the horrid complaints to God and testifying to their own lack of understanding about what God was doing. How could Cyrus be God's anointed servant? How could Israel or the remnant left in Babylon find any meaning in the role of a Suffering Servant called to be a light to the nations and to sacrifice themselves as a guilt offering for their people?

The final chapters of Isaiah (55–66) have a post-exilic Israel in view, a people who have returned from exile only to find their homeland is not paradise. They can well see themselves as having played the role of Suffering Servant for nothing. Has God tricked them with his promises? Have they endured the trip back to Palestine and the labor of building the temple only to find life no better, perhaps not as good, as life in exile? The Suffering Servant forces post-exilic Judaism to see that they must play an ongoing role. They cannot expect to suffer for a little while and prosper forever. They are to be a suffering people, giving witness and sacrifice for the nation and for the nations until God completes his work in fulfilling his promises.

Although each generation of Israel could find a calling and an identity in the servant of the Lord, none saw a true fulfillment of the prophetic hope. In fact, C. R. North is on target in writing, "It is probable that the prophet looked for the coming of one who would more perfectly embody the ideal of what Yahweh's servant should be" (IDB, 4, p. 293).

The Hebrew Bible became an integral part of the Christian canon. Here the church can see that no individual or community in Israel truly fulfilled the role of Suffering Servant. None had the attitude and the self-sacrificing spirit of the servant. The remnant of true Israel was ultimately reduced to one person, the man Jesus from Nazareth, who gained his messianic identity from Isaiah 53 and the other servant passages. He in reality became the guilt offering that solved the world's sin problem. He willingly bore our sins on the cross. In him we find healing, peace, hope, and a future. As Christians we look back to Jesus as the only true Suffering Servant of God, but we also look to the present.

As North advises us, "More important even than who the Servant was is the question, 'What was the Servant to do?' . . . The uniqueness of the Servant lies in this: he not only encountered and accepted suffering in the course of his work; in the final phase suffering became the means whereby he accomplished his work, and was effective in the salvation of others. He made himself an 'offering for sin' (53:10). . . . What happens is that the 'we' are moved to repentance, confession, and amendment" (IDB, 4, pp. 293–294).

The Suffering Servant called his church to take up the cross and follow him. That means he gave the church a mandate to be the Suffering Servant for our generation and for the nations of our era. The call and intent of Isaiah 53 is not complete with the life of Jesus. It takes on new power to compel the church to forsake the political, economic, and military games of the world's rise to prominence and success. It urges us to be faithful to the Suffering Servant by following willingly in his footsteps, taking on his identity and his unremarkable appearance for our generation. The work of the original Suffering Servant was declared finished on Calvary, but it is not complete until each of us has accepted the role of cross-bearing servants witnessing to the nations and bringing them to know Jesus as their offering for sin and Savior.

Apparently, then, the prophetic message gained few real followers when it was first announced to the people of Israel and when the later generations in Babylon and in post-exilic Jerusalem heard it. This message, like the rest of prophecy, was preserved for a new generation that would read and understand and follow. The words challenged each generation to assume the proper office of the servant of Yahweh with the call to carry the sins of the world, even unto death.

Finally, one lonely Galilean took upon himself the image of the Suffering Servant and followed its calling even to the cross of Golgotha. God, as he had promised the prophet, honored the commitment of his Son and gave him a portion with the great names of history, indeed installing him at the top of the list. Through that one name—Jesus—all the people of the world have been given the chance to unload their sins and find a new way of life. That new way of life continues to be the old way of the servant of Yahweh. The passage that molded the Master's way must also mold ours.

> **MAIN IDEA REVIEW:** *God's zeal for his people is revealed as he sends his servant to suffer and die for their sins.*

III. CONCLUSION

The Role of the Suffering Servant

The climax of the Book of Isaiah is a call to testify to the greatness of one who showed no marks of material greatness. It challenges the church to proclaim the marvelous good news of the death, burial, and resurrection of Jesus Christ. At the same time it boldly invites us to take up the cross of Jesus in our world and to be the Suffering Servant, ready to sacrifice our lives for the salvation of our generation.

PRINCIPLES

- God judges human powers who mock him and blaspheme his name.
- God's salvation brings songs of joy.
- God saves his people in world history for all people to see.

APPLICATIONS

- Bow yourself before God and acknowledge him as your King.
- Confess God as your only Savior.

- Thank God for sending his Suffering Servant to die for your sins.

- Commit yourself to take up your cross and follow the Suffering Servant in today's world with the same spirit and attitude that Jesus demonstrated to his world.

IV. LIFE APPLICATION

Jesus Our Substitute

Martin Luther wrote: "All the prophets did foresee in Spirit that Christ should become the greatest transgressor, murderer, adulterer, thief, rebel, blasphemer, etc., that ever was or could be in all the world. For he, being made a sacrifice for the sins of the whole world, is not now an innocent person and without sins . . . but a sinner." He was, of course, talking about the imputing of our wrongdoing to Christ as our substitute.

Luther continues: "Our most merciful Father . . . sent his only Son into the world and laid upon him . . . the sins of all men saying: Be thou Peter that denier; Paul that persecutor, blasphemer and cruel oppressor; David that adulterer; that sinner which did eat the apple in Paradise; that thief which hanged upon the cross; and briefly be thou the person which hath committed the sins of all men; see therefore that thou pay and satisfy for them. Here now comes the law and saith: I find him a sinner . . . therefore let him die upon the cross. And so he setteth upon him and killeth him. By this means the whole world is purged and cleansed from all sins."

The presentation of the death of Christ as the substitute exhibits the love of the cross more richly, fully, gloriously, and glowingly than any other account of it. Luther saw this and gloried in it. He once wrote to a friend: "Learn to know Christ and him crucified. Learn to sing to him, and say, 'Lord Jesus, you are my righteousness, I am your sin. You have taken upon yourself what is mine and given me what is yours. You became what you were not, so that I might become what I was not.'"

What a great and wonderful exchange! Was there ever such love? (adapted from Packer, *Your Father Loves You*).

V. PRAYER

Lord Jesus, you suffered and died for me. Show me the way the cross will guide me. Help me be the Suffering Servant for people to whom you lead me today and every day. Amen.

VI. DEEPER DISCOVERIES

The Servant of Yahweh

The Hebrew expression (*'ebed Yahweh*) along with brief forms such as "my servant" or "your servant" appears 268 times in the Old Testament by one count (TLOT, 2, pp. 820–821). The variety of applications of the terminology show us that this is not a technical term limited to one particular person or group or concentrated in one section of Old Testament literature. The following is a listing of the different persons or groups referred to as God's servant:

- Abraham (Gen. 26:24; Ps. 105:6,42)
- Abraham, Isaac, and Jacob (Exod. 32:13; Deut. 9:27)
- Ahijah (1 Kgs. 14:18; 15:29)
- David (2 Sam. 3:18; 7:8; 1 Kgs. 8:66; 1 Chr. 17:4,7,24; 2 Chr. 6:15–17,42; Pss. 18 title; 36 title; 78:70; 132:10; Isa. 37:35; Ezek. 34:23; 37:24–25)
- Eliakim (Isa. 22:20)
- Elijah (2 Kgs. 10:10)
- Foreign worshipers (Isa. 56:6)
- Individual (Isa. 41:9; 52:13)
- Isaac (Gen. 24:14)
- Isaiah (Isa. 20:3)
- Israel (Lev. 25:55; Deut. 32:43; Pss. 113:1; 135:1; Isa. 41:8; 44:1–2,21; 54:17)
- Jacob (Isa. 44:1–2; 48:20; Jer. 46:27–29; Ezek. 28:25)
- Job (Job 1:8; 2:3; 42:7–8)
- Jonah (2 Kgs. 14:25)
- Joshua (Josh. 24:29; Judg. 2:8)
- Moses (Exod. 14:31; Deut. 34:5; Josh. 8:31,33; 11:12,15; 13:8; 18:7; 1 Kgs. 8:53,56; 2 Kgs. 21:8; 1 Chr. 6:49; 2 Chr. 1:3; Neh. 1:7–8; 10:29; Dan. 9:11)
- Nebuchadnezzar (Jer. 25:9; 27:6)
- Prophets (2 Kgs. 9:7; 17:13; Ezra 9:11; Jer. 25:4; 35:15; Ezek. 38:17; Amos 3:7)
- Tobiah (Neh. 2:10)
- Zerubbabel (Hag. 2:23; Zech. 3:8)

To understand the term, one must see the wide range of applications of the term *'ebed* or "servant." It may mean "bondsman, subordinate, subject, vassal, mercenary, official, minister" according to the context and according to the relationship to the lord or master of the *'ebed*. In addition, one may use the term "your servant" or "my lord" as a polite manner of addressing oneself to a person of authority even though no official relationship of lord and servant exists (Gen. 32:5; 33:14).

The citizens of a nation were the slaves of the king. They chose to follow him in war (1 Sam. 27:5,12). The top government officials were referred to as servants of the king even when they were free men, not slaves, and were exercising high authority in international affairs. Such officials themselves owned servants of their own.

A nation conquered or made to pay tribute to another nation was considered enslaved (Deut. 5:15; Josh. 9; 2 Kgs. 16:7).

"Israel also shared, however, the ancient notion that slaves were property (as in the inventory of possessions in Gen. 12:16; 24:35)." Service as a slave could be mutually agreed upon as a short time arrangement (Gen. 29–31) or an enduring state of ownership (Exod. 21:2,6; Deut. 15:12). Even when the term meant a real sense of ownership and authority by a master, "the primary element of the existence of slaves was not captivity but membership and security" (Westermann, TLOT, pp. 822).

The phrase "servant of Yahweh" is one of many examples of transferring relationship terms on the human level to describe human relationship to God. God becomes the Lord or Master in such linguistic usage, and people become his slaves. Here again, the term may have quite different meanings. Applied to Moses or Abraham or Joshua, the term signifies a person of authority and respect who is totally dedicated to serving God. The Joshua narrative uses this term for Moses until the end of Joshua's life when he finally is called the servant of Yahweh (Josh. 29:29) as a title of respect for his faithful service.

"Being 'ebed to a person can signify the harshest limitation of existence, but being God's 'ebed always means having a good Lord. It can never mean servitude in the negative sense" (TLOT, 2, p. 826). "Any servant of Yahweh was a privileged person" (North, IDB, 4, p. 292).

The Book of Psalms speaks of God's servant(s) fifty-four times, often in prayers of lament. The servant cries to the Master for help and expresses trust in the Master's ability and willingness to help (Ps. 86:2; Num. 11:11).

The most significant use of "servant of Yahweh" occurs in the central section of the Book of Isaiah. Here Israel is commissioned as God's servant with a special task to accomplish, a task that can be summarized as being a light to the nations. This language personifies Israel as a member of God's court staff, a royal official with specific responsibilities and authority. "The description of Israel in these passages in the same way in which Moses is called Yahweh's servant indicates Israel's significance for others" (TLOT, p. 827).

Isaiah brings his concept of the servant to a climax in the so-called Servant Songs in which the servant of Yahweh speaks in first person (42:1–4; 49:1–6; 52:13–53:12; 50:4–9). The servant represents Yahweh to the nations as would a king. The servant witnesses to Yahweh's message as would a prophet. Finally, the servant offers himself as a guilt offering, the task of a priest. The servant is commissioned to establish justice (42:1–4), to be a light so Yahweh's salvation can reach to the ends of the earth (49:6), to suffer willingly until Yahweh vindicates him (50:4–9), and to suffer and die without complaint as the guilt offering for the people (53:10). All in all, North is correct in concluding that "the Servant is too complex a figure to be fitted into any single category" (IDB, 4, p. 293).

Israel is called "my servant" (41:8–10), and the servant is called Israel (49:3). Yet the servant has a mission to Israel. How can this be? North suggests, "He may be an individual or group in whom, so to speak, Israel is incorporated, as the king might be said to embody his people" (IDB, 4, p. 293).

Quite uniquely, the focus is on the servant's suffering (42:4; 49:7; 50:4–9; 52:13–53:12) leading to his sacrificial death for the sins of others. Reward and victory come only after death. Such language is startlingly new. "This is the first such statement in the Old Testament and it surpasses everything previously said of a servant in Yahweh's service" (TLOT, 2, p. 528).

Moses endured the complaints and rebellions of his people and died without entering the promised land. Jeremiah experienced much suffering as he delivered his message of treasonous surrender to Babylonia. The nation Israel suffered greatly under Assyria, then Babylonia, and even under Persia after the return from the exile. In a figurative way Moses, Jeremiah, and the nation as a whole could be said to have suffered and died for the survival of the remnant Israel. But none did so willingly and self-consciously as in the description of the servant of Yahweh. All these and others foreshadowed what it meant to be a true servant of Yahweh.

We find the Suffering Servant mentality and commission carried out fully and consciously only in Jesus of Nazareth. As North says, "It is true that he nowhere quotes directly from the passages which modern scholars delimit as the Servant Songs, though he did say of Isaiah 61:1–2a, which is so similar in spirit to the Songs that some scholars have included it in the song cycle: 'Today this scripture has been fulfilled in your hearing' (Luke 4:21). It is clear that Jesus thought of his sufferings as having been 'written of him' (Matt. 26:24,54,56; Luke 18:31), and it would be hypercritical not to include Isaiah 53 and the related passages among 'the scriptures' to which he referred. The 'many' of Mark 10:45 is strongly reminiscent of the fourfold 'many' in Isaiah 52:14–15; 53:11–12" (North, IDB, 4, p. 293).

Ultimately, then, Jesus is the Suffering Servant of Isaiah, but this is not the end of the story, as described in the commentary above. We must remember, with Richard J. Clifford: "All Israel becomes a servant when it embraces the divine will and plan as shown by the individual servants. When the people do not obey God's word, then the servant stands over against the people as a rebuke and as an invitation to conversion" (Clifford, ABD, 3, p. 499).

Jesus the individual servant sets the path for us to follow in becoming the Suffering Servant for our community and world. Should we refuse the calling, Isaiah 53 stands over us in condemnation as it did over a reluctant Israel. But it also stands as a new invitation to become what Jesus shows us we can be and must be if we are kingdom people.

VII. TEACHING OUTLINE

A. INTRODUCTION

1. Lead Story: The Transforming Power of Sacrificial Love
2. Context: Repeated appearances of the servant of the Lord have led to this climactic section of Isaiah's book. The servant has been Israel, a remnant within Israel, and a mysterious individual. Here the individual takes front and center. As we keep asking, who is this?, the text keeps calling us back to see what this servant is doing for us and what he is calling us to do for others.
3. Transition: The servant will succeed. That is God's opening and closing promise in this section. But how does one detect and define success? How does one react to this kind of success? Will you find a pattern for success for your life as you study the mission of the Suffering Servant? Will you find the way to salvation for your life?

B. COMMENTARY

1. Zealous for Zion (52:1–12)
2. Satisfaction for the Suffering Servant (52:13–53:12)

C. CONCLUSION: JESUS OUR SUBSTITUTE

1. Wrap-up: God's plan for salvation surprised Israel in Jerusalem and Israel in exile. Israel's king quietly disappeared from sight for the moment, replaced by a servant. This unique, mysterious figure rejected headlines and heroism. He stayed in the background, drawing no attention to himself. Only his hideous appearance and unmerciful suffering made people notice him. Then suddenly God's plan became clear, just as he had promised. Salvation came not through a military victory by a king but through the servant's humble suffering for others. His suffering resulted in his death. But that suffering and death spoke much louder than had anything in the servant's lifetime, because they made people testify: he died for us. He bore our sins.

With his suffering stripes we are healed and find peace. His death means God will see us as righteous and will give him the great reward he deserves.

2. Personal Challenge: You have met the Suffering Servant. You have seen that Israel never fully accepted the challenge and became what God called them to become. Only Jesus of Nazareth fulfilled the role of Suffering Servant. He died for your sins, so you would not have to die. Have you accepted his death and made him your Lord and Savior? Have you become his servant? Are you willing to take up the cross as he did and suffer so others may know his salvation?

VIII. ISSUES FOR DISCUSSION

1. According to your understanding, how did Jesus fulfill the role of the Suffering Servant?
2. Have you accepted the salvation that Jesus offers?
3. Does God really expect you to see the Suffering Servant as the role he expects you to take up in life? Why? Why not?

Isaiah 54–55

The Covenant of Comfort and Compassion

I. **INTRODUCTION**
The Text That Started World Missions

II. **COMMENTARY**
A verse-by-verse explanation of these chapters.

III. **CONCLUSION**
Beyond the Exile

An overview of the principles and applications from these chapters.

IV. **LIFE APPLICATION**
Expanding Our Territories

Melding these chapters to life.

V. **PRAYER**
Tying these chapters to life with God.

VI. **DEEPER DISCOVERIES**
Historical, geographical, and grammatical enrichment of the commentary.

VII. **TEACHING OUTLINE**
Suggested step-by-step group study of these chapters.

VIII. **ISSUES FOR DISCUSSION**
Zeroing these chapters in on daily life.

Isaiah 54–55

IN A NUTSHELL

God invites his abandoned wife to return and be fertile. The time of anger is over; compassion is the word of the day. Judgment is past history. God will rebuild their city and establish peace and righteousness. This will bring foreign nations scurrying to Israel as God calls people to seek him while he may be found. Those who turn to God, forsaking their evil ways, will find free pardon and mercy. Israel will escape captivity for God's glory and honor.

The Covenant of Comfort and Compassion

I. INTRODUCTION

The Text That Started World Missions

*T*his passage started the modern missionary movement. William Carey was a shoe repairman who was baptized at age twenty-two on October 5, 1783. Soon he began to preach for Baptist congregations. He was described as slight of stature, prematurely balding, and wearing an ill-fitting red wig. He preached all summer in a church at Olney and did so poorly the church refused to recommend him for ordination. He pastored small churches and continued to fix shoes and teach school. At his cobbler's bench he taught himself Greek, Hebrew, Dutch, French, and Latin. He read widely and soon gained a passion for the world far beyond England.

Carey preached his heart out in English Baptist churches, calling people to support a missionary movement to India. Isaiah 54:2 was his sermon text. He made two quick points: Expect great things from God. Attempt great things for God.

Finally people formed the Particular Baptist Society for Propagating the Gospel among the Heathen. Carey challenged congregations to start a mission fund even if it meant giving only one penny a week. The first offering raised thirteen pounds. When no one else answered the call to missions, Carey dedicated himself to go to India and teach people about the love of God in Jesus Christ. He faced one major hurdle: his wife Dorothy initially opposed his missionary efforts. She later relented and went to India, but at considerable expense to her family and health.

Only slowly through years of work did Carey have any success. One of his great accomplishments was translating the Bible into Bengali. But from his start, the world missionary movement began and continues to flourish today.

Surely no one seemed a more unlikely candidate than William Carey for starting such a monumental movement as world missions. Israel found that it had just as few skills, aptitudes, and resources as did Carey. God called Israel to take on a new adventure with him to reach the nations with the message of salvation.

II. COMMENTARY

The Covenant of Comfort and Compassion

> **MAIN IDEA:** *Having punished his people, God calls them to find comfort, peace, and compassion in his eternal covenant of blessing as they live out his righteousness.*

A Build Bedrooms for the Barren (54:1–17)

Oracle of salvation

> **SUPPORTING IDEA:** *Love, peace, compassion, and comfort are God's words for his people after he has punished them in his anger.*

54:1–3. The prophet used the language of Israel's worship to call the people to trust God's new promises. An opening hymn responded exactly to their laments (cp. Lam. 1). Zion had become like a widow without children. The hymn praised God for fulfilling his promise to Abraham again (Gen. 13:1–3). As with the barren Sarah of old, so God would bless the **woman, you who never bore a child**. Israel would experience a population explosion beyond anything imaginable. The people would have to build extensions to their houses to hold the new additions. Once again the nation Israel would loom large on the international scene. God promised they would **dispossess nations and settle in their desolate cities**.

54:4–8. This meant an oracle of salvation calling for Israel to fear not (NIV, **Do not be afraid**) was in order. The **shame** of exile was past history. Zion's **husband** had come to claim her. He could lay claim to the most impressive titles on earth, each of which showed his power and authority. He is **Maker**, Lord of Hosts (NIV, LORD **Almighty**), **Holy One of Israel, Redeemer, God of all the earth.** He was one with power to do whatever he desired on earth, because he had created both Israel and the **earth**. Israel had a right to complain. She had been forsaken, but that was only for a **brief moment** because of God's justified **anger**. Now a new day had dawned, a day of **deep compassion**. God would show the depth of emotion that a woman felt for a child who had just left her womb. (For God's compassion, see "Deeper Discoveries," chs. 13–14.) He would show the **everlasting kindness** or faithful love (Hb. *chesed*; for God's faithful love, see "Deeper Discoveries") that bound him in covenant to his people Israel. Love and compassion meant that his wife Israel could be sure that he would bring them back.

54:9–10. The only comparison that could be made had to go all the way back to the **days of Noah** (see Gen. 6–9) when God made a new beginning.

Then God made a new **covenant** with all mankind, a covenant centered in his work that established **peace** with his people Israel and promised to use them to be his light to the nations. Such new work of God was based on his **compassion** (see vv. 7–9; contrast the same term in 47:6). It is the deep devotion of a parent for children, which removes all momentary anger.

54:11–17. God had called for someone to comfort his people (ch. 40), but no one had come forward to do so. God would bring comfort in his own way. Because of his deep compassion, God would rebuild the majesty and glory of Jerusalem, reestablishing not only the outward splendor but also the inner stability. God would begin his own education program so the children would learn **peace** at a tender age. No longer would **tyranny** and **terror** rule the land. God would bring what he had sought all along—righteousness (cp. 1:17,21,26,27; for righteousness, see "Deeper Discoveries," chs. 50–51).

The emphatic note here is that such restoration would not be followed by another moment of anger. Rather, God would prevent any future enemy from harming his new creation. No **weapon** could prevail against Israel, since God formed those who made weapons. He also formed any potential enemy who might **work havoc.** This was the new inheritance (NIV, **heritage**; see 47:6), not just land but security. This was God's **vindication**—the same word translated "righteousness" in verse 14 and indicating the right order that God establishes in his world (see 42:6). No one would have reason to complain to God again. He would be vindicated as he saved his people.

Ⓑ Call to the Costless Covenant (55:1–13)

Street vendor's spiel

SUPPORTING IDEA: *God calls people to forsake their wicked lifestyle and return to him for pardon, compassion, and an everlasting covenant of blessing as they become his witnesses.*

55:1–5. Having tried the language of the courtroom, the temple, and the funeral parlor, the prophet finally turned to the language of the marketplace to summarize his appeal to his people. God offered the best buy of the day if they would take it. No store ever offered a better sale. Everything was free. The seller wanted **no money.** He simply wanted the trust and confidence of the buyer in his product. The product itself was not an unneeded frill. Rather, it represented the basic necessity of life itself! The seller guaranteed full life in all its dimensions. Who could resist such a bargain?

Yet, there was competition. The prophet knew that other salesmen were offering **what is not bread,** yet claiming it was the basic staple of life. He had to call the customers' attention away from such competitors so they would **listen to me.** The prophet offered an **everlasting covenant** with a lifetime guarantee. God would give the people in exile the same promise he had given

David. The covenant with David (2 Sam. 7) had become the subject of doubt and lamentation (Ps. 89:38–51). The prophet took the opportunity for a new sales pitch. God was renewing the Davidic covenant. He was not limiting it to one man or one office. The entire nation would fulfill the role once given to David. That role was now interpreted in a shocking manner. David was not simply to conquer the world and bring glory to Israel. David was to be a **witness** to the nations so they would follow his command and come to God. Israel in exile was to become such a witness that even unknown nations would **hasten** to her to find the **splendor** of her God. Israel was to be a blessing to the nations (see Gen. 12:2–3; 26:3–4).

55:6–11. The sales pitch took a subtle twist. The salesman called on the customers to do something quite unexpected. Instead of paying him money for their product, they had to **seek the LORD**. Was this possible? Normally the expression meant to go to the temple to worship (see Deut. 12:5; Ps. 105:4), but people in exile had no temple. The prophets changed this to mean to seek God's way of life, his lifestyle for his people (Amos 5:4–7,14–15).

For the people in exile, who were complaining that God had forgotten them and his promises to David, to seek the LORD had a very simple meaning: Quit your complaining. Quit thinking that Babylonia and its gods have won the victory. God is with you now, listening to you. **Call on him while he is near.** Repent, **turn** back to your God. **Forsake** your **wicked way** and **thoughts**. Start life over again with God. He is ready to forgive and forget, to turn over a brand new page in history. Anger is no longer God's attitude toward you. **He will have mercy** (the Hebrew word used earlier for "compassion"). **He will freely pardon** (or he will forgive a multitude of times).

Isaiah called on the exiles to realize that God was different from them. God made plans beyond their wildest imaginations. His new plan included them, if they were willing to fly high with him rather than stooping down in the misery of self-pity and hopelessness. How does one respond to this? Could a people exiled for a whole generation—most never having seen the homeland—believe God's prophetic word? What about all the propaganda they heard about the victorious gods of Babylonia? Why not believe it? Did not Babylonia control the world? Was evidence here and now with Babylonia more powerful than pointing back to creation and the Exodus? Had God had his day long ago, a day that could never return? Should we keep up to date with the gods of the present generation? Was this promise of a new deliverance for his people, a new exodus, anything but pipe dreams? Could God and his new word be trusted to bear fruit just as certainly as the **rain** from **heaven** produce fruit in the ground? God promised anew: **my word that goes out from my mouth: It will not return to me empty.**

God's **word** did have one condition. The fruit God's word produces is the fruit he plans, the **purpose** for which he sends his word. People cannot put conditions on God's word and make him act the way they think he ought to act. They must be willing to be a part of his plan the way God has described it through the prophetic word! Will you seek God under these conditions?

55:12–13. If you agree to the conditions, Isaiah declared, here's the product. God's people will escape their exile and go out in a glorious procession. **Joy** and **peace** will fill their hearts. Even the natural elements will take part. All of this will come to pass for one reason. The wilderness itself will be transformed from a place of **briers** and the **thornbush** to a place of **pine** and **myrtle**. It will make a name (the literal translation of **renown**) for God. This new exodus from exile will be a sign that can never be erased from history.

Here then is the summary of the message of chapters 40–55. God had planned salvation for his people. He sent his prophetic word to announce this salvation. The people must decide to climb out of the depth of despair to join the journey of joy along the wilderness way and to be a witness for the world to the glory of God.

> **MAIN IDEA REVIEW:** *Having punished his people, God calls them to find comfort, peace, and compassion in his eternal covenant of blessing as they live out his righteousness.*

III. CONCLUSION

Beyond the Exile

Exile is not the end. God has glory and joy for a people who see themselves doomed to depression. God's way of return from exile is not automatic. People have to respond. They must quit depending on the meaningless idols of the enemy and put new faith and trust in the promising word of God. Then the promises to Abraham will be fulfilled. The exodus of Moses will be repeated. The covenant of David will be renewed. New, full, joyous life is a real possibility—not only for Israel but for today. Do you believe God wants to do this for you?

PRINCIPLES

- No human weapon can harm the people whom God protects.
- God is transcendent with thoughts, plans, and ways we cannot comprehend.
- God's Word always accomplishes its purpose.

APPLICATIONS

- Thank God for his compassion and grace.
- Ask God to give you his spiritual food and water to nourish your soul.
- Praise God for forgiving your sins and giving you peace.

IV. LIFE APPLICATION

Expanding Our Territories

God stood ready to bless exiled Israel and expand their territory and their ministry in ways beyond their highest dreams. But the people had to accept God's gift, to take the water of life. They had to stretch out their tent curtains, lengthen their cords, strengthen their stakes, and thus enlarge their residences. They had to let God do things his way. God continues to call all people to experience the peace, love, and joy of his Spirit as the fruit of a life of faith in him. But we must give up our ways and live life according to his directions. Will you accept God's blessings and ask him to fill your life with the fruit of his Spirit?

V. PRAYER

Dear Father of all blessings, come and bless us today. Give us your food and drink that will sustain our bodies and our souls. Give us faith to launch out in ministry for you even when the way seems hopeless. Your word will not return to you empty. Your ways will work even though they are so different from my ways. I trust you. I depend on you. I give myself to follow your ways. Amen.

VI. DEEPER DISCOVERIES

God's Faithful Love (54:8)

Hebrew *chesed* is one of the most important words in the Old Testament, occurring 245 times, but only eight times in Isaiah. It represents love in action between two persons, each going beyond the normal community expectations to show concern for the other. Both humans and God can act in ways that demonstrate such faithful, loyal love. It is part of God's character (Exod. 34:6; cp. Num. 14:18; Neh. 9:17; Pss. 86:15; 145:8; Joel 2:13). This is not, however, a static abstract description of God. It is the dynamic, relationship-oriented side of God. It affirms God's goodness and faithfulness displayed in his saving actions for his people and for the world. *Chesed* is the basis for God's forgiveness for our sins (Num. 14:17–19). This saving action does not come automatically. In each new crisis those who are faithful to God cry to him to display his *chesed* and save them from their miserable condition, as is seen repeatedly in the Psalms. In turn the faithful commit themselves to obey God's teaching and laws (see Ps. 119).

This divinely-initiated relationship has "an expected reciprocity and mutuality that demands service, fear, and even a corresponding exercise of *chesed* in return" (NIDOTTE, 2, p. 213). On the human plane, *chesed* is "the love you show your friend" (2 Sam. 16:17)—the natural reaction of one person who cares for another without having to follow community customs or moral rules. This faithful devotion to a friend is "unfailing kindness like that of the LORD" (2 Sam. 9:3). *Chesed* is the faithful fulfillment of a caring relationship whatever the cost. In a political setting, *chesed* becomes the fulfillment of agreements, treaties, and covenants (1 Sam. 20:8). Here *chesed* is not "an aspect or ingredient of covenant as such. Rather, the covenant comes in to reinforce the commitment to *chesed* in a situation where its exercise is not naturally to be expected or is likely to be put under strain by future circumstances" (Baer and Gordon, NIDOTTE, 2, p. 212).

God expects his people to show this kind of faithful devotion to one another and to him. His charge against them is that "there is no faithfulness (Hb. *'emeth*), no love (*chesed*), no acknowledgment (or knowledge, Hb. *da'at*) in the land" (Hos. 4:1). These qualities, especially *chesed,* are far more important than the ritual parts of a people's relationship with God (Hos. 6:6,8). Isaiah shows that God is looking for "men who show faithful love" (literally men of *chesed*) although humans ignore the loss of such people (Isa. 57:1). Too often human *chesed* (NIV, "glory") dries up and fades away like "flowers of the field" (Isa. 40:6). This brings forth divine anger and judgment, but divine *chesed* brings forth love and compassion in place of momentary anger (Isa. 54:8; cp. Mic. 7:18). Thus anger is "for a moment" (Isa. 54:8), but *chesed* "for you will not be shaken" (Isa. 54:10; cp. Pss. 89:2,28,33; 117:2; Jer. 31:3). This echoes the familiar biblical refrain that God's *chesed* endures forever (1 Chr. 16:34,41; Ezra 3:11; Pss. 100:5; 107:1; Jer. 33:11).

Thus God's people witness to and tell about "the kindnesses of the LORD, the deeds for which he is to be praised" (Isa. 63:7). In an interesting turn of phrase, these "kindnesses of the LORD" are done "according to his many kindnesses" (Isa. 63:7, author's translation). Israel knows that their king is established on his throne only because of God's *chesed* and that any hoped-for future king will come to power only through such divine *chesed* (Isa. 16:5). God thus promises the exiled people that he will make "an everlasting covenant with you (plural), my faithful love (*chesed*) promised to David" (Isa. 55:3).

VII. TEACHING OUTLINE

A. INTRODUCTION

1. Lead Story: The Text That Started World Missions

2. Context: These two chapters conclude the middle or Babylonian section of Isaiah's book (chs. 40–55). They represent an impassioned plea for Israel to come back to a relationship of faith in God in which they trust his ways rather than their ways and rely on his faithful love and compassion to deliver them from exile. Thus the call to comfort of chapter 40 comes to a comforting end with the sovereign God's call to seek him while he may be found and to turn to him for mercy and pardon.

3. Transition: All people need comfort, hope, and forgiveness. These chapters point us to the source of such support. God is willing to stand on the street and hawk his wares to us because he loves us so deeply and wants us to know his compassion and comfort.

B. COMMENTARY

1. Build Bedrooms for the Barren (54:1–17)

2. Call to the Costless Covenant (55:1–13)

C. CONCLUSION: EXPANDING OUR TERRITORIES

1. Wrap-up: God has a deal for you—life at its fullest and best, free of charge. He asks you to turn to him in trust and faith to find mercy, compassion, comfort, and hope.

2. Personal Challenge: Will you accept God's free gift of life? To do so, you must accept the fact that he is going to run his world and yours according to his ways and his character, not according to yours. You must turn to God's ways and give up your ways. Will you do so now?

VIII. ISSUES FOR DISCUSSION

1. Describe a time when you felt rejected and deserted by God. What did he do to bring you back to him?

2. What have you done that can be called "spending money on what is not bread"? Have you found a more satisfying way?

3. What testimony can you give from your own experience to show that God's word does not return to him empty?

Isaiah 56–57

Justice or Judgment

I. **INTRODUCTION**
    A Storm with an Attitude

II. **COMMENTARY**
    A verse-by-verse explanation of these chapters.

III. **CONCLUSION**
    No Change

    An overview of the principles and applications from these chapters.

IV. **LIFE APPLICATION**
    Join God in the Battle

    Melding these chapters to life.

V. **PRAYER**
    Tying these chapters to life with God.

VI. **DEEPER DISCOVERIES**
    Historical, geographical, and grammatical enrichment of the commentary.

VII. **TEACHING OUTLINE**
    Suggested step-by-step group study of these chapters.

VIII. **ISSUES FOR DISCUSSION**
    Zeroing these chapters in on daily life.

"*L*earn to say no. It will be of more use to you

than to be able to read Latin."

Charles Haddon Spurgeon

Isaiah 56–57

IN A NUTSHELL

*G*od calls his people to maintain justice and do right, since his salvation is at hand. God will accept the worship and sacrifices of every person who trusts in him. But those responsible for Israel are blind and greedy. Those who are depending on idols will find no help, but God will give an inheritance to those who find refuge in him. So prepare the road home, because the high and holy God loves the lowly and contrite people. His anger at them will not last forever. God will heal and guide the faithful into his peace. But the wicked will not know peace.

Justice or Judgment

I. INTRODUCTION

A Storm with an Attitude

*B*ill Hybels recalls a great adventure he had with his dad during junior high days. They sailed together on Lake Michigan for an afternoon of fun and togetherness. Suddenly, a mischievous look appeared in the eyes of Bill's father. "What do you say we sail all night over to Chicago, just you and me?" A seventy-mile all-night sail sounded like the most fun in the world for a junior high kid with his dad. So they set sail for Chicago. So did a monumental storm. Hybels calls it a storm with an attitude. He realized just how great an adventure he faced when his dad came and tied him to the boat with a rope around his waist. They survived a furious all-night fight with the storm and saw the lights of Chicago just as morning broke. Finally they sailed into the harbor and docked the boat.

Hybels confessed, "For the first time in my life I had a vivid understanding of how wonderful a protected harbor can be. Three hundred yards away, a storm was spewing its bile on every boat trying to navigate Lake Michigan's waters. But in this protected bay we found refuge, a hiding place from the storm" (Hybels, *The God You're Looking For,* pp. 81–82).

Israel had its temple back and was living in the promised homeland again. But life remained a storm without peace and without the blessings expected by those who were returning from exile. The prophet had a peace promise for them, if they would listen.

The sad fact of history was that God's people believed the prophecies of salvation just as little as they did the declarations of doom. Cyrus did conquer Babylon in 538 B.C. and did allow the exiles to return to their homeland (see Ezra 1; 6). Only a small percentage agreed to go back. They began to rebuild the temple, but opposition and disorganization stopped the work until Haggai and Zechariah got it started again in 520 B.C.

The temple was finished and dedicated in 515 B.C. The prophetic sermons in Isaiah 56–66 deal with the problems of this period of history, as a people sought to gain their identity, encourage their scattered parts to come home to Zion and join in the task set out for them, and to find the lifestyle that God desired for them in the new historical situation. Finding peace with God proved just as hard for a people who had returned to the promised land with a rebuilt temple as it had for a people in exile who had never seen the temple.

II. COMMENTARY

Justice or Judgment

> **MAIN IDEA:** *God calls all people to prayer, worship, trust, obedience, and salvation, but some still rebel and face his judgment.*

A. Offer Open to the Outcasts (56:1–8)

Priestly instruction

> **SUPPORTING IDEA:** *God invites all people to join in prayer and worship without fear of rejection.*

56:1–2. The prophetic word challenged the community as they began their temple worship again and yet lamented their political situation. They had to learn what it meant to be the people of God and to maintain the hope of the people of God in their new situation. The new accomplishment of building the temple did not mean that **salvation** had arrived. Rather, salvation was still in the future (cp. 46:13).

The building of the temple did not mean that a new way of salvation, consisting of temple worship and sacrifice, had been found. Having built God's house for him to dwell in their midst, the people's first order of business was to build a lifestyle suitable for serving in the presence of the holy God (cp. 1:17). Such a lifestyle was separated into two parts: religious service and social **justice**. **Sabbath** worship had become especially important as a sign of Yahweh's people when they had no temple. God wanted such loyalty to the Sabbath to continue when the temple had been restored. But Sabbath loyalty could not replace doing what was **right** or keeping one's **hand from doing any evil**.

56:3–8. God had commissioned his servant to bring justice to the nations (42:1–4). Here is a clear word carrying out the first steps of that commission. Israel constantly argued about the role of foreigners in their worship life (see Deut. 23:2–9; Ezra 4:1–6; Neh. 9:2). Most agreed that a **foreigner** or a physically-impaired **eunuch** had no business entering God's house.

The **eunuchs** could not experience the blessing of a multitude of sons as promised in 54:1 but they would be given a greater blessing—a **memorial** plate in the **temple** which would hold them up as examples for coming generations. The **foreigners**, likewise, would be admitted to the temple and **accepted** by God. They would find the joy of worship in his **house of prayer**. Yes, foreigners could offer **burnt offerings and sacrifices** on the **altar** in the new temple.

What heresy this must have been for traditional members of God's people! They had a hard time learning that God's purpose is not to exclude but to include. This purpose must not be limited to one period of history. It continues so other outcasts can find the open door to God. Modern church doors too often have unwritten rules about who is expected to enter and who is not.

Just as with the people of God (v. 1), the new converts must find a new lifestyle that is suitable to the presence of God among them. This lifestyle has a very definite shape—regular Sabbath worship, making decisions that please him, being loyal and obedient to God's **covenant**, and binding **themselves to the LORD to serve him** rather than other gods. People who do this are welcome **to worship** God in his house, no matter what their origin, their language, their customs, or their racial heritage.

B Devouring the Wicked (56:9–12)

Prophecy of disaster

> **SUPPORTING IDEA:** *Even as God announces salvation, judgment comes to those who refuse to trust and obey him.*

56:9–12. The experience of Israel in exile did not substantially change the nation's upper class. They refused to learn. They had the commission to be **watchmen** who would protect God's people from outside enemies. Instead, they became the enemy from whom God's people needed protection. They were like **dogs** that could not **bark**. They had no **understanding** of their job assignment. They went to **sleep** on the job and worked only for their own **gain** rather than helping the people. A drinking song was their theme song (v. 12). They did not think that God held them responsible or that God could again punish a people who refused to be his people. So God shouted out the invitation: **Come, all you beasts of the field, come and devour, all you beasts of the forest.** A people who survived the Exile and returned from it faced a new fate: death by being devoured.

C The Illusion of Idolatry (57:1–13)

Courtroom trial

> **SUPPORTING IDEA:** *False worship brings destruction, but trust in God brings a divine inheritance.*

57:1–2. The religious condition changed as little as the political situation. The people tried to cover their bets on all sides by worshiping as many gods as possible, just like all their neighbors. The result: the truly **righteous** man died without anyone noticing or caring. The people were too busy trying to satisfy the demands of all the gods. **Peace** for the righteous man came to be an escape from the world's calamity into the **rest** of **death**. (For peace, see "Deeper Discoveries.")

57:3–10. All the while, the majority of mankind were **mocking** or making sport of (NAB) or ridiculing (TEV) such righteous fools. They were enjoying themselves amid the fertility cults that used sexual rites in an attempt to ensure the agricultural and personal fertility of the nation. They went so far as to **sacrifice** their own **children**.

The exact translation and interpretation of verses 8 and 9 remains unclear. A very literal translation reads: "And behind the door and the doorpost, you placed your memorial. For separated from being with me you uncovered and climbed up. You made your bed wide. You cut for yourself from them (a covenant understood?). You love their bed. A hand (euphemism for nakedness?) you saw. You traveled to the king (change vowels to read foreign God Molech?) with olive oil. You multiplied your perfumes. You sent your envoys unto the distance. You lowered (them?) clear into Sheol" (author's translation).

This reference is certainly to fertility worship of foreign gods and possibly practices involving necromancy, or seeking direction from the dead. Israel never learned the lessons which Hosea and Jeremiah and others tried to teach them.

In all of this, the people fooled themselves, thinking they had something when all they had was a pure illusion. They kept digging deep to find strength to go on in their perverse ways. Only Yahweh, the true God, could give hope, but they did not turn to him.

57:11–13. Having called the sinners to court (v. 3) and listed the accusations against them (vv. 4–10), the prophet asked the people to defend themselves. Did they refuse to worship Yahweh because he had been so patient with them and **long been silent** in spite of all their sins? Why were they in such awe, reverence, and **fear** of the gods whose worship was so morally repugnant? Why did they prefer those gods to their God?

The speech in verse 12 has a double meaning. The prophet would tell the defendants of their right and proper (legal?) actions. He would also describe their **righteousness** in performing all their religious acts. Nothing would **benefit** them at this point. The time for sentencing had come. The sentence was simple: God would leave them to the illusion of their **idols**. The sentence was also negative: The idols would vanish from the picture, carried off by a **mere breath**. They would not take part in the new inheritance that God planned to give to his people. This was God's judgment on those who were not faithful to him. They did not receive the gifts they thought their idols could give them, and they did not receive the inheritance that God promised his people.

Ⓓ Healing for the Humble (57:14–21)

Promise of salvation

SUPPORTING IDEA: *The holy, eternal God will revive and heal his punished people, but the wicked will never find peace.*

57:14–15. Return from exile did not remove all the obstacles in the way of the people of God. The prophet had to repeat the call to **prepare the road** for God's new work of salvation (cp. 40:3). God sought to build a path for his people in their own homeland as well as in foreign exile. God remained **high and lofty** (cp. 6:1). The high and **holy** God chose, however, to dwell not in heavenly isolation but with the humble and **contrite**. He would **revive** their hopes and dreams and show them the way to a new day. He wanted his people to accept the obstacles in their path and continue to trust their God until he had cleared the path for them.

57:16–19. The people continued to complain that God's **anger** was endless. The divine reply was simple. God was the Creator who had given the **breath** of life for men's nostrils (cp. Gen. 2:7). Anger and death could not be his final word. Divine anger had a justified cause—the covetousness, the **greed** of his creatures. God had tried to punish and bring his creatures back to himself, but that had not worked. Now God would work in a new way. He would **heal** the guilty ways and thus bring **comfort** (cp. 40:1). This would transform the words of mourning into words of **praise**.

So God pronounced a benediction of **peace** on his people, not just those in Jerusalem but those **far and near**. The healing would have an unexpected effect. It would not be limited to the small area around the rebuilt Jerusalem. It would encompass everything far and near, particularly those Jews who had not yet been faithful and had not returned to Jerusalem from their various places of exile.

57:20–21. Still, it was not universal healing. Some still followed the wicked ways described so vividly earlier in the chapter. They simply could not give up their wicked ways. The **wicked** would face judgment, not **peace**.

MAIN IDEA REVIEW: *God calls all people to prayer, worship, trust, obedience, and salvation, but some still rebel and face his judgment.*

III. CONCLUSION

No Change

The social and historical situations have changed drastically. Israel is back home. A new temple invites them to bring their sacrifices and offerings, celebrate their festivals, and look for God's promised Messiah. But one thing appears not to have changed. The people want to keep their religious options open. They celebrate God's history and God's victories in the temple. Then they go to the traditional worship places on the hills and under the trees and in the valleys. There they carry out the age-old religious practices of Baalism and other fertility cults. Let God protect our politics, they declare, while the other gods do what they do best—ensure the fertility of our land and our people.

"No way!" comes God's answer. "I am still the only God. My demands remain the same—righteousness, justice, worship of me and no one else. This applies to any person who wants to worship, no matter what his family or national history or culture. All may come to worship. When they do so, depending on me and on no other gods, then I promise peace and salvation. If they do not, then they are wicked and will receive the judgment I have always announced against the wicked."

PRINCIPLES

- God has an open invitation to all people to become part of his people.
- God's house is a house of prayer for all people, not just for a select group.
- God is a trustworthy refuge for people who are faithful to him.

APPLICATIONS

- Commit yourself to a life of justice and righteousness before God.
- Ask God to forgive you for specific actions that show you are selfish and materialistic.
- Separate yourself from anything that would become a false god in your life.

IV. LIFE APPLICATION

Join God in the Battle

Dr. Paul Carlson was a California doctor with a thriving practice. He agreed to join a relief agency to serve for six months as a medical missionary in what was then called the Belgian Congo. Returning to his lucrative practice in California, Carlson was a changed man. He could not brush the Congo experience out of his mind. He told another doctor, "If you could only see [the need], you wouldn't be able to swallow your sandwich." Soon the young doctor could do nothing else but uproot his family and move to the Congo.

In the most primitive conditions he set up a clinic and gave medical care to the Congo people—all for $3,230 a year.

After two years, Dr. Carlson met a situation he could not heal. Along with several other Americans, he was captured as a prisoner of war in an internal revolution. Seeing a chance to escape, he raced over to a wall and climbed to the top. A burst of bullets rang out and slashed into his body. He fell back off the wall, dead.

Time magazine reported the senseless killing: "Dr. Carlson's murder, along with the massacre of perhaps another hundred whites and thousands of blacks, had a special, tragic meaning. [He] symbolized all the white men—and there are many—who want nothing from Africa but a chance to help. He was no saint and no deliberate martyr. He was a highly skilled physician who, out of a strong Christian faith and a sense of common humanity, had gone to the Congo to treat the sick."

This is a dramatic illustration of what the humble, contrite believer does. The believer finds where God is at work meeting human needs, and he joins God in the battle against poverty, ignorance, sickness, superstition, injustice, and death. The humble believer does not count the financial cost. The humble believer only counts the cost of not doing what God says.

Is God calling you to get out of the materialistic rut of life and find a way to serve others with his love? Has he put something on your heart like he put the Congo on Dr. Carlson's? Does everything in the world say, "I can't do that; it does not make sense?" Remember, God's ways are not our ways. If God is pointing you in a "senseless" direction, take notice. It must make sense according to his ways.

V. PRAYER

God, you have shown me the need of people around the world who do not know Jesus Christ. You want me to do what is just and right in the larger picture of the world. I keep calculating only what is just and right for me and for my family. Teach me your ways. Show me where you want me to go, what you want me to do. Humble me. Give me a contrite heart so I will be willing to do things your way. Amen.

VI. DEEPER DISCOVERIES

Peace (Hb. *shalom*)

The Old Testament uses the term *shalom* 237 times, twenty-nine of those in Isaiah. Biblical peace is much more than the absence of war or fighting. The related Hebrew verb means "to repay or requite someone for something."

In one sense, *shalom* means repayment for something missed in life. From the human standpoint, such repayment may be good or bad. God creates light and darkness, prosperity (*shalom*) and disaster (literally, evil; Isa. 45:7). Suffering anguish may be for your peace, being God's way of showing his love and keeping you from the pit of destruction by putting all my sins behind your back (literal translation of Isa. 38:17). It is God's way of bringing you to obedience and faithfulness (Isa. 54:8). Peace is always something God establishes, not something that we humans achieve (Isa. 26:12).

After God's anger has brought discipline and punishment on your sin, then God promises to heal as he pronounces peace on all people far and wide (Isa. 57:19). He comforts his people in exile by restoring Zion to its place among the nations and extending "peace to her like a river" (66:12). This peace from God is not reserved for special people. He can even protect Cyrus of Persia as the foreign king pursues his enemies in battle and then moves on "unscathed" (literally, in *shalom*) "by a path his feet have not traveled before" (41:3).

God wants all people to come to him for refuge. They can do this only when they have made peace with him, when they have acknowledged him as the one God and have dedicated themselves to live life in his way and not in selfish, materialistic, worldly ways. Peace comes from a life dedicated to righteousness and lived in quietness and confidence (Isa. 32:17). Peace is "the deep commitment to the work of justice" (Healey, ABD, 5, p. 206).

Once you have become obedient and faithful to the righteous life, you can receive life and peace. God promises absolute peace to those who lean on him for support. Such a person trusts in God (Isa. 26:3). This life is a life filled with all that God desires (Exod. 18:23). It is a life with no incomplete parts, lacking nothing. It is a life of purpose and meaning without fear. It is a life "in peaceful dwelling places, in secure homes, in undisturbed places of rest" (Isa. 32:18). It is a life of success, good fortune, and material blessings (Gen. 29:6; Jer. 6:14). It is a life that a person likes and enjoys (Isa. 55:12). It is a life without war but with alliances of peace and mutual help (Judg. 4:17; Zech. 6:13). It is a life with all future peace guaranteed because children learn directly from God and thus experience great peace as they obey him (54:13).

Sometimes the life of peace cannot be found on this earth because wickedness is so strong. At that time righteous people find true peace only as "they lie in death" (57:2). Thus full and true peace is a life established only when God sends a new ruler, the Prince of Peace (Isa.9:6; cp. Zech. 9:9–10). He makes "peace your governor and righteousness your ruler" (60:17). Peace is a life that praises messengers who announce victory and peace that comes when God saves his people and reigns as their king (52:7). Most of all, peace comes through the Suffering Servant who was punished in our place so we may have peace (Isa. 53:5). This peace provided by God through his messianic king and Suffering Servant has "no end" either through time or through geographical space (Isa. 9:7).

Most people do not experience such peace, because they do not know "the way of peace . . . there is no justice in their paths" (Isa. 59:8). "Envoys of peace weep bitterly" because the worldly systems that seek to bring peace break down under human greed, selfishness, and hunger for power (Isa. 33:7). God does not allow the wicked to have peace (Isa. 48:22; 59:8). He has a day of vengeance, literally a day of payback (using a term related to *shalom*; 34:8). It shows how people come to experience peace and what robs them of peace. Even God's word of peace for the present may contain a proclamation of judgment for the future when we are more interested in our own situation than we are in that of the entire people of God.

"Peace according to the prophetic preaching is the result of restored righteousness and cannot be achieved while one is persisting in sin and evil (Isa. 32:17; 48:18; 54:13; 60:17)" (Nel, NIDOTTE, 4, p. 132). "Peace embraces the notion of the restoration of creation to justice, truth, and righteousness. Peace is a blessing and a sign of the blessed life of the new creation just as it was the hallmark of the first creation. . . . Peace is both a restoration of the divine plan of creation and the harbinger of the completion of life to come" (Healey, ABD, 5, p. 207).

VII. TEACHING OUTLINE

A. INTRODUCTION

1. Lead Story: A Storm with an Attitude

2. Context: God had invited his people to take the free gift of bread and drink, turn to him, and enjoy the salvation he had in store for them. The question remained, How well did they understand his offer? Would they accept it?

3. Transition: Chapters 57–58 spell out clearly the contents of God's offer of free bread and drink, of salvation for his people. Salvation means they will maintain justice and righteousness and receive peace. The alternative is to endure God's judgment again because they choose to go back to the false gods of their fathers. As you study these passages, you must determine your alternatives. What do you understand God to mean by salvation and peace? What components of your lifestyle bring down God's judgment? Which do you want: justice or judgment?

B. COMMENTARY

1. Offer Open to the Outcasts (56:1–8)
2. Devouring the Wicked (56:9–12)
3. The Illusion of Idolatry (57:1–13)
4. Healing for the Humble (57:14–21)

C. CONCLUSION: JOIN GOD IN THE BATTLE

1. Wrap-up: God extends his salvation offer to all people, no matter what their social, political, geographical, economic, or racial settings. In turn, he expects that they will work for justice and righteousness in his world. He also expects them to worship him at his chosen sanctuary in the ways he has commanded. To do so means to quit going to the worship places of other gods and participating in their immoral, unproductive, sinful worship. Those who accept God's offer will receive peace and salvation and become involved in his program for justice. Those who reject this offer face judgment.

2. Personal Challenge: Face the truth about your town. What injustice is practiced there? Are you willing to get involved, to do what is right, to fight for justice? If your answer is no, then you had better examine your relationship with God very carefully, because he always stands on the side of justice. Beware that you are not a blind watchman thinking that today will be just like yesterday, so let's drink and enjoy. Humble your heart and find God's peace.

VIII. ISSUES FOR DISCUSSION

1. Describe two conditions in your town that cry out for someone who will fight for justice and righteousness.
2. What characteristics mark a person with whom God is pleased?
3. Israel combined worship of God with the worship of idols. How do we do the same thing today in principle, even though we might not bow down to literal idols?

Isaiah 58–59

Fasting That Is Favored

"*S*in in the Old Testament is not a disturbance of the 'status quo' in nature or an aberration which destroyed the harmony of affairs in the cosmic state. It is the violation of communion, the betrayal of God's love, and a revolt against his lordship."

Ralph L. Smith

Isaiah 58–59

 I N   A   N U T S H E L L

*G*od commissions his prophet to warn his people of their sins as they blithely go through the routines of religion. They must learn what true fasting and worship is—seeking justice and compassion for the needy. When you practice that kind of fasting, the Lord will satisfy your needs. Your problem lies not in some inadequacy on God's part but in your sins. God will don his special kind of armor and pay back his enemies for their injustice. People who repent will find that God gives them his Spirit.

Fasting That Is Favored

I. INTRODUCTION

Mistaken Identity

We often pontificate proudly about something we know nothing about, only to find someone else who is willing to reveal our mistakes. So it was with the newspaper writer who described the marvelous accomplishments of a volleyball coach. According to the story, this woman had done everything possible in the world of volleyball. The writer described her personal background, her volleyball achievements, her coaching secrets, and the style of volleyball she insisted that her teams play.

The next day the newspaper ran a one-line note about the previous day's story. The coach was, in reality, a man.

Israel had the same type of mistaken identity about themselves. They had finally rebuilt the temple and were participating joyfully in all its rites and rituals, even the fasts that commemorated the destruction of Jerusalem. They saw themselves as very religious people who were carrying out God's instructions precisely. Then one day God decided to show them who they really were. God used a plethora of words for sin to depict Israel's true character. What a shock for a self-satisfied people of God! Look and study closely. You may need the same shock therapy. It could be that the identity you carry so proudly does not match God's opinion of you (adapted from Swindoll, p. 496).

II. COMMENTARY

Fasting That Is Favored

> **MAIN IDEA:** *God calls people to turn from sin, live in his righteousness, and discover that he answers prayer and brings healing.*

A Taps for the Transgressors (58:1–14)

Priestly instruction

> **SUPPORTING IDEA:** *Righteous living on behalf of needy people brings a relationship in which God hears and responds to prayer.*

58:1–2. Again the prophet assumed the role of a priest to tell Israel what was expected in their new day with their new temple. They thought they had to carry out precise fasting regulations to show what they were willing to give up in the name of religion. The word of God came with an important announcement. The announcement had to be shouted out with **trumpet**-like volume to be heard above the racket of religious ritual. The sin question, not public ritual, was central to religion. The people came to the temple in eagerness to encounter God and **know** his **ways**. They acted just like **a nation that does what is right**. God ignored all their religious doings. He noticed only one thing. This was a people who had **forsaken the commands of its God**. Coming to worship and asking what God wanted is not enough; God's people must do what God wants.

58:3–5. The people continued in their daily religious practices in the temple, putting on a great show as if they observed the rights and responsibilities which God placed upon them. They even went so far as to complain to God that he was not taking proper notice of all their good righteous acts. They **fasted** and **humbled** themselves, but God had **not noticed**.

The divine answer came clearly: "Your fasting is none of my business. Indeed, you are the ones who find pleasure in it, not me. You **exploit** your employees. You cause others to work all the time for you so they cannot participate in the worship services. You end up **quarreling** and fighting when you are supposed to be worshiping." God did not seek the precise fulfillment of regulations. He wanted people to show their religion through their concern and help for other people in need. A fast involved symbols of humility like putting on **sackcloth** and lying down in **ashes**. No, God declared, you are simply proud of your humility. This was not **a day acceptable to the LORD**.

58:6–7. If ritual fasting was simply boosting one's own religious ego, what was the key to divine blessing? What was acceptable to the Lord? God called for concrete action, helping others in need. Again the emphasis is on overcoming **injustice** with righteous acts. God does not want anyone under someone else's **yoke**. Here is the beginning of the fight against slavery of every kind. God hates oppression. He wants his people to set **oppressed** people **free**. God's people are dedicated to providing the basic needs of life to those who do not own them. We feed the **hungry** and provide **shelter** for the **poor**, homeless **wanderer**. We **clothe** those who cannot afford proper clothing, and we make sure we take care of our own **flesh and blood**.

God does not accept excuses from people who try to hide themselves and pretend needy family members do not exist (see Deut. 22:1–4). Note that *you* here through verse 14 is singular, pointing to individual blessings and responsibilities. The singular "you" is directed at each member of the people of God, so that the collective group becomes what each individual becomes.

58:8–10. When God's people learn that salvation for them means giving themselves to establish righteousness and justice for others, then God's promise and purposes will be fulfilled. The "light to the nations" (49:6) will dawn.

Healing for the nations and the needy will take place. The image here is of the quick appearance of a scab over a wound in the skin. God's **righteousness** revealed in our righteous acts will lead the parade that will bring in the Gentiles. God's **glory** (cp. ch. 6) will be the **rear guard** protecting the caravan (cp. 52:12). No longer are we talking of a march out of exile through the wilderness to Jerusalem as in chapters 40–55. Now we are talking of Israel taking up their mission for God and leading the parade to call the world to join in worship in Jerusalem.

Under these conditions, the faithful believer could **call** upon God and expect an answer (contrast v. 3). Just as the prophet had answered God's call to service with **Here am I** (6:8), so God will answer his obedient servants. God is present for his people only when his people are present for others. Such presence for others involves one's words and deeds. **Pointing** a **finger** of accusation and blame at another or gossiping maliciously about another is as wrong and sinful as refusing to provide for the **needs of the oppressed**. Then the **light** of God's salvation will break in like **noonday** for you, for the poor, and for the nations.

58:11–14. Creating righteousness for the poor and oppressed brings God's listening ear to Israel's prayers (v. 9) and God's guiding hand to **guide** them and to **satisfy** their needs. This would have national implications, since the rebuilding of Jerusalem and the nation could then continue. The disappointment of the returned exiles at the weakness and desolation of Jerusalem would end as God led an obedient people to fulfill their dreams as well as his. The good old days would return if proper respect for God and his worship ruled the **day**.

The prophetic lesson was complete. Prophetic religion had been defined. It was a combination of proper conduct in relationship to the world's needy and proper respect for the worship observances which God had set forth. True religion expressed in doing justice and righteousness would result in a new day for Jerusalem and new joy for God's people.

🅱 Separated from the Savior by Sin (59:1–15a)

Service of repentance

> **SUPPORTING IDEA:** *Sin is the only thing that separates a person from God.*

59:1–8. The people complained that God had lost the ability to **hear** and **save** or rescue (cp. 50:2). The prophet answered with a resounding No! Their **iniquities** had separated them from **God**. God did **not hear** because he had **hidden his face** from their sin. The sin is precisely described: oppressing the poor (see 1:15), lying and corrupting the legal processes (see 1:21–23), and scheming to hurt others in order to pad one's own pockets. The latter charge appears in proverbial language like that of Psalm 58:4 and Proverbs 1:16. Verse 8 succinctly summarizes their sin. They had no knowledge or concern for **peace** and **justice**. (For peace, see "Deeper Discoveries," chs. 56–57; for justice, see "Deeper Discoveries," ch. 1.)

59:9–15a. The prophet suddenly joined his people in a confession of sin. The people agreed that they could not expect God's order of **justice** and **righteousness** to reign among them when they had sinned as the prophet had described. Thus they groped helplessly in the **darkness** as if they were **blind**. They were as good as **dead**. They described the very essence of their sin. Outwardly it was directed toward the harm of other people and the health of their pocketbooks, but inwardly it was a rejection of God himself. In neglecting or opposing **justice** and **righteousness**, they were **turning** their **backs** on God.

Ⓒ The Almighty in Armor (59:15b-21)

Promise of salvation

SUPPORTING IDEA: *God arms himself to save and gives his Spirit to those who turn from sin.*

59:15b-17. God answered such confession with a promise of salvation. God was angry (literally, "it was evil in his eyes") at the lack of justice among his people. At the same time he was **appalled** that his people suffered without an intercessor (literal translation of **one to intervene**) able to restore the proper order. So the Divine Warrior equipped himself for battle. His strong right **arm** brought **salvation** or victory. His **righteousness** provided all the support or supplies he needed. He went out to achieve **vengeance** in his jealous **zeal** (the Hebrew term means both "jealous" and "zealous") against all those who had opposed him and his people in their mission to achieve justice. (For zeal of the Lord, see "Deeper Discoveries," chs. 9–11.)

59:18–21. God's purpose was to maintain his own respect and honor among the nations, reaching out even to the distant **islands**. The entire earth from **west** to east (**the rising of the sun**) would have the proper **fear** and awe in God's presence. Thus God promised to come to his people as their **Redeemer**, but only to those who would **repent of their sins**. His redemption was carefully defined in terms of a **covenant** promise. The prophetic **Spirit** and **words** would abide with his people forever.

Here is salvation—God's people hearing the prophetic word pointing out their sin, joining the prophet in confessing their sin, and hearing the word of divine promise that brings deliverance from their crisis situation. Only on the day of Pentecost did such a constant abiding Spirit come to the people of God

forever. (For God's redemption, see "Deeper Discoveries," chs. 60–61; for salvation, see "Deeper Discoveries," chs. 47–49.)

> **MAIN IDEA REVIEW:** *God calls people to turn from sin, live in his righteousness, and discover that he answers prayer and brings healing.*

III. CONCLUSION

Confession and Repentance

God opposes sin. He wants us to know our sin, confess our sin, and repent of our sin. We cannot expect God to hear and answer prayer or to rescue us from our enemies when we persist in sin. God wants to bring salvation, but he does so only when we are willing to serve him sincerely. God wanted Israel to demonstrate true faith by joining him in reaching out to the oppressed and needy. God has promised to avenge his people and give them his Spirit, but this comes only after confession and repentance.

PRINCIPLES

- God ignores a rebel's piety and judges his sin.
- Using and manipulating other people is a sin that God despises.
- God will not hear your prayers if your life is dedicated to sin.
- God hears the prayers of people who seek to bring justice and righteousness to this world.

APPLICATIONS

- Plan a way to help a specific person or group of persons who are suffering from oppression and injustice.
- Lead your Bible study group to plan a way to minister to hungry people in your community.
- Determine what God expects from you so you can meet his expectations and experience his joy.

IV. LIFE APPLICATION

Good in the Worst Sense

Some people are "good in the worst sense of the word," according to Mark Twain. Philip Yancey illustrates this with the experience of a mother who came to him for help. She told how she had recently stood in a church sanctuary with her fifteen-year-old daughter. The pastor's wife spied her and marched up. "I hear you are divorcing," she accosted the lonely lady. "What I can't understand is that if you love Jesus and he loves Jesus, why are you doing that?" Having never spoken to this pastor's wife before, the newly divorced woman stood stunned, as was her daughter. "The pain of it," the woman blurted out to Yancey, "was that my husband and I both did love Jesus, but the marriage was broken beyond mending. If she had just put her arms around me and said, 'I'm so sorry'" (Yancey, p. 31).

The pastor's wife was good in the worst sense of the word. She stood for the right so strongly that she could not reach out to help the person who was hurting and in need. A little girl was overheard praying, "Dear God, Make all the bad people good and the good people kind."

Isaiah spoke to a "good" people. They knew how to fast and call on God and point the finger of guilt and shame at other people. Isaiah reminds us strongly that God knows our sins and wants to forgive them and bring deliverance and salvation, but he will do that only when we repent of our sins. We repent in word and by joining God in his mission for justice and righteousness for all people. We need to offer love and grace to other people and provide their basic needs even when it costs us. Will you turn from being "good in the worst sense of the word" toward being just and fair and righteous, working for God's truth and waiting for God's deliverance and redemption?

V. PRAYER

Righteous and just Father of all truth, forgive me when I am so religious that I am good for nothing and for no one. I repent of my religious pride and my religious arrogance. Forgive me when I am so good that I judge others rather than freeing them from oppression and injustice. Show me today how to start being a part of your mission to bring justice, righteousness, freedom from oppression, and truth into this world. Amen.

VI. DEEPER DISCOVERIES

Israel's Vocabulary for Sin

Israel has a rich vocabulary that describes human sin which separates us from God. The following brief study of the major words for sin cannot begin to encompass the full nature of sin, because sin is not confined to a few words. Sin includes everything we do and every attitude we have that opposes the will and way of God.

Isaiah 58–59 include the following words for sin:

Pesha' is a crime that leads to punishment, a rebellion against the legal order. It includes the illegal possession of property that belongs to another (Exod. 22:8) and an offense against the person or property of another (Amos

1:3–2:6). Children rebel against their parents (Isa. 1:2; cp. 1:28). Israel's leaders, their spokesmen—those responsible for interceding with God for the people—rebelled against God (Isa. 43:27). The greatest sign of rebellion, however, is serving another God than the Creator of the world and the Redeemer of Israel (46:7–9). Such rebellion is not new. It goes back to the beginning of the nation's history, its birth (48:8).

Rebellion causes God to divorce his people, to sell them to another nation (50:1). God's people do not recognize their rebellion so God commissions the prophet to declare it to them (58:1). But God is willing to erase our rebellious behavior from his record (Isa. 43:25). We must confess that our rebellious actions and attitudes are not a once-in-a-while happening. Our sinful rebellions are many, so many they are ever before us (59:12). We must admit that such action is not simply a crime against another person; it is rebellion against God himself (59:13).

We must repent, turn away from such rebellion (59:20). His Suffering Servant let himself be registered on the census list of rebels (53:12). He was pierced and stricken for our rebellious behavior (53:5,8), but he still made intercession for us (53:12). Those who do not repent and accept the atoning work of the Suffering Servant face death and torment (66:24).

Chata'ah is the basic Old Testament word for "sin." It means "to miss the mark" as when one shoots an arrow at a target and misses (see Judg. 20:16). Sin may be committed against another person or against God (1 Sam. 2:25). It may be committed without conscious awareness (Gen. 20:9; Lev. 4–5; Ps. 41:4). It reaches back to the first person in Israel's history (either Adam, Abraham, or Jacob; 43:27); Still sin by its nature brings death (Num. 27:3; 2 Kgs. 14:16; Dan. 9:16). It makes God hide his holy face and not listen to the prayers of his people (59:2).

Sadly, God's people seem proud of their sin and let others know about it (Isa. 3:9). They sweep their sins into a pile, heaping up a collection of sins (Isa. 30:1). They hurt other people with their sinful words in the courtroom (29:21). They burden God with their sins (43:24), especially when their sinful hands make idols (31:7). Our sin makes God so angry that salvation seems an impossible dream (64:5). God must commission the prophet to let the house of Jacob know of their sins (58:1). A sinful people (1:4) have no hope of winning a case against God, because their sins testify against them (59:12).

The price of sin must be paid. Sinners will be broken (1:28). On the day of the Lord they face destruction (13:9). So they are terrified before the consuming, everlasting fire (33:14). God's people in their exile pay double for all their sin (40:2). Still, God wants to atone for our sin (Isa. 6:7; 27:9), sweep it away (44:22). He is the only one who can. He is ready to remember our sins no more (43:25). His Suffering Servant bore the sin of many (53:12).

'Awen means "harm" or "disaster" and is used to describe crimes and sins with disastrous results. It literally means "the power of disaster," describing a sinful act and its results. It also can mean "deception" or "nothing." In this latter usage, it refers often to false worship of idols (Isa. 41:29). In the Old Testament it appears eighty times, always in poetry rather than in prose. This type of disastrous, empty sin occupies the mind of the fool and leads the fool to oppose God (Isa. 32:6). The person whose life is marked by 'awen needs to change his way of thinking (Isa. 59:7). Such thinking produces talk that is dangerous and empty. Such talk must be transformed and done away with (Isa. 58:9).

This dangerous sin is committed when people become allies with a pagan political power rather than seeking help from God (31:2); when they pass evil, dangerous, meaningless laws (10:1); and when they manipulate the court system in the interests of injustice and personal gain (29:20). Such actions in the courts give birth to this sin (59:4). What such actions produce is harmful and evil (59:6).

In most cases the doer of 'awen wants "to harm a Yahweh worshiper by misusing their power, especially by slander, cursing, false accusations, and other sins of the tongue" (Carpenter and Grisanti; NIDOTTE, 1, p. 313). This person also must change his way of worship, because his public worship assemblies are all 'awen (1:13) even if the worship gathering is supposedly dedicated to the Lord. In actuality "the doer of 'awen seeks to unsettle or even kill any faithful member of the covenant community, especially the less fortunate individuals" (Carpenter and Grisanti, NIDOTTE, 1, p. 310).

'Awen has "general applicability to all types of unhealthy activity" and also to "their consequences." "The word essentially always envisions the totality of a catastrophic process" (Knierim, TLOT, 1, p. 61). It operates in all spheres of life—political, religious, legal, military.

God never creates or causes 'awen, so that it is not part of his discipline to his people. By contrast, rʿ is a calamity which comes from God (Jer. 4:6; 11:11,17, 23; Mic. 2:3).

"Every type of 'aœwen-act or 'aœwen-sphere is implicitly or explicitly ungodly and thereby always appears theologically disqualified. . . . the criterion for the disqualification is the notion that that which is called 'aœwen is a perversion of the salvation-effecting spheres of power and thereby of the salvation-effecting divine presence" (Knierim; TLOT, 1, p. 62). Still God offers people who practice such dangerous, harmful evil a new chance to repent and turn back to God (Isa. 55:7). They demonstrate this in concrete help for those whom they have cheated of justice and opportunity (58:10).

'Awon is "an act, or mistake, which is not right, unjust" (HALOT) as well as the consequences of that act, including the guilt incurred by and experienced by the person who commits the sinful act (Isa. 59:3). The word includes anything that is twisted, perverse, and outside the moral limits that God has placed on the universe. Also included in the term is the punishment that results from the sin (Isa. 64:7). The term occurs 331 times in the Old Testament, twenty-five times in Isaiah.

Every person has committed such twisted acts and deserves to be blown away with the wind (64:6). Our perverse acts weary God (43:24) and erect a dividing wall between us and him (59:2) so that he hides his face from us (64:7). They bring his punishment (13:11; 57:17), even on following generations (14:21). The nation seeks to transport its sin and guilt to its storehouses but uses "cords of deceit" (5:18). They do not trust God and his Word, so they face certain fall just like a besieged city with a bulging wall (30:13). These sinful acts weigh a nation down with a burden of guilt and punishment too heavy to bear (Isa. 1:4).

God's people recognize their sin and ask for God's anger to subside (64:9). Isaiah's personal experience showed that God was willing to forgive his guilt and unjust actions (6:7), although the time comes when God refuses to forgive (22:14). God shows the way to atonement for perverse acts of sin (27:9). In God's timing he announces that sin is forgiven and removed (40:2). God's Suffering Servant was crushed for our unjust, twisted acts of sin (53:5). The punishment for our disastrous actions fell on him (53:6), and he bore out sins (53:11).

VII. TEACHING OUTLINE

A. INTRODUCTION

1. Lead Story: Mistaken Identity

2. Context: Isaiah 56–57 promises hope to a people from a healing God who brings peace to his people but refuses to let the wicked experience peace. The following chapters retrace the steps of guilt one more time to remind Israel of their guilt and to show that more than outward religious rites are needed to find God's peace. A people can be eager to know God and can go through all the religious services and actions possible and still find themselves facing God's judgment.

3. Transition: How can a thoroughly religious people, even a people willing to endure fasting and rituals of mourning, be guilty and face God's judgment? Chapters 58–59 reveal the true components of religion that please God. They call on you to examine your life and see if you exhibit the components of true religion in your life. Or are you simply going through the motions of what the church requires without pleasing God?

B. COMMENTARY

1. Taps for the Transgressors (58:1–14)
2. Separated from the Savior by Sin (59:1–15a)
3. The Almighty in Armor (59:15b–21)

C. CONCLUSION: GOOD IN THE WORST SENSE

1. Wrap-up: A religious people may be a sinful people. Those who complain, mourn, and fast because of their dreadful situation may need to look closely at God's expectations and their daily lives. Failure to join God on his mission of righteousness and justice for all people is failure to experience God's salvation. Such sin separates you from the Savior and does not let you join the celebration when he straps on his armor to bring deliverance to his people.
2. Personal Challenge: Take a sin inventory of your life, using these chapters as a guide for discovering sin. Then repent of your sins, for the Savior is coming again.

VIII. ISSUES FOR DISCUSSION

1. In what ways do people try to hide their sinful lives behind religious activities? What does God say about this?
2. How do these chapters help you understand those times you cried to God for help and seemed to receive no answer?
3. Can you identify specific groups of people in your town who are objects of gossip and condemnation and who need to be recipients of Christian ministry?
4. What is involved in true confession and repentance of sins?

Isaiah 60–61

Showing the Splendor

I. **INTRODUCTION**
Seeing the Hand of God Today

II. **COMMENTARY**
A verse-by-verse explanation of these chapters.

III. **CONCLUSION**
A Nation of Priests

An overview of the principles and applications from these chapters.

IV. **LIFE APPLICATION**
Samson's Dream

Melding these chapters to life.

V. **PRAYER**
Tying these chapters to life with God.

VI. **DEEPER DISCOVERIES**
Historical, geographical, and grammatical enrichment of the commentary.

VII. **TEACHING OUTLINE**
Suggested step-by-step group study of these chapters.

VIII. **ISSUES FOR DISCUSSION**
Zeroing these chapters in on daily life.

"*G*od . . . is the light and sound and fragrance and food and embracement of my inner man—where that light shines into my soul which no place can contain, where time does not snatch away the lovely sound, where no breeze disperses the sweet fragrance, where no eating diminishes the food there provided, and where there is an embrace that no satiety comes to sunder. This is what I love when I love my God."

Augustine

Isaiah 60–61

IN A NUTSHELL

*G*od wakes Jerusalem up to receive foreign delegations who have come to worship him in their temple. They bring with them great riches to offer as sacrifices to God. God no longer shows anger but compassion to his people and uses the coming of the nations to teach his people that he is their Savior and Redeemer. Righteousness and peace will replace violence and destruction. God anoints his messenger to preach good news to the poor, to bind up the brokenhearted, to proclaim freedom for the captives, and to proclaim that God's day of vengeance has come. Ruined cities and devastated land will be restored. God's people will become priests for the world and experience everlasting joy. This is part of God's everlasting covenant. So God's messenger sings God's praise.

Showing the Splendor

I. INTRODUCTION

Seeing the Hand of God Today

*O*n Saturday, July 5, a plane carrying four men crashed. Three days of searching finally found the fragments of the plane. During all this Verdell Davis waited anxiously and prayed for her missing husband. She also prayed that somehow her children would see the hand of God in what was going on. Daughter Shawna held faithfully to her conviction that her daddy would be found alive and all would be well. Then the news came. Verdell had to place her arms around Shawna and relay the news that her father was dead. "I don't believe it," the daughter shouted.

Three days later in the church in Comanche, Texas, waiting for the funeral to begin, Verdell talked with the minister. Turning around, she saw her two boys kneeling in front of the casket. They had their arms around their sister, who knelt between them. Mother overheard her children praying to God that he would give them the kind of love for him that their dad had had. This assured their mother that God had answered her prayers and that she and the children could see the hand of God even in this tragedy.

Similarly, God tried to help Israel see the good that was coming from their tragic loss of Jerusalem and the years spent in exile. God was ready to begin all over again with Jerusalem and to bring all the nations to her gates to worship him and see his splendor. The question was, Would the people of Jerusalem see God's hand in tragedy and heed his call to mission in time of recovery? (Davis, p. 18).

II. COMMENTARY

Showing the Splendor

> **MAIN IDEA:** *God restores his people to righteous living and glorious worship and sends them as priests to the nations.*

A Gathering Around the Glow of God's Glory (60:1–9)

Promise of salvation

> **SUPPORTING IDEA:** *God will glorify his people by bringing them back to his house of worship.*

60:1–3. God's people had returned to their city and had tried to rebuild it and the temple. Something was missing. Their hopes and dreams had not been brought to reality. Despair and frustration began to set in. The prophet's words reassured his people and called them to attention. God was going to act for them. The **darkness** of despair and defeat would cover the earth, but God would shine his **glory** upon them, so that the **light** of his **glory** would attract the **nations** to Jerusalem. (For glory of God, see "Deeper Discoveries," chs. 6–8.)

60:4–9. The nations would bring the remainder of the exiles back to Jerusalem and would bring rich tribute—**the wealth on the seas, the riches of the nations**—to rebuild the city in all its glory. The nations included all those known to Israel, as far away as **Tarshish** (see this commentary, p. 141) and the distant **islands**. Yet the people of Zion must accept one small detail. These foreigners would also come to worship at the **temple**, and God would accept them (see 2:2–4; 55:5). The event would **honor** the **Holy One of Israel** (see "Deeper Discoveries," ch. 1), as the nations saw how he had **endowed** Zion with **splendor.**

B Recognizing the Redeemer (60:10–18)

Promise of salvation

> **SUPPORTING IDEA:** *God's victory over the nations will show that he is Savior, Redeemer, holy one, and mighty God.*

60:10–14. Israel would no longer have to labor to rebuild her city and temple to their former glory. Foreign nations and **kings** would supply the necessary financial resources and the manpower to **rebuild** the walls. How could this be? God had turned away from his **anger** toward his sinful people. Now he would show **compassion** to them (see "Deeper Discoveries," chs. 13–14). Zion would never have to shut her **gates** in fear. Rather, she would have to keep them open twenty-four hours a day to accommodate all the people bringing her gifts. Any nation that did not join in the **procession** to Zion would be **utterly ruined**—obliterated from the earth.

Lebanon, known for its glorious cedar trees, would bring its glory to Israel for the new temple (cp. 1 Kgs. 5:6–18). The temple was his footstool (1 Chr. 28:2; Ps. 99:5; Isa. 66:1; Matt. 5:35), and God would **glorify** that **place.** Israel, who lived in such great dread and fear of the nations who had so horribly mistreated them, would see these same **oppressors** come to Jerusalem **bowing** before Israel. They would recognize that this was **Zion of the Holy One of Israel.**

60:15–18. God's marvelous new day of salvation would not be a passing fancy, but it would be **everlasting**. Self-esteem and **joy** would again mark the people of Jerusalem. All this would come to pass so Israel might know Yahweh their God and rest assured that he was their **Savior**, not their silencer; their **Redeemer**, not their ruiner. (For God's redemption, see "Deeper Discoveries.") He remained the **Mighty One of Jacob**. That meant he was Israel's God as long as there had been an Israel, because Jacob also bore the name Israel (Gen. 32:28). From his twelve sons came the twelve tribes of Israel.

The day of salvation would be marked by top-quality goods rather than make-do materials. The buildings would no longer serve defense purposes. **Peace** and **righteousness** would rule the land. Defense walls would now be referred to as **Salvation**. **Violence** and **destruction** would vanish.

God Is Your Glory (60:19–22)

Promise of salvation

> **SUPPORTING IDEA:** *God is the eternal light and glory of his people, and he will establish peace and righteousness for them.*

Salvation would be so complete that Zion would no longer have to depend upon unpredictable natural phenomena for weather and **light**. God's glorious presence would outshine the **sun**, so that darkness would be no more. Thus their **days of sorrow** would end. Such marvelous new promises were possible only under one condition. The people themselves must be totally different. They would be **righteous**, part of the proper order of God's universe, turning away from the sins they had confessed in chapter 59. (For righteousness, see "Deeper Discoveries," chs. 50–51.) Then they would be able to claim possession of their **land forever**, without worry that an enemy might take it away or that God would again punish them for their sins.

Under such conditions, the promise to Abraham of many descendants could again be fulfilled. Such promises depend not upon human effort, but upon God's power. His people will gather for the glorious day when he will **display** his **splendor** among them (cp. 49:3; 61:3).

Gladness in God's Garden (61:1–11)

Commissioning report

> **SUPPORTING IDEA:** *God sends his messenger to bring good news and help to all those in need. He establishes his people as priests among the nations, celebrating the joy of his salvation.*

61:1–3. The prophet described his commissioning by God to minister to the needs of the post-exilic community (cp. 6; 42; 50:4–11). This became the text for Jesus' first sermon in Nazareth in which he identified the role given here as his role (Luke 4:16–21). The prophetic task centered in preaching to the **poor** and needy. The content was the action of God to meet their needs. **Freedom** is the term normally used to speak of releasing slaves during the Jubilee Year (Lev. 25:10,13; Jer. 34:8–10). The source of the task was the divine **Spirit** (see 59:21).

The time when God would show his **favor** remained indefinite, but sure. He would **comfort all who mourn** (note the use of the same Hebrew term in 1:24; 12:1; 22:4; 40:1; 49:13; 51:3,12,19; 52:9; 54:11; 66:13). The result was that the **mourning** and complaining of the people in Jerusalem would be stopped once and for all. A **crown**, probably of flowers, would replace the **ashes** which a mourner usually placed on his head. **Oil** for the skin could once again be used, bringing gladness instead of the sadness of the mourner who would not rub his skin with oil (cp. 2 Sam. 14:2). The purpose of the task was to **display** God's **splendor** (see 49:3). Splendor refers to that which brings praise and pride.

61:4–7. The long-term results would bring the restoration of Jerusalem and the surrounding **cities** that had long been in **ruins**. The new situation of salvation produced by the prophet's proclamation would bring foreign labor so that God's people could tend to the Lord's work. Not just those from Aaron's family but the entire nation would be **priests of the LORD**, being the **ministers** of God to the nations. **Foreigners** would not only do the hard work for God's people, but they would also bring such luxurious sacrifices that they would pay the expenses of the new nation of priests. **Riches, inheritance**, and **everlasting joy** would be the new traits and attitudes of God's people.

The text of verse 7 is difficult to translate. A literal reading is "instead of your (plural) shame double; and disgrace they will rejoice their portion; therefore in their land double they will possess; they will have joy of eternity" (author's translation). This appears to promise more land than ever in eternal **joy** rather than the **shame** they had suffered under the Babylonians and in the poor circumstances immediately after they returned to their homeland.

61:8–9. The prophet added to his promise of salvation a note on God's reasoning. God had decided to restore the **justice** he loved while doing away with the **iniquity** (or injustice) and **robbery** he hated, even while the people suffered because he was punishing them. God would pay the wages of suffering to his people and sign an eternal contract (or **covenant**) with them that promised his justice. This would mark them off so that everyone could notice they were different—they were God's people, **blessed** by him. Again, the result would be glory given to Yahweh.

61:10–11. The prophet reacted to his own message with a hymn of praise at the work that God was accomplishing through him (cp. ch. 12). God would cause his righteous order and the proclamation of his greatness to spring up as a plant so that all the **nations** could see it. God's messenger was dressed in such a way that those who saw him would see God's **salvation** and God's **righteousness**. Such finery rivaled the beauty of wedding garments. This was the goal toward which the man of God worked when God's Spirit anointed him to proclaim good tidings to the poor and afflicted.

> **MAIN IDEA REVIEW:** *God restores his people to righteous living and glorious worship and sends them as priests to the nations.*

III. CONCLUSION

A Nation of Priests

God had come to redeem his beleaguered people. His glory drew the nations to his city to bring rich offerings and to rebuild the ruins. His glory provided light and perfect weather for the city. He showed that his dominant side was compassion, not anger. His goal was redemption, not destruction or punishment. He sought to establish a righteous order of peace and justice. To do so he called his people as priests to the nations with a message of hope for the poor, broken, and needy.

Although Israel as a nation refused to accept the challenge and take on the identity that the prophet gave them, God did not fail his people. Jesus of Nazareth came, took up the messenger's appointed task, and brought new hope and salvation to the world. He now calls us as his people to take up the same mission he had and to give hope to the world's hopeless. As we do, we experience his blessings and know for sure that everlasting joy is ours. And we show God's splendor to the world.

PRINCIPLES

- God wants his people to be a light to all peoples of the world.
- God maintains sovereign control over all the nations of the earth.
- God wants to bring peace to his people so that all sorrow will vanish.
- God's plan is to bless his people through his everlasting covenant.

APPLICATIONS

- Tell someone else the experience you had when God became your personal Savior and Redeemer.
- Describe a mission God has called you to accomplish for him.
- Reject racial and ethnic prejudice.

IV. LIFE APPLICATION

Samson's Dream

Where do I see God's splendor displayed for the world? I see it in the face of a short, wiry Kenyan. Samson Kisia has shown me more of God's glory than any person I know. Samson is the acknowledged leader of Baptists and evangelicals in Kenya, although for several years he has held no elected position except pastor of his church. For four years now, we have sent volunteers to help Samson realize his dream. For three years he took us to the western-most outposts of Kenya. We tromped up one hill and down another, seeking people who needed to hear about Jesus Christ.

Samson wanted to win an entire section of his nation to Christ, so they, in turn, could take the message to the surrounding nations. Having carefully plotted out where churches were needed, Samson sent the volunteers into each of these areas to preach, witness, and start new churches. Samson found men whom God had called out to pastor these churches. Now western Kenya has over one hundred new churches because Samson followed the dream God gave him.

In 1997, nine people saw God bring 1,271 people to salvation. In 1998, twenty-nine volunteers witnessed God lead 5,963 people to Jesus as Lord. In 1999, eighty-six American volunteers experienced God's power changing the lives of 15,082 Kenyans. Then in 2001 Samson began working on another dream, going into northeastern Kenya to reach the northern neighbors. Sixteen volunteer missionaries let God use their testimonies to bring 1,913 people to Christ.

In October 2001 twenty-two more volunteers went to see what God was still doing in Kenya. Samson had already sent the maps showing precisely where to witness, where new churches needed to be started. He had already trained a translator and a person to take down names to work with each volunteer from the United States. He enlisted new pastors for new churches that would exist. Samson saw God's splendor dotting the Kenyan countryside with churches filled with new believers so all of Kenya and the surrounding nations would recognize Jesus as Lord and see his glory.

Samson was simply doing what Isaiah preached, what Jesus took as his personal mission, and what God still calls his church to do. He calls each person who knows him as Savior and Lord to catch a vision like Samson's and to work to bring people to know him as Lord. Have you caught the vision? Are you an instrument God is using to show his splendor to your part of the world?

V. PRAYER

Glorious God, words cannot describe your splendor, glory, and majesty. We stand amazed in your presence. We also stand amazed that you have chosen to use us to show your splendor and majesty to the world. Open our eyes to your vision. Show us the poor, needy, broken-hearted prisoners to whom you want to minister through us. Forgive us our limited visions. Fill us with your dreams for a redeemed world. Show us how to join you at work fulfilling those dreams. Amen.

VI. DEEPER DISCOVERIES

God's Redemption (60:16)

Isaiah's vision is that God is the Redeemer of his people. God knows the awful plight they have faced and the problems they still face. He has begun his work of redemption by bringing them back to their homeland from exile. He wants to continue that work of redemption by using them to be priests and witnesses to the nations. But exactly what is the prophet saying as he talks about the Redeemer bringing redemption?

Hebrew uses a verb (*ga'al*) to speak of redemption and a participle form of the verb (*go'el*) for Redeemer. The verb's basic meaning and application is "to buy something back" whether that is a house (Lev. 25:33), a person sold to pay his debts (Lev. 25:48–49), a sacrificial animal (Lev. 27:13), a house previously dedicated to God (Lev. 27:15), or a field or other property (27:19–26). Jeremiah 50:34 applies this usage to God (cp. Job 19:7–25; Ps. 119:154).

Go'el becomes a technical term in family law and functions, in the case of a husband dying and leaving behind a wife without children. The closest male relative was bound by custom and law to marry the widow and raise up children in the name of the deceased man (Gen. 30:1; Ruth 4:4,6). The male relative who fulfilled this responsibility was called the *go'el* or redeemer.

In criminal law a person who committed a crime against another person was responsible for paying back the cost of his crime. If the injured party for some reason was not available to receive restitution, then the nearest relative was to receive it and was called the *go'el* (Num. 5:8).

In capital punishment cases, the closest relative was responsible for avenging the death of his relative. This avenger was called a *go'el* of blood, but to prohibit such a custom from getting out of hand and becoming an uncontrolled vendetta, the cities of refuge were set up to protect the person accused of murder (Num. 35:12; Josh. 20:3–9; cp. 1 Kgs. 16:11). Thus in

Israel's law redemption was "to redeem that which belongs to the family from outside jurisdiction" (Stamm, TLOT, 1, p. 291).

God used the image of redemption to describe what he did for his people as he brought them out of Egyptian slavery and gave them freedom (Exod. 6:6; cp. Pss. 74:2; 78:35; 107:2; Jer. 31:11; Hos. 13:14). This figure of the divine Redeemer becomes a central theme in the Book of Isaiah in addressing the situation of exiled Israel (chs. 40–55) and Israel returned from exile but still disappointed (chs. 56–66). The idyllic period of redemption through the exodus soon came to an end when God's people rebelled and grieved his Holy Spirit (63:9–10). "By recalling the first Exodus . . . the prophet portrays future events as a new exodus, which frees Israel from slavery and restores them to their rightful, original owner" (Hubbard, NIDOTTE, 1, p. 792). God told his people not to fear, because as their Redeemer he would help them (41:14). He admitted that they faced the current problems because he punished them in his anger, but that moment was over, and now his compassion for them was in control (54:8).

They might still face the problems of exile, being hated and abused by everyone, but God had redeemed them and claimed them as his own (49:7). He knew their shame and disgrace, but they can now forget that (54:4–5). He has a plan to overcome all obstacles and take them home (43:1–2). He will take care of Babylonia no matter how strong that enemy appears (43:14). Thus God issued the command for Israel to leave Babylon (48:20), letting all the world know, "The Lord has redeemed His servant Jacob." Not only has he redeemed Israel in Babylon; he has also redeemed Jerusalem (52:9), so international leaders and rulers will recognize God's power, come there, and bow down before his people (49:7,26). They will give nourishment to God's people, because he is their Redeemer (60:16).

As Israel's Redeemer, God has no peer; no other god is like him (44:6–7). He rules all the earth (54:5). As God's servant, Israel can rejoice, for God has not forgotten them; rather, he has redeemed them, forgiving their sins (44:22–24). Their Redeemer is the world's Creator, so Israel has no reason to fear the nations and their powerless gods (44:24–25). Israel can raise their hurts and frustrations in prayer to God their Redeemer (63:16).

But Israel's Redeemer was not satisfied with just any Israel. He had expectations for them, and plans for those who fulfilled those expectations (48:17–19). They must turn from their transgressions (59:20). Finally, in the final chapter of world history, Israel will truly be called "the redeemed of the Lord" (62:12). They will live in a land without vicious beast but with everlasting joy (35:9–10). Isaiah thus "anchors the end of Israel's history in its beginning" (see 41:8–9; 51:1–3). . . . . "For as *go'el* Yahweh does not purchase strange goods; rather he regains that which has always—since the time of Abraham—belonged to him. Yahweh lays claim to his ancient right to Israel;

he actualizes a claim that was his because he has created and chosen this people and he is its king" (TLOT, 1, p. 294).

VII. TEACHING OUTLINE

A. INTRODUCTION

1. Lead Story: Seeing the Hand of God Today
2. Context: God has redeemed Israel from exile, but he wants to do more. He wants to restore life in Jerusalem so God's people will recognize their mission to the nations and become priestly witnesses who display God's splendor. Chapters 60–61 call Israel to recognize God's continued action in redeeming them and challenge them to accept a new role in their worship and witness.
3. Transition: Israel back home in Jerusalem likes to complain just as much as did Israel in exile in Babylon. God has an answer for those complaints and an astounding picture of the new Jerusalem he wants to create in order to show his splendor to the world. We look today to see the mission God has for us in witnessing to the nations and being part of God's plan to let the world see his splendor and glory.

B. COMMENTARY

1. Gathering Around the Glow of God's Glory (60:1–9)
2. Recognizing the Redeemer (60:10–18)
3. God Is Your Glory (60:19–22)
4. Gladness in God's Garden (61:1–11)

C. CONCLUSION: SAMSON'S DREAM

1. Wrap-up: God's plan is bigger than ours. We seek redemption for ourselves and our people, but he seeks redemption and salvation for the entire world. We complain about the situations we face. He calls us to watch for his miracles of bringing our enemies to fall at our knees. We complain that we have too much to do. He calls us to be his priests to the nations and let all the world join us in transforming his temple and his worship. But the task involves more than going to temple worship. It also means telling good news to the poor, needy, and broken-hearted who stay away from our worship. It means showing God's splendor to the rich nations who come to us and showing God's splendor to the impoverished needy of the world.
2. Personal Challenge: Where do you stand in the picture Isaiah has painted? Are you part of the nations that live without knowing or

recognizing God? You need to come to his worship and discover that he wants to be your Redeemer. Are you part of God's people who complain about the way things are going? You need to hear God's call to be a priest, telling the world about God's splendor. Are you in contact with poor people, broken-hearted people, prisoners? You need to tell them the good news that God loves them and has a plan for their lives.

VIII. ISSUES FOR DISCUSSION

1. Describe contacts you have with people of other nations who do not know God. How can you show them God's splendor?
2. What complaints have you been raising to God? Is he calling you to move beyond your complaints and join him in ministering to others who need his good news?
3. List the names of five to ten people who are suffering from grief, poverty, imprisonment, and hunger. What will you do to show these people that God can bring them justice, hope, and love?

Isaiah 62–64

The Savior Is Not Silent

I. INTRODUCTION
The Silent Friend

II. COMMENTARY
A verse-by-verse explanation of these chapters.

III. CONCLUSION
God's Eternal Plan

An overview of the principles and applications from these chapters.

IV. LIFE APPLICATION
"Are You Ready to Listen?"

Melding these chapters to life.

V. PRAYER
Tying these chapters to life with God.

VI. DEEPER DISCOVERIES
Historical, geographical, and grammatical enrichment of the commentary.

VII. TEACHING OUTLINE
Suggested step-by-step group study of these chapters.

VIII. ISSUES FOR DISCUSSION
Zeroing these chapters in on daily life.

Isaiah 62–64

IN A NUTSHELL

*G*od answers Israel's complaints by breaking his silence and promising renewed greatness and glory for Israel. He calls Israel to prepare the way for nations to come to Jerusalem and worship, because God is making his people into a holy people. God comes from Edom in blood-stained clothes, showing he is already at work defeating the enemies and showing himself mighty to save for Israel. The prophet gives Israel a lament in which they remember God's great saving deeds of the past and how they grieved God's Spirit, making him their enemy. So Israel calls on God to quit hardening their hearts with the result that they did not walk in his ways. They ask him to return to them and restore them as he did in the ancient past. Confessing their sins, Israel asks God not to be angry and to forgive their sins. They wonder if God will keep silent and keep punishing them.

The Savior Is Not Silent

I. INTRODUCTION

The Silent Friend

I have a dear friend who brings great joy and happiness into my life. We do many things together and share our hearts with each other. Only one thing impedes our relationship. This friend has a habit of lapsing into silence. For long periods, even hours at a time, conversation ceases. In such times many thoughts and fears race through my mind. What have I done to make my friend so angry? Why won't this dear pal say anything? Have I lost a friend forever? What can I do to bring our relationship back to normal and get conversation going again?

Israel had such a time in their relationship with God. Israel could remember the many wonderful times when God had been near to them and had fought their battles and blessed them. But the times came when God was silent. They found no way to get through to him. The enemy prevailed, and God did nothing. Strings of questions plagued Israel. They shouted and pouted, trying to find an answer to God's silence. Isaiah 62–64 pictures one time when God broke his silence and renewed his promise to save Israel in a mighty way. Here we learn much about God's silence, about human sin, and about future salvation.

II. COMMENTARY

The Savior Is Not Silent

> **MAIN IDEA:** *God will win the victory over his enemies and transform his people into a righteous community as they quit their pouting, confess their sins, and ask for a new relationship with the heavenly Father.*

The Restless Redeemer (62:1–12)

Promise of salvation

> **SUPPORTING IDEA:** *God will bring salvation to his people in clear view of the nations and will create a holy, righteous people.*

62:1–5. The community continued to complain that God had not fulfilled his promises. Instead he had been **silent**. God responded to his people's plea by promising to act to reestablish her **righteousness** and **salvation** (or her right order and her state of deliverance; see NEB). Such work would not occur in secret but in view of all the **nations** and their leaders. Jerusalem's reputation would be transformed, because God would rename her. Rather than a heap of ruins at the mercy of the nations, Jerusalem would be the **crown** adorning God himself and resting in his **hand**. Her new name would be **Hephzibah** (NIV footnote, **my delight**) rather than **Deserted**, and **Beulah** (NIV footnote, **married**) rather than **Desolate**. The marriage imagery is then taken a step further. The **land will be married . . . so will your sons marry you**.

This has caused a great variety of interpretations from Bible students. No one can be sure of having the correct interpretation here. To me it appears God is reinforcing his fertility promise from 60:21–22. "Zion," "Jerusalem," "the land" are all terms representing the people of Israel. The people who have been in exile away from the land will now be married to that land, staying with it forever. Just as the marriage blessing is to be fruitful and multiply and fill the land (or earth; Gen. 1:28), so the promise here is that the permanent marriage of people and land will lead to a multitude of offspring among God's blessed people. **God** would be the happiest one of all those rejoicing at the great wedding feast. His joy would be that of a **bridegroom** with a new **bride**.

62:6–9. God repeated his promise with yet another image. He would set **watchmen** to protect the **walls** of **Jerusalem**. Whether these are angelic, prophetic, or military, he did not say. They would imitate God in never being **silent** (cp. vv. 1 and 6). Their task would be unique. They were to serve as the private secretary reminding God of his engagement calendar, so he would not forget what he had promised to do for **Jerusalem**. Again, the purpose of his work was to bring **praise** to himself by bringing Jerusalem praise and fame among the nations of the **earth**.

God underlined the intensity of his commitment with a solemn oath. **Never again** would **foreigners** rule Jerusalem. **Never again** would her **enemies** demand her products and profits as tribute and taxes. Instead, her produce would be used in the great worship festivals in the newly-built temple **sanctuary**.

62:10–12. Having sworn his promise, God called the people to action, using the same language he had used earlier for the people during the Exile (cp. 40:3). A new **highway** must be constructed, but this one would **prepare the way** for worship in the temple. A new signal to the nations (see 49:22) would call the kings to recognize what Yahweh had done; then they would bring the proper tribute (see 60:2). Zion would not have to wait any longer for her wages (see 61:8; 49:4). Again, the **reward** would correspond to a new nature, because the people would be known as the **Holy People**, those

Redeemed of the LORD. (For God's redemption, see "Deeper Discoveries," chs. 60–61.) The nations would thus seek Israel out rather than laughing at how their God had deserted them (cp. v. 4).

The people of God were thus called to quit their complaints over God's silence and to get ready for God to fulfill his promise. Could they wait with praise rather than pouting?

B Our Warrior Wreaks His Wrath (63:1–6)

Response to a watchman

SUPPORTING IDEA: *The Divine Warrior fulfills his promises by releasing his anger on his enemies.*

63:1–2. Unable to convince his audience that God was going to fulfill his promises, the prophet painted one of the most gruesome pictures in all of literature. He took up the role of the lone sentry watching the international border. He spied movement from the southeast.

"Hark! Who goes there on the border with **Edom**?" (For Bozrah as capital of Edom, see commentary on 34:6; see Jer. 49:13,22; cp. Gen. 36:33.) "Is one of our enemies attacking?" (See 34:5; Obadiah; for Edom as a people descended from Jacob's brother Esau, see Gen. 36; cp. Num. 20:14–21; 1 Kgs. 11:14–22; Ps. 137:7; Ezek. 25:12–13; Lam. 4:21–22; Amos 1:11.) "Is that the royal **crimson** that I see moving in the shadows?"

"No, don't shoot. **It is I** who have promised to **save** you."

"Can it be the Divine Warrior? But why are you so **red**?"

63:3–6. "I have done to the enemy just what you have claimed I did to you. I **trampled** them to death like I was pressing grapes to make wine. Remember my promise (61:2). I had to do it all **alone**, but I was able even with **no one to help**. You have nothing more to fear from all your enemies. I am with you to fulfill what I promised." Yes, God's **day of vengeance** has come (see 34:8; 61:2). It is the **year** of **redemption**, that is the time for God to pay back the enemies for what they have done to Israel and to restore Israel fully to what God had always intended them to be.

Quit complaining, people. God is not silent. The Divine Warrior is on the way. He has decided it is time to act. No one can stop him. He has already started. His garments are red with enemy blood. **I trampled the nations in my anger; in my wrath I made them drunk and poured their blood on the ground.**

ⓒ Petition for Paternal Promises (63:7–64:12)

Lament

SUPPORTING IDEA: *God's people react to his punishment by confessing their sins and asking for a new relationship with the heavenly Father.*

63:7–9. The prophet not only responded to the cries of his audience with answers from God; he also provided appropriate language for the people to express their frustration and uncertainty to God (cp. chs. 12; 25; 61:10–11). This is one of the marvelous elements of biblical prayer so often ignored by the people of God today. The Psalms and other biblical prayers express quite openly and dramatically the depth of anger and frustration that people of God often feel in moments of crisis and tension. The prayer here begins like a hymn, describing God's **kindnesses** or faithful love (see "Deeper Discoveries," chs. 54–55), praiseworthy **deeds**, and **compassion** (see "Deeper Discoveries," chs. 13–14).

The people could know these by looking back at what tradition said about God. He had done so much for them. Trusting them to be trustworthy **sons**, in the Exodus he **became their Savior** (Exod. 1–15; cp. Isa. 59:1; 60:16; for salvation, see "Deeper Discoveries," chs. 47–49). He shared their **distress**.

Interpreting this passage has been difficult from earliest times. The Septuagint, the earliest Greek translation of the Old Testament, provides a variant Hebrew text tradition: "In all the affliction, not an ambassador nor a messenger (or angel) but the Lord himself saved them." In either reading, the emphasis is upon the action of God as the one whose **presence saved** his people (cp. Exod. 33:2). He did everything possible for them, redeeming them because he loved the people like a father (see 43:4). So throughout the wilderness **days of old** and beyond, **he carried them** like a child riding his father's back.

63:10–14. Hymnic overtones suddenly vanished. Israel shattered God's expectation. They **rebelled**. They could not be trusted to be true to God (see v. 8). They **grieved his Holy Spirit**. The verbal form here occurs one other time in the Old Testament, in Psalm 56:5. It can be translated literally, "All the day they found fault with, hurt my word (or my thing)" (author's translation). The verb implies bringing deep worry and distress through personal hurt or affront. Israel did this to God by rebelling against him, by not responding to the Father's love with a child's obedient affection. God in turn responded by becoming Israel's **enemy** instead of the Divine Warrior who acted as their Savior.

This caused Israel to stop and take account. The text of verse 11 raises some questions, reading literally, "And he remembered days of forever, Moses and his people. Who is "he"? (author's translation). The closest reference point would be God in the previous verse, and some Bible students read the text this way. Others see Moses as the subject, or Moses and his people, a possible reading in Hebrew syntax. Apparently, however, as often in Hebrew narrative, the writer assumes the audience knows he means "Israel" is the subject without specifically naming Israel.

In this interpretation, Israel **recalled** their history with God, especially the central saving event of the exodus. Israel used it to raise questions about their present. Where was the God of **Moses** who had divided and led them through the **sea** (Exod. 14–15)? Where was the **Spirit** he had placed **among them** and where was the One who had given **rest** to his people when he brought them out of the wilderness into his promised land (cp. Exod. 33:14; Deut. 3:20; 25:19; Josh. 1:13–15; 22:4)? Why did God no longer act to **gain for himself everlasting renown** (more literally, "to make for himself an everlasting name")?

63:15–19. In spite of the absence of any signs of God's activities in the present, the people still asked him to act—the basic request in any lament. They recognized God's basic nature as holy and full of glory. (For Holy One of Israel, see "Deeper Discoveries," ch. 1; for the glory of God, see "Deeper Discoveries," chs. 6–8.) They called upon the compassionate, fatherly care of God, not upon their righteousness. They could not even call upon their membership in the people of God, because their own patriarchal ancestors did not claim them. Their only hope was in their history with God: their **Redeemer from of old** and his zealous protection of them. (For zeal of the Lord, see "Deeper Discoveries," chs. 9–11.)

Perplexity plagued Israel. God, who had been their Redeemer, had now become their enemy. In so doing he had hardened their hearts (see ch. 6). Israel had only one alternative. They ran to God with the plea, **Why?**—the central component of all laments. "You are the only God," they declared. "You control history. You are our Father and Creator. Why did you drive us away from you so that we no longer stand in awe and respect before you? Why did you let us get in the state we are in?" So Israel pleaded with God to come back: "We have lost all identity, and you have lost your home. We were your holy people. Now we are no different from any one else. Help!"

Note the differing translation possibilities for verse 19. Most translations add an English word or two to make sense of a difficult Hebrew text that reads literally: "We were (became) from eternity; You did not rule over them; your name was not called over them. If only you would tear apart the heavens; you would come down; from your presence the mountains would quake" (author's translation).

64:1–5. The translation and interpretation of verses 2–6 represent one of the most difficult tasks in all the Book of Isaiah, as a look at several translations and commentaries will confirm. The call for help is phrased in drastic terms: "Do what you used to do. Tear the **heavens** apart and **come down** to us." (Note that in the Hebrew text this is the conclusion to 63:19.) "Show the **enemies** your terrible presence. Let them know **your name**, which they have forgotten since it has been so long since you have done anything important in human history."

Meditation on how God used to act and how he might act again led the people to stand in silent awe for a moment before the unique **God**, who **acts** for his obedient, expectant people, **who wait for him**. Finally, the people recognize what God has tried to teach so often: He is totally different from all other gods. This difference lies precisely in his ability to act in and control human history. But such meditation only brought to mind the present state. God was **angry** at the **sin** of the people. In spite of the claim that God had caused his people to sin (63:17), Israel confessed that they had chosen to sin. Their sin was exactly what the prophet had preached throughout his book: It was **against them**, that is, against **those who gladly do right**, who remember God's ways. Israel must ask the rhetorical questions, **How then can we be saved**? Israel knew the logical answer—we have no reason to expect salvation at all.

64:6–7. Israel turned lament into confession of sin, dramatically listing their sins. This was not a scattered few. **All of us have become like one who is unclean**. The people were religious. They carried out **righteous acts**. But such acts earned no reward. They were as useless as **filthy rags** that were used for cleaning. Their sins swept them away to destruction. No one any longer called on Yahweh's **name** or tried to "lift himself up to grasp hold of you" (author's translation). No one prayed and sought God's will. This lament in 63:11 to 64:12 is thus a groundbreaking event in prayer for this generation. Understandably, God had **hidden** his face, or withdrawn his presence, from his people and let them suffer the consequences of their **sins**.

64:8–12. But God's people could not simply give up. They came back to God, pleading for his fatherly compassion. This is one of the few places in the Old Testament where God is called **Father** (see Deut. 32:6; 2 Sam. 7:14; 2 Kgs. 2:12; Pss. 68:6; 89:27; Isa. 63:16; 64:8; Jer. 31:9; Mal. 1:6; 2:10). Could the Creator forget his creature? (Note Isaiah's use of the potter and clay imagery in 29:16; 41:25.) Could God be eternally angry? (Note the reversal here of God's argument in 45:9.) Did God know how to forgive and forget? Did he remember **we are all your people**? The people described the condition of God's land to him, becoming especially pitiful and poignant as they pictured the **ruins** of his beautiful dwelling place, **our holy and glorious temple where our fathers praised you**. Jerusalem was exactly what God had promised it would not be (62:4). Could God **keep silent** forever?

The people thus had a prayer given them by the prophet to appeal to the Father's love and the Creator's pride as well as to confess their own sin and faithlessness. Now what would happen? Would the people be faithful to pray to God and acknowledge their condition before him? Would God answer? Or would the people continue their pouting and complaining?

MAIN IDEA REVIEW: *God will win the victory over his enemies and transform his people into a righteous community as they quit their pouting, confess their sins, and ask for a new relationship with the heavenly Father.*

III. CONCLUSION

God's Eternal Plan

Pouting Israel was wrong. God had not been eternally silenced. He still had a plan for them. Once more God, working on his own time schedule, would act in history, win the victory, and transform his people into the righteous community he had planned all along. In fact, the Lord has already marched into battle against archenemy Edom, showing himself mighty to save. Now would Israel grieve God's Holy Spirit as in the wilderness days and continue their lamentation, or would they add to their lament a confession of their sins and ask for forgiveness?

Today, God's people often sense God's silence. This section of Scripture challenges us to believe God will again spring into action if we put away pouting and confess our sins. It calls on us to be the righteous people of faith whom God seeks to create to perform his mission among the nations.

PRINCIPLES

- God has a plan to create a righteous people in whom he can delight.
- God is mighty to save his people, and he delights in them.
- God can win all victories by himself without help.
- When his people suffer distress and anguish, God does, too.
- Salvation comes only because God loves and has mercy on his people.

APPLICATIONS

- Express your trust to God in his plan for the future, no matter how dark the present looks.
- Look for your Savior to come again.
- List ten reasons you have to praise God.
- Ask God to forgive every sin you have committed.

IV. LIFE APPLICATION

"Are You Ready to Listen?"

My given-to-silence friend often breaks the long conversation lulls with a simple question, "Are you ready to listen, now?" Suddenly, I realize that I had been talking about my subjects, carrying on about my problems, and ignoring the friend's interests and needs. Or I have responded to my friend's questions in ways that were totally inappropriate, showing that I had not really listened to what was being asked. I thought I was on top of the situation and knew everything going on, when I was actually out of the situation living in my own dream world and ignoring the reality my friend was describing. My friend wanted to help me but could not get me to face reality or to pay attention to the side of the situation I wanted to ignore.

Israel was God's chosen people. He had done so many things to create the nation, give it land, raise up leaders, and establish its reputation among the nations of the world. All the while, Israel sought ways to keep God on their side and still enjoy life like the rest of the world did. They were not faithful to God. So God had to teach them a lesson. He did so by being silent, doing nothing for them. Israel pouted and complained about God's silence for a while. Eventually they came to the point of listening to God's side of the picture. He was ready to act if they were ready to be righteous. They needed to describe their sinful history as well as his salvation history. Confessing their sins, they found God already in action, mighty to save.

The complaint that God is silent also has a modern ring. So many people refuse to believe in God because they have not seen him do anything lately. God's people, you and I, have a bad day or a bad week and decide God is on vacation. He has forgotten us. Perhaps it is time for us to stop complaining and listen. God calls us to confess our sin, commit ourselves to his righteous purposes, and wait for him to act according to his timetable. Lamentation is acceptable for a season, but with lamentation comes the call to confession, repentance, and renewal.

V. PRAYER

O silent God, we have a hard time understanding you and your ways. We see so much you have done for us in the past. We can recount our testimony of being saved, being baptized, even being rescued from disastrous situations. But now we seem to find only a deaf ear as we pray and lament about the horrors of the present. We confess our sin. We know we have failed you in so many ways, trying to follow you and the world at the same time. We repent of our sins. We turn back to you. Forgive us. Renew us. Break your silence, and save us. Amen.

VI. DEEPER DISCOVERIES

Spirit of God

Studying and defining the "Spirit of God" or the "Spirit of the Lord" in the Old Testament is a difficult assignment in many ways.

First, Christians come to the Old Testament with a New Testament understanding of the Holy Spirit given on Pentecost and tend to read that understanding back into the Old Testament.

Second, the Hebrew word *ruach* occurs 378 times in the Old Testament (fifty-one in Isaiah) and means not just God's Spirit but also "spirit, wind, breeze, breath." Thus God's *ruach* may be his breath (Exod. 15:8,10; Isa. 11:15), which in turn may represent what comes from his lips, namely, his word (Isa. 11:4). Here is a mystery of revelation, because God must show his people or his inspired writer when and how the wind represents his breath. In those cases where the wind is recognized as God's breath, God himself is present with his people in the wind.

Third, *ruach* is a constituent not only of God but also of all living creatures, including humans. The relationship between the creature spirit/breath and the divine Spirit/breath is not always clear and easy to separate. Although in Genesis 2:7, the Hebrew text says God breathed into Adam the "breath of life," *ruach* does not appear there. The Hebrew term is *neshemah*. Genesis 6:17 and 7:15 do use *ruach* for the breath of life in all creatures and in humans. Genesis 7:22 says the *neshmah* (breath) of the *ruach* of life was in all creatures—human and animal. Isaiah 42:5 describes God giving humans breath with *ruach* (cp. 57:16). In Zechariah 42:5 God gives man *ruach*, but this may be seen either as breath or as spirit. In Job 27:3 the breath in human nostrils is the *ruach* of God.

The human *ruach* may extend beyond breath and vital life forces to "describe an entire range of human frames of mind, from the strongest emotions to the failure of all vitality" (Albertz and Westermann, TLOT, 3, p. 1210). (See Josh. 2:11; 5:1; Isa. 25:4; 57:15; 65:14.)

Fourth, the wind is an instrument that God created (Amos 4:13) and uses to bring punishment and destruction, so that often the wind is the *ruach* of God (cp. Ps. 35:5; Isa. 27:8; 57:13; Jer. 4:11–12; Ezek. 13:11,13; 19:12; Hos. 13:15). He also directs the wind to bring salvation (Num. 11:31) and appears to his people in the wind (2 Sam. 22:11; Dan. 7:2).

Fifth, the wind can be used by God to transport his prophets, but here the distinction between wind of God and Spirit of God becomes quite blurred.

The English translator must choose either wind or Spirit, but the Hebrew terminology comprehends both meanings (1 Kgs. 18:12; Ezek. 3:12,14; 11:1,24; 43:5; cp. Acts 8:39).

Sixth, *ruach* can describe an external or internal power with emotional and psychological effects, most of these being negative in character (Num. 5:14; Hos. 4:12; Zech. 13:2). Such may be called "an evil spirit from (or of) the LORD" (1 Sam. 16:14–16,23; 19:9; cp. 2 Kgs. 19:7). The human *ruach* can also be the intellectual center that leads to human will and human action (2 Chr. 36:22; Jer. 51:11).

Humans thus need a "new *ruach*" (Ezek. 11:19; 36:26). This would also come from God.

Thus, *ruach* is a part of human existence and experience, a part created and directed by God. In some sense this inner "ruach" of humans is God's working among them both for good and for bad, for blessing and for punishment. More directly, the Old Testament speaks of God's *ruach*. It gave Joseph ability to interpret dreams (Gen. 41:38). The prophets had a special spirit (2 Kgs. 2:9,15), but this was not always seen as good, since a "man of the spirit" could be called "demented" or "mad" (Hos. 9:7, literal translation). God could put a deceiving spirit in the mouths of the prophets, who could debate how the spirit could move from one prophet to another, causing different utterances in the name of the same God (1 Kgs. 22:24; 2 Chr. 18:23).

The term *ruach* of the Lord occurs twenty-seven times. At times this is the wind (Isa. 40:7; Hos. 13:15). The Spirit of the Lord can be impatient, giving God a psychological element (Mic. 2:7). It can be the divine mind that never needs counsel (Isa. 40:13). The Spirit led Israel into the promised land and brought rest (Isa. 63:14). The Spirit came on the judges as they ruled Israel and led armies to battle (Judg. 3:10; 11:29) or as Samson perfected feats of strength (Judg. 13:25; 15:14). It could transform Saul into a man of the spirit prophesying with the other prophets in a seemingly ecstatic manner (1 Sam. 10:6). It provided the wisdom and strength for young David to become king, but departed from Saul, replaced by an evil spirit from the Lord (1 Sam. 16:13–14). The Spirit inspired David (2 Sam. 23:2), Ezekiel (Ezek. 11:5), Micah (Mic. 3:8), Jahaziel (2 Chr. 20:14), and the messenger of Isaiah 61:1 as they wrote, sang, or prophesied. The Spirit will also be the moving force behind the promised Messiah (Isa. 11:2).

The *ruach* of God (Hb. *'elohim*) occurs sixteen times (including Gen. 41:38; Ezek. 11:24). Genesis 1:2 includes the Spirit in the work of creation, although many Bible students understand the meaning here as "wind." The Spirit of God gives the artisan skill and wisdom in his craftsmanship (Exod. 31:3; 35:31). It allowed Balaam, Saul, Saul's messengers, Asa, and Zechariah to prophesy (Num. 24:2; 1 Sam. 10:10; 19:20,23; 2 Chr. 15:1; 24:20). It drove Saul into angry action (1 Sam. 11:6).

Over thirty other passages also refer to the Spirit of Yahweh with pronouns or other markers of the divine name. The Spirit is the force in creating people and renewing the earth (Ps. 104:30; cp. Job 33:4). Israel's plans should be done through God's Spirit, but too often are not (Isa. 30:1). God thus instructed his people coming out of Egypt through his Spirit (Neh. 9:20; cp. Isa. 63:11) and shared his Spirit that he had placed on Moses with the seventy elders (Num. 11:17, 25). Joshua also had the Spirit (Num. 27:18). He tried to change the evil ways of the people by giving the Spirit to the prophets (Neh. 9:30). After the Spirit caused men to prophesy, Moses had prayed that all God's people might be prophets (Num. 11:26–29), and God's prophet knew the Spirit had sent him to God's people (Isa. 48:16). But God's rebellious people grieved his Spirit (Isa. 63:10; cp. Zech. 7:12).

God's Spirit does direct the work of his servant (Isa. 42:1), and the psalmist asked for the Spirit's guidance (Ps. 143:10). The psalmist prayed for forgiveness, asking that God cleanse him and not take his Holy Spirit from him (Ps. 51:11). The other side of the picture is that the psalmist knew he could never escape God's Spirit (Ps. 139:7). God through his Spirit resurrected the dry, dead bones of Israel in exile (Ezek. 37:14). God promised to pour his Spirit on Israel's descendants so they would multiply as in the promise to Abraham (Isa. 44:3). God renews his covenant with his people, including placing his Spirit on them and his words in their mouth so they can obey him (Ezek. 36:27). The Spirit poured on them is a sign of God's promise to be with them and never to hide his face again (Ezek. 39:29).

In the final days God's Spirit will bring all his people to prophesy, even the slaves (Joel 2:28–29), and will transform the land into a place of fertility and righteousness (Isa. 32:15–16).

In the Old Testament then, the Spirit of God is one way of expressing God's powerful presence in his world to create, communicate, and chastise his people. It is also his promise of a new day in which God's people will know God's will, be able to communicate it to others as prophets, and will find God fulfilling his promises for a new creation and a new people of righteousness.

VII. TEACHING OUTLINE

A. INTRODUCTION

1. Lead Story: The Silent Friend
2. Context: Israel is pouting over God's silence and their frustration at having to live in poverty, although they have returned from exile. God breaks the silence and marches forth covered in enemy blood to show he still intends to create a righteous nation.

3. Transition: What makes God's people pout and complain? Will a pouting people hear God's word and respond? What does God have to say to a people who are content to complain? This study may wake us up from our period of justifying ourselves at God's expense. It may take the pout off our face and make us face up to God's expectations, even when things do not go just as we think they should.

B. COMMENTARY
1. The Restless Redeemer (62:1–12)
2. Our Warrior Wreaks His Wrath (63:1–6)
3. Petition for Paternal Promises (63:7–64:12)

C. CONCLUSION: "ARE YOU READY TO LISTEN?"
1. Wrap-up: God sometimes faces his people in silence. They respond with shouting, pouting, and lament. Finally, on his time schedule God renews his conversation with his people and shows that he is already taking action for them. God's people must change their lament to confession of sin and repentance and plead for forgiveness.
2. Personal Challenge: Are you experiencing a time of God's silence? Tell him about it. Read the laments of the psalms to God and let them express your anger and frustration. Then examine your own life, confess your sins, ask for forgiveness, and wait patiently for God to act according to his plan and in his time.

VIII. ISSUES FOR DISCUSSION

1. Do you believe God has times of silence? Or does our sin separate us from him so we cannot hear his voice? Or can both of these be true?
2. Share with your Bible study group your experiences with God during a time of his silence. What happened in your experience to reopen the conversation with God?
3. God broke silence with Israel through military action against their enemies. In what ways does God show us today that he has broken his silence and is with us in a mighty way?

Isaiah 65–66

A Future for the Faithful

Quote

"*T*his true kind of worship is summed up in the phrase calling by my name. To pray in God's name means to submit to him and to pray in terms of his revealed character and will."

John D. W. Watts

Isaiah 65–66

IN A NUTSHELL

*G*od scolds Israel for not being available when he came calling and then lists the sins that preoccupy them. God threatens to carry out the written threat to destroy Israel but backs off by promising to save a remnant. Still this means many people face disaster, and God will create a new, faithful people. Indeed, he will create a new heaven and a new earth, rejoicing over Jerusalem and delighting in his people. No evil will threaten the people in the new paradise. At home in heaven, God needs no earthly home built for him. He simply wants humble, contrite people rather than evil people who delight in religious rituals. He will repay his enemies who trouble his faithful people but will multiply the faithful miraculously. He will be Jerusalem's comforter, but will show fury to his foes. He will send his people to the far reaches of the world so all will know his glory. Thus all people will come to Jerusalem to worship the true God.

A Future for the Faithful

I. INTRODUCTION

People the Church Did Not Want

*W*illiam Booth used the time his wife was teaching a Bible class to stroll through the east end of London. Every fifth building was a pub. Some bars had steps so small children could climb up and order a drink. Each time he went Booth saw the same men there, drinks in hand, wasting the day and their families' financial resources. This led an indignant Booth to open a Christian mission nearby in 1865. He ministered to those people the churches ignored as too far gone for them to worry with. The churches opposed Booth so strongly that he had to form his own church so the people he helped could confess their sins, repent, and accept God's salvation in Jesus. From this experience, of course, grew the Salvation Army (Yancey, p. 254).

God had a similar experience with Israel. He called them to see what he was doing, and they ignored him. They went about their daily routines and extravagant worship rituals unaware that God wanted something else from them. God gave his blessings and promises to the faithful few who were scorned by the religious majority. The others he invited to his ritual of death. A study of these chapters will remind us of the blessings God has in store for his people. But they will also warn us that the obviously religious sometimes are so busy in God's house that they miss God's presence. God is often at work far away from where the church gathers in his name.

II. COMMENTARY

A Future for the Faithful

MAIN IDEA: *God is creating a new world of peace, joy, and prosperity from the remnant of his people. But he will punish those who ignore him and continue in their sin, especially their sin of observing religion without devotion.*

A Snapping the Silence Because of Sinful Sacrifices (65:1–7)

Promise of salvation and judgment

SUPPORTING IDEA: *God calls a sinful people back but finally punishes them when they ignore him and continue in their meaningless religious rites.*

65:1–7. God had a reply ready for the prayer of his people, but it was not exactly what they expected. He did not say, "Yes, your Father loves you. What can I do for you, my child?" Instead, he drew back in a scolding tone and asked, "Where have you been all this time? I have been waiting for you to **call.** You were too busy with all your other gods, worshiping at their **altars** and participating in their horrendous religious practices."

God **revealed himself** (literally, "let himself be sought"), but no one was asking anything about God. God "let himself be **found**" (author's translation), but no one was seeking him. This was dangerous, because God's invitation implored them to "seek the Lord while he may be found" (55:6). One did not have to find God now. He was there screaming, "**Here am I.** Call on me for help." God planned a day when his people would give thanks and call on his name (12:4), but this nation refused to call to ask God for help and to proclaim the name of God in praise and witness. A foreign conqueror called by Yahweh would call on his name (41:25), but Israel would not. God had called Israel by name (43:1), but Israel would not pronounce the name of Yahweh in their worship (cp. 64:7).

Why did Israel not call? Because Israel was not obeying. They pursued **their own imaginations,** not God's **ways.** It was as if they had sneered at God as they followed pagan religious practices. They continued the practice Isaiah condemned from the beginning—fertility worship in **gardens** planted for pagan gods (see 66:17). **Altars of brick altars** apparently were connected to fertility cults, possibly that of Asherah. Sitting by the **graves** was a pagan way of seeking prophetic oracles from the dead and was expressly forbidden in Deuteronomy 18:11 (cp. 1 Sam. 28). Eating **pigs** was against the laws of Leviticus 11:7 and Deuteronomy 14:8. This was especially repugnant if, as is probable, these had been sacrificed to a pagan god.

Unclean meat is a general term used elsewhere in Leviticus 7:18; 19:7; and Ezekiel 4:14. It apparently refers to meat that had been kept more than three days and was not good enough to use in sacrifices. Here it includes a variety of sacrifices made to pagan gods. In such horrid religious folly, this generation followed the example of their forefathers, who **burned sacrifices on the mountains and defied me on the hills.** This is another reference to worship at pagan shrines.

These people not only disobeyed God's law and refused to listen to his revelation; they also said they were **sacred.** Thus they claimed a peculiar holiness. Such holiness could make them (1) better than other people, (2) unable to associate with other people for fear the holy ones would be contaminated, (3) somehow bring contamination upon God (see Lev. 21:6), or (4) bring holiness upon other people which would endanger those people's lives (see Ezek. 44:19). God judged such worshipers, making them a continual burnt offering to himself. He did this on the basis of written prophecies, probably referring to

62:1 and 59:18. The new generation had repeated the sins of the fathers and had not prayed as the prophet suggested. God would **pay back in full**.

Ⓑ Ready Reply for the Remnant (65:8–16)
Prophetic promise and threat

SUPPORTING IDEA: *God will not destroy all the people he has chosen but will preserve a remnant who will be his servants and receive his blessings.*

65:8–10. Judgment was not God's final word. He decided not to **destroy them all**. A farmer may decide to keep a bad batch of **grapes** because he finds a little bit of **juice** which "can be a blessing" (author's translation; NIV, **there is yet some good in it**)—that is, it can provide income. In similar fashion, God had found some reason for hope in Israel. He renewed the promise to Abraham about multiplying his seed (see Gen. 12:1–3). Once Israel had forfeited the promise (48:19), but God renewed it (see 54:3). Here was the holy seed of the stump of Israel (6:13), the promised blessing on Israel's descendants (44:3). Here was the fulfillment of the promise to the Suffering Servant that he would see his seed (53:10). Here God reaffirmed Israel as his chosen people who would regain the inheritance of the land first given by Moses and Joshua. They would possess both the western valley, **Sharon**, and the eastern **Valley of Achor**. But this was for a different people from those of verse 1. This was for a **people who seek me**.

65:11–12. A great distinction had to be made. The early prophets had pronounced judgment on the entire nation. After the exile things would change. Salvation was promised the servants who still produced blessing, while judgment was brought down on those who rebelled against God. The individual choice became much more important among a people who had no political power. Judgment came because the people left the temple—**my holy mountain**—to worship pagan gods of **Fortune** (Hb., *Gad* as in Baal-Gad in Josh. 11:17 and in Phoenician inscriptions) and **Destiny** (Hb. *Meni*, an abbreviated form of the Arabic god Manat). Doom was their destiny. The reason for doom remained the same as in the opening verses of the chapter—not paying attention to, praying to, or obeying God.

65:13–16. God then pronounced blessings on the righteous and curses on the guilty (vv. 13–15), climaxing in destruction of the guilty, but the gift of a new **name** for the righteous. The other side of the picture was that human blessings and curses could be made only in the name of Yahweh, because worship of all other gods would have disappeared from the **land**. God had indeed **forgotten** the **past troubles**. No longer is God hiding his face (8:17; 54:8; 64:7). No longer is Israel hiding behind falsehood and lies (28:15–17). No longer do their sins hide God's face from them (59:2). No longer would

Israel have to labor to hide their plans from God (29:15). No longer could Israel complain that their way was **hidden** from the Lord (40:27) or that God spoke in secret hiding (45:19). No longer would God's servant have to hide his face from mocking and spitting (50:6). Now the only thing in hiding was the forgotten past and its problems.

ⓒ Joy over Justice in Jerusalem (65:17–25)

Promise of Salvation

SUPPORTING IDEA: *In God's new creation, sadness and weeping will vanish, replaced by joy, prosperity, and peace.*

65:17–19. The new condition of salvation for only a portion of God's people could occur because God had created something entirely **new**. The new creation would differ greatly from the old one, being dominated by **joy** instead of mourning and **weeping**. The joy would be shared by the **people** and by God. This new creation would share some features with the old. It would still have both **heavens** and **earth**. And it would center in the holy city of **Jerusalem**.

65:20–23. The injustices of life would disappear. Long life would be the rule for God's people, death at **a hundred** being like an infant's death that could only be explained as the death of a sinner. All of God's people would live to a ripe old age and enjoy the fruits of their life. The age of Messiah would clearly have dawned (cp. 11:6–9). No longer would people lose their property and crops to foreign invaders. Each of God's faithful people would **enjoy the works of their hands**. Labor would be rewarded in the field and in the birth place. Every newborn would escape the "horror of sudden disaster" (author's translation; NIV, **misfortune**). Curses would disappear. Every generation would be **blessed** by God.

65:24–25. But how could all this take place for such a people as the prophet faced? It all centered on the communication of prayer. God had an answer ready even before they called (cp. v. 1). If God's people would only hurry up and pray! When they did, paradise could be restored (cp. 11:6–9). Now the gardens and brick altars would go unused. Pagan shrines would disappear from the land. Life would center on God's **holy mountain**. So many things are possible when God's people get rid of their gripes and turn to the Lord in honest prayer! One day God's praying people will see a new heaven and a new earth, paradise restored, with no more violence, no more injustice, and peace and joy for all.

$\boxed{\text{D}}$ Righteous Ritual Renewed (66:1–4)

Prophecy of disaster

> **SUPPORTING IDEA:** *The heavenly Father does not need sacrifices or anything else from his people.*

66:1–2. The post-exilic community came to attach too much importance to the temple. They thought it assured instant success and power. They interpreted the prophecies of Haggai and Isaiah 61 incorrectly and demanded that God fulfill his promises immediately, no matter the attitude of the people. God had another word. He took up the language they themselves had used in worship to remind them that God was the heavenly Father who was not dependent upon human beings for anything. He did not need a **place** to sleep. Anything they built was simply a part of his creation. If they wanted to do something that deserved divine attention, they must fulfill the demands of prophetic religion.

One important element of that religion is underlined here: close attention to the divine **word**. The emphasis is on the prophetic promise that the people continued to doubt and the prophetic warnings that they ignored.

66:3–4. The grammar of these verses is not clear. The original text does not have **is like** in any of the verses. The prophet saw the human tendency to choose their own way rather than God's. They did follow God's guidelines in some matters, but then they brought in pagan rites. Their way was full of **abominations** (Hb. *shiqquts,* "a monster," "something to abhor," "a horror"; the same term used in Daniel 12:11 for the "abomination that causes desolation"). Nothing had changed from the situation in 65:1. No one was home when God called. No one paid attention to God's word. God would make his choice—he would **bring upon them what they dread.**

$\boxed{\text{E}}$ Rendering Righteous Recompense (66:5–6)

Oracle of salvation

> **SUPPORTING IDEA:** *God will deliver his faithful people by condemning those who refuse to believe his word.*

66:5–6. The post-exilic community in Jerusalem quickly became split into camps, as has so often happened in the history of the people of God. One camp began charging the other with all sorts of sins and plots. Apparently one group refused to accept the other as part of the people of God. The center of contention was the prophetic **word,** particularly the words of 60:1; 55:12; and 61:6–7,10. The group the prophet condemned apparently had lost faith that any such grand predictions would ever be fulfilled, while the faithful few clung to their faith in God's word. The unbelieving group called on the others to get God to fulfill his word so he would be **glorified** and the faithful ones would have **joy**.

The prophet assured his followers that the **brothers** would be embarrassed beyond measure; indeed, he called his followers to listen for the sound of battle that would show that the coming of God's payday had been announced in the **temple**. Their **enemies**, who were also his enemies, would receive payment in full.

F Birth Brings Bounty (66:7–16)
Promise of salvation

SUPPORTING IDEA: *God will satisfy and bring joy to his children but will bring judgment on his enemies.*

66:7–12. The prophet described the salvation he expected and why he expected it. The rapid increase in the population of Jerusalem brought the **birth** imagery to mind. Such a population explosion was unique, almost unbelievable. If God had brought this to pass, would he stop there? There could be only one logical response: join in the great birthday celebration. Become part of the family. Let **Jerusalem** satisfy your needs. Here the prophet implicitly called the feuding parties to reconcile their differences. He called **all** of Jerusalem to forget their complaining to God and **rejoice** in what he was planning for Jerusalem. In Jerusalem all their needs would be met. The promises of chapter 61 would certainly come to pass.

66:13–16. Jerusalem would be able to nourish and raise her multitude of children. Israel would be comforted (51:12,19). The claim that God was silent and had deserted his servants (see 64:12) would no longer be raised. God would truly come to judge his enemies. (For God's anger, see "Deeper Discoveries," ch. 12.)

The prophet had spoken. Would his new word reconcile the bickering parties in Jerusalem? Or would it simply fan the fire, giving new hopes to one and new reasons for the other to mock and laugh at the foolish hopes the prophet raised?

G Sanctifying Servants for the Savior (66:17–24)
Promise of salvation

SUPPORTING IDEA: *God will gather people from all nations to worship him but will bring torment to those who sin against him.*

66:17. The Book of Isaiah ends with what we might call a prophetic sandwich. Between two pronouncements of judgment on those who rebelled against Yahweh (vv. 17,24), the prophet painted a glorious picture of God's salvation (vv. 18–23). Judgment would come on those who participated in the worship of other gods (cp. 65:3). Special attention is paid to a prominent leader of such worship. The people were **following** him, although we know nothing else about such a person.

66:18. Such abominable worship brought the divine decision to reveal his **glory** once and for all. (For glory of God, see "Deeper Discoveries," chs. 6–8.) Again, Yahweh planned to act for the entire universe, not just a small portion of it. Now **all nations and tongues . . . will . . . see my glory**, a privilege denied the great Moses (see Exod. 33).

66:19. God would send the survivors of his people to gather the **nations** to see his **sign**. Here the sign is not defined or explained (see 7:14; 55:13). The nations mentioned are only the most exotic lands on the edges of the known world. (For the nations, see "Deeper Discoveries.")

66:20–21. The mission to the nations would have immediate results. The nations would return the Israelites still in exile to their homeland. This would represent the acceptable sacrifice for the foreign nations (cp. 60:6–7). But God had something more radical. The foreigners who came would not just deliver the remaining exiles and go back home. Some of the foreigners would become **priests and Levites**, serving in the temple itself (cp. 61:5–6). Native Israelites had no more privileges that they could proudly hold to themselves as their rights from God. God would finally achieve his purpose of extending the light to the nations.

66:22–23. These verses describe the new creation of God (see 65:17). The descendants of all the foreign nations can remain people of God who participate not just in one unique service of worship but in the regular weekly **Sabbath** worship services in the temple. This was the prophetic dream, a challenge to the complacency and racial pride of his people and a continual challenge to the people of God to reach out into all the world with the good tidings of God's comfort for all people (see Matt. 28:18–20).

66:24. Such a dream was not separated from reality. It was in touch with the other side of the picture. Not everyone would accept God's invitation to gather as part of his people (v. 18). God's people would have to see the horrible results of rebellion against God (v. 24; for judgment for rebellion, see "Deeper Discoveries"). Those who **rebelled** would not even receive burial, but would suffer shame as **worms** ate at their corpses, as the fires of the garbage heaps of Jerusalem burned them, and they became a symbol of God's judgment upon the wicked (cp. Jer. 7:30–8:3; Mark 9:48).

MAIN IDEA REVIEW: *God is creating a new world of peace, joy, and prosperity from the remnant of his people. But he will punish those who ignore him and continue in their sin, especially their sin of observing religion without devotion.*

III. CONCLUSION

A New Heaven and a New Earth

God's plan for world mission and his promises to deliver his people from trouble prove divisive. Some people believe and follow these principles. Others ridicule the believers and scorn God himself. Still God refuses to keep silent. He thrusts the prophetic word before us and forces us to take sides. Do we believe the word and expect God to create a new heaven and a new earth for us? Or do we think that word is only a pipe dream so that we go about our daily routine in the world's way, ignoring God? God has spelled out the horrid punishment you face when you ignore him. Do you really want to endure such punishment? Trust God and his promises. Get ready for a new heaven and a new earth.

PRINCIPLES

- God goes the extra mile to encourage his people to follow and obey him.
- God has given his people his written word to let them know what brings his judgment.
- God's plan is to work through a faithful remnant of his people to bring salvation to the world.
- God's salvation plan is to create a new heaven and a new earth where sin and suffering do not exist.

APPLICATIONS

- List religious or superstitious practices that have an attraction for you, although you know God condemns them.
- Express your dependence on God and acknowledge that you do not have the power to accomplish anything without him.
- Get yourself ready to experience God's final judgment of the world.
- Dedicate yourself to participate in one volunteer mission trip for God.

IV. LIFE APPLICATION

A Transforming Vision

Gary Smalley and John Trent invite us to imagine the worst football team in the nation. Their athletic director has scheduled them against the defending national champions. The game is played, of course, on the champions' home field. All the athletic director expects is to get a sizable paycheck that will meet the year's athletic budget for his small school. The team hustles onto the field to a smattering of applause and a large number of boos from the home fans. Then thunderous cheers announce the arrival of the national champions. The visiting players realize why their opponents are champions. They are huge, fast, strong, and play with great confidence. The visitors feel their own confidence level sink.

Suddenly, the entire visitors' squad looks up and sees a vision. It is more real than anything they have ever witnessed before. They see themselves—exhausted, sweat-streaked, dirty, bruised, bandaged. Yet they are cheering wildly. How could this be? Then they see the scoreboard:

HOME CHAMPIONS	13	QUARTER: 4TH
VISITORS	14	TIME 00:00

The vision disappears. Back to reality. A stadium full of fans, fanatically yelling for their opponents. A team with twice as many players, all of them much bigger and stronger facing them. But now, they are a different team. They have changed inside. Encouragement and wild elation flow through their minds and emotions. Now they can play with energy and confidence. They absorb the hits as they run to the ball, gang tackle, block with bone-jarring tenacity, and sacrifice everything they have for this one moment in history. They had seen a picture of what could be. They were ready to make it happen.

Tell the same vision to the home team and their fans, and you get an entirely different reaction—laughter, scorn, disbelief, ridicule. A little vision could not make the difference. Their big boys would run over the small school kids with ease (Smalley and Trent, *Leaving the Light On,* p. 188).

Or would they? Each person needs a vision of the end—the final goal—of life. Such a vision determines much of how we live each day of life. Isaiah gave Israel a major vision of what God wanted—a people with trust, obedience, hope, righteousness, and justice. Most of Israel saw only the reality of a Jerusalem far from its glory days without fortifications, without a true army, without hope against the powerful nations of the world. Isaiah saw a glorious God who wanted to share his glory with all the nations. He wanted to bring all the nations to Jerusalem to bow before him in sacrifice and service.

Which side would you have joined if you had been listening to Isaiah's message? Which side are you on today? Do you live in expectation of a new heaven and a new earth? Or do you expect life to go on as usual forever? Your vision will determine how you live.

V. PRAYER

God of vision and glory, help me share your vision and trust your word. Forgive me when I let the world dominate my thinking and thus my acting. You are the only God. You still control all the world, every nation, and every day of the future. I trust you. I will live for you and carry your vision to the nations. Amen.

VI. DEEPER DISCOVERIES

A. The Nations (66:19)

The following are the nations to whom God's heralds will be sent to invite these people to be witnesses of God's glory:

Tarshish was apparently in the far west, a shipping port of Spain perhaps (see 60:9; Ps. 72:10; Ezek. 27:12; Jonah 1:3). The next country was apparently Libya or another section of Africa (most all translators make a slight change in the Hebrew text here following the Septuagint). Hebrew *Lud* may also be in Africa or it may possibly refer to Lydia in western Asia Minor (Jer. 46:9; Ezek. 30:5). Tubal is in eastern Asia Minor near Cilicia southeast of the Black Sea (Ezek. 27:13; 39:1). The Hebrew term *Javan* refers to the Greeks from Ionia (Joel 3:6). Their territory included the cities of Ephesus and Smyrna. No one was to be excluded in God's attempt to let all the world know his glory.

B. Judgment for Rebellion (66:24)

The early Jewish community did not like the horrible note on which the Book of Isaiah ended and so directed that in worship when the book was read, 66:23 should be repeated after 66:24. Ever since, people have sought ways to avoid the biblical message of judgment. But the biblical word continues to remind God's people that God's promises contain two sides—salvation for the faithful and condemnation for the rebels.

VII. TEACHING OUTLINE

A. INTRODUCTION

1. Lead Story: People the Church Did Not Want

2. Context: Isaiah concludes his book with two chapters that deal with God's reaction to the complaint that he is silent. He speaks to a nation that has seldom been united in its worship of him and that at the moment is strongly divided. What word can God have for a divided people?

3. Transition: God notes the division in his house, and says that he will no longer treat the people as one group. He now has a remnant of true Israel within the nation as a whole. He has a promise of salvation, of a new heaven and a new earth, but only for part of the people. How do you know which part of the people you belong to? How do you know whether God is promising you a blessing or a curse? Do you still have a chance before God? These two chapters will help you answer these questions.

B. COMMENTARY

1. Snapping the Silence Because of Sinful Sacrifices (65:1–7)
2. Ready Reply for the Remnant (65:8–16)
3. Joy over Justice in Jerusalem (65:17–25)
4. Righteous Ritual Renewed (66:1–4)
5. Rendering Righteous Recompense (66:5–6)
6. Birth Brings Bounty (66:7–16)
7. Sanctifying Servants for the Savior (66:17–24)

C. CONCLUSION: A TRANSFORMING VISION

1. Wrap-up: The book is finished. It has appealed to three distinct generations of Israel's people to trust Yahweh in every moment of history, no matter how dark. It has finally described Israel as two peoples, not one. This is not a political division but a religious division. Some people believe and obey. Others sneer and act like the rest of the world, secure in their understanding that they are people of Yahweh, even if he says they are not. God has a future for the faithful but only worms and wounds for the worldly wise.

2. Personal Challenge: You must stand up and be counted. What vision of life drives you each day? What promises or threats do you believe? Is the word you read in the Bible about a new heaven and a new earth a word of hope for you? Or is it so unreal you can merely laugh and say, "I will believe it when I see it"? That will be too late. Get on God's side today, even if it means enduring scorn and derision.

VIII. ISSUES FOR DISCUSSION

1. What does the promise of a new heaven and a new earth mean to you?
2. In what ways do people ignore the calling and seeking of God?
3. What does a large, lovely new church building represent to God? What may it represent for the people who built it?
4. What promises has God given you that are the most meaningful in determining how you live your life each day?

Glossary

atonement—God's way of overcoming sin through Christ's obedience and death to restore believers to a right relationship with God

Babylon—Name of an evil city and empire in the sixth century B.C.; a code name for another evil city in Revelation

confession—Admission of personal sin and seeking forgiveness from others

consecration—Setting apart for God's use

conversion—God's act of changing a person's life in response to the person's turning to Christ in repentance and faith from some other belief or from no belief

covenant—A contract or agreement expressing God's gracious promises to his people and their consequent relationship to him

creation—God's bringing the world and everything in it into existence from nothing

day of the Lord—God's time of decisive intervention in history and the final day of judgment in the end time

election—God's gracious action in choosing people to follow him and obey his commandments

evil—Anyone or anything that opposes the plan of God

exile—Israel's life in the Assyrian kingdom after 722 B.C. and Judah's life in Babylon after 587 B.C.

exodus, the—The most important act of national deliverance in the Old Testament when God enabled the Israelites to escape Egypt

fall, the—The result of the first human sin which marred the image of God in humans and created an environment for and a tendency toward sin for all people

foreknowledge—God's eternal knowledge of the future

forgiveness—Pardon and release from penalty for wrongdoing; God's delivery from sin's wages for those who repent and express faith in Christ; the Christian act of freeing from guilt and blame those by whom one has suffered wrong

Gentiles—People who are not part of God's chosen family at birth and thus can be considered "pagans"

glorification—God's action in the lives of believers, making them able to share the glory and reward of heaven

grace—Undeserved acceptance and love received from another, especially the characteristic attitude of God in providing salvation for sinners

holy—God's distinguishing characteristic that separates him from all creation; the moral ideal for Christians as they seek to reflect the character of God as known in Christ Jesus

Holy Spirit—The third person of the Trinity; the presence of God promised by Christ and sent to his disciples at Pentecost representing God's active presence in the believer, the church, and the world

idolatry—The worship of that which is not God

Jerusalem—Capital city of Israel in the Old Testament; religious center of Judaism in the New Testament; also name of the heavenly city John describes in Revelation (New Jerusalem)

judgment—God's work at the end time involving condemnation for unbelievers and assignment of rewards for believers

justification—The act or event by which God credits a sinner who has faith as being right with him through the blood of Jesus

Glossary

Law—God's instruction to his people about how to love him and others; when used with the definite article "the," *law* may refer to the Old Testament as a whole but usually to the Pentateuch (Genesis through Deuteronomy)

mercy—A personal characteristic of care for the needs of others; the biblical concept of mercy always involves help to those who are in need or distress

Messiah—The coming king promised by the prophets; Jesus Christ who fulfilled the prophetic promises; Christ represents the Greek translation of the Hebrew word "messiah"

mission—The God-given responsibility of the church and each believer to bring God's love and the Christian gospel to all people through evangelism, education, and ministry; missions is used especially to refer to work done by Christians outside their own culture

obedience—Hearing and following instructions and directions from God; expected of believers

omnipotent—God's unlimited power to do that which is within his holy and righteous character

omnipresence—God's unlimited presence in all places at all times

omniscience—God's unlimited knowing

prophet—One who speaks for God

redemption—The act of releasing a captive by the payment of a price; Jesus' death provided our redemption from sins power and penalty (Heb. 9:12)

repentance—A change of heart and mind resulting in a turning from sin to God that allows conversion and is expressed through faith

righteousness—The quality or condition of being in right relationship with God; living out the relationship with God in right relationships with other persons

salvation—Deliverance from trouble or evil; the process by which God redeems his creation, completed through the life, death, and resurrection of his Son Jesus Christ

shalom—Hebrew word for peace and wholeness meaning fullness of life through God-given harmony with God, the world, others, and oneself

sin—Actions by which humans rebel against God, miss his purpose for their life, and surrender to the power of evil rather than to God

sovereignty—God's freedom from outward restraint; his unlimited rule of and control over his creation

spirit—The quality, power, or force within persons that makes them open to relationship with God; the Spirit of God

transcendence—God's quality of being above or beyond his creation

wrath of God—God's consistent response opposing and punishing sin

Zion—Another name for Jerusalem

Bibliography

Commentaries

Achtemeier, Elizabeth. *The Community and Message of Isaiah 56–66*. Augsburg, 1982.

Allis, Oswald T. *The Unity of Isaiah*. Presbyterian and Reformed Publication Co., 1950.

Blenkinsopp, Joseph. *Isaiah 1–39*. AB 19. Doubleday, 2000.

Brueggemann, Walter. *Isaiah 1–39*. Westminster Bible Companion. Westminster/John Knox, 1998.

Childs, Brevard. *Isaiah*. OTL. Westminster/John Knox, 2001.

Clements, R. E. *Isaiah 1–39*. NCB. Eerdmans, 1980.

Elliger, Karl. *DeuteroJesaja 40:1–45:7*. BK. Neukirchener Verlag, 1978.

Grogan, Geoffrey W. *Isaiah*. EBC 6. Zondervan, 1984.

Gray, George Buchanan. *A Critical and Exegetical Commentary on the Book of Isaiah i–xxvii*. ICC. T. & T. Clark, 1912.

Hanson, Paul. *Isaiah 40–66*. Interpretation. John Knox, 1995.

Keil, C. F., and Delitzsch. *Isaiah*. Commentary on the Old Testament, VII–VIII. Trans. James Martin. Eerdmans, 1954.

Knight, George A. E. *Isaiah 40–55: Servant Theology*. ITC. Eerdmans, 1984.

Knight, George A.E. *Isaiah 56–66: The New Israel*. ITC. Eerdmans, 1985.

Mauchline, John. *Isaiah 1–39*. Torch Bible Paperbacks. SCM, 1962.

McKenzie, John L. *Second Isaiah*. AB 18. Doubleday, 1968.

North, Christopher R. *The Second Isaiah*. Clarendon Press, 1964.

Oswalt, John. *The Book of Isaiah*. 2 vols. NICOT. Eerdmans, 1986, 1997.

Sawyer, John F. A. *The Daily Study Bible: Isaiah*. 2 vols. Westminster, 1984, 1986.

Seitz, Christopher R. *Isaiah 1–39*. Interpretation. John Knox, 1993.

Smith, Ralph L. *Old Testament Theology*. Broadman & Holman, 1993.

Sweeney, Marvin A. *Isaiah 1–39 with an Introduction to Prophetic Literature*. FOTL XVI. Eerdmans, 1996.

Watts, John D. W. *Isaiah*. 2 vols. WBC 24, 25. Word Books, 1985, 1987.

Westermann, Claus. *Isaiah 40–66*. OTL. Westminster, 1969.

Whybray, Norman. *Isaiah 40–66*. NCB. Oliphants, 1975.

Widyapranawa, S. H. *Isaiah 1–39 The Lord Is Savior*. ITC. Eerdmans, 1990.

Young, Edward J. *The Book of Isaiah*. 3 vols. NICOT. Eerdmans, 1965.

Reference Works

Ancient Near Eastern Texts Relating to the Old Testament. Ed. J. B. Pritchard. 2nd ed. Princeton University Press, 1955.

Anchor Bible Dictionary. Ed. David Noel Freedman. 6 vols. Doubleday, 1992.

Brisco, Thomas C. *Holman Bible Atlas.* Broadman & Holman, 1998.

Brueggemann, Walter. *Theology of the Old Testament.* Fortress, 1997.

Clements, R. E. *Isaiah and the Deliverance of Jerusalem.* JSOTS 13. JSOT Press, 1980.

Dictionary of Classical Hebrew. Ed. David J. A. Clines. Vols 1–5+. Sheffield Academic Press, 1993–2001.

Hebrew and Aramaic Lexicon of the Old Testament. Ed. Ludwig Koehler and Walter Baumgartner; rev. Johann Jakob Stamm. Trans. M. E. J. Richardson. 4 vols. 1994–1999.

Holman Bible Dictionary. Ed. Trent C. Butler. Holman Bible Publishers, 1991.

Holman Bible Handbook. Ed. David Dockery. Holman Bible Publishers, 1992.

Interpreter's Dictionary of the Bible. Eds. George Arthur Buttrick; Keith Crim. 5 vols. Abingdon Press, 1962, 1976.

Kaiser, Walter. *A History of Israel.* Broadman & Holman, 1998.

Kitchen, Kenneth A. *The Third Intermediate Period in Egypt.* Aris & Phillips, 1973.

McBeth, Leon. *A Sourcebook for Baptist Heritage.* Broadman Press, 1990.

Monumental Inscriptions from the Biblical World. Eds. William B. Hallo and K. Lawson Younger, Jr. *The Context of Scripture.* Vol. 2. Brill, 2000.

New International Dictionary of Old Testament Theology and Exegesis. Ed. Willem A. VanGemeren. 5 vols. Zondervan, 1997.

Theological Dictionary of the Old Testament. Eds. G. Johannes Botterweck, Helmer Ringgren, Heinz-Josef Fabry. 11+ vols. Eerdmans, 1974–2001+.

Theological Lexicon of the Old Testament. Eds. Ernst Jenni and Claus Westermann. Tr. Mark E. Biddle. 3 vols. Hendrickson Publishers, 1997.

Sources of Illustrative Materials

Arthur, Kay. *As Silver Refined.* Waterbrook Press, 1997.

Augustine. *Confessions.* Thomas Nelson, 1999.

Breathnach, Sarah Ban. *Something More: Excavating Your Authentic Self.* Warner Books, 1998.

Blackaby, Henry, and Claude King. *Experiencing God.* Broadman & Holman, 1994.

Christenson, Evelyn. *What Happens When Women Pray?* Victor Books, 1975.

Crabb, Larry. *Connecting.* Word, 1997.

Davis, Verdell. *Riches Stored in Secret Places.* Word, 1994.

Dobson, James. *When God Doesn't Make Sense.* Tyndale House, 1993.

Gordon, Ernest. *Miracle on the River Kwai.*

Graham, Billy. *Hope for the Troubled Heart.* Word, 1991.

Hybels, Bill. *The God You're Looking For.* Thomas Nelson, 1997.

Kempis, Thomas à. *Imitation of Christ.*

Lucado, Max. *The Applause of Heaven.* Word, 1996.

Lucado, Max. *In the Grip of Grace.* Word, 1996.

Miller, Calvin. *The Empowered Leader.* Broadman & Holman, 1995.

Miller, Calvin. *Until He Comes.* Broadman & Holman, 1998.

Packer, James. *Your Father Loves You.* Harold Shaw Publishers, 1986.

Patterson, Dorothy Kelley. *Beatitudes for Women.* Broadman & Holman, 2000.

Schuller, Robert. *Tough Times Never Last, But Tough People Do.* Thomas Nelson, 1983.

Shepherd, Sheri Rose. *Life Is Not a Dress Rehearsal.* Broadman & Holman, 1997.

Smalley, Gary, and John Trent. *Leaving the Light On.* Multnomah, 1994.

Sproul, R. C. *The Soul's Quest for God.* Tyndale, 1992.

Swindoll, Charles R. *The Finishing Touch.* Word, 1994.

Templeton, John Marks. *Discovering the Laws of Life.* Continuum, 1995.

Vos Savant, Marilyn. *Reader's Digest Quotable Quotes,* 1997.

Wilkerson, Bruce. *The Prayer of Jabez.* Multnomah, 2000.

Yancey, Philip. *What's So Amazing About Grace.* Zondervan, 1997.

Zecharias, Ravi. *Cries of the Heart.* Word, 1998.